Social Justice Counseling

I (Rita Chi-Ying Chung) dedicate this book to my parents:
Jack Tai Hing Chung and Daphne Chung (Young Lai Yung), who taught me
everything I know about social justice and instilled in me the passion, the strength, the courage,
and the fearlessness to speak up and speak out against social injustices and human rights violations.

I (Fred Bemak) dedicate this book to my parents, Walter and Ruth Bemak,
who have, in the most profound and deepest way, shown the path for the next generation
to somehow help this world be a better place, and to my incredible daughters, Amber and Lani,
for carrying social justice into the next generation and helping me know that it was and is all worth it.

Social Justice Counseling

THE NEXT STEPS BEYOND MULTICULTURALISM

Rita Chi-Ying Chung
Frederic P. Bemak
George Mason University

Los Angeles | London | New Delhi
Singapore | Washington DC

Los Angeles | London | New Delhi
Singapore | Washington DC

FOR INFORMATION:

SAGE Publications, Inc.
2455 Teller Road
Thousand Oaks, California 91320
E-mail: order@sagepub.com

SAGE Publications Ltd.
1 Oliver's Yard
55 City Road
London EC1Y 1SP
United Kingdom

SAGE Publications India Pvt. Ltd.
B 1/I 1 Mohan Cooperative Industrial Area
Mathura Road, New Delhi 110 044
India

SAGE Publications Asia-Pacific Pte. Ltd.
33 Pekin Street #02-01
Far East Square
Singapore 048763

Acquisitions Editor: Kassie Graves
Editorial Assistant: Courtney Munz
Production Editor: Eric Garner
Copy Editor: Cate Huisman
Typesetter: C&M Digitals (P) Ltd.
Proofreader: Sally Jaskold
Indexer: Maria Sosnowski
Cover Designer: Bryan Fishman
Marketing Manager: Katharine Winter
Permissions Editor: Adele Hutchinson

Copyright © 2012 by SAGE Publications, Inc.

Printed in the United States of America

Library of Congress Cataloging-in-Publication Data

Chung, Rita Chi-Ying.

Social justice counseling : the next steps beyond multiculturalism/Rita Chi-Ying Chung, Frederic P. Bemak

p. cm.
Includes bibliographical references and index.

ISBN 978-1-4129-9952-6 (pbk.)

1. Cross-cultural counseling. 2. Psychiatry, Transcultural. 3. Social justice. I. Bemak, Fred. II. Title.

BF636.7.C76C48 2012
616.89′14—dc23   2011031258

This book is printed on acid-free paper.

11 12 13 14 15 10 9 8 7 6 5 4 3 2 1

CONTENTS

ACKNOWLEDGMENTS

This book would not have come about without the support and dedication of many people. We would like to thank Diana Ortiz and Mandi Gordon, who have been invaluable in assisting us with the preparation of this book. We would also like to thank Reston Bell, Liz Davis, Jan Weng, Kate Golkow, Rodolfo Marenco, Candace Fleming, Brad Pabian, Hollie Jones, and Diana Ortiz for their powerful narratives, which help the book come alive with true life stories about social justice. We would also like to thank our colleagues at SAGE—Kassie Graves, who through her constant support and encouragement helped to bring this book to completion; and Cate Huisman, who one can only dream about having as a copy editor.

In addition we would both like to deeply thank all of the many students who have taken up our challenge and dared to take the risk and find the courage to confront themselves and others regarding multicultural social justice issues. You are the pathway for the next generation of multicultural social justice counselors, and we write this book in your honor.

I (Rita Chi-Ying Chung) would like to thank my coauthor, colleague, and partner Fred Bemak for his continuous support and dedication to social justice work, who has led by example in walking his talk. And in turn, I (Fred Bemak), would extend my deepest appreciation and gratitude to my coauthor, colleague, and partner, Rita Chi-Ying Chung, for being the absolute embodiment of living a life filled with social justice values and being an incredible model for multicultural social justice work.

PART I

INTRODUCTION TO COUNSELING AND SOCIAL JUSTICE

1

INTRODUCTION

We must become the change we want to see in the world.

(Mahatma Gandhi)

The writing of *Social Justice Counseling: The Next Steps Beyond Multiculturalism in Application, Theory, and Practice* has taken place during the last ten years. It has been a journey that parallels the multicultural social justice movement within the mental health field, fraught with strong reactions to the content of the book. These have been both highly laudatory and—in the earlier years of writing—strongly critical about the place of social justice within the context of counseling, psychology, and social work. Over the ten years since this book became an idea, the mental health field has broadened to more easily include issues of social justice as integral to the work of psychologists, counselors, and social workers, and the criticism about social justice as a fundamental aspect of counseling has diminished, albeit not disappeared. Based on our work, our experiences, and our commitment to justice, equality, and equity for all people, and the critical issue of redistributing power and privilege as a means toward social justice, we have stayed the course with this book and are delighted to share with you our thoughts and experiences related to multicultural social justice counseling.

This book has a foundation in the amazing work of many colleagues who have paved the way in the field for multicultural counseling and psychology (e.g., Joseph Aponte, Patricia Arredondo, Manuel Casas, William Cross, Michael D'Andrea, Judy Daniels, Juris Draguns, Janet Helms, Farah Ibrahim, Allen Ivey, Teresa LaFromboise, Anthony Marsella, Thomas Parham, Paul Pedersen, Joseph Ponterotto, Don Pope-Davis, Issac Prilleltensky, Maria Root, Derald Wing Sue, Stanley Sue, Joseph Trimble, Clemont Vontress, and many others). The chapters in this book build on the incredible work and efforts of the pioneers in the multicultural field and present ways to embed social justice as the next step in the counseling, psychology, and social work fields. This book is a first step in systematically looking at how to integrate social justice into the mental health field without it being absorbed and diluted in the multicultural work that has taken root and now constitutes a cornerstone of contemporary counseling with an emphasis on cultural diversity and plurality.

Social inequities that are rooted in oppression, intolerance, privilege, power, and inequities are not new. For a long time, discrimination, oppression, and intolerance have methodically excluded people based on race, ethnicity, culture, sexual orientation, socioeconomic status, gender, age, religion, physical disability, mental disability, and so forth, and this has created obstacles to access, opportunity, and participation. Counselors, psychologists, and social workers are constantly working with clients, families, communities, and schools that experience profound issues of oppression, discrimination, social inequities, unfair treatment, and disproportionate privilege, as well as unequal social, political, and economic access. Yet, consistent with the origins of Western psychology, we frequently focus on the individual and her or his pathology or strengths, rather than the broader social, economic, political, and ecological context.

The unintended result of our mental health tradition has created a situation in which we often neglect larger critical issues that impact mental health, and we make conscious decisions to deemphasize those aspects of our clients' lives. Incorporating social justice into our work does exactly the opposite—it helps us in examining and helping our clients to address vital life circumstances and issues that affect them and become salient components in counseling and psychotherapy. Social, economic, ecological, historical, and political issues and concerns, and social action as well, subsequently become key ingredients in the psychotherapeutic relationship.

The attention to cultural diversity has moved the field of mental health toward greater responsiveness in the 21st century. In the United States, where Latinos and Asians are the fastest-growing groups nationally, 12% of the population is foreign born, and projections indicate that by 2042, people of color will outnumber Whites, with the nation projected to be 54% minority in 2050 (U.S. Census Bureau, 2008). While in some circles there is greater acceptance of cultural diversity, there is at the same time a growing polarity in attitudes and values regarding the acceptance of ethnic and racial diversity, tolerance for differences in religious beliefs, and acceptance of differences in sexual orientation. These differences, coupled with the world shrinking through globalization, media and technology, and the vast migration of people all around the world, counselors, psychologists, and social workers by necessity must become knowledgeable and sensitive to issues of diversity.

In turn, mental health professionals must acquire distinctive skills to accompany their growing awareness in order to effectively work with culturally diverse populations. This requires a growing acceptance of, respect for, and appreciation of the dignity and uniqueness of race and ethnicity, physical and mental disabilities, gender, religion, sexual orientation, age, and socioeconomic status. Even with emergent approval of cultural diversity, there has not been systematic attention as to how to link culturally responsive mental health work with social justice counseling. This book provides an examination of how to move to the next steps that go beyond the combination of social justice and multicultural counseling, presenting ideas about social justice application, theory, practice, and research. In addition, this book is different from other books on social justice in providing a foundation of the theories, skills, and techniques that are critical to understand being a competent multicultural social justice mental health provider, examining issues that we believe must be understood by social justice mental health professionals as key components of their work. These issues are typically separated and addressed as separate components of social justice work, and therefore separate books are written specifically focusing on a component. But this book uniquely brings together the next steps beyond multiculturalism for the first time, to include a comprehensive look at them. Issues that are included in this book include the integration of multiculturalism and social justice, models of intervention, relevant socioeconomic and political issues, change theory, advocacy, leadership, empowerment, interdisciplinary collaboration, social action research, training, and global issues.

Three common questions that are asked in multicultural social justice work are as follows:

1) What is social justice?

2) What are the differences between multicultural counseling and social justice counseling?

3) How does a multicultural social justice counselor, psychologist, or social worker actually provide counseling?

The intent of this book is to answer these critical questions; the answers are essential in taking the next steps to move beyond multicultural counseling. Over the past few decades, we have established a body of literature, including excellent research and theory, along with guidelines about becoming an effective multicultural practitioner.

The book is divided into six sections. It begins with Part I, which includes the current chapter, an introduction to counseling and social justice. Chapter 2 reviews the theories of multicultural counseling and presents how this body of literature relates to social justice work. Next, Chapter 3 presents social justice as a fifth force and outlines definitions, theories, historical perspectives, models, and characteristics of a social justice counselor, psychologist, and social worker.

In Part II, there is a description of the Multi-Phase Model (MPM) of psychotherapy, counseling, human rights and social justice, a social justice counseling model that we have developed as a framework from over 50 years of combined experience. This part begins with Chapter 4, a discussion on the development, rationale, and prerequisites for effectively utilizing the MPM model. It is followed by Chapter 5, in which we describe the MPM.

Part III shares the deeply personal social justice journeys of each of the two authors as well as a number of graduate students. The inclusion of our respective personal narratives and the students' narratives was to reach you, the reader, on a more personal level, with hopes that you can identify your own social justice journey. The stories describe several individuals' journeys in becoming social justice mental health practitioners and share the power of transformation through training and practice.

Following the personal narratives is Part IV, which describes the critical intersection between social change and social justice. Chapter 9 examines dimensions of change, including an exploration

of process, power, and resistance to change. The next two chapters describe what we consider critical qualities of a competent multicultural social justice counselor. Chapter 10 provides a close look at leadership, leadership styles, issues of gender, and characteristics of a social justice leader. Chapter 11 examines advocacy within the framework of social justice counseling. It includes an overview of the history of advocacy, qualities of an effective advocate, and challenges of being a counseling social justice advocate. Chapter 12 continues with an examination of one of the most important markers for working from a multicultural social justice perspective, that is, empowerment. Given that nowadays in counseling, psychology, and social work, there are no critics of empowerment, and that everyone is supportive of empowering clients, families, and communities, the chapter takes a critical look at how mental health professionals sometimes inadvertently disempower others under the guise of empowerment. To more closely examine these issues, this chapter discusses what we call *authentic empowerment* and describes its relationship to social justice counseling. Finally in Part IV, Chapter 13 focuses on interdisciplinary collaboration. We have found that remaining within one's own sphere of counseling, psychology, or social work is highly limiting in doing social justice counseling. To address this, we have included this chapter on the importance of working across disciplines, and we have included guiding principles for interdisciplinary collaboration.

One of the criticisms of social justice counseling has been the scarcity of evidence-based research to support incorporating social justice into counseling. To address this, we have incorporated Part V, Social Justice Applications, which includes chapters on social action research and training. Chapter 14 examines the dimensions of social action research that is geared toward social change, looks at descriptors of social action research, and considers how social action research relates to counseling, psychology, and social work. Chapter 15 discusses a social justice training model to assist educators in developing graduate training models that emphasize multiculturalism, social justice, and human rights. This chapter provides ideas, suggestions, and recommendations on how to train the next generation of multicultural social justice counselors, psychologists, and social workers.

Part VI is the final section of the book. Chapter 15 examines the importance and relevance of social justice in a global environment that assists counselors, psychologists, and social workers to "think globally, and act locally." The chapter underscores the impact of globalization on social justice and the interaction between national and global injustices and mental health work. Finally, Chapter 17 concludes the book with a discussion of the realities of social justice work and how to "feed one's soul" when working on injustices. It is crucial that helping professionals practice self-care so that they are able to continue with courage and passion when battling against social injustices.

We believe that this book is the first to present how to take the next steps beyond the incredible multicultural strides we have taken in the mental health field. We also feel that the inclusion of several topical areas that are essential to social justice mental health work in one book comprehensively synthesizes the knowledge and material necessary to move to the next steps of application, theory, and practice that will move us forward to a more equitable, just, and healthy society and world.

We wish you success in your social justice work, and as Mahatma Gandhi said, "A small body of determined spirits fired by an unquenchable faith in their mission can alter the course of history."

REFERENCE

U.S. Census Bureau. (2008). *An older and more diverse nation by midcentury.* Retrieved from http://www.census.gov/Press-Release/www/releases/archives/population/012496.html

2

THEORIES OF MULTICULTURAL COUNSELING AND ITS RELATIONSHIP TO SOCIAL JUSTICE

The nation will be more racially and ethnically diverse by midcentury, according to projections released by the U.S. Census Bureau. Minorities, now roughly one-third of the U.S. population, are expected to become the majority in 2042, with the nation projected to be 54% minority in 2050. By 2023, minorities will comprise more than half of all children. (U.S. Census Bureau, 2008)

The Latina/o population is projected to nearly triple, from 46.7 million to 132.8 million during the 2008–2050 period. Thus, nearly one in three U.S. residents would be Latina/o. The African American population is projected to increase from 41.1 million, or 14% of the population in 2008, to 65.7 million, or 15% in 2050. The Asian population is projected to climb from 15.5 million to 40.6 million—a rise from 5.1% to 9.2%. American Indians and Alaska Natives are projected to rise from 4.9 million to 8.6 million (or from 1.6 to 2%). The Native Hawaiian and Other Pacific Islander population is expected to more than double, from 1.1 million to 2.6 million. The number of people who identify themselves as being of two or more races is projected to more than triple, from 5.2 million to 16.2 million. (U.S. Census Bureau, 2008)

WARM UP EXERCISE

1. *When was the first time you noticed race or ethnicity?*

2. *When were you in a setting that was multicultural? Did you reach out to others from culturally diverse backgrounds that were different than your own?*

3. *Can you recall major historical events that impacted cultural diversity in the United States? How about events that had a global impact on cultural diversity?*

4. *When you have had professional or personal contact with people from cultures different from your own, did you use different communication skills than you use with people from your own culture? If not, why not? If you did, please describe the difference.*

5. *Do you believe that having exposure and relationships across different cultures enriches one's life? Why?*

Social justice is at the very core of multicultural counseling. To understand social justice and human rights within the mental health domain, multicultural counseling must be thoroughly examined. Therefore this chapter will begin with an overview of the history, theory, and practice of multicultural counseling; this will be followed by an examination of the development of the multicultural counseling competencies. Throughout the chapter, we will discuss the relationship between multicultural counseling and social justice and human rights.

In recent decades, there has been an enormous increase in the literature regarding multicultural counseling (e.g., Arredondo, Rosen, Rice, Perez, & Tovar-Gamero, 2005; Arredondo & Toporek; 2004; Constantine, 2007; Pedersen, 2000; Ponterotto, Casas, Suzuki, & Alexander, 2001; Pope-Davis & Coleman, 1997; Roysircar, Sandhu, & Bibbin, 2003; Sue, Arredondo, & McDavis, 1992; Sue et al., 1998). With the recognition of the dramatically changing racial, ethnic, and cultural demographics of the United States (Chung, Bemak, Ortiz, & Sandoval-Perez, 2008; U.S. Census Bureau, 2002), and the effects of information technology and globalization, we as mental health professionals can no longer ignore the influence of culture on our clientele. This is consistent with the great likelihood that we will see clients from different racial, ethnic, and cultural backgrounds and that our families, communities, schools, and regions will be affected by cultural differences. As a result, there has been an increase in multicultural counseling training in the past 25 years (Brown, Parham, & Yonker, 1996; Kiselica, Maben, & Locke, 1999). In fact, multicultural training courses in counseling programs were projected to be the fastest growing new courses offered in the 1991 to 1995 period (Hollis & Wantz, 1990, 1994), leading us to our current practices in the 21st century.

Given the importance and the profound impact of multicultural counseling, it has become the "fourth force" in the counseling profession (Pedersen, 1999). According to Pedersen (1999), multicultural counseling being the fourth force does not imply that it is competing with other counseling theories but rather is complementary to current counseling theories. He contends that the multicultural counseling emphasis actually underscores the importance of culture and therefore places culture in a central position in relationship to the other three forces, which are the psychodynamic, behavioral, and humanistic aspects of counseling.

HISTORICAL PERSPECTIVES

Multiculturalism is not a new or recent concept. For centuries, dating back to ancient civilizations, there has been recognition of barriers, challenges, and potential problems in communicating and interacting with people from different cultural and diverse backgrounds (Jackson, 1995). One difference from the past is that cultural diversity has expanded globally and can be found to varying degrees throughout the world. Given the rapid expansion of cultures across national and international borders, vast movements of people who are voluntarily and involuntarily migrating, advancing technology, and swiftly growing globalization, multiculturalism is not only a prominent worldwide phenomenon, but also a complex and multidimensional issue. Therefore, it becomes even more important for us as counselors and psychotherapists to be aware of, understand, and acknowledge the complexity of multiculturalism as it relates to ourselves and our clients, and the potential influence it has on our work as counselors and therapists.

The history of multicultural counseling spans several decades. In the 1950s, there were few journal articles on multicultural counseling. During that time period, scholars of color faced barriers in getting published in professional journals. Professional publications were dominated by a small group of nationally known authors who were predominantly of European-American descent, and generally there was a lack of interest in the field (Walsh, 1975). However, in the 1960s, with the growing importance of the civil rights movement, multicultural counseling began to develop and generate more professional interest. A new political and social awareness of issues of racism, prejudice, and discrimination strongly influenced counselors and psychotherapists to reexamine the field in relation to social injustices. Notions, such as the inferiority of minority or ethnic and racial groups compared to the majority group, were questioned (Jackson, 1995). During this era, multicultural counseling blossomed, in part due to the support of White mental health professionals who had obtained a new sense of awareness and sensitivity to unfair treatment, inequities, and race. Questions were raised regarding whether psychological and counseling theories, models, and techniques that were based on European-American traditions would be applicable to clients from different ethnic, racial, and cultural backgrounds. Hence, a newly articulated concern arose that questioned whether services provided by mental health professionals would be effective for *all* clients.

Adding to this awareness and sensitivity perpetuated by the civil rights movement was an increase in opportunities for higher education for racial and ethnic groups and a simultaneous growing interest in the helping professions. One result was an expanding group of racially and culturally diverse helping professionals who were trained during this time period, and who raised serious questions about the responsiveness of mental health professionals to cultural differences within the increasingly diverse population (Aubrey, 1971). The impetus that was established in the 1960s continued in the 1970s, with many more researchers investigating multicultural and cross-cultural issues in counseling and psychotherapy. Funding came from the federal government, state governments, and private foundations as this momentum promoted a surge of rapid growth in cross-cultural research in the 1980s and 1990s. This growth has continued into the 21st century, with professionals conducting research and writing about diversity and multicultural issues in record numbers (Jackson, 1995). It is obvious, from the steady growth in research and increasing recognition of the importance of being culturally responsive, that multicultural counseling is not only here to stay, but it is indeed the fourth force in the helping profession.

CULTURAL COUNSELING PARADIGMS

Although helping and supporting individuals has been going on since the earliest times of humankind, professional counseling was developed in Western, first-world countries, and it provides the basis for counseling and psychotherapy, emphasizing individual treatment that is fundamental to European-American cultures. Sue and Sue (1990) identified three models that have addressed culture from very different standpoints and belief systems; these models include the genetic deficiency model, the cultural deficiency model, and the culturally diverse model.

The *genetic deficiency model* purports that people of color are intellectually inferior to White European-Americans. Initially, this view was supposedly supported by Arthur Jensen's studies (e.g., Jensen, 1969; Nyborg & Jensen, 2000) that examined the differences between African Americans' and Whites' levels of intelligence; more recently, it has been supported by the concept of the bell curve (Hernstein & Murray, 1994). Although these theories promoting a view of inferior intelligence based on race were very popular at one time, it is important to be aware that Jensen's studies have been discredited while Hernstein and Murray's findings have also been disputed (Valencia & Suzuki, 2001).

The *cultural deficiency model* that Sue and Sue identify takes a monocultural view. Monoculturalism begins with an assumption that all people are the same (or should be the same) and hold similar cultural beliefs, values, attitudes, and worldviews. In this model, the majority European-American White cultural group in Western developed countries is considered the baseline for comparisons with all other culturally diverse groups. Thus, standards for all cultural groups are defined and measured as compared to the majority culture (White European-American) and are viewed as culturally deprived or deficient if they do not hold to those standards. Hence, people of color, immigrant and refugee populations with linguistic differences, gay and lesbian populations, and other diverse populations who are not part of the mainstream are perceived to be culturally deprived and lacking the attributes of the majority culture. This perspective provides a basis for the therapeutic encounter that is highly ethnocentric, with narrow beliefs that advocate for the superiority of one group over others.

The third model, the *culturally diverse model,* supports the concept of multicultural counseling and differences in culture. Being from a non-mainstream cultural group and having differences from it are not perceived as limitations or disadvantages. One is not judged in this model from the perspective of White European-Americans or the majority culture, so that differences are viewed as indicating one is deficient, weak, or flawed. Instead, different cultural perspectives are valued, respected, and appreciated. The culturally diverse model with its focus on multiculturalism does not view cultural differences as debilitating, as the two previous models do, but rather as positive, healthy, vital, and indispensable components of society (Robinson & Howard-Hamilton, 2000). The culturally diverse model that embraces multiculturalism therefore supports and values awareness, respect, understanding, acknowledgment, acceptance, and appreciation of racial, ethnic, gender, sexual orientation, religion, disabilities, and other cultural differences. Helping professionals who adhere to this model therefore recognize that cultural differences should be acknowledged and celebrated, and they bring this value into their work.

The Development of Multicultural Counseling Competencies

As we discussed previously, the past few decades have brought a substantial increase in the literature about multicultural counseling training, practice, and research. The world of counseling and psychotherapy has been comprehensively examined and critiqued through a multicultural lens. A variety of authors have addressed issues such as acculturation (e.g., Chun, Organista, & Marin, 2002), barriers to accessing mainstream services (e.g., U.S. Department of Health and Human Services, 2001), trust and empathy (Chung & Bemak, 2002), culturally responsive prevention programs, culturally specific interventions, and theories based on multiculturalism, as well as culturally embedded skills and techniques (e.g., Aponte & Wohl, 2000; Atkinson & Hackett, 2004; Bernal, Trimble, Burlew, & Leong, 2003; Constantine, 2007; Ivey, D'Andrea, Bradford Ivey, & Simek-Morgan, 2002; Pedersen, Draguns, Lonner, & Trimble, 2002; Ponterotto et al., 1996;

Sue & Sue, 2003). This body of research has focused on how we, as helping professionals, can be culturally responsive to clients from different racial, ethnic, and cultural backgrounds. Part of this work has been to develop psychological measurements of multicultural constructs, such as worldviews (Ibrahim, Roysircar-Sodowsky, & Ohnishi, 2001).

Simultaneously, an understanding of the challenges encountered by diverse populations—such as the "isms" (e.g., sexism, classism, and ageism), disabilities, and sexual orientation—has been cultivated (Atkinson & Hackett, 2004). Mental health professionals have also developed tools, such as the concept of racial and ethnic identity (e.g., Cross & Vandiver, 2001; Helms, 1995; Phinney, 1992), White identity theory (Helms, 1995), sexual orientation development (e.g., Dube & Savin-Williams, 1999; Espin, 1994), and biracial and multiracial identity (e.g., Root, 1992, 1996; Winters & DeBose, 2003) to assist us in understanding not only our clients' backgrounds, but also our very own cultural backgrounds, biases, prejudices, and privileges as they relate to the work we do within the therapeutic relationship.

The 1980s brought greater consciousness and a movement to help professionals become aware of the need to be culturally responsive to clients from different cultural backgrounds. It was during that time period that the profession began to establish guidelines and standards for multicultural competencies. These competencies are important to understand; they provide a context for our current work and a foundation in the integration of social justice into everyday practice and training. The history and evolution of these competencies are described below.

Multicultural Competencies

The development of the multicultural competencies (also known as MCC) originated in 1981, when Division 17 (Counseling Psychology) of the American Psychological Association (APA) established a committee to develop a position paper defining multicultural competencies. The

position paper identified 11 competencies that came under three dimensions: beliefs/attitudes, knowledge, and skills (Sue et al., 1982). The position paper was accepted, but interestingly, was not endorsed by the Division 17 Executive Committee. However, it was published in *The Counseling Psychologist* (Sue et al., 1982) and provided the helping profession with the first set of guidelines on the requirements for becoming a competent multicultural counselor. The position paper was important as a baseline for later work, serving as a template for subsequent refinement and expansion of the competencies (e.g., Arredondo et al., 1996; Sue et al., 1992; Sue et al., 1998).

It was 10 years after the publication of the position paper that a list of 31 multicultural counseling competencies was published (Sue et al., 1992). The 1992 competencies were endorsed by three APA divisions (current names are the Society of Counseling Psychology [Division 17], Society for the Psychology of Women [Division 35], and the Society for the Psychological Study of Ethnic Minority Issues [Division 45]) and six American Counseling Association (ACA) divisions (Association for Adult Development and Aging [AADA], Association for Counselor Education and Supervision [ACES], Association for Gay, Lesbian, and Bisexual Issues in Counseling [AGLBIC], Association for Multicultural Counseling and Development [AMCD], American School Counselors Association [ASCA], Association for Specialists in Group Work [ASGW], and the International Association of Marriage and Family Counselors [IAMFC]). Although APA did not endorse the competencies, the APA Board of Ethnic Minority Affairs did publish the Diversity Guidelines (APA, 1993). Furthermore, the recognition of the importance for psychologists to have multicultural competencies when working with clients from different ethnic, racial, and cultural backgrounds caused changes to be made in the APA Ethical Principles of Psychologists and Code of Conduct so that multicultural competencies were included (APA, 1992).

Amazingly, it took 20 years for the multicultural competencies to be endorsed by the Executive Committee of Division 17 (Society of Counseling

Psychology) (Arredondo et al., 1996; Sue et al., 1992). There were three professional organizations that played a major role in contributing to establishing the multicultural competencies: Division 17 of the APA—the Society of Counseling Psychology, Division 45 of the APA—the Society for the Psychological Study of Ethnic Minority Issues, and the Association for Multicultural Counseling and Development (AMCD), a division of the ACA. The original 11 multicultural competencies (Sue et al., 1992) evolved into the 31 multicultural competencies (Sue et al., 1992) that were operationalized (Arredondo et al., 1996) as well as two additional competencies that addressed issues of racial identity (Sue et al., 1998), making a total of 33 competencies. These 33 multicultural counseling competencies served as a template for the Multicultural Guidelines (APA, 1993). It was not until 2002 that the APA Council of Representatives finally endorsed the multicultural competencies (Arredondo & Perez, 2003), while ACA endorsed them in March 2003 (ACA, 2003).

Since there is substantial literature and comprehensive descriptions of the multicultural counseling competencies (e.g., Arredondo et al., 1996; Pope-Davis & Coleman, 1997; Sue et al., 1992; Sue et al., 1998), only a brief description of the competencies will be provided here. Multicultural competencies have been defined as counselors' attitudes/beliefs, knowledge, and skills in working with clients from a variety of ethnic, racial, and cultural groups (e.g., groups defined by gender, social class, religion, sexual orientation, disabilities, etc.) (Sue et al., 1992; Sue et al., 1998). The competencies are structured into a three by three matrix consisting of three dimensions and three levels (see Figure 2.1). The three dimensions are as follows: (1) counselor awareness of his/her cultural values and biases, (2) counselor awareness of the client's worldview, and (3) culturally appropriate intervention strategies. The three levels include (a) attitudes/beliefs, (b) knowledge, and (c) skills. Figure 2.1 is a diagram of the three dimensions and the three levels within each.

Figure 2.1   Multicultural Competencies for Counselors and Psychotherapists

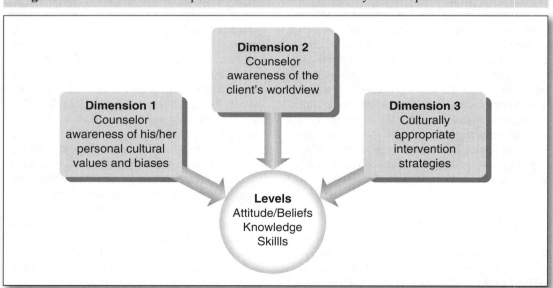

Source: Adapted from Arredondo et al. (1996).

Note: Attitude/beliefs, knowledge, and skills in working with clients will vary under each dimension.

Dimension 1: Counselors' and psychotherapists' awareness of personal cultural values and biases. Level 1, *Attitudes/Beliefs*, covers the need for counselors and psychotherapists to develop an awareness of their own cultural heritage, values, beliefs, attitudes, worldviews, experiences, perceptions, privileges, biases, prejudices, identity, and other psychological processes. It is critical for counselors and psychotherapists to be culturally aware of and sensitive to their own cultural backgrounds and how these backgrounds influence and impact the therapeutic relationship. Additionally, counselors and psychotherapists must be aware of their positive and negative responses to people from other cultures. An example would be the mental health professionals who have an awareness that within their own culture there is implicit and explicit discrimination against a particular ethnic or racial group. Knowing their own biases is important in their ability to effectively work with clients or students from that ethnic or racial group.

Hence, knowing about one's attitudes and beliefs requires that culturally skilled counselors and psychotherapists move from being culturally unaware to being aware of, and sensitive to, the complexity of their own cultural heritage and its interrelationship to that of other cultures. Mental health professionals must achieve this while valuing and respecting differences and recognizing the limits to their own competence and expertise in working across cultures (Sue et al., 1998). With this awareness and acceptance, the concept of "cultural superiority" is eliminated, and practitioners adopt a deep-rooted sense of truly valuing, appreciating, and respecting the differences in others. Counselors and psychotherapists are therefore comfortable with race, ethnicity, and differences within themselves and their clients.

Level 2, *Knowledge,* involves culturally skilled counselors and psychotherapists having knowledge about their own racial and cultural heritage and how it personally and professionally affects them in the counseling processes. Knowing the traditions, rituals, and beliefs that accompany certain life events is very helpful in understanding the meaning and context behind one's own behaviors, thoughts, and feelings. This means that counselors and psychotherapists acquire knowledge from both personal and professional perspectives about the history and impact of stereotyping, oppression, racism, and discrimination as it relates to their own cultural backgrounds as well as clients' backgrounds. Hence, counselors and psychotherapists acknowledge their own racist attitudes, beliefs, and feelings related to race, ethnicity, sexual orientation, and other aspects of cultural diversity. It is important to note that this is sometimes difficult for us to admit to ourselves and takes courage, deep honesty, and openness to address tough personal and professional issues.

According to Helms (1995), it is important for White counselors and psychologists to understand the direct and indirect benefits that result from implicit and explicit value systems that are embedded within individual, institutional, and cultural racism. In line with a social justice model, we would suggest that it is essential that counselors and psychotherapists are aware of privilege related to their race, ethnicity, or gender, and that they understand the social and personal impact this has on others, particularly given its potential for creating a power differential within the therapeutic relationship. Concurrently, it is important that they are knowledgeable about cultural differences in communication styles, realizing how their own and others' styles may inhibit or facilitate the counseling process. An example of this was a White mental health professional from a suburban background who came from a person-centered framework and was confused and disconcerted when facilitating groups with African American clients from urban backgrounds. The clients were far more direct, assertive, and confrontational in their approach to each other than the practitioner expected, so the person-centered approach was ineffective in this milieu.

In Level 3, *Skills,* counselors and psychotherapists are able to work effectively with culturally diverse clientele. They use their knowledge, awareness, and understanding of history, culturally specific help-seeking behaviors, values, worldviews, religious and spiritual beliefs, and the social context to adapt interventions to effectively respond to clients, while at the same time recognizing the limitations of their abilities and competencies. Thus, supervision, consultation, education, and training experiences are pursued and welcomed, since these experiences enrich their understanding and effectiveness in working with culturally different clientele. For example, a mental health professional may seek consultation, further training, or education about working with a client from Somalia, get help when working with a transgender client, refer clients from El Salvador to a Central American psychotherapist, or call a Native American mental health colleague to ask about cultural practices related to a Native American client.

Dimension 2: Counselor awareness of client's worldview. In Level 1, *Attitudes/Beliefs*, counselors and psychotherapists gain competencies by proactively learning about and understanding the worldviews of their culturally different clients. They are aware of their negative emotional reactions toward other racial, ethnic, and cultural groups and have insight into personal stereotypes, prejudices, biases, and preconceived notions. For example, a counselor who comes from a religious background that is strongly against homosexuality must be aware of how these deeply rooted values impact her or his counseling of individuals who are struggling with issues of sexual identity. Fostering awareness does not imply that we must adopt the worldview of the clients, but rather generate an awareness, understanding, acknowledgment, and acceptance of our client's worldview as another valued and legitimate perspective in their lives.

In Level 2, *Knowledge*, counselors and psychotherapists are aware of and have knowledge and information about the client's background. Life experiences, cultural heritage, sociopolitical issues, and historical context are all important as we strive to understand the client's life. This competency is strongly linked to racial/ethnic identity development models (Sue et al., 1998) that enable us as mental health professionals to comprehend how race, ethnicity, and culture affect personality formation, vocational choices,

manifestations and expressions of psychological disorders, help-seeking choices and behaviors, treatment expectations and outcomes, and the appropriateness or inappropriateness of counseling approaches, skills, interventions, and techniques. We must also know how sociopolitical and historical factors have influenced and continue to influence the lives of racial, ethnic, and cultural groups. For example, issues such as immigration, racism, poverty, stereotyping, hopelessness, and powerlessness are all likely to lead to distrust in us as professionals and distrust of others that will certainly influence the therapeutic process. This example becomes more concrete when we see a recent immigrant from a war-torn country who is fearful and paranoid when authority figures ask personal questions. Understanding immigrant clients' reluctance to respond to the personal questions may require an understanding of how they witnessed or knew about questioning of family members, friends, or others by government officials that resulted in these others being taken away and incarcerated, disappearing, or being publicly or privately harassed, raped, or beaten.

In Level 3, *Skills*, gaining multicultural competency requires the counselor or psychotherapist to be familiar with current research regarding the mental health of various ethnic, racial, and culturally diverse groups. Mental health professionals therefore must continually seek out learning experiences that enrich their knowledge, understanding, and cross-cultural skills, and they must be actively involved with ethnic, racial, and cultural groups outside of the counseling or academic setting. Examples of multicultural encounters may involve attending community events, going to social and political functions, and participating in celebrations.

Dimension 3: Developing culturally appropriate interventions strategies. Level 1, *Attitudes/Beliefs*, requires counselors and psychotherapists to respect, without judgment, clients' cultural, spiritual, and religious beliefs and values regarding physical and mental functioning. They should also respect indigenous helping practices and community help-giving and support networks. For example, both of us (Fred and Rita) have collaborated with spiritual healers from local communities when working with clients who believed in spiritual practices rooted in traditions of their culture. In addition, bilingualism and multilingualism are also respected, and therefore counselors and psychotherapists do not perceive a client's use of another language as an impediment or detrimental to counseling (Chung & Bemak, 2007).

A great example of this occurred when I (Fred) was on a research fellowship through the World Rehabilitation Fund at the National Institute of Mental Health and Neuro Sciences (NIMHANS) in India. NIMHANS was instituting a national pilot program in working with mental illness that had a family residential component whereby the full extended family from throughout India came and lived for three-week treatment periods. Given the many languages throughout India, there were five different languages spoken at the intensive group counseling sessions, with simultaneous translations being made from client or family member to client or family member to client or family member and so on. And it worked with multiple translations going back and forth in five languages! A similar situation for Rita occurred when she was running a psychoeducational group for Southeast Asian refugees. After I (Rita) spoke in English, I translated what I said into Chinese, while four other translators simultaneously translated into four other Southeast Asian languages. The important lesson in these two examples is not to be daunted by multiple languages and to appreciate and respect the differences that language can bring.

In Level 2, *Knowledge*, counselors have a clear and explicit knowledge and understanding of how traditional counseling and therapy may clash with the cultural values of various ethnic, racial, and cultural groups. For example, if we were to emphasize independence for someone who comes from a culture where interdependence and loyalty to one's family is highly valued, it would be inappropriate and contrary to the fabric of the cultural background of the client.

In this level there is an awareness and understanding of institutional barriers that prevent diverse groups from accessing mainstream mental health services, and there is also an understanding of the potential cultural biases in assessment and diagnostic instruments. When using tests, it is essential that we keep in mind the cultural variables and linguistic capabilities of the clients.

In addition, mental health professionals must understand the unique cultural aspects of family structure, hierarchies, values and beliefs, and the interrelationship of families with the larger social community and the majority culture. This in turn requires knowledge about racial/ethnic identity models and an awareness of how these models relate to counseling and psychotherapy. We must ask ourselves important questions such as, "Where are our clients in terms of their racial identity, and how is that impacting the issues that they present to us and their response to me as a therapist?"

In Level 3, *Skills*, counselors and psychotherapists recognize that helping styles and approaches may be culturally bound, and they have the ability to engage in a variety of verbal and nonverbal helping responses that are appropriate means of cross-cultural communication. Thus, instead of being bound to only one approach for all clients, they are versatile and can move adeptly within various cultures to foster more effective communication. For example, in Native American and some Asian cultures, eye contact may be seen as offensive. Thus, to gauge the intensity and amount of eye contact with Native American or Asian clients would be important, and the amount would be different than when working with a White client who would expect more eye contact and reciprocate accordingly.

Another attribute of Level 3 is the ability of helping professionals to seek consultation with traditional healers or religious and spiritual healers in the treatment of culturally different clients when it is appropriate. Thus, if the client believes that a *curandero* or *shaman* is important with their healing, it is essential that the mental health professional support the utilization of this spiritual healer as a partner in the therapeutic process. For example, when I (Fred) was providing clinical consultation for a mental health center for Latina/os, the clinicians asked me about taking the client we were discussing to a *curandero*. They believed that this would be helpful, but they were unsure of its appropriateness as part of treatment in a mental health facility. The fact that I, as the consultant, was in full agreement and supported this intervention was crucial in the client resolving some of the issues that he was facing and had been stuck with while participating *only* in Western psychotherapy.

In addition, if there is a language difference between the counselor and client, counselors must assume responsibility for either seeking a translator with cultural knowledge and an appropriate professional background or refer the client to a knowledgeable and competent bilingual counselor. Counselors and psychotherapists must also be sensitive to issues of oppression, sexism, and racism, and therefore be cognizant of the relevance and impact of sociopolitical issues when they are conducting evaluations and providing interventions.

We as mental health professionals need to take responsibility for educating our clients about psychological processes, so they understand the goals of therapy, what to expect when they engage in counseling, their legal rights, and our orientation and ways of practicing. While we take into account our own level of racial identity development, we must tailor our relationship-building strategies, intervention plans, and referral considerations to the particular stage of identity development of the client. Finally, we must be able to combine our clinical role with psychoeducational work and interventions in larger systems that impact the client, so that we become consultants, advocates, advisors, teachers, facilitators of indigenous healing, and so on.

In summary, there has been enormous support for the multicultural competencies that are important to integrate in all aspects of our counseling practice, supervision, training, and research (e.g., Casas, Ponterotto, & Gutierrez, 1986; Ibrahim & Arredondo, 1986; Pope-Davis & Coleman, 2001; Pope-Davis, Reynolds, & Vazquez, 1992). The tremendous research, training, and interest in these issues have been consistent with the significant increase in attention to multicultural issues within the helping professions over the past few decades (e.g., Constantine, 1997; Hills & Strozier, 1992; Ladany, Inman, & Constantine, 1997; Pedersen, 1991; Ponterotto, 1997; Quintana & Bernal, 1995).

MULTICULTURAL COUNSELING COMPETENCY ASSESSMENTS

It is clear in the field of mental health that psychology and counseling graduate training programs have integrated multicultural issues into their academic curriculums. This has occurred in varying degrees that range from the inclusion of multicultural counseling and psychotherapy through one required course to an infusion of multiculturalism throughout the curriculum. Based on different interpretations of how to operationalize cross-cultural work in graduate level training, questions have been raised regarding how to ensure effective multicultural counseling training (Coleman, 1996; Constantine, Ladany, Inman, & Ponterotto, 1996). Both Pope-Davis and Dings (1995) and Constantine and Ladany (2001) have conducted comprehensive reviews and assessments of the instruments that assess multicultural counseling competencies. Given the importance and relationship of multicultural counseling to social justice and human rights, this section will provide a brief overview of their findings. The multicultural counseling competencies have been evaluated in three different ways that include self-reports, portfolios, and observer-rated indices. These methods each examined the effectiveness of multicultural counseling training in graduate programs and have relevance to social justice work.

SELF-REPORT ASSESSMENTS

We want to provide you with a brief overview of results from three self-report instruments that were designed to measure the multicultural competencies of helping professionals, so you have a clear sense of where these assessments stand in the field (see Table 2.1). The Multicultural Awareness/Knowledge/Skills Survey (MAKSS) was developed by D'Andrea, Daniels, and Heck (1991). The 60-item scale consists of three subscales that include broad categories of awareness, knowledge, and skills. Each subscale contains 20 items with reported reliabilities of .75, .90, and .96 for each of the subscales respectively. Items are rated on a 4-point Likert scale. Although the authors report that the instrument is valid, it has been suggested that the MAKSS needs to provide more evidence of validity (Pope-Davis & Dings, 1995).

The Multicultural Counseling Inventory (MCI) by Sodowsky, Taffe, Gutkin, and Wise (1994) was developed "in order to operationalize some of the purposed constructs of multicultural counseling competencies" (p. 139). The 40-item instrument is rated on a 4-point Likert scale and consists of four subscales: Multicultural Counseling Skills (11 items), Multicultural Awareness (10 items), Multicultural Counseling Knowledge (11 items) and Multicultural Counseling Relationship (8 items). The MCI is unique in that it expands on the multicultural counseling competencies to include multicultural counseling relationships, thus having more bearing on the therapeutic relationship. Internal consistency reliabilities and correlations were reported with a mean Cronbach's alpha of .87 for the total score of the entire measure, and of .78, .77, .80, and .68 for each of the subscales respectively (Sodowsky, Kuo-Jackson, Richardson, & Corey, 1998). The instrument focuses on behaviors rather than attitudes and has been reported to have good content, construct, and criterion-related validity (Sodowsky et al., 1998).

The Multicultural Counseling Knowledge and Awareness Scale (MCKAS) is a 32-item instrument developed by Ponterotto, Gretchen, Utsey, Rieger, and Austin (2002). The items are rated on a 7-point Likert scale. The MCKAS is a revised version of the Multicultural Counseling Awareness Scale–Form B (Ponterotto et al., 1996) and consists of two factors: Awareness (12 items) and Knowledge (20 items). It was reported that each subscale has a coefficient alpha of .85, and it has good content, construct, and criterion-related validity (Ponterotto et al., 2002).

Table 2.1 Self-Report Assessments for Multicultural Competency

	Multicultural Awareness/Knowledge/ Skills Survey (MAKSS)	*Multicultural Counseling Inventory (MCI)*	*Multicultural Counseling Knowledge and Awareness Scale (MCKAS)*
Developed by	D'Andrea, Daniels, and Heck (1991)	Sodowsky, Taffe, Gutkin, and Wise (1994)	Ponterotto, Gretchen, Utsey, Rieger, & Austin (2002)—Revised version of multicultural counseling Awareness Scale-Form B (1996)
What it measures	Broad categories of awareness, knowledge and skills	To operationalize some of purposed constructs of multicultural counseling competencies	Awareness and knowledge
Number of items	60 items with 3 subscales (20 each)	40 items with 4 subscales: multicultural counseling	32 items with 2 subscales: awareness (12 items)

(Continued)

Table 2.1 (Continued)

	Multicultural Awareness/Knowledge/ Skills Survey (MAKSS)	Multicultural Counseling Inventory (MCI)	Multicultural Counseling Knowledge and Awareness Scale (MCKAS)
		skills (11), multicultural awareness (10), multicultural counseling knowledge (11), multicultural counseling relationship (8)	and knowledge (20)
How it is scored/rated	4-point Likert scale	4-point Likert scale	7-point Likert scale
Reliability/validity	Subscales have respective reliabilities of .75, .90, & .96 and have good validity	Mean Cronbach's alphas of 87 and .78, .77, .80, & .68 for respective subscales—focuses on behaviors, not attitudes, and has good content, construct, and criterion-related validity	Each subscale had a coefficient alpha of .85 and has good content and criterion-related validity

Limitations of self-report assessments. In any self-report measures, there are inherent limitations. One limitation relates to the fact that respondents may provide anticipated or socially desirable responses rather than actual behaviors or attitudes (Pope-Davis & Dings, 1995; Sue, 1996), so that the respondent may be trying to please the researcher by doing or saying the "right thing." This type of limitation supports studies that found no significant relationship between self-reported multicultural counseling competence and demonstrated competence (Constantine & Ladany, 2000; Ladany, Inman, & Constantine, 1997), in which the self-report is not reflective of the demonstration of skills. Another factor in finding discrepancies between what the counselor or psychotherapist reports and what is objectively demonstrated is the fact that respondents may be from selected sample groups rather than random or anonymous samples, resulting in a feeling that some level of personal or professional credibility and importance is at stake (Pope-Davis & Dings, 1995).

Therefore, researchers need to control and account for attitudes of social desirability when examining correlates of self-reported multicultural counseling competencies. In addition, respondents may interpret the items differently than intended by the test developers. Researchers (e.g., Constantine & Ladany, 2001; Ponterotto & Alexander, 1996; Pope-Davis & Dings, 1995) have also suggested that for all three instruments, there is a need for more evidence on the various types of validity, and that given the lack of validity-related evidence, it is unclear what each instrument measures. Constantine and Ladany (2001) also stated that although the three instruments have similar objectives of assessing perceived multicultural counseling competence, these measures tend to vary in the number of factors that compose the overall construct and therefore may be confusing about what the instruments actually assess. Although studies comparing the three measures found some degree of correlation, they still appear to measure different constructs (Pope-Davis & Dings, 1995). Also, if the three instruments are reliable and valid as purported, then the question arises as to the degree of interchangeability of the instruments (Pope-Davis & Dings, 1995).

Another limitation of the self-reported multicultural counseling competence measures is the criticism that the aim of the measures is not quite accurate. The measures claim to assess the respondent's ability to work with a range of ethnic, racial, and cultural groups; however, a review of the items found that they focused mainly on working with people of color (Constantine & Ladany, 2000). Constantine and Ladany (2001) raise an important issue, pointing out that the competence measures have focused on demonstrating multicultural counseling competencies in individual counseling; they do not include counseling and psychotherapy in a wider context, such as with groups and families, and other interventions such as outreach, consultation, and advocacy. Furthermore, although the multicultural counseling competencies have been expanded upon and operationalized, they have not been assessed for their effectiveness. Future studies could help provide a better understanding of how the multicultural counseling competencies correspond with social justice and human rights, especially since these concepts are at the very core of multicultural counseling.

Alternative Multicultural Counseling Competency Assessments

Another method of assessing students' multicultural counseling competencies is the use of the portfolio (Coleman, 1996). Given that a portfolio is a collection of a student's work that demonstrates effort, progress, and achievement in specific areas, portfolios can also be used to reflect counselors' competence in multicultural counseling during their training (Coleman, 1996). We would suggest that this can also be a tool for assessing students' reflections on issues of social justice and human rights. The portfolio is unique in that it has the potential to demonstrate a counselor's abilities within the three multicultural counseling competence levels (awareness, knowledge, and skills) and across the various kinds of counseling interventions. This may be evident in the student's work with individuals, groups, and families and in consultation (Coleman, 1996),

where counselors can document through a portfolio their multicultural counseling competence using different treatment modalities.

A primary strength in using the portfolio is the ability to identify and evaluate competencies based on a broad range of behaviors. For example, the portfolio could document that the student has demonstrated self-awareness of his or her own attitudes regarding a client's use of an indigenous healer, or it could show that the student has knowledge about help-seeking behaviors in a particular culture. The use of a portfolio may be contrasted to single assessment instruments, such as watching a videotaped session with culturally diverse clients, which have been construed as more limited (Constantine & Ladany, 2001). It is also important to keep in mind the limitations of using portfolios; it may be time-consuming to develop and review them and problematic to define consistency and reliability for scoring and evaluation (Coleman, 1996; Collins, 1992; O'Neil, 1992).

ASSESSMENTS OF MULTICULTURAL ISSUES IN TRAINING PROGRAMS

Two instruments have been developed for faculty or training directors to assess program-based multicultural training for students. These instruments are useful tools in encouraging discussion and exploration of multicultural issues within training programs and providing program information about areas that need multicultural enhancement (Constantine & Ladany, 2001). One instrument is the Multicultural Competency Checklist (MCC) developed by Ponterotto, Alexander, and Grieger (1995). This is a 22-item checklist focusing on racial and ethnic diversity issues in training programs; it consists of six categories: Minority Representation, Curriculum Issues, Counseling Practice and Supervision, Research Considerations, Student and Faculty Competency Evaluation, and Physical Environment.

A second instrument developed by Pope-Davis, Liu, Nevitt, and Toporek (2000), the Multicultural Environmental Inventory–Revised (MEI–R), has 27 items that assess graduate students' perceptions of their academic training program in terms of its multicultural focus. The MEI–R has sound construct validity and has four factors: Curriculum and Supervision, Climate and Comfort, Honesty in Recruitment, and Multicultural Research. The limitation for both of these instruments is their use of self-report measures, but it may be valuable to those who are training students at the university or supervising trainees on the job.

SUPERVISOR RATINGS OF MULTICULTURAL COUNSELING COMPETENCE

The Cross-Cultural Counseling Inventory–Revised (CCCI-R) developed by LaFromboise, Coleman, and Hernandez (1991) is a 20-item instrument designed for supervisors to assess their trainees' cross-cultural counseling competence. The items are rated on a 6-point Likert scale and consist of just one factor, which includes items that represent three areas: cross-cultural counseling skills, sociopolitical awareness, and cultural sensitivity. The single factor is reported to have a coefficient alpha of .95 and to have demonstrated good content, construct, and criterion-related validity (LaFromboise et al., 1991; Sabnani & Ponterotto, 1992). One major limitation of this measure is that the rater, who is the supervisor, must be multiculturally competent.

SUMMARY

Social justice and human rights are at the very core and provide a foundation that is the heartbeat of multicultural counseling. It is essential that helping professionals working within the realm of social justice and human rights have a thorough knowledge and awareness of the issues and evaluation instruments that are fundamental to multicultural counseling. It is also critical that professionals working on social justice in counseling and psychotherapy are able to apply the multicultural skills they have acquired and recognize the importance of the multicultural counseling

competencies, many of which are rooted in traditions of social justice and human rights.

We would suggest that understanding oneself and others; knowing about the sociopolitical, historical, and economic factors that contribute to social inequities; understanding the impacts of globalism, technology, ethnic and racial identity, and nationalism; and having an overall knowledge of the impact of the psychosocial and ecological context for any client, family, and community are fundamental to employing a social justice model in counseling and psychotherapy. In the next chapters we will discuss social justice as the "fifth force" in counseling.

DISCUSSION QUESTIONS

1. How would you describe your level of cultural awareness? How do you think you can increase your understanding of cultural diversity and the worldviews and beliefs of others?

2. What is a racial or ethnic group that you would like to learn more about? What steps do you plan to take to learn more about that group?

3. The fourth force in counseling has been identified as multiculturalism. What, in your opinion, is the relationship and impact of multiculturalism to the other three forces in psychotherapy? Provide a case example about an area in which you would consider multiculturalism, and indicate any aspects of the case where you believe that cultural diversity would *not* be a factor. In responding to the question, think about the following:

   a. What are some of the factors you would take into consideration?
   b. What does this mean in terms of how you would change the way you approach your client/student?
   c. What elements of therapy would be different?
   d. How do you think your client/student would react?

4. Think about your own race and ethnicity. When considering the genetic deficiency model and the cultural deficiency model (monoculturalism) how would you be compared and measured?

   a. Would you be in a position of privilege or a disadvantaged position?

   b. What are some current practices that are still based on such models?

5. Take a look at two journals of your preference. Review the most recent editions as well as one from 10 years ago.

   a. Observe how many articles address multicultural practices.

   b. Take a look at the edition from 10 years ago. Do you see any differences in the articles? Are cultural diversity and culturally responsive practice and research discussed more or less in the current issue? How, if at all, are these issues discussed differently?

   c. Review the multicultural competencies. What are some of the competencies that you have as a mental health professional?

   d. What are some areas for your own growth? What are some of those competencies that are still challenging for you to understand?

   e. Would you add any other competencies to the list?

   f. How has your training program been helping you and working with you to be a culturally competent counselor? (Or, if you have completed your training, how did the program help you in this regard?)

REFERENCES

American Counseling Association. (2003, March). *ACA governing council meeting minutes.* Alexandria, VA: Author.

American Psychological Association. (1992). *Ethical principles of psychologists and code of conduct.* Washington, DC: Author.

American Psychological Association. (1993). Guidelines for providers of psychological services to ethnic, linguistic, and culturally diverse populations. *American Psychologist, 48,* 45–48.

American Psychological Association. (2002). Ethical principles of psychologists and code of conduct. *American Psychologist, 57,* 1060–1073.

Aponte, J. F., & Wohl, J. (2000). *Psychological intervention and cultural diversity* (2nd ed.). Needham Heights, MA: Allyn & Bacon.

Arredondo, P., & Perez, P. (2003). Expanding multicultural competence through social justice leadership. *The Counseling Psychologist, 31*(3), 282–290.

Arredondo, P., Rosen, D. C., Rice, T., Perez, P., & Tovar-Gamero, Z. G. (2005). Multicultural counseling: A 10-year content analysis of the Journal of Counseling and Development. *Journal of Counseling and Development, 83,* 155–161.

Arredondo, P., & Toporek, R. (2004). Multicultural counseling competencies. *Journal of Mental Health Counseling, 26*(1), 44–55.

Arredondo, P., Toporek, R., Brown, S. P., Jones, J., Locke, D. C., Sanchez, J., Stadler, H., et al. (1996). Operationalizing of the multicultural counseling competencies. *Journal of Multicultural Counseling and Development, 24,* 42–78.

Atkinson, D. R., & Hackett, G. (2004). *Counseling diverse populations* (3rd ed.). Boston, MA: McGraw-Hill.

Aubrey, R. F. (1971). Historical development of guidance and counseling and implications for the future. *Personnel and Guidance Journal, 55*(1), 288–295.

Bernal, G., Trimble, J. E., Burlew, A. K., & Leong, F. T. L. (2003). Introduction: The psychological study of racial and ethnic minority psychology. In G. Bernal, J. E. Trimble, A. K. Burlew, & F. T. L. Leong (Eds.), *The handbook of racial & ethnic minority psychology* (pp. 1–12). Thousand Oaks, CA: Sage.

Brown, S., Parham, T. A., & Yonker, R. (1996). Influence of a cross cultural training course on racial identity attitudes of white females and males: Preliminary perspectives. *Journal of Counseling and Development, 74,* 510–516.

Casas, J. M., Ponterotto, J. G., & Gutierrez, J. M. (1986). An ethical indictment of counseling research and training: The cross-cultural perspective. *Journal of Counseling and Development, 64,* 347–349.

Chun, K. M., Organista, P. B., & Marin, G. (2002). *Acculturation advances in theory, measurement, and applied research.* Washington, DC: American Psychological Association.

Chung, R. C-Y., & Bemak, F. (2002). The relationship of culture and empathy in cross-cultural counseling. *Journal of Counseling & Development, 80,* 154–159.

Chung, R. C-Y., & Bemak, F. (2007). Immigrant and refugee populations. In M. G. Constantine (Ed.), *Clinical practice with people of color: A guide to becoming culturally competent* (pp. 125–142). New York, NY: Teachers College Press.

Chung, R. C-Y., Bemak, F., Ortiz, D. P., & Sandoval-Perez, P. A. (2008). Promoting the mental health of immigrants: A multicultural/social justice perspective. *Journal of Counseling & Development, 86,* 310–317.

Coleman, H. L. K. (1996). Portfolio assessment of multicultural counseling competency. *The Counseling Psychologist, 24,* 216–229.

Collins, A. (1992). Portfolios for science education: Issues in purpose, structure, and authenticity. *Science Education, 76*(4), 451–463.

Constantine, M. G. (1997). Facilitating multicultural competency in counseling supervision: Operationalizing a practical framework. In D. B. Pope-Davis & H. L. K. Coleman (Eds.), *Multicultural counseling competencies: Assessment, education and training, and supervision* (pp. 310–324). Thousand Oaks, CA: Sage.

Constantine, M. G. (2007). *Clinical practice with people of color.* New York, NY: Teachers College Press.

Constantine, M. G., & Ladany, N. (2000). Self-report multicultural counseling competence scales: Their relation to social desirability attitudes and multicultural case conceptualization ability. *Journal of Counseling Psychology, 47,* 155–164.

Constantine, M. G., & Ladany, N. (2001). New visions for defining and assessing multicultural counseling competence. In J. G. Ponterotto, J. M. Casas, L. A. Suzuki, & C. M. Alexander, *Handbook of multicultural counseling* (2nd ed., pp. 482–498). Thousand Oaks, CA: Sage.

Constantine, M. G., Ladany, N., Inman, A. G., & Ponterotto, J. G. (1996). Students' perceptions of multicultural training in counseling psychology programs. *Journal of Multicultural Counseling and Development, 24,* 241–253.

Cross, W. E., Jr., & Vandiver, B. J. (2001). Nigrescence theory and measurement: Introducing the Cross Racial Identity Scale (CRIS). In J. G. Ponterotto, J. M. Casas, L. A. Suzuki, & C. M. Alexander (Eds.), *Handbook of multicultural counseling* (pp. 371–393). Thousand Oaks, CA: Sage.

D'Andrea, M., Daniels, J., & Heck, R. (1991). Evaluating the impact of multicultural counseling training. *Journal of Counseling and Development, 70,* 143–150.

Dube, E. M., & Savin-Williams, R. C. (1999). Sex identity development among ethnic sexual-minority male youths. *Developmental Psychology, 35,* 1389–1398.

Espin, O. M. (1994). Feminist approaches. In L. Comas-Diaz & B. Greene (Eds.), *Women of color: Integrating ethnic and gender identities in psychotherapy* (pp. 265–286). New York, NY: Guilford Press.

Helms, J. E. (1995). An update of Helms's white and people of color racial identity models. In J. G. Ponterotto, J. M. Casas, L. A. Suzuki, & C. M. Alexander (Eds.), *Handbook of multicultural counseling* (1st ed., pp. 181–198). Thousand Oaks: CA: Sage.

Hernstein, R. J. & Murray, C. A. (1994). *The bell curve: Intelligence and class structure in American life.* New York, NY: Free Press.

Hills, H. I., & Strozier, A. A. (1992). Multicultural training in APA-approved counseling psychology programs: A survey. *Professional Psychology: Research and Practice, 23,* 43–51.

Hollis, J. W., & Wantz, R. A. (1990). *Counselor preparation 1990–92: Program, personnel, trends* (7th ed.). Muncie, IN: Accelerated Development.

Hollis, J. W., & Wantz, R. A. (1994). *Counselor preparation 1993–95: Vol. 2: Status, trends, and implications* (8th ed.). Philadelphia, PA: Accelerated Development.

Ibrahim, F. A., & Arredondo, P. M. (1986). Ethical standards for cross-cultural counseling: Counselor preparation, practice, assessment and research. *Journal of Counseling and Development, 64,* 349–352.

Ibrahim, F. A., Roysircar-Sodowsky, G., & Ohnishi, H. (2001). Worldview: Recent developments and needed directions. In J. G. Ponterotto, J. M. Casas, L. A. Suzuki, & C. M. Alexander (Eds.), *Handbook of multicultural counseling* (pp. 425–456). Thousand Oaks, CA: Sage.

Ivey, A. E., D'Andrea, M., Bradford Ivey, M., & Simek-Morgan, L. (2002). *Theories of counseling and psychotherapy: A multicultural perspective* (5th ed). Boston, MA: Allyn & Bacon.

Jackson, M. L. (1995). Multicultural counseling: Historical perspectives. In J. G. Ponterotto, J. M. Casas, L. A. Suzuki, & C. M. Alexander (Eds.), *Handbook of multicultural counseling* (pp. 3–16). Thousand Oaks, CA: Sage.

Jensen, A. (1969). How much can we boost IQ and school achievement? *Harvard Educational Review, 39,* 1–123.

Kiselica, M. S., Maben, P., & Locke, D. C. (1999). Do multicultural education and diversity appreciation training reduce prejudice among counseling trainees? *Journal of Mental Health Counseling, 21,* 240–254.

Ladany, N., Inman, A. G., & Constantine, M. G. (1997). Supervisee multicultural case conceptualization ability and self-reported multicultural competence as functions of supervisee racial identity and supervisor focus. *Journal of Counseling Psychology, 44,* 284–293.

LaFromboise, T. D., Coleman, H. L. K., & Hernandez, A. (1991). Development and factor structure of the Cross-Cultural Counseling Inventory–Revised. *Professional Psychology: Research and Practice, 22,* 380–388.

Nyborg, N., & Jensen, A. (2000). Black-white differences on various psychometric tests: Spearman's hypothesis tested on American armed services veterans. *Personality & Individual Differences, 28*(3), 593–599.

O'Neil, J. (1992). Putting performance assessment to the test. *Educational Leadership, 49*(8), 14–19.

Pedersen, P. (1991). Multiculturalism as a fourth force in counseling. *Journal of Counseling and Development, 70*(1), 6–12.

Pedersen, P. (1999). *Multiculturalism as a fourth force.* Philadelphia, PA: Brunner/Mazel.

Pedersen, P. (2000). *Handbook for developing multicultural awareness* (3rd ed.). Alexandria, VA: American Counseling Association.

Pedersen, P., Draguns, J. G., Lonner, W. J., & Trimble, J. E. (2002). *Counseling across cultures* (5th ed.). Thousand Oaks, CA: Sage.

Phinney, J. S. (1992). The multigroup ethnic identity measure: A new scale for use with diverse groups. *Journal of Adolescent Research, 7,* 156–176.

Ponterotto, J. G. (1997). Multicultural counseling training: A competency model and national survey. In D. B. Pope-Davis & H. L. K. Coleman (Eds.), *Multicultural counseling competence: Assessment, education and training, and supervision* (pp. 227–241). Thousand Oaks, CA: Sage.

Ponterotto, J. G., & Alexander, C. M. (1996). Assessing the multicultural competence of counselors and clinicians. In L. A. Suzuki, P. J. Meller, &

J. G. Ponterotto (Eds.), *Handbook of multicultural assessment* (pp. 651–672). San Francisco: Jossey-Bass.

Ponterotto, J. G., Alexander, C. M., & Grieger, I. (1995). A multicultural counseling checklist for counseling training programs. *Journal of Multicultural Counseling and Development, 23,* 11–20.

Ponterotto, J. G., Casas, J. M., Suzuki, L. A., & Alexander, C. M. (Eds.). (2001). *Handbook of multicultural counseling* (2nd ed.) Thousand Oaks, CA: Sage.

Ponterotto, J. G., Gretchen, D., Utsey, S. O., Rieger B. P., & Austin, R. (2002). A revision of the Multicultural Counseling Awareness Scale. *Journal of Multicultural Counseling & Development, 30*(3), 153–180.

Ponterotto, J. G., Rieger, B. P., Barrett, A., Sparks, R., Sanchez, C. M., & Magids, D. (1996). Development and initial validation of the Multicultural Counseling Awareness Scale. In G. R. Sodowsky & J. C. Impara (Eds.), *Multicultural assessments in counseling and clinical psychology* (pp. 247–282). Lincoln, NE: Buros Institute of Mental Measurements.

Pope-Davis, D. B., & Coleman, H. L. K. (1997). *Multicultural counseling competencies: Assessment, education and training, and supervision.* Thousand Oaks, CA: Sage.

Pope-Davis, D. B., & Coleman, H. L. K. (Eds.). (2001). The intersection of race, class, and gender in multicultural counseling. Thousand Oaks, CA: Sage.

Pope-Davis, D. B., & Dings, J. G. (1995). The assessment of multicultural counseling competencies. In J. G. Ponterotto, J. M. Casas, L. A. Suzuki, & C. M. Alexander (Eds.), *Handbook of multicultural counseling* (pp. 312–330). Thousand Oaks, CA: Sage.

Pope-Davis, D. B., Liu, W. M., Nevitt, J., & Toporek, R. L. (2000). The development and initial validation of the Multicultural Environmental Inventory: A preliminary investigation. *Cultural Diversity and Ethnic Minority Psychology, 6,* 57–64.

Pope-Davis, D. B., Reynolds, A. L., & Vazquez, L. A. (1992). *Multicultural counseling: Issues of ethnic diversity* (Film). Available from the University of Iowa Video Center, C-215 Seashore Hall, Iowa City, IA 52242, or call 1-800-369-4692.

Quintana, S. M., & Bernal, M. E. (1995). Ethnic minority training in counseling psychology:

Comparisons with clinical psychology and proposed standards. *The Counseling Psychologist, 23*, 102–121.

Robinson, T. L., & Howard-Hamilton, M. F. (2000). *The convergence of race, ethnicity, and gender: Multiple identities in counseling.* Upper Saddle River, NJ: Prentice-Hall.

Root, M. P. P. (Ed.). (1992). *Racially mixed people in America.* Thousand Oaks, CA: Sage.

Root, M. P. P. (Ed.) (1996). *The multiracial experience: Racial borders as the new frontier.* CA: Sage.

Roysircar, G., Sandhu, D. S., & Bibbin, V. E. (2003). *Multicultural competencies: A guidebook of practices.* Alexandria, VA: Association for Multicultural Counseling and Development, American Counseling Association.

Sabnani, H. B., & Ponterotto, J. G. (1992). Racial/ethnic minority instruments in counseling research: A review, critique, and recommendation. *Measurement and Evaluation in Counseling and Development, 24*, 161–187.

Sodowsky, G. R., Kuo-Jackson, P. Y., Richardson, M. F., & Corey, A. T. (1998). Correlates of self-reported multicultural competencies: Counselor multicultural social desirability, race, social inadequacy, locus of control, racial ideology, and multicultural training. *Journal of Counseling Psychology, 45,* 256–264.

Sodowsky, G. R., Taffe, R. C., Gutkin, T. B., & Wise, S. L. (1994). Development of the Multicultural Counseling Inventory: A self-report measure of multicultural competencies. *Journal of Counseling and Development, 41,* 137–148.

Sue, D. W. (1996). ACES endorsement of the multicultural counseling competencies: Do we have the courage? *Spectrum, 57*(1), 9–10.

Sue, D. W., & Sue, D. (1990). *Counseling the culturally different: Theory and practice.* New York, NY: Wiley.

Sue, D. W., Arredondo, P., & McDavis, R. (1992). Multicultural counseling competencies and standards: A call to the profession. *Journal of Multicultural Counseling and Development, 20,* 64–88.

Sue, D. W., Bernier, J. B., Durran, M., Feinberg, L., Pedersen, P., Smith, E., & Vasquez-Nuttall, E. (1982). Position paper: Cross-cultural counseling competencies. *Counseling Psychologist, 10,* 45–52.

Sue, D. W., Carter, R. T., Casas, J. M., Fouad, N. A., Ivey, A. E., Jensen, M., LaFromboise, T., et al. (1998). *Multicultural counseling competencies: Individual and organizational development.* Thousand Oaks, CA: Sage.

Sue, D. W., & Sue, D. (2003). *Counseling the culturally diverse: Theory and practice* (4th ed.). New York, NY: Wiley.

U.S. Census Bureau. (2002). *United States Census 2000.* Washington, DC: U.S. Department of Commerce, Economics and Statistics Administration.

U.S. Census Bureau. (2008). *An older and more diverse nation by midcentury.* Retrieved from http://www.census.gov/Press-Release/www/releases/archives/population/012496.html

U.S. Department of Health and Human Services. (2001). *Mental health: Culture, race, and ethnicity.* A supplement to *Mental health: A report of the surgeon general.* Rockville, MD: U.S. Department of Health and Human Services.

Valencia, R. R., & Suzuki, L. A. (2001). *Intelligence testing and minority students: Foundations, performance, factors, and assessment issues.* Thousand Oaks, CA: Sage.

Walsh, W. M. (1975). Classics in guidance and counseling. *Personnel and Guidance Journal, 54*(4), 219–220.

Winters, L. I., & DeBose, H. L. (2003). *New faces in a changing America: Multiracial identity in the 21st century.* Thousand Oaks, CA: Sage.

3

Social Justice as the Fifth Force: Theories and Concepts

Everyone has the right to work, to just and favourable conditions of work and to protection for himself and his family (and) an existence worthy of human dignity. . . . Everyone has the right to a standard of living adequate for the health and well being of himself and his family, including food, clothing, housing and medical care. (U.N. Universal Declaration of Human Rights, 1948)

The smart way to keep people passive and obedient is to strictly limit the spectrum of acceptable opinion, but allow very lively debate within that spectrum—even encourage the more critical and dissident views. That gives people the sense that there's free thinking going on, while all the time the presuppositions of the system are being reinforced by the limits put on the range of the debate. (Chomsky, 1998)

WARM UP EXERCISE

1. *When you were a high school student, did you ever observe a social injustice? Do you remember what you thought and felt? Did you do anything? Why or why not?*

2. *Do you believe you have power in any part of your life? If so, how do you use this power? What does this feel like?*

3. *Are there social injustices that you wish you could change? If so, what are they?*

4. *Civil rights leaders; outspoken critics of war, slavery, and oppression; leaders of the women's movement; advocates for the poor and disenfranchised; activists promoting same sex marriages; environmental activists; and so many others have taken major steps that frequently placed themselves in danger and at high levels of risk. To what degree would you "step out" and place yourself at risk to fight for a social justice issue you believed in?*

The issues of social justice and human rights draw people from different professions and different walks of life. These concerns transcend socioeconomic boundaries, race, ethnicity, culture, religion, age, and gender. Many people who enter the mental health profession do so based on apprehensions about a variety of social justice issues, such as racism, sexism, poverty, discrimination, and interpersonal violence. The concept of "social justice" is not found in the dictionary. However, there is a definition for the term *justice* in Merriam-Webster's online dictionary that includes the following:

> The maintenance or administration of what is just . . . the administration of the law . . . the establishment or determination of rights according to the rules of law or equity . . . the quality of being just, impartial, or fair . . . the principle or ideal of just dealing or right action. (http://www.merriam-webster .com/dictionary/justice)

It is clear from the definition that the concept of *justice* is most frequently associated with the legal system, with an underlying assumption that justice equates to equal rights, access, and fair treatment.

Based on the definition of *justice,* the concept of *social justice* refers to a just society and expands beyond the legal interpretation of justice and the law. Rather, the concept of social justice, when considered within the context of counseling and psychotherapy, is based on the idea that society gives individuals and groups fair treatment and an equal share of benefits, resources, and opportunities. Striving for justice remains a continuing struggle, since not all individuals or groups receive the same justice, opportunities, or rights in similar situations. This chapter will examine the concept of social justice within the context of the mental health field, with an aim to provide clarity regarding the concept itself and the importance and relevance of social justice and human rights in the work we do as psychologists and professional counselors.

What is Social Justice?

When we consider "social" justice in the mental health field, we are examining a broader perspective than is covered by the more narrowly defined legal aspect of justice. Social injustice incorporates social issues that involve the individual, the family, the community, the wider society, and even the international community. It refers to unfair treatment or inequities that have resulted from racism, sexism, socioeconomics, sexual orientation, religion, ableism, and other "isms," all of which affect quality of life. Social justice constitutes the right to fairness and equity (Bell, 1997).

Social injustices may be experienced in a variety of different ways, ranging from personal affronts to broader kinds of violations that are institutionally based. A social injustice may be a clear and overt inequity—such as denial of entry to a private club based on race, gender, or religion, or a hate crime directed at the person—such as the word *JAP* recently seen by the authors scratched onto the hood of a parked car. Other forms of social injustice may manifest more covertly, such as institutional unwritten policies that prevent people of color and/or women from advancing to senior positions, or discrimination that results in lower pay raises for people who are gay or lesbian or are physically challenged. Table 3.1 provides some examples of the inequalities and unfair treatment of specific groups.

As these examples show, social inequities may arise when there is a lack of acceptance and tolerance for differences, such as intolerance for differences in race, ethnic and cultural group, religion, language barriers, socioeconomic status, disabilities, age, gender, and sexual orientation. These intolerances may lead to discrimination, biases, prejudice, unfair treatment, and, at times, interpersonal violence. Subsequently, social justice is determined by social conditions, and by definition it includes concepts of justice, fairness, and righteousness. In effect, social justice is a response to social conditions that produce inequalities in how people in any given society

Table 3.1 Examples of Inequalities and Unfair Treatment of Specific Groups

Growing Discrimination Among Pregnant Workers

Even though birth rates are declining, more and more women are saying that they have been discriminated against at work because they are pregnant. This issue has become one of the fastest growing types of discrimination addressed by the Equal Employment Opportunity Commission. The range of jobs in which it is experienced is quite large, from entry level employment to positions that are higher up.

Lawyers believe that in many situations, employers do not realize they are discriminating, but pregnant women have been fired, denied promotions, and pushed to terminate their pregnancies. Employment lawyers also mention that smaller organizations have a fear that women will go on maternity leave during an important time, or that many women will leave at once, leaving behind extra work for their coworkers. One woman was fired a week after telling her manager she was pregnant, because the manager felt she would not be able to drive, which was part of her job. Another woman was laid off shortly after her maternity leave.

The rise in discrimination is important, since women make up more than half of the total work force, and their share in it is expected to grow even more. This type of discrimination also has the potential to cost companies money if the women against whom they discriminate press charges. Pregnancy discrimination has become more prevalent, because of the challenges of the current economy, because more pregnant women are staying at work longer into their pregnancies, and because of stereotypes about pregnant women.

Source: Armour (2005).

Transgender Person, Duanna Johnson, Murdered in Memphis, TN

Duanna Johnson was found shot to death in the street in North Memphis, Tennessee. A witness heard a gun fire and saw three people fleeing the scene, but the police do not have any suspects. A lawyer, Murray Wells, confirmed that Johnson was his client, saying that she was often in the neighborhood where she was killed. Murray also stated that Johnson was trying to move back to her hometown of Chicago, because she could not afford to live in Memphis any longer. Her apartment did not have electricity, and Murray was helping her buy a bus ticket back to Chicago.

Just months before her death, Johnson was arrested on prostitution charges. She stated that one police officer beat her while another one held her down after making derogatory comments about her sexuality. The beating was videotaped, and the two officers were fired from the police department.

Source: Margetts (2008).

Teenage Boys Not Responsible for the Death of Immigrant, Luis Ramirez

Two teenage boys were found not guilty of the death of Mexican immigrant, Luis Ramirez. Ramirez died of blunt force to the head, but defendants Derrick Donchak, 19, and Brandon Piekarksy, 17, were acquitted of all charges except for simple assault. The jury that acquitted them was made up of six white women and six white men.

Lawyers for Donchak and Piekarksy put the blame on other teens who were involved in the confrontation with Ramirez and also made Ramirez out to be the aggressor. The night Ramirez died, the group of teens had been drinking and provoked Ramirez and his friend with racial comments, according to the prosecutors. The argument ended with Ramirez dying in the hospital two days after the encounter.

A spokeswoman for the Mexican-American Legal Defense and Education Fund stated that this case sends the dangerous message that a person of a different national origin is less valuable in our society. It also sends the message that people can brutally beat other people to death and get away with it.

Source: Grinberg (2009).

gain access and rights to advantages and disadvantages (Miller, 1999). King Davis (1996) nicely summarizes social justice, stating that social justice is

> a basic value and desired goal in democratic societies and includes equitable and fair access to societal institutions, laws, resources [and] opportunities, without arbitrary limitations based on observed, or interpretation of, differences in age, color, culture, physical or mental disability, education, gender, income, language, national origin, race, religion or sexual orientation. (p. 1)

One way to understand social justice is to examine social injustices. To illustrate social injustices, we have chosen a recent example from the U.S. media related to a police arrest. An arrest was made of two faculty members on a major campus in the Southwest region of the United States for an alleged robbery. Two African American faculty members were walking across campus after leaving their offices. Police had reports of two African American men robbing a facility on campus, and the police were searching for the culprits. They stopped the two faculty members for questioning about the robbery. The subsequent denial of involvement and strong responses by the two faculty members led to the police increasing their use of physical force and the ultimate arrest of the two "suspects." After more extensive investigation, the two faculty members were released when it became clear that they did not commit the robbery.

A question that was raised was, what if the robbers had been White? Would the arresting officers have responded differently to the suspects' protestations of innocence and assertions that they were faculty members at the university? Would they have let such suspects go rather than making an arrest and conducting an interrogation? Interestingly, the authors of this book are familiar with a story to this effect, where two male colleagues, both White, were walking across campus at another university. Police approached them and confronted them about a robbery that had just occurred. The colleagues vehemently denied any involvement in the robbery, told police about their positions as professors, and were quickly judged innocent by the officers.

These were two similar situations with two different races that had two different outcomes. This story is multiplied by the thousands with the effects of differences in race, ethnicity, gender, sexual orientation, social class, disabilities, age, and so forth, and it is substantiated by research: There are biases and prejudices so that people, based on who they are, do not always receive equal treatment (Adams et al., 2000).

To further illustrate the robbery situation noted above, let's say one African American man and one White American man were taken into custody regarding the robbery. It may appear that both men were subjected to the same legal process. However, the type of legal process may differ in several ways. For example, the treatment they receive from the initial contact with law enforcement (e.g., how they are questioned, taken into custody, etc.), the type of legal representation they receive, the type of sentencing they receive (if found guilty) or the penalty given may be totally different according to their race or ethnicity. (See Table 3.2 for more information regarding minorities on death row.) Researchers (e.g., Harris, 2002; Mauer, 1999; Miller, 1996; Walker, Delone, & Cassia, 2003) have found that African Americans tend to receive

Table 3.2 Percentages of Minorities on Death Row as of 2003

Jurisdiction	Percentage
U.S. military	86%
Colorado	80%
U.S. government	77%
Louisiana	72%
Pennsylvania	70%

Source: American Civil Liberties Union (2003).

more negative and prejudicial treatment from law enforcement and the legal system than White Americans. For example, Sommers and Ellsworth (2001) found that White jurors are more susceptible to making prejudiced decisions regarding Black accusers. In fact, in 82% of the death penalty sentencing reviewed by the U.S. General Accounting Office (1990), the victim's race was found to influence the likelihood of the perpetrator being charged with capital murder or receiving the death penalty. That is, those who murdered Whites were found more likely to be sentenced to death than those who murdered African Americans.

Relationship Between Power and Social Justice

The concept of social justice has an interesting relationship with power. People in positions of power can perpetuate social injustices, intentionally or unintentionally, if they are intolerant, hold prejudicial beliefs, harbor a desire to maintain the status quo, or lack awareness or understanding about racial, ethnic, and cultural differences. They can maintain their power, positions, and wealth by both consciously and unconsciously, and intentionally or unintentionally, treating designated groups of people unfairly.

At times, people in positions of power and privilege may disregard those who are less powerful. This may be due to ignorance, lack of awareness, or simply not being concerned about the lives of people who are powerless. These types of actions frequently contribute to a continuation of unfair treatment and inequity in services, resulting in continued oppression and personal behaviors and decisions that support and cultivate discrimination and unequal institutional policies and practices. The perpetuation of the power differential is underscored by the fact that many of those in power have the information, knowledge, and skills to access resources and peers who have the ability to influence policies and funding priorities that could promote greater equity, equal opportunities, and fairness.

There is great potential to access support toward change, equality, equal treatment, and similar resources for all people.

A good example of this is the inequity in wealth and power in the United States. Only a small group, the top 10% of the U.S. population, receives nearly 50% of all the income earned in the United States (Saez, 2009). The same type of power base can be seen when we examine representation in positions of power; in modern-day America, people of color and women are still grossly underrepresented in Congress and as CEOs. Women make up 51% of the U.S. population. In Congress, however, in 2009, 83% of members of the House of Representatives and Senate were male (Center for American Women and Politics, 2009). Breaking these figures down by race shows that 77% of members of Congress are White, with 76% in the House and 81% in the Senate ("The United States Congress," 2009). Currently, only 25 women head Fortune 1000 companies—this represents only 2.5% of all Fortune 1000 CEOs (Catalyst, 2011), and 23% of college presidents at private institutions are women (American Council on Education, 2007). Similarly, in 2008, women made up 46.7% of all law students but only 34.4% of all lawyers and 18.7% of all partners (Catalyst, 2009). On the global level, the top 400 income earners in the United States make as much in a year as the entire population of the 20 poorest countries in Africa—over 300 million people (Project Censored, 2005). Imbalances such as these continue to promote an unequal distribution of power and have the strong potential to both maintain and promote social injustices and human rights violations.

THEORIES OF SOCIAL JUSTICE IN PSYCHOLOGY AND COUNSELING

Given the numerous examples of social justice, Lee and Walz (1998) concluded that it is psychotherapists' and counselors' moral responsibility to address significant social, cultural, and economic challenges that may have a negative impact on the psychosocial well-being and development of clients. We would concur, suggesting that mental health professionals and counselors have an ethical and moral obligation to work toward social justice and address larger social problems within the therapeutic context. This requires that the mental health professional be able to understand the relationship between their clients' cognitive and affective functioning and their behaviors and interactions within their larger world milieu.

What this means for psychologists and counselors is that the larger environmental issues that negatively impact a client's life, the broader systemic factors that influence a client's psychological health, and the effect of institutions such as schools or the workplace must all be viewed within the larger perspective of psychological well-being. When working toward social justice and human rights, these ecological variables provide a broad, deep context that shapes and contributes to an individual's mental health. Within a social justice model, these variables play a key role in the therapeutic interventions of helping professionals.

Humphreys (1996) argued that psychologists can effectively provide more in-depth, sustained benefit to society through the betterment of social institutions and changes in social policy rather than through psychotherapy. Vera and Speight (2003) purport that counseling psychology is uniquely positioned to shift gears toward social justice work, given an emphasis on personal strengths and resilience and on psychoeducational practices, interactions, and dynamics within the larger ecological context, fostering a generally broader, more holistic view of people. We would concur, and we suggest that client problems are frequently reactions and responses to deep-seated issues rooted in the social, cultural, political, and economic world of the client. Hence it is important that we as psychologists and counselors look at the larger or macro picture.

Figure 3.1 illustrates the influence and impact of societal and environmental factors on individuals and their families and communities. As the figure demonstrates, individuals and their families do not live in isolation, and what affects society may also influence them directly or indirectly. For example, being discriminated against due to religious differences may be experienced on multiple levels, from an individualized situation of being verbally or physically abused to a broader social situation in the community, where there may be experiences of harassment, differential treatment in the workplace or school, stereotypical views from the media, unfair treatment in the health and legal systems, a difference in the quality of services, and so on. Each of these situations impacts the individual's psychological well-being and quality of life.

Reducing the problem to simply an intrapsychic or isolated personal issue without consideration of the larger systemic issues may be in one sense "band-aiding" a presenting problem. This results in a short-term solution at the expense of addressing deeper-rooted social issues, subsequently running the risk of insidiously perpetuating the circumstances that created the problem in the first place. For example, when a client came to me (Fred) to discuss his frustration and anger about being poor, it was unacceptable to only help him come to terms with his feelings about living in poverty. Taking a deeper look at the social and economic circumstances that contributed to this client being poor and continuing to be poor, I worked not only with the presenting feelings but also helped the client employ strategies to get himself out of poverty, to assist his family in breaking the cycle of poverty, and to facilitate skills that would promote successful ways to become an advocate for himself and his family to change his situation. I took this tack in psychotherapy rather than simply helping the client come to terms with his feelings of frustration and anger about being poor.

Examples like this are endless, (see Table 3.3) and we would agree with our colleagues and strongly assert that it is our moral, social, and

Figure 3.1   Macro Approach to Social Justice and Human Rights

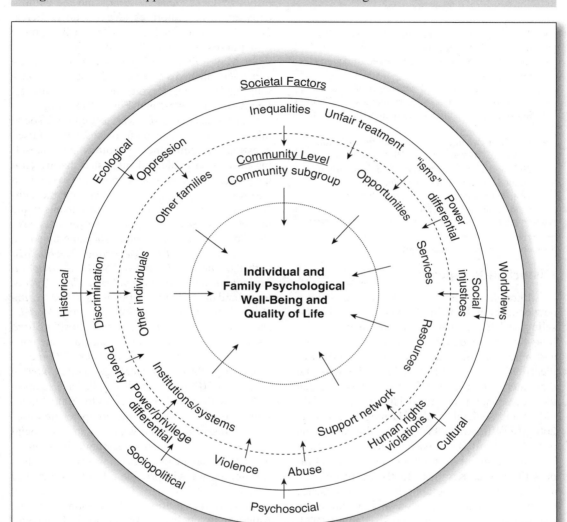

ethical responsibility to more directly address these issues in a proactive manner, rather than ignore larger contextual issues that affect our clients' psychological well-being. To fully understand and appreciate how the field has moved from an individual perspective to larger social justice issues, an overview of the historical perspective of social justice is discussed below.

Table 3.3 U.S. Poverty Statistics, 2009

- The official poverty rate in 2009 was 14.3%, up from 13.2% in 2008.
- In 2009, 43.6 million people lived in poverty, up 3.8 million from 2008.
- Poverty rates remained unchanged for Asians (12.5%) and increased for Hispanics (25.3%), non-Hispanic Whites (9.4%), and Blacks (25.8%).
- For children under 18 years old, the percentage in poverty increased from 19.0% in 2008 to 20.7% in 2009. The poverty rate for children under 18 remained higher than that of 18-to-64-year olds (12.9%) and that of people aged 65 and over (8.9%).

Source: U.S. Census Bureau (2010).

Historical Perspective

Although the issue of social justice is not a new concept in the field of psychology and counseling, it has taken professionals in the field a long time to recognize this concept in training and practice. The concept of social action was identified in the writings of Frank Parsons and then later Carl Rogers, who both advocated that the profession respond to social injustices at individual and societal levels (Hartung & Blustein, 2002; McWhirter, 1998). During the same time period, Clifford Beers was advocating for more humane treatment of individuals with mental illness (Tenety & Kiselica, 2000). Early feminist and multicultural scholars criticized the absence of approaches to oppression and inequities in traditional psychological work (Espin, 1994; Sparks & Park, 2000; Sue & Sue, 2008).

In the 1960s there was a strong movement in the United States toward civil rights and against the Vietnam War. These political movements raised the social and political consciousness of many people, including psychologists and counselors. As a result, ethnicity- and race-specific associations were developed in the 1960s and 1970s that responded to erroneous, so-called scientific hypotheses about the intellectual inferiority of Blacks (Jensen, 1969), and the cultural deprivation of minorities (Arredondo & Perez, 2003; Riessman, 1962). See Chapter 2 for more in-depth discussion of this issue.

In May 1971, the *Personnel and Guidance Journal* published a special issue entitled "Counseling and the Social Revolution" edited by Michael Lewis, Judith Lewis, and Edward Dworkin. The aim of the special issue was to highlight social injustices in the counseling profession. It raised questions regarding the psychology and counseling profession's role and suggested that psychotherapists and counselors must not assume a passive role by simply understanding the concerns without becoming active participants in the movement of social change. Other journals have since published special issues focusing on social justice, including *The Counseling Psychologist* with the May 2003 edition, "*Social Justice and Multicultural Competence in Counseling Psychology,*" and the November 2004 issue, "*Integrating Psychology and Social Justice: A Training Model.*" More recently the *Journal on Counseling and Development* has published a special issue entitled "*Multiculturalism as a Fourth Force in Counseling: Reviewing our Progress and Charting Our Future*" (D'Andrea, Foster, & Pedersen, 2008). As we discussed in Chapter 2, multicultural counseling and the multicultural competencies provided a foundation from which to address social justice issues. To better understand the foundations of social justice work in psychology and counseling, we will provide a brief summary of its history.

In 1981, the president of Division 17 of the American Psychological Association (APA), counseling psychologist Allen Ivey, commissioned Derald Wing Sue to chair a committee to develop the multicultural competencies. Even though the report was eventually published (Sue et al., 1982), as mentioned in Chapter 2, it was 20 years before the Executive Committee endorsed the multicultural counseling competencies (Arredondo et al., 1996; Sue, Arredondo, & McDavis, 1992). Also, it was not until 2002 that the APA Council of

Representatives unanimously endorsed the multicultural competencies (Arredondo & Perez, 2003). In 1987, the American Association for Counseling and Development published a significant position paper on human rights that called for counselors to be advocates for social change (American Association for Counseling and Development, 1987). However, the American Counseling Association (ACA) did not endorse the competencies until March 2003 (ACA, 2003).

Philosophical Tenets of Social Justice for Mental Health Professionals and Counselors

The philosophy behind social justice is founded on the precepts of liberty and equality that can be traced back to John Locke's libertarian justice model, which emphasized the connection between merit and liberty (Hartnett, 2001; Nozick, 1974; Stevens & Wood, 1992). In Locke's model, it was the responsibility of individuals to make their own decisions and determine their own lives, which is consistent with capitalism, where the premise is that all individuals have an equal opportunity and freedom to determine their own lives and outcomes. A major criticism of Locke's premise was that the idea that everyone had an opportunity was more important than any inequitable outcomes, so that, for example, if social class, racial, or gender inequities became evident, they would not be a problem as long as individuals had opportunities to change the inequalities.

Others have challenged and expanded upon Locke's assertions. Rousseau argued that the freedom of choice should not create unequal opportunities in a society and become institutionalized as status quo (Rawls, 1971). He claimed that government should play a major role in preventing social inequalities even while supporting freedom of choice. The communitarian approach to social justice highlights the process by which power, privilege, and oppression become forces (Young, 1990), emphasizing that there is a need

to transform the interplay and progression of dynamics that leads to inequalities rather than address the outcome itself or actual inequalities. Liberation psychology proposes that the field prioritize what has to happen in the future rather than the discrimination and oppression of the past (Martin-Baro, 1994). In contrast, distributive justice (Prilleltensky, 1997) describes the importance of working within the larger sociopolitical context rather than emphasizing the individual as the means to overcome injustices, requiring equality and fairness as an essential component that will foster cultural diversity.

RELATIONSHIP BETWEEN MULTICULTURAL COMPETENCIES AND SOCIAL JUSTICE

As previously discussed in Chapter 2, recent decades have generated significant increases in the literature on multicultural counseling and multicultural counseling competencies. The multicultural counseling competencies provide guidelines for psychologists, counselors, and social workers to be culturally responsive and effective with clients from different racial, ethnic, and cultural backgrounds. We would assert that if helping professionals are committed to multicultural counseling competencies, then there is a natural link to also being committed to social justice. As Derald Wing Sue and his colleagues (1998) stated, "Multiculturalism is about social justice, cultural democracy, and equity" (p. 5). Others (e.g., D'Andrea & Daniels, 1999; Helms & Cook, 1999; Lee & Walz, 1998; Parham & McDavis, 1987; Ridley, Mendoza, & Kanitz, 1994; Thompson & Neville, 1999; Toporek & Reza, 2001) have agreed and advocated for social justice in the mental health field.

To expand on the discussion about the multicultural competencies in Chapter 2, this section will highlight the relationship between multicultural competencies and social justice. In Chapter 2 we discussed the development and the importance of multicultural counseling competencies to provide a foundation for examining social justice and human rights as it relates to multiculturalism in counseling and psychology. It is important to note that the multicultural counseling competencies have been criticized for not fully integrating issues of social justice (Vera & Speight, 2003). It has been argued that although the idea of social justice has been incorporated into the competencies, and the commitment to social justice is evident, the competencies provide minimal attention to operationalizing the work toward social justice. We would suggest that multicultural counseling competencies and social justice/human rights go hand in hand, so that a clearer understanding of a pathway to integrate and operationalize the two is critical.

Arredondo (1999) explored ways in which the multicultural counseling competencies addressed oppression and racism by identifying such issues as privilege, values, stereotyping, and oppression as key to personal awareness, to knowledge of the effect of sociopolitical influences on self-concept and identity, and to understanding institutional obstacles and diagnostic cultural biases as impediments to social justice. Thus, not only do we as professionals need to be aware of, understand, and acknowledge our personal and clients' cultural backgrounds, value systems, beliefs, prejudices, biases, and privileges, but we must also have the knowledge and skills regarding individual, group, family, community, and system levels of interaction to work toward social justice and human rights and be proactive as social change agents. We concur with Arredondo in our belief that the multicultural counseling competencies have clearly established a foundation for social justice and human rights and truly are the core of ongoing and future work in the integration of mental health with social justice and human rights.

One caution is that we do not fool ourselves as we move forward into the social justice arena. As well-meaning, well-trained, and well-intentioned counselors and psychotherapists, we may have knowledge and awareness of—and in some cases even skills in—multicultural counseling, yet lack a deeper understanding of how this awareness, information, and skill fit into doing social justice and human rights work. Given the requirements of the Council for Accreditation of Counseling and Related Educational Programs (CACREP) and of the APA for training in multiculturalism, and the adoption of the multicultural counseling competencies by APA and ACA, we would assume that accredited and licensed counselors and psychologists have a basic awareness and knowledge of the multicultural counseling competencies, and hopefully a basic level of skill as well.

Even so, many colleagues' awareness, knowledge, and abilities do not extend to a comprehensive understanding of the profound historical, socioeconomic, political, and ecological issues that impact and drive the need for effective implementation of the multicultural counseling competencies. Furthermore, if there is an understanding of how social justice issues impact our clients, their families, and their communities, there is a lack of knowledge of how to actually do social justice work. As the editors of the Journal for Social Action Counseling and Psychology (Tod Sloan and Rebecca Toporek) have stated, "Our colleagues need more concrete examples of what social change work looks like and of how one might go about reflecting systematically on that" (personal communication, November 7, 2008).

For example, training for some of us may not have included an in-depth, rigorous examination of our own cultural background, privileges, prejudices, and biases; such an examination would contribute to effective multicultural and social justice work. A result of this may be an inadvertent contribution to maintaining the status quo that perpetuates oppression and discrimination, particularly of people who have a history of marginalization and being oppressed (Martin-Baro, 1994; Prilleltensky, 1997). The complexity of these multiple factors that influence our lives and experiences and the subsequent interaction with people who have been or are oppressed and disenfranchised, combined with the multifaceted intersection of these variables in the world of counseling and psychotherapy, would lead us to say that an essential aspect of training in multicultural counseling is learning how to integrate multicultural competency training and skill development with social justice and human rights work. In fact, leaders in the multicultural movement have established an institute (National Institute of Multicultural Competencies [NIMC]) to assist training programs in addressing multicultural and social justices in their curriculum, teaching, training, and research.

In summary, given the unequal distribution of resources and the historical, sociopolitical, cultural, and ecological factors involved in discrimination and oppression, counselors and psychotherapists can no longer focus only on the intrapsychic dynamics of the client. Traditionally, psychotherapists and counselors have focused solely on individuals and have been apolitical (Brown, 1997), with psychologists supporting this position by arguing that there is a need to focus on the individual in order to understand family and social behavior that promotes injustices (Martin-Baro, 1994; Prilleltensky, 1997). I (Fred) saw an example of this with a client who was experiencing racial discrimination at her employment site. The client was in a work situation where there were subtle and negative comments made to her and others based on their racial backgrounds. For me to work with her by focusing only on intrapsychic issues and helping her adjust to a hostile and oppressive environment would be to assist her with fitting into and adapting to a racist environment. It was my belief that to address this issue in psychotherapy as the client's problem would unconsciously be sanctioning the racism she found in her work environment, and implicitly communicating to her that it was, in fact, her problem. To move beyond the traditional individual framework, I worked with the client on becoming her own advocate for changing the environment and

helped her not only to deal with personal feelings and reactions to the situation, but to assume a role with her colleagues and develop proactive strategies to change the discriminatory and hostile environment.

As this example shows, the interplay between the client's own individual problems and the larger social, political, historical, economic, and ecological world are keys in social justice work. Traditional psychology and counseling have ignored and disregarded the community's and society's overt and covert contributions to the experiences and behavior of clients and families, placing the blame on the individual (Ryan, 1971). Multicultural counseling competencies have clearly set the stage for professionals to "open their eyes" and examine presenting problems, behaviors, and responses not only from the individual's point of view, but also from the macro, ecological, and contextual viewpoints. Thus, in undertaking an analysis of clients' behaviors and their presenting problems, it is critical to include *all* variables, such as the interaction of the family, community, historical, and political perspectives as well as the surrounding ecosystem. These are all important elements that contribute to clients' lives and influence our assessment and intervention strategies.

Social justice is at the very core of multicultural counseling competencies, making it essential that professionals have both the ability to perceive accurately ecological factors that influence clients, and the skills to challenge and address systemic barriers that impede the client's growth, development, quality of life, and psychological well-being (Constantine, Hage, & Kindaichi, 2007; Fondacaro & Weinberg, 2002; Hage, 2003; Prilleltensky & Prilleltensky, 2003; Vera & Speight, 2003). Social justice can be seen as evolving from the civil rights movement, the feminist movement, and the war on poverty, and it is rooted in distributive justice and fair distribution of societal resources (Fondacaro & Weinberg, 2002), so that advantages and disadvantages are equally distributed to individuals or groups in society (Miller, 1999).

The multicultural counseling competencies have similar roots and therefore embrace societal issues and concerns for equity, equal access, and fairness.

GOALS FOR SOCIAL JUSTICE WORK

The goal of social justice work is to eliminate unfair treatment, inequities, and injustices in order to create a society where *all* members—regardless of their race, ethnicity, culture, sexual orientation, gender, religion, socioeconomic status, disability, age, or other distinguishing characteristic—are on the same playing field. This requires that *all* people, not just a privileged few, receive an equal distribution of resources, are psychologically and physically safe and secure (Bell, 1997), and have equal access to available resources. Examples of unequal distribution of resources in the United States and globally have been presented.

Economic injustices lead to multiple social injustices. The 10% of the individuals and their related institutional bodies that have the majority of wealth and power in the United States have substantially greater control of what happens within the society compared to the 90% majority of the population who have significantly less wealth and power. The gap between those who have (the rich) and those who do not have (the poor) wealth, resources, and power is widening and is now bigger than it has been since the 1930s (Wolff, 2003). In fact, the middle class in the United States is shrinking, and its former members are joining the ranks of the poor (Dugas, 2003; NOW, 2004). According to the U.S. Census Bureau (2010) 1 in 7 (14.3%—44 million) Americans and 1 in 5 (21%—15.5 million) children are living in poverty. The number of Americans who do not have health insurance is growing (Krieger, 2003), increasing 15.6% in 2004 (Connolly & Witte, 2004) and has now soared to 50.7 million in 2010 according to the U.S. Census Bureau (2010).

The economic decline is particularly acute for the more subordinate, oppressed, or marginalized groups who have less voice or power and greater needs. To illustrate this point, as of 2002, the median net worth of White American households was $88,651, 11 times greater than that of Latina/o families ($7,932) and 14 times greater than that of African American families (Witte & Henderson, 2004). Therefore, ethnic families are far less likely to own their own homes. The home ownership rate for Whites is 74%, while it is 47% for the latter two groups. More than a quarter of African American and Latina/o households own no assets beyond a car (Goldenberg, 2004). Thus, the 10% who have the greatest wealth and power also inherently carry more privilege in a society that allows them to wield their position to establish policies that can enhance or limit opportunities and access to resources for disenfranchised groups of people. Examples of this can be seen with millions of citizens in the United States who have limited health care and mental health care, diminished social services, inadequate housing, lower-quality education in poorer urban and rural school districts, fewer employment opportunities, restricted political representation, unfair judicial treatment, fewer legal rights, and generally reduced human rights.

Those in power not only have more say about immediate issues as noted above, but they also have a significant impact on the future of others and may use their status and wealth to contribute to maintaining directives that are beneficial to those with wealth and power (see Figure 3.2). For example, the wealthiest 10% contribute to political campaigns and influence who will gain access to political control and power. This in turn contributes to financial decisions that may or may not benefit disenfranchised groups and may have deleterious effects on human services such as mental health services, which in turn impacts our work as counselors and psychologists.

Figure 3.2 Classism in the United States: The Intersection of Race/Ethnicity, Gender, and Class

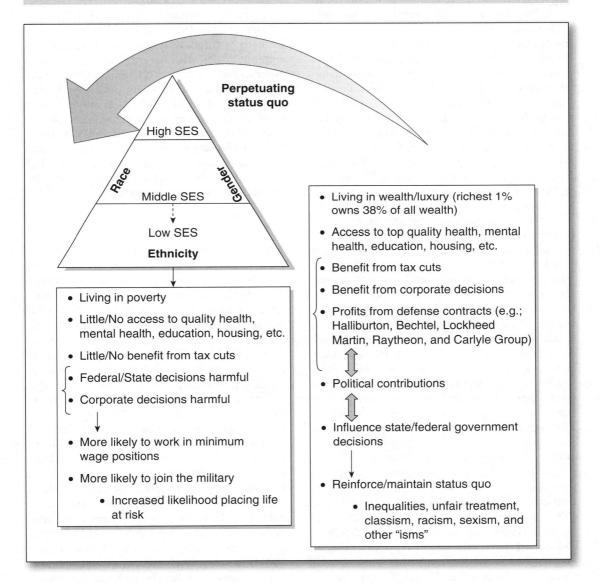

MODELS IN SOCIAL JUSTICE

To address larger social issues, a number of theories of social justice have been proposed. Collaborative models of change have been driven by system and feminist theories, which have helped redefine power relationships. In turn, restructuring power redefines the dynamics within the therapeutic encounter, so that the therapist-client relationship changes, particularly as one strives for social equity. It has also been argued that counseling and psychotherapy must include a belief in and commitment to social obligation, which countermands the dynamic of mental health services directly or indirectly cultivating oppressive and unequal power relationships within the therapeutic relationship. Prilleltensky (1997) speaks about the redistribution of power as a communitarian justice model. Others have strongly promoted combating racism (e.g., Carter, 2007; D'Andrea & Daniels, 1999; Helms & Cook, 1999; Sue et al., 2007), and sexism (e.g., Apfelbaum, 1999) in counseling and psychology. Lewis, Lewis, Daniels, and D'Andrea (1998) presented a model to more effectively work with issues of oppression that incorporated consulting, advocacy, education, and being an agent of change in public policy.

An example of this type of social justice work would be to rally mental health proponents to vote for legislation that would provide better funding for a women's shelter. Similarly, Atkinson, Thompson, and Grant (1993) developed a multicultural model to more effectively deal with oppression that expands the counselor's role to embrace being a change agent, advocate, advisor, and consultant. All the above models have a common theme, regardless of their approach, in that they strive to effectively deal with inequalities and unfair treatment through changing the role of the mental health professional in a way that goes beyond traditional counseling and psychotherapy.

In this book, we are proposing a model that synthesizes other models of social change and our own work in social justice and human rights. The model directly targets social justice and human rights and is called the Multi-Phase Model of Psychotherapy, Counseling Human Rights, and Social Justice (MPM). This model is more fully discussed in Chapter 5 and presents a definitive outline for how we as mental health professionals can change from our traditional roles to more effectively and proactively respond to social injustices and potential human rights violations. The model includes various levels that incorporate social justice and human rights

interventions at micro, meso, and macro levels in an effort to more clearly define how one does social justice and human rights work in the mental health field. This next step forward to more formally incorporate social justice and human rights into our work is particularly important; Helms (2003) criticized the multicultural counseling literature for focusing primarily on integrating social justice principles at the micro level while ignoring the larger systemic levels. The MPM emphasizes the interplay between micro, meso, and macro levels and subsequently addresses historical, social, political, personal, familial, economic, and community issues that impact the individual and the larger society.

SOCIAL JUSTICE AND ETHICS

Traditionally in the United States, ethical standards for counseling and psychology are established according to legal precepts that guide moral behavior. But many unethical behaviors are subtle and less available to legal interpretation. In the United States, professional codes of ethics have been established for both counseling and psychology that are aimed at ensuring and protecting clients' rights. One criticism of these ethical codes has been that they are idealistic and too general (Remley, 1985). The ethical standards have also been criticized for being too legalistic, accentuating linear thinking, being too objective at the expense of interplay between subjective and objective linkages, maintaining an emphasis on protection rather than growth, sustaining the status quo rather than focusing on change, and leaning too heavily on legal sanctions (Rowley & MacDonald, 2001). The criticisms lead toward a mentality of *fear in working,* whereby professionals live in fear of being sued and therefore are afraid to take important risks that may be therapeutically beneficial to their clients. Of interest is that the ethical standards generally do not address social justice or human rights issues but rather refer to overarching legal implications and the law about the "do's and don'ts" in the practice of counseling and psychotherapy.

One fascinating example of defining ethics from a very different standpoint is the *Ethical Framework for Good Practice in Counselling and Psychotherapy* of the British Association for Counselling & Psychotherapy (BACP, 2002). This document presents a national code of ethics from the standpoint of considering values, principles, and personal moral qualities that are more closely aligned with respect for human rights and human dignity, rather than from the standpoint of punishment, consequences for unethical behaviors, and the law. Some of the key concepts of the BACP ethical framework include ensuring the integrity of practitioner-client relationships, fostering a sense of self that is meaningful to the person(s) concerned, enhancing the quality of relationships between people, appreciating the variety of human experience and culture, and striving for the fair and adequate provision of counseling and psychotherapy services. The BACP ethical principles of counseling and psychotherapy go on to list things such as fidelity, client autonomy, a commitment to avoiding harm to the client, and justice and fair treatment for all clients. Finally the ethical framework cites personal moral qualities such as empathy, sincerity, integrity, competence, fairness, and wisdom as part of its framework. The approach is in dramatic contrast to the legalistic perspective taken by similar guiding ethical codes in the United States and other countries, where there is an emphasis on right and wrong behaviors and subsequent punishment for violations.

Although we appreciate the need for and importance of a legalistic approach, given the emphasis in the United States on litigation, we are concerned that the U.S. ethical codes do not address the "human aspects" of mental health services in a proactive and positive manner. When I (Fred) served seven years on a state licensure board for professional counselors, I was party to reviews of all the professional violations for counselors in the state. It was striking that there were no guidelines that promoted healthy client-counselor relationships such as

those in the UK, but rather strict laws that guided ethics and professional behavior. Consequently the professionals knew when they did something wrong, but they did not have guidelines for a more positive approach to their work that would provide a framework for promoting the healthier and more positive psychological well-being of their clients. Our comments in this section about ethical guidelines present a different way of thinking about what we normally take for granted—in this case ethical codes—and suggest that we could theoretically incorporate other perspectives that move more toward a social justice and human rights paradigm.

United Nations Universal Declaration of Human Rights

It is appropriate at this point to mention the Universal Declaration of Human Rights, although international human rights and social justice issues will be discussed in Chapter 15. Although the U.N. may seem far removed from the work you may do in your local community, region, or even nationally, its broad international perspective has implications for our work as counselors and psychotherapists. The thread that connects the Universal Declaration of Human Rights to psychology and counseling, particularly when we assume a position of incorporating social justice into our work, is the fundamental theme of equality, human rights, and social justice for all people. Inherent in both the Universal Declaration of Human Rights and the practice of psychotherapy and counseling is an individual or group's basic needs and rights to food and nutrition, accessible housing, education, medical care, the opportunity to vote and participate in the democratic process, the right to a safe and productive life free of discrimination and oppression, and opportunities to exercise free choice and free speech.

Since the mental health profession does not have documents that provide guidelines and precepts to follow with regard to human rights, the Universal Declaration of Human Rights offers interesting and appropriate guiding principles that can help define our work. The helping profession's fundamental aim is similar to that of the declaration in ensuring first and foremost that individuals or groups have a right to meet their basic needs that is underscored by physical and psychological safety and protection. Once this fundamental baseline of human rights is achieved, then individuals can move on to address more complex levels or stages of development, fostering optimal personal, cultural, and social growth and development and psychological well-being.

Similar to the focus of the U.N. declaration, the focus of the mental health professional should be proactive or purposeful to prevent and intervene in situations that create inequities and injustices for individuals and groups of people. Thus, in the absence of an existing human rights document for the United States, the Universal Declaration of Human Rights provides a framework from which mental health professionals can address issues of injustice and equality and promote the social, psychological, physical, and spiritual health of individuals, families, communities, and organizations. This relates to cultivating diversity and acceptance of all individuals despite their socioeconomic status, age, disability, gender, ethnicity, sexual orientation, or racial background, and is imperative in ensuring maximum growth and the development of potential for individuals and marginalized groups of people.

For example, mental health professionals and counselors can assist individuals to access their right to education, their right to social services, their right to due process of the law, or their right to accessible housing. In any of these areas, individuals have the right to equal opportunities to achieve success, to grow, and to access services despite their gender, ethnicity, socioeconomic background, living conditions, religious beliefs, sexual orientation, political beliefs, and so forth.

In summary, while the U.N.'s Universal Declaration of Human Rights and the fields of psychology and counseling are vastly different, there are distinctive parallels and overlaps between the two. The declaration provides a much needed guideline regarding social justice and mental health that is thus far absent in the mental health field in the United States. The declaration has the potential to help us think differently about our role as mental health professionals, striving for equality for all and the opportunity for optimal growth and development within a safe environment. (The Universal Declaration of Human Rights is appended in its entirety to the end of this chapter.)

SOCIAL JUSTICE: A FIFTH FORCE

Traditional psychology and counseling training has focused on theories and skills, with little attention to other variables that are related to psychotherapy and counseling process and outcome. The primary purpose of psychotherapy and counseling is to promote an individual's well-being and mental health. Given the challenges of daily life, globalization, changes, and transitions, it is clear that for mental health professionals and counselors to be truly effective, they need to move beyond their traditional role of providing psychotherapy and counseling. What may appear to be effective during psychotherapy and counseling is limited, since it is easily erased once clients leave counseling sessions and interact with the real world outside of therapy.

As we always tell our graduate students in training and the counselors and psychologists that we supervise, "Much of the real work happens outside of therapy." It is important that we find out how the benefits of the hard work and countless hours we spend with clients in actual psychotherapy can be sustained once they leave us. How do we help clients to maintain their progress, and not have the change and hard work they are doing be undermined by compelling circumstances once they are back in their families, workplaces, schools, and communities? This is particularly important given that traditional helping paradigms have focused on individual psychotherapy regardless of the therapist's theoretical orientation (e.g., cognitive, behavioral, humanistic) toward changing the individual's behavior, thoughts, and/or feelings. The social justice model framework suggests that, with the emphasis on changing *only* the individual, we, as mental health professionals, have neglected to look beyond the individual to the other important and highly influential factors in clients' lives.

One reason for the overemphasis on individuals in psychology and counseling may be the underlying assumption that individuals maintain full and ultimate control over their lives and subsequently their environment. But unfortunately not everyone starts on an equal playing field, and some people have many rights and privileges, while other people have minimal or sometimes no rights or privileges (see Table 3.4). This can be seen where laws forbid gay or lesbian individuals to marry, where there is a paucity of educational resources and licensed teachers in urban poor public schools as compared to schools in richer suburban communities, or where large numbers of American citizens do not have access to health care and mental health care insurance in order to receive the support they desperately need.

These types of injustices require larger systemic changes in order to affect *all* individuals from diverse cultural, racial, and ethnic backgrounds. Such change requires mental health professionals to go beyond their traditional role of changing only the individual, and to understand and advocate for equality and justice in the larger society, hence changing systems (Pedersen, 1987). It has been argued that by providing traditional services, mental health professionals are "being hand-maidens of the status quo" and are therefore unintentionally helping "to perpetuate various forms of oppression in our society" (D'Andrea, 2002, p. 4), a role of which they are probably unaware.

Awareness regarding multiculturalism has been heightened during the past decade so that most counseling and psychology training programs have a multicultural component. However, the extent and depth to which multiculturalism and diversity are addressed varies from program to program (Pieterse, Evans, Risner-Butner, Collins, & Mason, 2008). Regardless, multiculturalism and diversity in the mental health field have been important concepts during the late 20th century and are now important in the 21st century, as the demographics in the United States become

Table 3.4 Discrimination Against Same-Sex Couples

Fairness and Equality for All

Nancy Gill, who had been employed with the U.S. Postal Service for 21 years, was not able to insure her spouse under her health plan. Randell Lewis-Kendell was denied a Social Security payment when his spouse of 30 years passed away. Keith Toney could not change his last name on his passport after he got married. They were all married to same-sex partners in the state of Massachusetts and still live in the state, but they are unable to receive spousal benefits under the Defense of Marriage Act (DOMA). This act states that in order to receive these benefits, the marriage must be between a man and a woman. These three couples, along with twelve other couples, sued the federal government, arguing that DOMA denies them equal protection under the law. These couples are not arguing that they should be allowed to get married. They are already married in the state of Massachusetts and should therefore receive the benefits and full rights of marriage. President Obama is opposing DOMA, but this lawsuit brings up questions about the fairness of denying benefits to same-sex couples, married or not.

Source: "The Benefits of Fairness" (2009).

increasingly diverse, and inequities become more marked and identified by marginalized populations.

The multicultural competencies (Sue et al., 1998) provide core components for us as psychologists and counselors to use to become more culturally responsive. Although awareness of ourselves and our clients is an essential ingredient of being culturally responsive, it is important that, along with understanding, acknowledging, accepting, and appreciating cultural differences, we go the next step and become proactive in addressing issues of equity, "isms," oppression, discrimination, power differentials, and institutionalized oppression. The focus is therefore not on changing the individual (Pedersen, 1987), but changing systems and policies on multiple levels. All of this leads us to take on somewhat different roles than our training and/or typical protocols have defined, as we redefine ourselves within a social justice paradigm that emphasizes being proactive in changing systems and establishing a more equitable distribution of power and resources so that all people can live with the same rights, dignity, safety, and resources (Goodman, 2001).

As a result of the above, a new professional affiliate group, Counselors for Social Justice (CSJ), was established in the American Counseling Association (ACA). CSJ recognized that for the counseling profession to remain a viable and relevant part of the mental health care system in the 21st century, it must move beyond the traditional helping paradigm and adopt a new role that includes not only counseling individuals, groups, and families, but also being proactive in advocacy and social change. Thus, CSJ promotes embracing and endorsing a new perspective by acknowledging cultural oppression—such as heterosexism, racism, sexism, ageism, and ableism, and by providing culturally sensitive counseling while working toward eradicating these types of oppression in the wider society. Furthermore, CSJ embraces multicultural, feminist, postmodern, constructivist, and gay/lesbian/transgender theories rather than traditional counseling theories, since these nontraditional theories more

adequately address issues of oppression and injustice (D'Andrea, 2002).

Twenty-five years ago, the group Psychologists for Social Responsibility (PsySR) was created. PsySR is an independent, nonprofit organization that applies psychological knowledge and skills to build cultures of peace with justice. The membership consists of psychologists, students, and other social justice advocates in the United States and around the world. The goal of PsySR is to develop and promote resources for creative, nonviolent, participatory approaches to the most pressing social issues of our time (http://psysr.org).

Multicultural counseling has been identified as the fourth force in counseling and psychology (Pedersen, 1991). Given the strength and importance of acting on social issues, social justice in our opinion is definitely the fifth force in counseling and psychology as suggested by others (Pack-Brown, Tequilla, & Seymour, 2008; Ratts, D'Andrea, & Arredondo, 2004). This would relate to social justice charting new territory and focusing on social issues within society. Although multicultural competencies and the multicultural movement address many of the issues related to social justice and human rights, the specific emphasis on social inequities and social change is not their primary focus; thus we would suggest expanding the multicultural movement to a fifth force, social justice and human rights.

The Role of Social Justice Counselors

To truly address social injustices in the 21st century, we as counselors and psychotherapists must move beyond our traditional roles of individual counseling that historically have neglected social problems. It is important that our work incorporates the promotion of change through advocacy for clients and their families and communities, and that it involves taking risks and challenging injustices at organizational, institutional, and societal levels. We must move beyond the role of remediation particularly, as D. W. Sue (1995) pointed out, when counselors and psychotherapists are often working with clients who are victims of oppressive policies that fail to achieve equality. This requires graduate programs to do more effective training of students regarding (a) organizational change and systems skills, (b) strategies to access systems, (c) different ways of practicing our trade as mental health professionals, (d) new models of supervision that go beyond traditional individual therapeutic precepts, and (e) associated research to substantiate evidence-based mental health and social justice outcomes.

In this new role, it is important that psychotherapists and counselors view clients from more of an ecological viewpoint. To omit environmental influences on clients' lives and their experiences of oppression and discrimination, and to emphasize solely their intrapsychic issues, would be ineffective in addressing social justice and human rights issues and would essentially maintain and reinforce the status quo (Prilleltensky, 1997). We have one cautionary note, though, about determining the influences on our clients' lives and the aspects of inequity, unfairness, discrimination, or oppression that have affected them: We must ensure that we consult and clarify with clients what these issues are before we make judgments and decisions about how to empower them, and about what issues are important for them within the social justice and human rights areas.

Ironically, we have noticed that there is a great deal of discussion and agreement about empowering clients, while the professional makes all the decisions regarding the problem, diagnosis, treatment, and follow-up. True therapeutic partnerships are an integral part of social justice and mental health work, so that one must avoid hiding behind the *cloak of professionalism*. Full participation of the client in the process of counseling or psychotherapy is fundamental to social justice and human rights work, whereby the professional is an active, highly engaged participant in the change process and partners with

an equally active and highly engaged client or group of clients.

This was highlighted over 30 years ago in Freire's (1973) work, when he posed the question of whether or not the client is best prepared "to understand the significance of an oppressive society? And who suffer the effects of oppression more than the oppressed?" (p. 22). A more recent example was given in two articles we wrote outlining a process of empowerment for African American high school girls through the Empowerment Groups for Academic Success (EGAS) approach (Bemak, 2005; Bemak, Chung, & Siroskey-Sabdo, 2005). In these articles, we described true empowerment that went beyond rhetoric. Another way to talk about empowerment is to look at helping professionals who truly understand and address issues of social justice as people doing so *with* their clients rather than *for* their clients.

For mental health professionals and counselors to ignore the rich wealth of knowledge that clients bring to the mental health encounter creates a power differential and reliance on the professional for expertise. This "banking concept" that was coined by Freire (1973) implies that clients are helpless and passive recipients who are reliant on the counselor or psychotherapist to "deposit" information and help change the client's world when there is a need for systemic intervention. The banking concept generates unhealthy dynamics between therapists and clients and more insidiously reinforces a traditional status quo, maintaining clients as dependent without equal power, and professionals in a position of control over clients' lives.

If we are to be successful in promoting social change aiming toward greater justice and rights, then it is essential that we develop alliances with people who are marginalized and oppressed (Nelson, Prilleltensky, & MacGillivary, 2001). An example can be seen in an African American female client who comes to us wanting to improve her life as a parent and wife, but feels disempowered in her relationship with her husband and her supervisor at work. The social justice work with this client would be to foster her own power within and outside of the therapeutic relationship so that she feels increasingly comfortable to assert herself with the therapist as well as with those in the world around her. Thus, the dynamics are consistent—the client is powerful within and outside of therapy.

A new role for counselors and psychotherapists would also emphasize other types of responses that go beyond traditional psychotherapy and counseling, such as advocacy, the development of prevention and intervention programs, outreach programs, the promotion of social action in partnership with clients and their families and communities, and so on. These new roles would be as important as the traditional role and not in any way be secondary or of less importance. This is consistent with Sue's (1995) contention that engaging in proactive and preventative approaches is essential to address historical and current oppression.

We would concur and suggest that individual counseling and psychotherapy may offer only a superficial "band-aid" that neither heals the client nor addresses the deeper social and political problems facing clients, that maintains a professional passivity, and that often focuses on remediation. In fact, Prilleltensky (1997) has called therapeutic remediation reprehensible, while Albee (2000) has strongly criticized remedial treatment that doesn't change social conditions. Taking the example of the female client above, to ignore her oppression as a Black woman and simply discuss how she might feel better with her husband and supervisor at work would not touch the deeper issues related to being a woman, to being African American, and to the interaction between race and gender and feelings of powerlessness. We would assert that her ability to advocate for herself and receive our support in undertaking self-advocacy is critical in the therapeutic relationship. Developing strategies that help her to prevent the feelings of helplessness in the future, and to change the dynamics of her relationships with her family members and supervisor, should be regarded as equally important as and not mutually exclusive to psychotherapy and counseling (Vera & Speight, 2003). This will be further discussed in Chapter 5 on the Multi-Phase Model of Psychotherapy, Counseling, Human Rights, and Social Justice (MPM).

CHARACTERISTICS OF A SOCIAL JUSTICE WORKER

Mental health professionals and counselors are in an ideal role to take on social justice work. We have been trained in counseling to sharpen communication and listening skills to more effectively work with our clients, their families, and community concerns. In addition, we also understand group dynamics and group process as well as system dynamics. However, additional qualities are needed for social justice and human rights work. Chapter 10 presents the characteristics of a social justice leader. Below is a discussion of the unique characteristics of social justice workers.

Counselors and Psychologists as Political and Social Activists

As we have discussed, we as counselors and psychologists have a responsibility to address the social issues that affect our clientele. To simply ignore the social problems and the political decisions and priorities that provide a context for those social ills is to contribute to many of the problems that bring our clients to us in the first place. Domestic violence, lead poisoning, substance abuse, racial discrimination, sexual harassment, environmental health concerns, poverty, and so forth, all lead to individual, family, and community mental health problems. For example, ignoring political decisions about policies and funding allocations means that we are treating the symptoms and not the source.

There are endless examples of such issues that are relevant for counselors and psychologists. Defining a county budget for education defines the quality and priority of what is funded for a school district. Funding has implications for afterschool programs, which in turn have ramifications for the opportunities that are available for students in the afternoons and weekends. Districts with more activities, and more diverse activities, reach more children, who then do not have idle and unproductive time after school and on weekends. This has been demonstrated with chess programs, school-organized community volunteer programs, weekend and midnight basketball games, and so forth.

Another example is the recent controversy about torture. To stipulate that as professionals, counselors and psychologists should not weigh in regarding their opinions and should take a neutral stance, is to play a part in allowing and sanctioning the use of mental health trained professionals to engage in the practice of torture.

A third example relates to budgeting. If we as counselors and psychologists do not share our beliefs and opinions about mental health needs with legislators, we are excluded from the discussion about funding allocations. Instead, it is critical that we provide feedback and input to our county, state, and national elected officials and to our professional associations, rather than just passively assume that these decisions are made without input. We are in a unique position to see patterns and trends of social problems, and we have the potential to contribute to the discourse and direction of our local and national society. It is important for us to be active, take a stand, and have our voices heard about these types of political and funding situations in order to address the social problems that underscore many mental health issues.

DISCUSSION QUESTIONS

1. Think about what social justice means to you. How would you describe social justice? After reading this chapter, has your definition of social justice changed?

2. Think of a social justice issue that you would like to address as a psychologist or counselor. What would be the first step that you would take to address this issue?

3. Approach someone in your family and one of your friends, and ask them what they believe about social justice.

   a. Do they have similar or different definitions of social justice?

   b. Do they have different definitions than you have?

4. Find a local newspaper, and locate an article that you believe describes an injustice for an individual or a larger group of people.

   a. Is the injustice clearly understood by those who are affected by this issue or not?

   b. What do you imagine would be the role of a mental health professional in this situation?

5. When you read some of the statistics in this chapter about imbalances in income, salaries, access to health care, education, and so forth,

   a. How do these statistics impact you?

   b. Are any of these statistics new to you?

6. Your client is Mrs. Fox. She is a 72-year-old African American woman. Her family doctor referred her to the community agency you work for. Mrs. Fox seems to be forgetting things; she is very sad, irritable, and "bored." It seems Mrs. Fox has been having arguments with her relatives more frequently, and she does not feel she is useful anymore. Mrs. Fox used to help to take care of her grandchildren, but she started to get sick and forget important things, and she got very impatient. Her family doctor prescribes ibuprofen for her complaints. Her insurance does not cover any type of psychological assessment, and her family seems to struggle financially. Her doctor thinks she might be developing some sort of dementia or depression.

   a. Can you identify some of the social injustices in this case? List them.

   b. What are some of those injustices that are institutional or part of the system? Are some of them based on race, age, or gender?

   c. What is your ethical and moral role as counselor/psychologist?

7. The chapter discusses how the multicultural counseling competencies have set the stage for professionals to "open their eyes" to face the real problems from a systemic and ecological perspective.

   a. How is social justice "opening your eyes" to human rights?
   b. What are some of those prejudices and barriers you still need to work on?
   c. How will this new information help you to challenge the status quo of today's systems?

REFERENCES

Adams, M., Blumenfeld, W. J., Castaneda, R., Hackman, H. W., Peters, M. L., & Zuniga, X. (Eds.). (2000). *Readings for diversity and social justice: An anthology of racism, anti-Semitism, sexism, heterosexism, ableism and classism.* New York, NY: Routledge.

Albee, G. W. (2000). Commentary on prevention and counseling psychology. *The Counseling Psychologist, 28,* 845–853.

American Association for Counseling and Development. (1987). *Human rights position paper.* Alexandria, VA: Author.

American Civil Liberties Union. (2003). *Race and the death penalty.* Retrieved from http://www.aclu.org/capital-punishment/race-and-death-penalty

American Council on Education. (2007). *Annual Report 2007.* Retrieved from http://www.acenet.edu/Content/NavigationMenu/About/Annual Report/2007AnnualReport.pdf

American Counseling Association. (2003, March). ACA governing council meeting minutes. Alexandria, VA: Author.

Apfelbaum, E. (1999). Twenty years later. *Feminism & Psychology, 9*(3), 300–313.

Armour, S. (2005, February 16). Pregnant workers face growing discrimination. *USA Today.* Retrieved from http://www.usatoday.com/money/work place/2005-02-16-pregnancy-bias- usat_x.htm

Arredondo, P. (1999). Multicultural counseling competencies as tools to address oppression and racism. *Journal of Counseling & Development, 77*(1), 102–108.

Arredondo, P., & Perez, P. (2003) Expanding multicultural competence through social justice. *Counseling Psychologist, 31*(3), 282–289.

Arredondo, P., Toporek, R., Brown, S. P., Jones, J., Locke, D. C., & Sanchez, J. (1996). Operationalization of the multicultural counseling competencies. *Journal of Multicultural Counseling and Development, 24*(1), 42–78.

Atkinson, D. R., Thompson, C. E., & Grant, S. K. (1993). A three-dimensional model for counseling racial/ethnic minorities. *The Counseling Psychologist, 21*(2), 257–277.

Bell, L. A. (1997). Theoretical foundations for social justice education. In M. Adams, L. A. Bell, & P. Griffin (Eds.), *Teaching for diversity and social justice* (pp. 3–15). New York, NY: Routledge.

Bemak, F. (2005). Reflections on multiculturalism, social justice, and empowerment groups for academic success: A critical discourse for contemporary schools. *Professional School Counseling, 8*(5), 401–406.

Bemak, F., Chung, R. C-Y., & Siroskey-Sabdo, L. (2005). Empowerment groups for academic success: An innovative approach to prevent high school failure for at-risk, urban African American girls. *Professional School Counseling, 8*(5), 377–389.

The benefits of fairness: A lawsuit tests the federal protections owed to same-sex couples. (2009, March 21). *Washington Post.* Retrieved from http://www.washingtonpost.com/wp-dyn/content/article/2009/03/20/AR2009032003183.html

British Association for Counselling and Psychotherapy. (2002). *Ethical framework for good practice in counselling and psychotherapy.* Rugby, UK: Author.

Brown, D. (1997). Implications of cultural values for cross-cultural consultation with families. *Journal of Counseling and Development, 76,* 29–35.

Carter, R. T. (2007). Racism and psychological and emotional injury: Recognizing and assessing race-based traumatic stress. *Journal of Counseling Psychology, 35,* 13–105.

Catalyst. (2009). *Women in law in the U.S.* Retrieved from http://www.catalyst.org/publication/246/women-in-law-in-the-us

Catalyst. (2011). *Women CEOs of the Fortune 1000.* Retrieved from http://www.catalyst.orublication/322/women-ceos-of-the-fortune-1000

Center for American Women and Politics (CAWP). (2009). *Women in the U.S. Congress 2009.* Retrieved from http://www.cawp.rutgers.edu/fast_facts/levels_of_office/documents/cong.pdf

Chomsky, N. (1998). *The common good.* Berkeley, CA: Odonian Press.

Connolly, C., & Witte, G. (2004, August 27). Poverty rate up 3rd year in a row: More also lack health coverage. *The Washington Post,* p. A01.

Constantine, M. G., Hage, S. M., & Kindaichi, M. M. (2007). Social justice and multicultural issues: Implications for the practice and training of counselors and counseling psychologists. *Journal of Counseling & Development, 85*(1), 24–29.

D'Andrea, M. (2002). Counselors for social justice: A revolutionary and liberating force in the counseling profession. *Counselors for Social Justice Newsletter, 2*(2), 3–6.

D'Andrea, M., & Daniels, J. (1999) Exploring the psychology of White racism through naturalistic inquiry. *Journal of Counseling and Development, 77,* 93–101.

D'Andrea, M., Foster, E., & Pedersen, P. (Eds.). (2008). Multiculturalism as a fourth force in counseling: Reviewing our progress and charting our future. *Journal of Counseling and Development, 86*(3), 259–382.

Davis, K. (1996). What is social justice? Perspectives on *Multicultural and Cultural Diversity, 6,* 1–3.

Dugas, C. (2003, September 15). Middle class barely treads water: More are going under, even with two incomes. *USA Today.* Retrieved from http://www.usatoday.com/educate/netgain/lessons/NetGain1.pdf

Espin, O. M. (1994). *Feminist approaches.* In L. Comas-Diaz & B. Greene (Eds.), *Women of color: Integrating ethnic and gender identities in psychotherapy* (pp. 265–286). New York, NY: Guilford Press.

Fondacaro, M., & Weinberg, D. (2002). Concepts of social justice in community psychology: Toward a social ecological epistemology. *American Journal of Community Psychology, 30*(4), 473–492.

Freire. P. (1973). *Education for a critical consciousness.* New York, NY: Seabury Press.

Goldenberg, S. (2004, October 19). *U.S. wealth gap grows for ethnic minorities.* Retrieved from http://www.guardian.co.uk/world/2004/oct/19/usa.suzannegoldenberg

Goodman, D. J. (2001). *Promoting diversity and social justice: Educating people from privileged groups.* Thousand Oaks, CA: Sage.

Grinberg, E. (2009). Some satisfied, others outraged with verdict for immigrant's death. *CNN Justice.* Retrieved from http://articles.cnn.com/2009-05-02/justice/pa.immigrant.beating_1_brandon-piekarsky-derrick-donchak-teens?_s=PM:CRIME

Hage, S. M. (2003). Reaffirming the unique identity of counseling psychology: Opting for the "road less traveled by." *The Counseling Psychologist, 31,* 555–563.

Harris, D. (2002). Profiles in injustice: Why racial profiling cannot work. New York, NY: New Press.

Hartnett, D. (2001). *The history of justice.* Paper presented on the Social Justice Forum, Loyola University, Chicago, IL.

Hartung, P., & Blustein, D. (2002). Reason, intuition and social justice: Elaborating on Parson's career decision-making model. *Journal of Counseling and Development, 80*(1), 41–47.

Helms, J. (2003). A pragmatic view of social justice. *The Counseling Psychologist, 31,* 305–313.

Helms, J., & Cook, D. (1999). Using race and culture in counseling and psychotherapy: Theory and process. Needham Heights, MA: Allyn & Bacon.

Humphreys, K. (1996). Clinical psychologists as psychotherapists. *American Psychologist, 51,* 190–197.

Jensen, A. (1969). How much can we boost IQ and school achievement? *Harvard Educational Review, 29,* 1–123.

Krieger, D. (2003). Economic justice for all. Retrieved from http://www.wagingpeace.org/articles/2003/05/23_krieger_econ-justice.htm

Lee, C., & Walz, G. R. (1998). *Social action: A mandate for counselors.* Alexandria, VA: American Counseling Association.

Lewis, J. A., Lewis, M. D., Daniels, J. A., & D'Andrea, M. J. (1998). *Community counseling: Empowerment strategies for a diverse society.* Pacific Grove, CA: Brooks/Cole.

Lewis, M. D., Lewis, J. A., & Dworkin, E. P. (1971). Counseling and the social revolution. [Special issue]. *Personnel and Guidance Journal, 49*(9), 64–76.

Margetts, J. (2008). Homicide victim identified as transgendered person, Duanna Johnson. *ABC 24.* Retrieved from http://www.abc24.com/news/local/story/Homicide-Victim-Identified-as-Transgendered/CX278wImn0ygMyufj8owGA.cspx

Martin-Baro, I. (1994). *Writings for a liberation psychology.* Cambridge, MA: Harvard University Press.

Mauer, M. (1999). Race to incarcerate: The sentencing project. New York, NY: New Press.

McWhirter, E. H. (1998). An empowerment model of counselor education. *Canadian Journal of Counselling, 32*(1), 12–26.

Miller, D. (1999). *Principles of social justice.* Cambridge, MA: Harvard University Press.

Miller, J. G. (1996). Search and destroy: African-American males in the criminal justice system. New York, NY: Cambridge University Press.

Nelson, G., Prilleltensky, I., & MacGillivary, H. (2001). Building value-based partnerships: Toward solidarity with oppressed groups. *American Journal of Community Psychology, 29,* 649–677.

NOW. (2004). Who is the middle class? Retrieved from http://www.pbs.org/now/politics/middle classoverview.html

Nozick, R. (1974). *Anarchy, state, and utopia.* New York, NY: Basic Books.

Pack-Brown, S., Tequilla, T., & Seymour, J. (2008). Infusing professional ethics into counselor education program: A multicultural/social justice perspective. *Journal of Counseling and Development, 86*(3), 296–302.

Parham, T., & McDavis, R. (1987). Black men, an endangered species: Who's really pulling the trigger? *Journal of Counseling & Development, 66*(1), 24–27.

Pedersen, P. (1987). Ten frequent assumptions of cultural bias in counseling. *Journal of Multicultural Counseling and Development, 15*(1), 16–24.

Pedersen, P. (1991). Multiculturalism as a fourth force in counseling. *Journal of Counseling and Development, 70*(1), 6–12.

Pieterse, A. L., Evans, S. A., Risner-Butner, A., Collins, N. M., & Mason, L. B. (2008). Multicultural competence and social justice training in counseling psychology and counselor education: A review and analysis of a sample of multicultural course syllabi. *The Counseling Psychologist, 37,* 93–115.

Prilleltensky, I. (1997). Values, assumptions, and practices: Assessing the moral implications of psychological discourse and action. *American Psychologist, 52*(5), 517–535.

Prilleltensky, I., & Prilleltensky, O. (2003). Synergies for wellness and liberation in counseling psychology. *The Counseling Psychologist, 31,* 273–281.

Project Censored. (2005). *Wealth inequality in 21st century threatens economy and democracy.* Retrieved from http://www.projectcensored.org/publications/2005/1.html

Ratts, M., D'Andrea, M., & Arredondo, P. (2004). Social justice counseling: A "fifth force" in the field. *Counseling Today, 47,* 28–30.

Rawls, J. (1971). *A theory of justice.* Cambridge, MA: Belknap Press/Harvard University Press.

Remley, T. P., Jr. (1985). The law and ethical practices in elementary and middle schools. *Elementary School Guidance and Counseling, 19,* 181–189.

Ridley, C. R., Mendoza, D., & Kanitz, B. (1994). Multicultural training: Reexamination, operationalization, and integration. *The Counseling Psychologist, 22*(2), 227–289.

Riessman, E. (1962). *The culturally deprived child.* New York, NY: Harper & Row.

Rowley, W. J., & MacDonald, D. (2001). Counseling and the law: A cross-cultural perspective. *Journal of Counseling and Development, 79,* 422–429.

Ryan, W. (1971). *Blaming the victim.* New York, NY: Pantheon.

Saez, E. (August 5, 2009). Striking it richer: The evolution of top incomes in the United States. Retrieved from http://elsa.berkeley.edu/~saez/saez-UStopincomes-2007.pdf

Smith, P. (1971). Black activists for liberation, not guidance. *Personnel & Guidance Journal, 49*(9), 721–726.

Sommers, S. R., & Ellsworth, P. C. (2001). White juror bias: An investigation of prejudice against Black defendants in the American courtroom. *Psychology, Public Policy and Law, 7*(1), 201–229.

Sparks, E., & Park, A. (2000, October). *Facilitating multicultural training of counseling psychology graduate students: Experiential learning in a diverse setting.* Paper presented at the First Annual Diversity Challenge Conference, Institute for the Study and Promotion of Race and Culture, Boston College, Boston, MA.

Stevens, E., & Wood, G. H. (1992). *Justice, ideology, and education: An introduction to the social foundation of education.* New York, NY: McGraw-Hill.

Sue, D., Arredondo, P., & McDavis, R. (1992). Multicultural counseling competencies and standards: A call to the profession. *Journal of Multicultural Counseling and Development, 20,* 64–88.

Sue, D., Parham, T., & Santiago, G. B. (1998). The changing face of work in the United States: Implications for individual, institutional and societal survival. *Cultural Diversity and Ethnic Minority Psychology, 4*(3), 153–164.

Sue, D. W. (1995). Multicultural organizational development: Implications for the counseling profession. In J. G. Ponterotto, J. M. Casa, L. A. Suzuki, & C. M. Alexander (Eds.), *Handbook of multicultural counseling* (pp. 474–492). Thousand Oaks, CA: Sage.

Sue, D. W., Bernier, J. B., Durran, M., Feinberg, L., Pedersen, P., Smithe, E. & Vasquez-Nuttall, E. (1982). Position paper: Cross-cultural counseling competencies. *The Counseling Psychologist, 10,* 45–52.

Sue, D. W., Capodilupo, C. M., Torino, G. C., Bucceri, J. M., Holder, A. M. B., Nadal, K. L., &

Esquilin, M. (2007). Racial microaggressions in everyday life. *American Psychologist, 62,* 271–286.

Sue, D. W., Carter, R. T., Casas, J. M., Fouad, N. A., Ivey, A. E., Jensen, M., LaFromboise, T., et al. (1998). *Multicultural counseling competencies: Individual and organizational development.* Thousand Oaks, CA: Sage.

Sue, D. W., & Sue, D. (2008). *Counseling the culturally different: Theory and practice* (5th ed.). New York, NY: Wiley.

Tenety, M., & Kiselica, M. S. (2000). Working with mental health advocacy groups. In J. Lewis & L. Bradley (Eds.), *Advocacy in counseling: Counselors, clients & community* (pp. 139–146). Greensboro, NC: ERIC Clearinghouse on Counseling and Student Services.

Thompson, C., & Neville, H. (1999). Racism, mental health, and mental health practice. *The Counseling Psychologist, 27*(2), 155–223.

Toporek, R., & Reza, J. (2001). Context as a critical dimension of multicultural counseling: Articulating personal, professional, and institutional competence. *Journal of Multicultural Counseling and Development, 29*(1), 13–30.

United Nations. (1948, December 10). *The universal declaration of human rights.* Retrieved from http://www.un.org/en/documents/udhr/

The United States Congress quick facts. (2009). This Nation, American Government & Politics Online.

Retrieved from http://www.thisnation.com/congress-facts.html

U.S. Bureau of Census (2010). Income, Poverty and Health Insurance Coverage in the United States: 2009. Retrieved from: http://www.census.gov/newsroom/releases/archives/income_wealth/cb10-144.html

U.S. General Accounting Office. (1990, February). Death penalty sentencing: Research indicates pattern of racial disparities. *Report to Senate and House Committees on the Judiciary.* Retrieved from http://archive.gao.gov/t2pbat11/140845.pdf

Vera, E., & Speight, S. (2003). Multicultural competence, social justice, and counseling psychology: Expanding our roles. *Counseling Psychologist, 31*(3), 253–272.

Walker, S., Delone, M., & Cassia C. S. (2003). The color of justice: Race, ethnicity, and crime in America (3rd ed.). Belmont, CA: Wadsworth.

Witte, G., & Henderson, N. (October 18, 2004). Wealth gap widens for Blacks, Hispanics: Significant ground lost after recession. *The Washington Post.* Retrieved from http://www.washingtonpost.com/wp-dyn/articles/A40455-2004Oct17.html

Wolff, E. (2003). The wealth divide: the growing gap in the United States between the rich and the rest. *Multinational Monitor, 24,* 5.

Young, I. (1990). *Justice and the politics of difference.* Princeton, NJ: Princeton University Press.

United Nations Universal Declaration of Human Rights

December 10, 1948 –Universal Declaration of Human Rights
The United Nations

Article 1.

All human beings are born free and equal in dignity and rights. They are endowed with reason and conscience and should act towards one another in a spirit of brotherhood.

Article 2.

Everyone is entitled to all the rights and freedoms set forth in this Declaration, without distinction of any kind, such as race, colour, sex, language, religion, political or other opinion, national or social origin, property, birth or other status. Furthermore, no distinction shall be made on the basis of the political, jurisdictional or international status of the country or territory to which a person belongs, whether it be independent, trust, non-self-governing or under any other limitation of sovereignty.

Article 3.

Everyone has the right to life, liberty and security of person.

Article 4.

No one shall be held in slavery or servitude; slavery and the slave trade shall be prohibited in all their forms.

Article 5.

No one shall be subjected to torture or to cruel, inhuman or degrading treatment or punishment.

Article 6.

Everyone has the right to recognition everywhere as a person before the law.

Article 7.

All are equal before the law and are entitled without any discrimination to equal protection of the law. All are entitled to equal protection against any discrimination in violation of this Declaration and against any incitement to such discrimination.

Article 8.

Everyone has the right to an effective remedy by the competent national tribunals for acts violating the fundamental rights granted him by the constitution or by law.

Article 9.

No one shall be subjected to arbitrary arrest, detention or exile.

Article 10.

Everyone is entitled in full equality to a fair and public hearing by an independent and impartial tribunal, in the determination of his rights and obligations and of any criminal charge against him.

Article 11.

(1) Everyone charged with a penal offence has the right to be presumed innocent until proved guilty according to law in a public trial at which he has had all the guarantees necessary for his defense.

(2) No one shall be held guilty of any penal offence on account of any act or omission which did not constitute a penal offence, under national or international law, at the time when it was committed. Nor shall a heavier penalty be imposed than the one that was applicable at the time the penal offence was committed.

Article 12.

No one shall be subjected to arbitrary interference with his privacy, family, home or correspondence, nor to attacks upon his honour and reputation Everyone has the right to the protection of the law against such interference or attacks.

Article 13.

(1) Everyone has the right to freedom of movement and residence within the borders of each state.

(2) Everyone has the right to leave any country, including his own, and to return to his country.

Article 14.

(1) Everyone has the right to seek and to enjoy in other countries asylum from persecution.

(2) This right may not be invoked in the case of prosecutions genuinely arising from non-political crimes or from acts contrary to the purposes and principles of the United Nations.

Article 15.

(1) Everyone has the right to a nationality.

(2) No one shall be arbitrarily deprived of his nationality nor denied the right to change his nationality.

Article 16.

(1) Men and women of full age, without any limitation due to race, nationality or religion, have the right to marry and to found a family. They are entitled to equal rights as to marriage, during marriage and at its dissolution.

(2) Marriage shall be entered into only with the free and full consent of the intending spouses.

(3) The family is the natural and fundamental group unit of society and is entitled to protection by society and the State.

Article 17.

(1) Everyone has the right to own property alone as well as in association with others.

(2) No one shall be arbitrarily deprived of his property.

Article 18.

Everyone has the right to freedom of thought, conscience and religion; this right includes freedom to change his religion or belief, and freedom, either alone or in community with others and in public or private, to manifest his religion or belief in teaching, practice, worship and observance.

Article 19.

Everyone has the right to freedom of opinion and expression; this right includes freedom to hold opinions without interference and to seek, receive and impart information and ideas through any media and regardless of frontiers.

Article 20.

(1) Everyone has the right to freedom of peaceful assembly and association.

(2) No one may be compelled to belong to an association.

Article 21.

(1) Everyone has the right to take part in the government of his country, directly or through freely chosen representatives.

(2) Everyone has the right to equal access to public service in his country.

(3) The will of the people shall be the basis of the authority of government; this shall be expressed in periodic and genuine elections which shall be by universal and equal suffrage and shall be held by secret vote or by equivalent free voting procedures.

Article 22.

Everyone, as a member of society, has the right to social security and is entitled to realization, through national effort and international co-operation and in accordance with the organization and resources of each State, of the economic, social and cultural rights indispensable for his dignity and the free development of his personality.

Article 23.

(1) Everyone has the right to work, to free choice of employment, to just and favourable conditions of work and to protection against unemployment.

(2) Everyone, without any discrimination, has the right to equal pay for equal work.

(3) Everyone who works has the right to just and favourable remuneration ensuring for himself and his family an existence worthy of human dignity, and supplemented, if necessary, by other means of social protection.

(4) Everyone has the right to form and to join trade unions for the protection of his interests.

Article 24.

Everyone has the right to rest and leisure, including reasonable limitation of working hours and periodic holidays with pay.

Article 25.

(1) Everyone has the right to a standard of living adequate for the health and well-being of himself and of his family, including food, clothing, housing and medical care and necessary social services, and the right to security in the event of unemployment, sickness, disability, widowhood, old age or other lack of livelihood in circumstances beyond his control.

(2) Motherhood and childhood are entitled to special care and assistance. All children, whether born in or out of wedlock, shall enjoy the same social protection.

Article 26.

(1) Everyone has the right to education. Education shall be free, at least in the elementary and fundamental stages. Elementary education shall be compulsory. Technical and professional education shall be made generally available and higher education shall be equally accessible to all on the basis of merit.

(2) Education shall be directed to the full development of the human personality and to the strengthening of respect for human rights and fundamental freedoms. It shall promote understanding, tolerance and friendship among all nations, racial or religious groups, and shall further the activities of the United Nations for the maintenance of peace.

(3) Parents have a prior right to choose the kind of education that shall be given to their children.

Article 27.

(1) Everyone has the right freely to participate in the cultural life of the community, to enjoy the arts and to share in scientific advancement and its benefits.

(2) Everyone has the right to the protection of the moral and material interests resulting from any scientific, literary or artistic production of which he is the author.

Article 28.

Everyone is entitled to a social and international order in which the rights and freedoms set forth in this Declaration can be fully realized.

Article 29.

(1) Everyone has duties to the community in which alone the free and full development of his personality is possible.

(2) In the exercise of his rights and freedoms, everyone shall be subject only to such limitations as are determined by law solely for the purpose of securing due recognition and respect for the rights and freedoms of others and of meeting the just requirements of morality, public order and the general welfare in a democratic society.

(3) These rights and freedoms may in no case be exercised contrary to the purposes and principles of the United Nations.

Article 30.

Nothing in this Declaration may be interpreted as implying for any State, group or person any right to engage in any activity or to perform any act aimed at the destruction of any of the rights and freedoms set forth herein.

Source: Retrieved from http://www.un.org/en/documents/udhr/index.shtml

PART II

Multi-Phase Model of Psychotherapy, Counseling, Human Rights, and Social Justice

4

DEVELOPMENT, RATIONALE, AND PREREQUISITES OF THE MULTI-PHASE MODEL (MPM) OF PSYCHOTHERAPY, COUNSELING, HUMAN RIGHTS, AND SOCIAL JUSTICE

All compromise is based on give and take, but there can be no give and take on fundamentals. Any compromise on mere fundamentals is a surrender. For it is all give and no take.

(Mahatma Gandhi)

Believe and act as if it were impossible to fail.

(Charles F. Kettering)

WARM UP EXERCISE

1. *Do you have good communication skills? Do you think you are more a listener or a talker, or do you have a good balance?*

2. *When someone is sharing pain or deep distress with you, how do you manage it? How do you feel?*

(Continued)

(Continued)

3. *Would you characterize yourself as more pessimistic or optimistic? How do you imagine this will affect you as a counselor or psychologist?*

4. *Do you have any fears related to interacting with others? Discuss how these fears might affect you as a counselor or psychologist.*

5. *Sometimes counselors or psychologists must be confrontational or challenging and promote discomfort that eventually results in healing. How do these qualities fit with your personality?*

Before we present the Multi-Phase Model (MPM) of Psychotherapy, Counseling, Human Rights, and Social Justice in the next chapter, this chapter will examine the rationale for developing the MPM and discuss how to put the model into practice.

It is important that we consider applying the MPM within an ecological context of today's world that includes the social, historical, psychological, economic, political, environmental, and cultural aspects that influence everyday life (Bemak & Conyne, 2004). The very nature of these dimensions, which affect each individual, is such that they will come into play and have a significant impact in the therapeutic relationship. Some examples of factors that are important to consider within an ecological framework include globalization, the worldwide movement of people, changing ethnic and racial demographics, growing diverse lifestyles, religion and religious beliefs, increased inter- and intragroup conflict, terrorism, escalating interpersonal violence and abuse, high rates of divorce, growing rates of poverty, and a widening technological gap.

Other areas such as global warming also affect clients, clients' families, and their communities (Chung & Bemak, in press). This can be seen through the projections that global warming will stimulate the mass movement of people who will no longer have the natural resources to survive in their native regions, and the emergence of new diseases that will contribute to equity issues in accessing healthcare. Mental health professionals must consider these issues as we move into the future, requiring us to reassess training, practice,

skills, techniques, interventions, and supervision. The (MPM) was designed to address these issues and help mental health professionals more effectively include these issues in their work. The MPM is an extension of the Multi-Level Model of Psychotherapy, Counseling, Human Rights, and Social Justice (MLM) that was originally created for providing culturally responsive services for immigrants and refugees (Bemak & Chung, 2008a; Bemak, Chung, & Pedersen, 2003).

RATIONALE FOR THE MPM

Currently there is no model in the field of psychotherapy and counseling that integrates mental health with social justice and human rights while taking into consideration a relevant ecological framework. Our concern, as we discussed in previous chapters, relates to the lack of applicability of traditional models and pedagogy to contemporary issues that we face as psychologists and counselors. Furthermore, there is a marked absence of social justice and human rights within the framework of traditional mental health interventions. Thus, we designed the MPM with these parameters in mind.

The MPM is based on the following three assumptions. The first assumption is that traditionally, professional mental health principles and practices are rooted in precepts of individualism that have origins in European and European American constructs. The emphasis on individualistic society provides an underpinning for cultural values that permeate Western society and influence every aspect of life, including mental health and psychological well-being. The prominence of individualism in mental health theory and practice is juxtaposed with the fact that only about 30%, or less than one third, of the world's population comes from individualistic societies. More than two thirds of the world has origins in collectivistic societies that value interdependence and a social orientation that emphasizes family, community, and group traditions (Triandis, 1994). Differences between individualistic and collectivistic cultures can be seen in the United States, where 1 of every 8 people is an immigrant (Camarota, 2007) who was foreign born, while many other U.S.-born individuals come from ethnic and racial groups that have their origins in collectivistic cultures. The ensuing tension between the culture where one lives and the values that are derived from one's culture of origin may generate an inherent conflict.

A second assumption that led us to develop the MPM is based on the fact that individualistic constructs provide a foundation for Western perspectives on mental health. Western psychotherapy is firmly rooted in individualistic constructs, based on precepts of European psychoanalysis, psychopathology, and mental illness. Thus, individuals who seek mental health treatment in the West talk to psychotherapists independent of their families and communities. They receive diagnoses that label their problems and work to resolve difficulties on their own rather than in conjunction with significant others in their lives. Modern manifestations of Western mental illness correlate with the medical disease model, which includes interpretations of biochemical and genetic disorders that view medication as the means of treatment.

The disease model does not incorporate substantive sociopolitical concepts such as justice, equity, and fairness, nor is it concerned with human rights. Furthermore, researchers have found that the medical model orientation, which requires diagnoses to determine effective medication interventions and treatment, is culturally biased and inaccurate when working across cultures (Chung & Kagawa-Singer, 1995; Draguns, 2000; Phillips & Draguns, 1969). Thus, it presents formidable

obstacles when working with ethnically and racially diverse groups of people. In fact, a World Health Organization international study found that people with schizophrenia in poorer nations had a better recovery rate than those in Western industrial countries due to family and community support (Sartorius, Gulbinat, Harrison, Laska, & Siegel, 1996). These findings are consistent with those of a U.S. study that found social support was a buffer for mental illness (Kessler, Chiu, Demler, & Walters, 2005).

The third assumption related to the development of the MPM is based on the reality that historically, mental health has not considered issues of social justice or human rights. Neglecting social justice and human rights in mental health work has been, in our opinion, a glaring deficit, given that hundreds of millions of people around the world suffer as a result of inequities, unequal opportunities, inequalities, and injustices. One difficulty of including attendance to social justice issues within what is expected of mental health professionals is that there is no theoretical basis for incorporating social justice and human rights into the mental health domain, nor is there any training to integrate human rights into mental health practice. Despite the lack of a theoretical framework, we strongly believe that it is the psychologist's and counselor's moral and ethical obligation to address and incorporate these issues in their work.

Findings from research data complement these three assumptions, pointing out the need to address social justice and human right issues. Below is a brief description of four areas that illustrate the types of social justice and human rights issues that have a significant impact on our clients' and their families' lives and that impact their psychological well-being.

1. Growing Rates of Poverty

The United States has one of the highest standards of living in the world. However, the disparity between the rich and poor is widening, with the average income of the poorest fifth of the population down 6% and the average income of the top fifth up 30% over the 20 years leading up to the end of the last century (Bernstein, McNichol, Mishel, & Zahradnik, 2000). In fact, the gap between rich and poor is now wider than it has been since the 1930s (Lewis, 2003). For example, the richest 1% of households owns 38% of all wealth. In 2001, 7.8% of White Americans, 22.7% of African Americans, 21.4% of Latina/o Americans, and 10.2% of Asian Americans lived in poverty (Bernstein, 2002). One in six U.S. children (16.7%) lives in a family whose income is below the poverty line (Children's Defense Fund [CDF], 2004). This all adds up to the fact that poverty in the United States continues to be higher than that of most industrial nations (Center on Budget and Policy Priorities [CBPP], 1999; CDF, 2004; U.S. Census Bureau, 1999). It has been well established that poverty is detrimental to psychological well-being and mental health, with findings indicating that low-income individuals are two to five times more likely to suffer from a diagnosable mental disorder than those in the highest socioeconomic status group (e.g., Bourdon, Rae, Narrow, Manderchild, & Reiger, 1994). (See Table 4.1 for more information regarding low-income families.)

As Mahatma Gandhi stated, "Poverty is the worst form of violence."

2. Interpersonal Violence

Every day in the media we see or hear stories of interpersonal violence, whether it is an argument with a loved one, bullying, aggravated assault, robbery, rape, sexual abuse, child neglect, kidnapping, gang activity, homicide, suicide, or something else (see Table 4.2). When we read this list, it is scary to think that these things go on every day, and many of our clients will have been perpetrators and/or victims of these events. Interpersonal violence affects all individuals, regardless of their socioeconomic status, religion, race, ethnicity, culture, gender, disability, or sexual orientation. Strikingly, in 1993, youth violence was declared an epidemic (U.S. Department of Health and Human Services [U.S. HHS], 2001). An increase of violence globally prompted the World Health Organization to write a report addressing violence on multiple levels (Krug, Dahlberg, Mercy, Zwi, & Lozano, 2002). Once again, the experience and exposure to interpersonal violence has a significant impact on a client's psychological well-being.

Table 4.1　Report Finds That 1 in 4 Working Families Is Low-Wage

Between 2002 and 2006, the ranks of low-wage working families increased by 350,000.

Nearly 9.6 million (more than 1 in 4) of the nation's working families with children are low-wage income families.

Low-wage families are defined as those earning less than double the poverty rate. For a family of four, an annual income of $41,228 or less is considered to be low-wage.

One reason for the increase might be the growth in low-paying jobs.

As their wages are falling, families are struggling to pay for basics, such as health care, food, and housing.

More than one in five jobs in 2006 paid poverty-level wages.

Less pay does not equal less work. On average, 2,552 hours per year were worked in each family, which is the equivalent of one and one quarter full-time workers per family.

The report stated, "Low-income families must become better educated if they are going to move up economically."

While more than half of the jobs in the United States require more than a high school education, 88 million adult workers have only a high school education or less.

Source: Fletcher (2008).

Table 4.2 Interpersonal Violence

Many reports were received during the two years before her alleged murder that 13-year-old Alexis "Lexie" Agyepong-Glover was being abused by her adoptive mother. But somehow, the girl remained in the home, and nothing was ever done. The reports included descriptions of bruises on wrists and forearms as if she had been tied up, of an attempt to get on the bus in her underwear, of wandering the neighborhood wearing nothing but a grill cover, and of being locked in the trunk of her mother's car, among others. The Prince William County (Virginia) police department stated that they did not believe Lexie to be in serious danger; however, the state Department of Social Services was called to conduct an investigation. But the Department of Social Services would not comment on the matter.

Lexie's mother, Alfreedia Gregg-Glover, dumped Lexie in a creek, where she drowned. Gregg-Glover was then charged with murdering her daughter, lying to the police, and child abuse. Those who tried to help Lexie in the months leading up to her death are angered that no one bothered to take their calls seriously. Lexie would run away to neighbors' houses in hopes that the police could help her. The neighbors would call the police, but Lexie was never pulled from her adoptive mother's home. Gregg-Glover reported that Lexie had run away again, and two days later a man found her dead body in a creek.

Source: Mummolo (2009).

3. Racism and Discrimination

Accompanying the migration of racially and ethnically diverse refugees and immigrant groups to Western countries and high birth rates for some racial and ethnic minority groups, there are significant demographic shifts in Western countries. For example, it is projected that by 2050, the current White majority in the United States will become a minority, and demographics for the United States as a whole will be similar to those that now exist in Florida, California, and Texas (U.S. Census Bureau, 2002). With the demographic shift, there is the loss of majority status for the White population, raising issues of tolerance and acceptance of racial, ethnic, cultural, and religious differences for all diverse groups. Compounding racial intolerance are the heated debates on immigration issues in general, and specifically on illegal or undocumented immigrants (Chung, Bemak, & Kudo Grabosky, 2011; Chung, Bemak, Ortiz, & Sandoval-Perez, 2008) (see Table 4.3).

These issues are underscored in the FBI hate crime statistics for 2005 (U.S. Department of Justice, 2006), which showed a dramatic increase (20.7%) from 2000 to 2001 in hate crimes. The breakdown of these hate crimes is interesting.

Racial bias represented 54.7% of the hate crimes, while 13.9% of the hate crimes were driven by ethnic/national origin bias. Religious intolerance comprised 17.1% of the crimes, sexual orientation bias 14.2%, and disability bias 0.7%. It is essential that psychologists and counselors attend to these issues when working with ethnically and racially diverse clientele.

4. Health Care and Mental Health Care Access and Quality of Treatment

The accessibility of mental health care and treatment presents a major problem for many individuals in the United States. Kessler et al. (2005) found that 25% of all Americans had a mental health problem. Alarmingly, less than half of the 25% received some type of treatment. Of equal concern was the finding that the actual counseling and treatment services rendered for this small percentage of individuals was found to be inadequate. The study concluded that the lack or inadequacy of treatment was due to a number of factors. This included an inattention to early warning signs, inadequate health insurance, and the stigma regarding mental illness. The study also provided a picture of how the United States compares to other countries with regard to mental

Table 4.3 Racism and Discrimination

Poor Latina/os are continuously discriminated against nationwide, but especially in the South. According to the Southern Poverty Law Center, Latina/os are paid less than Whites for the work they perform, are denied basic health care, and experience racial profiling. Latina/o immigrants have been jailed and had money stolen. One woman was raped, but the rapist was not charged, because the woman was an undocumented immigrant.

Latina/os are being treated poorly by the police and sexually harassed because they are beyond the protection of the law. The president of the Georgia Latino Alliance for Human Rights stated that there is the general idea in society that discrimination against Latina/os is acceptable, because these people are here illegally and do not have the right to be in this country.

Arizona has also experienced a large amount of discrimination in three main forms: racial profiling by the police, workplace issues, and problems in the rental housing market. But John McManus, president of John Birch Society, feels that this is not the case. He says that the Southern Poverty Law Center likes to exaggerate information. But Southern Poverty Law Center President Richard Cohen feels that this matter concerns basic human rights. Abuse and discrimination are unacceptable in our society and will lead to Latina/o immigrants being invisible in the eyes of the law.

Source: Brice (2009).

health disorders: The United States is ranked as the number one country in the world with the highest levels of mental health problems. (See Table 4.4 for an example of how racism can impact mental health.)

Aggravating the problem of access to quality health care is the growth in medical costs, which far outpaced the growth of wages for the eighth straight year in 2004, when medical costs grew nearly four times as fast as wages (Connolly, 2005). This leaves health care essentially unaffordable for people with middle-level or lower salaries. The inability to afford health care is further exacerbated by businesses such as the airline

Table 4.4 Mental Health

A recent study shows that students in fifth grade are more likely to experience symptoms of mental disorders if they have been treated poorly based on the color of their skin. Study subjects included more than 5,000 children in Birmingham, Houston, and Los Angeles. It has been shown that racial discrimination can increase the chances of adolescents and adults developing mental health problems, but this is the first study to look at children's mental health with regard to various races.

The study does not prove that the racial discrimination was the cause of emotional problems among the children, because they were not followed over long periods of time. There is a chance that discrimination can damage a child's mental health, but there is also a chance that certain kids prompt more negative remarks from their peers or that children with emotional problems observe more bias.

There is a strong link between mental health disorders and perceived racial discrimination. Prejudice was evident for 20% of African Americans, 15% of Latina/os, 7% of Whites, and 16% of other study subjects. Latina/os had the worst mental health problems out of all groups. But about four out of five Latina/os who felt racial discrimination had parents who were not born in the United States. Parents of color may help their children learn to deal with racial discrimination better and to prepare for it.

Source: Elias (2009).

industry scaling back or dropping health coverage for their employees. If this trend continues, a substantial decline in the number of people with health insurance in the United States is projected (CBPP, 2006). It is evident that those with lower incomes cannot afford private health insurance, and with the steady increase in health care costs, it is projected that middle-level income earners will also be affected.

In 2005, 46.6 million Americans, or approximately 15.9% of the population, were uninsured and therefore lacking health care coverage (CBPP, 2006). The difficulty of paying for and accessing mental health services is an important element in the lives of many clients, and it is important to address this issue in psychotherapy and counseling. In addition, disparities have also been found in the quality of care between Whites and people of color, with the latter group receiving significantly lower-quality care in health facilities (Agency for Healthcare Research and Quality, 2000).

CHANGING DEMOGRAPHICS AND UNDERUTILIZATION OF MAINSTREAM MENTAL HEALTH SERVICES

The changing demographics in the United States offer a poignant example of the need to reexamine current mental health practices and training. The demographics for ethnic populations are changing quickly and have significance for mental health services (see, e.g., Sue, Fujino, Hu, Takeuchi, & Zane, 1991; U.S. HHS, 2001) as we mentioned above. The U.S. 2000 census reported that three in ten people in the United States are ethnic minorities, one in five people were born in another country or have at least one parent who was born in another country, and Latina/o Americans and Asian Americans are the fastest growing ethnic groups (U.S. Census Bureau, 2002). These demographics have the potential for a significant impact for the mental health field, with projections that the racial and ethnic makeup of our future clientele will also proportionately change.

In contrast to previous censuses, the 2000 U.S. Census for the first time allowed individuals to check off multiple racial/ethnic categories, resulting in new information and the collection of statistics on biracial/multiracial populations. It was found that 6.8 million or 2% of the U.S. population reported that they were in this category (U.S. Census Bureau, 2002). Projections for 2050 demographics indicate 54% of the population will be minority. Latina/o will constitute approximately 30% of the total U.S. population, and Asian Americans will make up 9% to 10% (U.S. Census Bureau, 2008a). Furthermore, the U.S. Census Bureau (2008b) reported that as of January 2009, immigration was expected to add one person every 36 seconds to the U.S. population, and the overall increase in the total U.S. population (from immigration and birth) was expected to be one person every 14 seconds. Such rapid growth underscores the demographic shifts that will necessitate new and responsive mental health services.

Despite the large and growing numbers of ethnic minority groups, findings have shown that ethnic minority populations tend to underutilize mainstream Western mental health services (U.S. HHS, 2001), either not accessing the services at all or dropping out early in the therapeutic process due to a lack of culturally appropriate responsiveness from mental health practitioners (Sue et al., 1991). A number of factors may contribute to these findings. One factor may be the tendency for psychologists and counselors to misdiagnose racial and ethnic clients as a result of racial and ethnic stereotyping (U.S. HHS, 2001). Another reason may be language barriers. A number of psychologists and counselors are unable neither to speak the native language of their clients, nor—of equal importance—to understand the nuances of effectively working with bicultural interpreters (Bemak, Chung, & Pederson, 2003; Raval & Smith, 2003).

The inability of Western trained psychologists and counselors to go beyond traditional training and practice in a culturally sensitive manner may also contribute to the underutilization of services by diverse racial and ethnic clients. Another factor may be a lack of accessibility of services. The location of service system facilities far from where clients live, and the costs of transportation to them, may be impediments for clients with fixed or restricted incomes. Finally, another reason for underutilization of mental health services may be the stigma attached within one's own racial or ethnic community to seeing a psychologist or counselor for support.

Changing demographics and subsequent diversification of the U.S. population have a significant relationship to therapeutic outcomes. Studies found that 40% of variations in outcomes were due to client extratherapeutic factors, or factors outside of the actual therapy or counseling, including social support networks (Lambert, 1992; Lambert & Bergin, 1994). The importance of social support is evident in collectivistic cultures, where family and community are more highly valued than the individual and play a significant role in helping and healing.

It is interesting that researchers have found that almost half of the therapeutic outcome is derived from factors external to the actual therapy. When combining this with the significant number of ethnic populations who underutilize mainstream mental health services, it becomes crucial that we as counselors and psychologists incorporate these research findings into our work and pay greater attention to what happens outside the actual therapy within the social support network of the family and community. The importance of social support networks has been supported in recent studies (e.g., Kessler et al., 2005; Sartorius et al., 1996) that showed that social support has a direct relationship to positive mental health.

In summary, training, practice, and research in the mental health field has focused on Western traditional views that emphasize working with individuals. The assumptions that an individual's problems are biomedically based, and that there is a universality in the conceptualization, manifestation, and treatment of psychological problems regardless of racial, ethnic, or cultural backgrounds, provide the foundation for mental health treatment. Consequently there is a lack of

understanding and acceptance of social justice and human rights issues as they relate to psychological well-being. Typically the psychologist or counselor who sees a client for counseling will not be considering issues of social justice, human rights, or inequities, but rather will focus more exclusively on the client's individual mental health, ignoring the broader social justice and human rights issues that are pertinent within the therapeutic relationship.

To more effectively address these inconsistencies and the absence of social justice work in counseling and psychotherapy, we expanded our prior model, the Multi-Level Model (MLM) (Bemak & Chung, 2008a; Bemak, Chung, & Pedersen, 2003) and developed the MPM, which is inclusive of social justice and human rights as an integral part of mental health work. The goal of developing the model was to offer psychologists and counselors a framework that will deal with today's rapidly changing society and that will work effectively with the myriad contemporary, complex, and interrelated issues that affect both human rights and mental health. The MPM is challenging, requiring that psychologists and counselors move beyond their traditional roles in individually focused work, and demanding a broader and more comprehensive view of mental health and psychological well-being that involves multiple levels of personal, social, and systemic change.

The Need for a Social Justice Mental Health Model: The Development of the MPM

Many clients come into the counseling relationship affected by local, regional, national, and even international events and situations. The recent earthquake and tsunami in Japan; the 2010 earthquake in Haiti; the attacks of September 11th, 2001; the train and bus bombings in Madrid and London; the 2008 shootings in Mumbai; the tsunamis in India, Indonesia, and Sri Lanka; the attacks of the Unabomber in the United States; the sniper in Washington, D.C.; the terrorist bombing during the World Cup finals in Kampala; and school shootings at Virginia Tech, Columbine, Minnesota, and Red Lake—each of these events has an impact on our clients. With mass media and technology providing volumes of information and opening up the world around us, many clients come to us with a heightened awareness of the world around them and the impact of that world on their lives. Clients internalize sociopolitical issues and injustices, yet in traditional models of mental health we have not paid much attention to these issues. Rather, there is a fundamental emphasis on personal issues, sometimes with an intrapsychic focus, frequently disregarding the importance and relevance of sociopolitical, historical, and economic factors that contribute to mental health.

We can see this in the wars in Iraq and Afghanistan or the current civil strife in Syria or Libya. The fighting is greatly impacting many individuals' psychological well-being as a result of what they've seen or heard in the media or of their personal experiences or those of their friends and relatives. Many people watch their own sons, daughters, nephews, nieces, husbands, wives, friends, neighbors, colleagues, and coworkers being called to war, and some have had relatives who died as a result of these wars. Other individuals have strong reactions to the war, prompting clients and therapists alike to want to do something. Frequently there are reactions that go beyond working out personal psychological issues, encompassing; strong feelings to do something or take action. For example, recently soldiers' wives have formed a group that has become a very important social support group. As the fear and anger of having their husbands away at war was brought up in counseling sessions, these sessions could have provided support and impetus for this idea, rather than ignoring it.

It is our contention that this type of personal call to action is appropriately addressed in counseling. This does not mean that one ignores deeper psychological issues and problems raised by individuals. But it requires a careful assessment and consideration of when and how to address social and political responses within the therapeutic relationship, and how to balance personal psychological concerns with a client's desire to proactively do something.

Another good example of balancing personal concerns with action can be seen in a school where a large number of ethnic and racial minority students were placed in a special education class, and the school counselor and school psychologist were working with a group of angry parents who were demanding some answers. Rather than help the parents accept and come to terms with the school practices, the counselor and psychologist raised a question as to whether or not there was a disproportionate placement of students of color in special education classes, and if this was in fact the case, what the counselor, psychologist, and parents constructively could do to review this situation and change the practice.

Generally, the social justice and human rights issues are broader issues that relate to the betterment of our society and have social implications that affect larger groups of people, communities, and the society at large. The issues are typically neither addressed nor attended to in mental health work. In fact, we would suggest that individual counseling and psychotherapy has taken a passive and often insidious role by focusing on changing the individual at the expense of changing the larger systems. The danger with this approach is that there is a perpetuation and implicit condoning of the status quo, which historically maintains unfair and unequal power and resource differentials that may in turn reinforce and contribute to social injustices.

To address these concerns, incorporate the human rights dimension into psychotherapy, and consequently improve the responsiveness of mental health professionals to the pressing needs for social justice, we developed the MPM (Bemak & Chung, 2008a; Bemak et al., 2003). The purpose of the MPM is to assist mental health professionals in being effective with *all* groups and *all* clients from all racial, ethnic, and cultural backgrounds as well as those who diverge from the mainstream in other ways (e.g., in sexual orientation, religion, gender orientation, socioeconomic status, disabilities, age, etc.) in working toward social justice and human rights. Inherent in the model is the focus on proactive attention to issues such as discrimination, racism, sexism, social responsibility, interdependence, self-determination, and oppression, as well as poverty, interpersonal violence, and other social conditions that inhibit personal and social development and growth.

The model speaks to the need for professionals to have unique skills—as well as sensitivity to and awareness, understanding, acknowledgment, and acceptance of—the historical, sociopolitical, sociocultural, and ecological backgrounds of clients and their families and communities. It further calls for a profound understanding of psychological realities, deeply rooted trauma and loss, poverty, racism, oppression, violence, self-determination, social responsibility, and discrimination. This understanding is of particular importance, since clinical training and supervision in counseling and psychology rarely addresses these issues. The MPM also incorporates a holistic approach that views a diverse clientele from both macro and micro perspectives as well as cross-cultural, multicultural, social justice, and human rights perspectives. Finally, the MPM reconceptualizes traditional Western training within a universal social justice and human rights framework that includes global cross-cultural perspectives. It presents therapeutic applications that are culturally responsive, using effective clinical interventions that keep these basic principles in mind.

REQUIREMENTS OF THE MPM APPLICATION

To effectively provide mental health interventions using the MPM, the mental health professional and counselor must have a variety of skills, techniques, and experiences, as well as a clear sense of how social justice and human rights impact one's psychological well-being. Figure 4.1 depicts the skills, experiences, techniques, and awareness that are essential to employ the MPM.

Clients' Experiences

Cultural sensitivity is a cornerstone of the MPM, with psychologists and counselors welcoming and working with clients' family and community worldviews, cultural values, beliefs, attitudes, customs, language, and spiritual dimensions. Concurrently, it is essential to consider the direct and indirect influential factors in the client's life experiences, such as the historical, sociopolitical, psychosocial, ecological, and cultural experiences that constitute the foundation and worldview for a person's life. For example when I (Fred) provided clinical consultation for 2½ years on a Native American reservation, it was essential that I kept in mind such things as the history of genocide, modern political oppression facing the nation, the nation's interaction with the surrounding mainstream society, and the effect of my being a White male working with a Native American group of professionals (which was discussed in depth). All of these issues had a great impact on the mental health issues facing the Native American clientele and were important to keep in mind as we worked toward wellness, healing, and mental health.

Other mediating factors that one must consider include past and present stressors, traumatic experiences, psychosocial adaptation and adjustment, level of acculturation and racial/ethnic identity, cultural support systems, spirituality, cultural beliefs in the conceptualization of mental health and resulting cultural manifestations or expressions of symptoms, cultural preferences and expectations with respect to help-seeking and treatment, experiences of discrimination and racism, and potential future human rights violations. It is essential to reflect on and keep in mind these parts of a client's life when applying the MPM.

Psychotherapy/Counseling Skills and Techniques

To complement the awareness of the client's experiences in a broader social context, there must also be a thorough knowledge and understanding of traditional Western psychotherapy

Figure 4.1 Requirements for Effective MPM Application

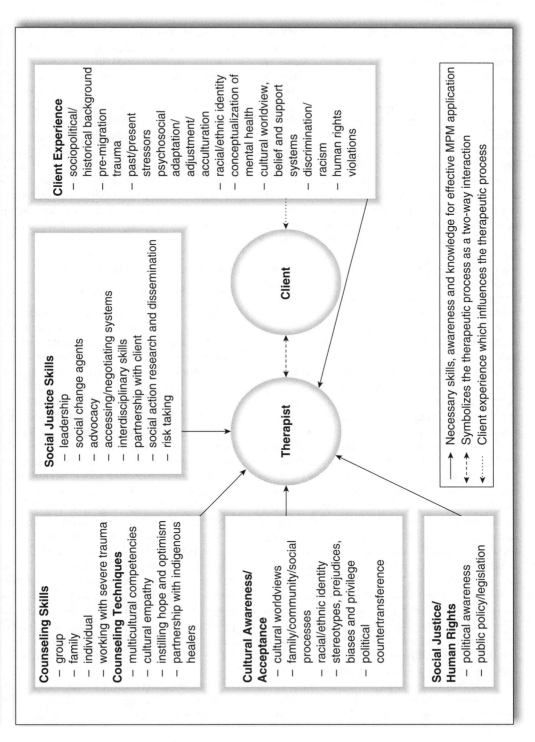

Client Experience
- sociopolitical/historical background
- pre-migration trauma
- past/present stressors
- psychosocial adaptation/adjustment
- acculturation
- racial/ethnic identity
- conceptualization of mental health
- cultural worldview, belief and support systems
- discrimination/racism
- human rights violations

Client

Social Justice Skills
- leadership
- social change agents
- advocacy
- accessing/negotiating systems
- interdisciplinary skills
- partnership with client
- social action research and dissemination
- risk taking

Therapist

Counseling Skills
- group
- family
- individual
- working with severe trauma

Counseling Techniques
- multicultural competencies
- cultural empathy
- instilling hope and optimism
- partnership with indigenous healers

Cultural Awareness/Acceptance
- cultural worldviews
- family/community/social processes
- racial/ethnic identity
- stereotypes, prejudices, biases and privilege
- political
- countertransference

Social Justice/Human Rights
- political awareness
- public policy/legislation

→ Necessary skills, awareness and knowledge for effective MPM application
⤍ Symbolizes the therapeutic process as a two-way interaction
⋯ Client experience which influences the therapeutic process

and counseling within a multicultural framework. Being culturally competent in the various skill areas of group, family, and individual counseling provides a basis for applying the MPM, but the mental health professional must also be able to adapt, modify, alter, expand, and/or change traditional skills and techniques into practices that are effective from a social justice/human rights perspective. This is especially important when working with people from different racial, ethnic, socioeconomic, and cultural groups. As mentioned previously, "talk therapy" may be foreign to certain groups, and therefore the psychotherapist must adapt traditional psychotherapy and counseling skills and techniques accordingly. For example, one of the ways I (Fred) have worked with a number of refugees from Africa and Asia has been to discuss dreams and semi-guided imagery fantasies that are applicable to the problems and struggles being faced by individuals.

It is very important that therapeutic and counseling relationships are viewed from cross-cultural and multicultural perspectives. Aspects such as empathy, boundaries, personal space, confidentiality, greeting of clients and their families, and clients' preferences to use indigenous healing methodologies need to be taken into account. For example, problems may arise if the psychologist or counselor is displaying Western or traditional methods of empathy such as direct eye contact or physical touch. This type of nonverbal behavior may be highly offensive to clients from Asian, Latina/o, Native American, Arab, or other cultures, and it may not be perceived as a way of intensely engaging or caring. Furthermore, eye contact between an older and a younger person, or between women and men, may be considered a cultural taboo.

Knowing about these issues beforehand, or being willing to learn about these cross-cultural differences while on the job, is crucial to fostering a sense of openness and awareness while working across cultures. Using the example of empathy, counselors and psychologists must be able to display empathy while considering cross-cultural interpersonal and communication variables (Chung & Bemak, 2002) and maintaining awareness that traditional Western displays of empathy may be inappropriate and even objectionable for many clients.

We would also suggest that in working with clients on social justice and human rights issues, it is important for the helping professional to have knowledge regarding working with trauma. This is especially important given the traumatic life events and experiences many clients have undergone who have felt their rights were violated. Thus, we believe it is essential that there is an understanding of working with post-traumatic stress disorder (PTSD) and related therapeutic issues, such as loss, grief, and bereavement.

The Element of Hope and Optimism within the MPM

When working with people whose human rights have been violated, the accumulation of negative and oppressive experiences may result in despair, helplessness, and hopelessness. It is our experience, when working with clients who are oppressed or have experienced different levels of trauma and personal and social violations, that hopefulness is critical in the healing process. One study of therapeutic outcomes has shown that 15% of the outcome is attributed to the placebo effects of hope and expectations, while other studies have emphasized the importance of optimism (or hope) as it correlates with positive psychological well-being (Frank, 1968; Lambert, 1992; Snyder, 1994). Consequently, we believe it is also necessary that psychologists and counselors be hopeful for their clients and project this positivism in their work. A negatively inclined psychologist or counselor transmits messages of hopelessness, frustration, and despair. On the other hand, mental health professionals who feel positive and see possibilities to influence the future reflect a viewpoint that there is the possibility of change on personal, social, and community levels.

Thus, when you are working with an adolescent who wants to stop taking drugs and is trying to take the difficult step to end long-standing friendships with other drug users, or when you are seeing someone who continues to experience discrimination about her or his sexual orientation at work, it is important for you as a psychologist or counselor to believe that these clients can make those steps and change themselves as well as have an impact on the external circumstances that are psychologically harmful. Therefore, confidence for a positive outcome becomes fundamental in the therapeutic relationship, whereby you, the psychologist or counselor, become a facilitator and partner for change with aspirations for a different and healthier outcome. This parallel process of hope becomes embedded in the therapeutic relationship, so that your level of optimism and expectations for change may be mirrored by the client's own beliefs and feelings.

An excellent example of this can be seen with the refugee population. Given the degree of inhuman and oppressive premigration experiences encountered by many refugees, it is critical that hope is a part of their lives. A counselor or psychologist who does not share a positive outlook, and who is not hopeful about the refugees' adjustment or ability to solve their problems in the resettlement country, may contribute to the refugee client's internalizing psychological difficulties and adopting feelings of despair. In contrast, when the psychologist or counselor is hopeful about the refugees' situation, the client is more inclined to mirror the therapist's attitude and have a positive outlook toward the potential for resolving the difficulties.

Cultural Awareness and Acceptance

As we have been discussing, mental health professionals and counselors working toward social justice and human rights must have more than the traditional requisite skills and go beyond using the usual techniques. To work with the complex issues of equity and justice, counselors and therapists must have a deeply rooted understanding of themselves that includes an understanding of their cultural heritage. This understanding must go beyond the customary awareness of themselves as human beings and extend to incorporate

their views, experiences, and perspectives about social change, social justice, social responsibility, and social activism. In turn, it is essential to understand on a deeper level how these personal, social, and political issues intersect and interrelate with the reality of their own lives. We would suggest that the impact of these multiple perspectives manifests in the therapeutic relationship and subsequently in the therapeutic process.

This may become evident when working with clients from different racial, ethnic, or cultural backgrounds or with lesbian, gay, bisexual or transgender clients, who have experienced racial and/or sexual discrimination. To understand this more clearly, consider a White mental health professional working with a client from a different racial or ethnic group. The White counselor or therapist would need not only to understand racial/ethnic identity theory (Helms, 1995) as it relates to the client, but also how White identity theory relates to the psychologist or counselor working across cultures (Helms, 1992). This is consistent with Helms's writings about how racial and ethnic identity theories were originally established for clients of color in the United States. These theories were developed to assess the adaptation of clients of color in a predominantly White society, in which there were inequalities and injustices toward members of ethnic and racial groups based on the assumption of White superiority and privilege and ethnic inferiority. These discriminatory attitudes and assumptions are not only perpetrated on the individual level but are also sanctioned in institutions and larger systems. Consequently, models have been developed to describe the adaptation of Whites as members of the dominant group through White identity theory.

Therefore, White identity theory assumes that White psychologists and counselors may undergo a developmental process of creating meaning about their identities as Caucasians, particularly in terms of how they think about, respond to, react to, and interact with clients from different racial/ethnic groups (Helms, 1984). For these psychologists and counselors, understanding their responses to issues of privilege, bias, racism, discrimination, and oppression is key in the therapeutic encounter. The same would hold true for psychotherapists and counselors from other cultural backgrounds, should their race, ethnicity, sexual orientation, or gender differ from that of their clients. For example, Asian counselors must undergo a similar process if their clients are African American, Latina/o, White, Arab, Native American, or of some other non-Asian group, and they must take into account race, ethnicity, age, sexual identity, religion, gender, socioeconomic status, and so forth. In addition, counselors and psychologists must acknowledge the intersection of multiple variables for each client, such as an African American *lesbian* client or a *male* Muslim client who has a disability.

Inherent in Helms's theory and relevant to cultural awareness and acceptance is an outline of different statuses that White psychologists and counselors may undergo with regard to social inequities. Initially, White psychologists and counselors may be oblivious to and unaware of racial and ethnic injustices; then they move through a progression of understanding toward a nonracist White identity. This process requires the mental health professionals' awareness, acknowledgment, acceptance, and understanding of their own biases and prejudices toward, beliefs about, and stereotypes of different racial, ethnic, cultural, religious, and other groups as well as an understanding of their own privileges and racism.

Although initially White identity theory was established to assist White mental health professionals to assess their own racial biases, prejudices, stereotypes, and countertransference, we would, as stated previously, expand upon this and suggest that it is critical for any mental health practitioner working with clients from a different racial, ethnic, or cultural group or different sexual orientation to have this level of awareness. (For a discussion of political countertransference, see p. 69.) Issues of privilege, biases, prejudices, and countertransference are not limited to any one group but affect all psychologists and counselors regardless of race, ethnicity, gender, age, class, religion, sexual orientation, disability, and so on. For example, a Latina therapist may have

stereotypical views of African Americans, a counselor who has strong religious beliefs may be negatively predisposed to gay clients, or a Jewish therapist may have negative countertransference issues with a Palestinian client. Regardless of the situation, it is mental health professionals' ethical duty to ensure that they are aware of and understand, accept, and acknowledge potential biases in their counseling and ways to work toward eliminating such biases.

In summary, to be effective when working with inequities, the MPM requires counselors and psychologists to undergo a deep self-examination of their values, beliefs, and worldviews while coming to terms with their stereotypes, biases, prejudices and privileges that may interfere with providing effective treatment (U.S. HHS, 2001).

The Relationship Between "isms" and Mental Health

Long-standing issues affecting clients are racism, sexism, classism, and the numerous other "isms." Racism has been identified as a natural consequence of Westernized individualism (Pedersen, 2000), and it may be possible to extrapolate this conclusion to other isms. Psychologists and counselors cannot ignore the impact that racism, sexism, and other forms of discrimination and oppression have on their clients, families, and communities. For example, it has been found that experiences of racism, prejudice, and discrimination are negatively related to psychological well-being and affect people from diverse ethnic, racial, and cultural backgrounds, impacting self-regard, interpersonal relationships, and adaptation to the broader social environment (Constantine, 2006; Steele, Spencer, & Aronson, 2002; Sue, 2003).

Impaired self-esteem and poor academic performance are frequently cited as psychological consequences of racism and discrimination (Asamen & Berry, 1987; Brantley, 1983; Hughes & Demo, 1989). In addition, racism and discrimination also contribute to substance abuse (Lopez-Bushnell, Tyer, & Futrell, 1992), child abuse, suicide (Horejsi, Craig, & Pablo, 1992), and domestic violence (Ho, 1990). Yet the traditional therapeutic interventions focus more on the presented problem (e.g., suicide or substance abuse) than on the ways to address discrimination and racism in a larger context. This same phenomenon can be seen in relationship to the other isms and consequent social injustices.

Psychologists and counselors who presume that they are free of discrimination, prejudice, racism, and other biases underestimate the social impact of their own socialization and their inherited and, in some instances, subtly ingrained unintentional covert discrimination and racism. Taking racism once again as an example, we can see in many instances that racism emerges as an unintentional attitude among well-meaning, right-thinking, good-hearted, caring professionals who are probably no more or less free from cultural biases than other members of the general public (Pedersen, 2000, p. 53). Thus to avoid acting on and internalizing isms consciously and unconsciously, and to be effective with all clients, it is important for psychologists and counselors to be aware of, understand, acknowledge, and respect their clients' and their own worldviews, life experiences, and cultural identities.

Political Countertransference

When assuming a social justice and human rights perspective, one is not only working with clients to promote psychological health and wellness but also working with much broader political issues that impact clients' lives as described earlier in this chapter. When one acknowledges and is aware of these broader ecological and political issues, the outlook for a client's mental health becomes more complex and interrelated with a wide range of associated issues that impact the client. For example, we became aware of a school where African American students receive detention, suspension, and expulsion at greater rates than White or Latina/o students for the exact same infractions. This raised issues about an institutional response to African American students' behavior that we believe cannot be ignored

within the counseling context. It is important that mental health practitioners be aware not only of their personal response to clients but also of their personal reactions at another level that we have named *political countertransference* (Chung, 2005; Chung et al., 2008). Political countertransference occurs when we as psychologists and counselors have personal reactions to the political context in which we work with clients, and this impacts our work with the clients. It is important to be aware of our own political countertransference given the potential impact it has on the therapeutic relationship.

Two examples provide an illustration of how political countertransference works. The first example relates to terrorist attacks. The September 11th, 2001 (9/11), attacks on the World Trade Center in New York and the Pentagon in Washington D.C., the October 12th, 2002, Bali bombings, the March 11th, 2004, attack in Madrid, the July 7th, 2005, attack in London, and the November 7th, 2008, terrorist attack at the Taj Mahal Hotel in Mumbai represent only a fraction of the deaths and havoc created by terrorist assaults. Focusing on one of the incidents, 9/11, psychologists and counselors within the United States and globally had strong feelings about the attacks, the victims of the attacks, and the losses experienced by the victims' families.

These reactions contributed to intense feelings accompanied by political convictions and possibly even negative perceptions of Muslims or people of Islamic faith. Counselors and psychologists working with clients from Islamic countries or with clients who held strong religious beliefs about Islam may have had strong reactions, particularly after 9/11 or one of these other terrorist events. These strong reactions on the part of the therapist or counselor would be their political countertransference, or their reactions to the devastation and trauma of that day's event. These reactions have the potential to interfere in the therapeutic relationship.

The second example relates to counseling someone who holds a firm religious belief that abortion is wrong. If you as a psychologist or counselor hold equally firm convictions that women should have the right to choose or that couples or partners should have the freedom to make choices about pregnancy, we would suggest that the reaction is not only rooted in a response to the client, but in a response to a highly charged political issue. Again, we would call this political countertransference. It is essential that psychologists and counselors be aware of political countertransference as another dimension of countertransference that has an impact on the work they do with clients.

Culture of Fear

Given the events of 9/11 in the United States and other terrorist attacks, it is now clearly established that we live in a world of global terrorism. When we live in an unpredictable environment where our sense of everyday safety is threatened, a culture of fear is created (Chung, in press; Chung et al., 2008). The culture of fear is reinforced by the constant reminders of 9/11 and other attacks by continual reports and associated changes in the "terrorist alert" levels. The terrorist alerts provide a constant reminder of the question: "How safe are we?" Feeling unsafe is a byproduct of the culture of fear, which then permeates other areas of our lives. In turn, the sense of underlying fear feeds and fuels potential social injustices and human rights violations.

Social Justice Action Self-Assessment

To genuinely address social justice issues and effectively utilize the MPM, psychologists and counselors need to undergo a social justice action self-assessment, asking themselves, "To what degree am I willing to address social justice issues?" Some psychologists and counselors believe that they are actively addressing these issues by simply talking about them, but this does not involve challenging existing systems or individuals who support these injustices. In our opinion, using the MPM requires us to closely examine what level of risk we are willing to take: "Am I willing to risk minor discomfort with my

colleagues? Would I be able to handle stronger feelings of resistance or discomfort? Would I place my job on the line for a social injustice?" and so forth.

Nice Counselor Syndrome

The nice counselor syndrome (NCS) refers to counselors and psychologists who take a neutral stance in an attempt to avoid upsetting others or the system; they maintain balance and harmony with coworkers, supervisors, and organizations. Counselors and psychologists with the NCS avoid conflict or unpleasant realities by giving positive reinforcement and feedback even when the situation warrants criticism, challenges, and confrontation (Bemak & Chung, 2008b). Yet to address injustices means that mental health professionals and counselors must sometimes challenge systems by rocking the boat. Challenging individuals and systems requires courage and risk taking and is not always easy. There are consequences in challenging the status quo; one might be labeled a troublemaker (Bemak & Chung, 2008b) or not a team player. We identify those who avoid social justice and human rights issues because of their concern for creating tension and dissonance as having NCS. To effectively employ the MPM, mental health professionals must move out of the NCS. The NCS will be discussed in more detail in Chapter 11.

Social Justice/Human Rights Awareness

Employing the MPM requires that mental health professionals be aware of current global, national, governmental, state, regional, and political issues that impact clients and their families and communities. Often clients do not talk about concerns that originate outside themselves, such as a policy that limits access to housing benefits, immigration restrictions on reunification of family, same-sex partners and marriage, or repeated experiences of institutional discrimination against women, persons with disabilities, or gay, lesbian, or transgender individuals. Yet these are underpinnings for clients' experience and everyday lives.

For example, given the current worldwide terrorist threats, in the United States there is ethnic profiling by law enforcement with specific groups, there are restrictions on visas and immigration for specific ethnic or cultural groups, and there are concerns about human rights violations regarding detainment of prisoners from the Iraq and Afghanistan wars. It is essential that counselors and psychologists be aware of the psychological impact of such policies on clients and address, rather than ignore, these factors within the therapeutic relationship.

Thus, to simply discuss with refugee clients from Afghanistan their anger over human rights violations toward Afghan detainees, and to try to help them in resolving those feelings, would not be the endpoint of treatment when using the MPM. Rather, it would be critical that the therapist talk about the context of these feelings within the larger Afghan community, the repercussions experienced by the clients in their everyday lives by virtue of the fact that they are from Afghanistan, the family pressures and reactions to the situation that influence their feelings, their desire or lack of desire for involvement in political actions within the Afghan community to address concerns about the war, and so forth.

People's views, perceptions, attitudes, and tolerance toward cultural, ethnic, and racial differences have been shaped in some respects by globalization and information access. Today we know many of the intimate details about the war in Iraq, the brutal killing of a gay man in the Midwest, or the racial tensions in a small town in the South that would not have been possible years ago. Through technology and the media, there is increasing exposure to cultural diversity. The rapid and instant technological transportation of images of and information about global and national situations, and increasing coverage of diverse groups of people, has created a situation where people develop opinions, perceptions, and attitudes toward individuals, groups, communities, and even countries with limited and often biased information.

Global situations that affect human rights are often politically charged and may be presented in a biased manner in the media. Hence, a simplistic or politically slanted view of a complex situation may result in a skewed perception and intolerance of specific cultural, ethnic, and racial groups. For example, the current worldwide terrorist threats have created an unfounded perception that specific cultural and ethnic groups may be terrorists, leading to cases of ethnic and racial profiling. Similar situations could arise given politically charged issues, such as gay marriage, that may increase the frequency of attacks on lesbian, gay, bisexual, transgender, or questioning (LGBTQ) individuals. Global reactions such as the United States' strong concern about the nuclear threat by North Korea may also instigate negative stereotyping toward all Asians, who may be viewed as both Korean and militaristic. Although the LGBTQ clients or the Arab or Asian American clients may not introduce or speak about these meta-level issues in psychotherapy and counseling, we would suggest that counselors must address them as an integral part of the clients' lives and the therapeutic process.

Redefining the Mental Health Role in Traditional Western Psychotherapy: Social Justice Skills

We have previously suggested that a thorough knowledge and understanding of traditional Western psychotherapy provides a basis for the MPM. It is essential that mental health practitioners have a core understanding of knowledge and skills from which to expand, alter, change, and adapt when using the MPM. Moving beyond traditional training to incorporate a parallel understanding of our own privilege, worldview, attitudes, values, beliefs, biases, and prejudices is necessary to work with a broader social and political context. The need to incorporate theories, techniques, and self-awareness in a culturally sensitive manner is essential in working toward social justice.

Thus, we would suggest that it is important to move beyond the apolitical framework in which we currently practice psychotherapy and counseling and reconstruct our roles as psychologists and counselors. As we are suggesting in this book, counselors and psychologists must become politically knowledgeable in a way that goes beyond their own political rights and choices. We believe that it is critical for counselors and psychologists to understand how to incorporate into their practice the mutually intertwined goals of social justice and mental health in working with clients. Psychologists and counselors must learn how to become human rights advocates. This requires them to take on newly defined proactive roles as leaders, change agents, and advocates for client(s).

Furthermore, helping professionals must acquire skills to work across disciplines with anthropologists, social workers, public health professionals, politicians, journalists, educators, lawyers, economists, geographers, historians, other helping professionals, sociologists, and community leaders. Thus, it is helpful for counselors and psychologists to know about social change and garner organizational development skills, negotiation skills, group process skills, and systems skills. Skills of this nature are helpful when working with clients to figure out how to deal with the justice system, educational systems, health and mental health systems, juvenile justice services, social services, housing services, equal rights offices, children's services, and so forth. Detailed descriptions of the above skills will be provided in later chapters of this book.

Newly defined roles will create different relationships with clients. Power, equity, access, unfairness, and inequities are viewed in a new light, as clients are assisted to become self-determining individuals within a broader social construct and to become advocates for themselves and others. Inherent in this newly defined role is the need for counselors and psychologists to focus on prevention and intervention that creates broader changes in their clients' lives and goes beyond individual adjustment and change. Instead, helping professionals form collaborative partnerships with clients to achieve equity and justice within a larger family and community context and to challenge, to the best of their ability, human rights violations that clients, their families, and their communities may encounter. As these newly constructed roles emerge, they add an element of partnering with clients to facilitate advocacy and social change (Bemak & Chung, 2005).

Consequently, traditional roles must be reexamined and adapted to better suit cross-cultural human rights perspectives. Western skills, techniques, interventions, models, and theories need to be aligned to be culturally sensitive. Redefining the counselor's or psychologist's role must also be considered and driven by existing research, such as findings that estimated that the therapeutic alliance accounts for 30% of a successful outcome (Lambert, 1992). This recharacterization of the role of the counselor and psychologist fosters an attention to and a respect for social justice and human rights issues that are important to the client.

CONCLUSION

The Multi-Phase Model of Psychotherapy, Counseling, Human Rights, and Social Justice (MPM) is designed to focus on mental health interventions that emphasize social justice and human rights. Through the combination of research findings and our own personal and professional experiences, we have a firm conviction that working with clients requires a broad ecological context for therapy, whereby the wider sociopolitical and economic framework that relates to humanitarian concerns and social justice are taken into account. The MPM is founded on principles of cross-cultural counseling that has relevance to different ethnic, racial, and cultural groups.

Issues that are considered fundamental to the therapeutic process in the MPM include taking into account clients' cultural conceptualizations and frameworks for understanding and defining mental illness and mental health, their cultural belief systems and worldviews, and the complexity of their historical and sociopolitical backgrounds. Furthermore, clients' past and present stressors; their levels of acculturation and racial identity; the psychosocial, cultural, and ecological barriers affecting their mental health and psychological well-being; and their experiences of discrimination, oppression, racism, and human rights violations are all important considerations that factor into clients' lives and are important in the MPM.

Within this model, it is critical that psychologists and counselors be culturally sensitive and responsive and have the capacity to redefine their professional roles and practice to incorporate proactive leadership, social change, and advocacy. These changes are essential to the prevention of and intervention against social injustices and human rights violations their clients may encounter. The next chapter will discuss the MPM and its application.

DISCUSSION QUESTIONS

1. You are requested to develop an intervention in a family homeless shelter in your local community. Considering the model proposed by the authors, which incorporates social, historical, psychological, economic, political, environmental, and cultural concerns, what are some of the factors that will influence the design and implementation of your intervention?
   a. Are there differences that you can imagine if your intervention had taken place five years ago in the same community?
   b. What would be the main differences in each dimension?

2. What are three assumptions on which the premise of the MPM is based?

3. Can you think of a current issue where social justice and human rights concerns interrelate with mental health? Consider such issues as poverty, interpersonal violence, racism, discrimination, mental health care access, and quality of mental health treatment.

4. Imagine yourself in 2050, when according to the U.S. Census, 54% of the population will be composed of minority groups. Given your racial and ethnic background, do you envision your life to be different than it is today? If so, how? How does access to services and resources need to change and adapt to shifting demographics?

5. Examine a copy of a current major newspaper or magazine. Count the number of news items referring to terrorism, fear, and violence, and share this with colleagues.

6. Think of a personal experience you have had that inspired you to either take action or want to take action to effect change. What action did you take or want to take? Looking back on this situation would you do anything differently?

7. When applying the MPM, it is important to be culturally sensitive and aware of your own biases. Conduct the following self-assessment, examining your current biases and reflecting on how you would manage them in a counseling relationship.
   a. What values/beliefs are most important to you?
   b. What stereotypes or prejudices do you currently have about other groups or your own?
   c. What privileges do you have that other groups do not have?
   d. What privileges do other groups have that you do not have?

8. What part(s) of the MPM application is/are the easiest for you to utilize? What part(s) will be the most difficult? Why?

9. Discuss your opinion of the "culture of fear." How do you think this will impact counseling relationships, and what approaches can you take to help your client deal with this culture of fear?

REFERENCES

Agency for Healthcare Research and Quality. (2000). *Addressing racial and ethnic disparities in healthcare.* AHRQ Publication No. 00-PO41. Retrieved from http://www.ahrq.gov/research/disparit.htm

Asamen, J. K., & Berry, G. L. (1987). Self-concept, alienation, and perceived prejudice: Implications for counseling Asian Americans. *Journal of Multicultural Counseling and Development, 15,* 146–160.

Bemak, F., & Chung, R. C-Y. (2008a). Counseling refugees and migrants. In P. B. Pedersen, J. G. Draguns, W. J. Lonner, & J. E. Trimble (Eds.), *Counseling across cultures* (6th ed., pp. 325–340). Thousand Oaks, CA: Sage.

Bemak, F., & Chung, R. C-Y. (2008b). New professional roles and advocacy strategies for school counselors: A multicultural/social justice perspective to move beyond the nice counselor syndrome. *Journal of Counseling & Development, 86,* 372–382.

Bemak, F., & Chung, R. C-Y. (2005). Advocacy as a critical role for school counselors: Working towards equity and social justice. *Professional School Counseling,* 196–202.

Bemak, F., & Chung, R. C-Y. (in press). The impact of global warming on the counseling profession. *Journal of Counseling & Development.*

Bemak, F., Chung, R. C-Y., & Pedersen, P. (2003). *Counseling refugees: A psychosocial cultural approach to innovative multicultural interventions.* Westport, CA: Greenwood Press.

Bemak, F., & Conyne, R. K. (2004). Ecological group work. In R. K. Conyne & E. P. Cook (Eds.), *Ecological counseling: An innovative approach to conceptualizing person-environment interaction.* (pp. 195–217). Alexandria, VA: American Counseling Association.

Bernstein, J., McNichol, E. C., Mishel, L., & Zahradnik, R. (2000). The characteristics and needs of sheltered homeless and low-income housed mothers. *Journal of the American Medical Association, 276,* 640–646.

Bernstein, R. (2002). *Poverty rate rises, household income declines.* Retrieved from http://www.census.govt/Press-Release/www/2002/cb02-124,html

Bourdon, K. H., Rae, D. S., Narrow, W. E., Manderchild R. W., & Reiger, D. A. (1994). National prevalence and treatment of mental and addictive disorders. In R. W. Manderchild & A. Sonnenschein (Eds.), *Mental health: United States* (pp. 22–51). Washington, DC: Center for Mental Health Services.

Brantley, T. (1983). Racism and its impact on psychotherapy. *American Journal of Psychiatry, 140*(12), 1605–1608.

Brice, A. (2009, April). Poor Latinos are victims of abuse nationwide, activists say. *CNN U.S.* Retrieved from http://articles.cnn.com/2009-04-22/us/latino.abuse_1_poor-latinos-discrimination-immigrants?_s=PM:US

Camarota, S. A. (2007, November). *Immigrants in the United States, 2007: A profile of America's foreign-born population.* Center for Immigration Studies. Retrieved from http://www.cis.org/immigrants_profile_2007

Center on Budget and Policy Priorities. (1999). *Low unemployment, rising wages fuel poverty decline.* Washington, DC: Author.

Center on Budget and Policy Priorities. (2006). *The number of uninsured Americans is at an all-time high.* Washington, DC: Author.

Children's Defense Fund. (2004). *The state of America's children 2004.* Washington, DC: Author.

Chung, R. C-Y. (2005). Women, human rights, and counseling: Crossing international boundaries. *Journal of Counseling & Development, 83,* 262–268.

Chung, R. C-Y. (in press). The culture of fear. *Journal of Counseling Psychology.*

Chung, R. C-Y., & Bemak, F. (2002). The relationship between culture and empathy in cross-cultural counseling. *Journal of Counseling and Development, 80,* 154–159.

Chung, R. C-Y., & Bemak, F. (in press). Global warming: Counselors' responsibilities and action. *Journal of Counseling & Development.*

Chung, R. C-Y., Bemak, F., Ortiz, D., & Sandoval-Perez, P. (2008). Promoting the mental health of immigrants: A multicultural/social perspective. *Journal of Counseling & Development, 86,* 310–317.

Chung, R. C-Y., Bemak, F., & Kudo Grabosky, T. (2011). Multicultural-social justice leadership strategies: Counseling and advocacy with immigrants. *Journal of Social Action in Psychology and Counseling, 3*(1), 86–102.

Chung, R. C-Y., & Kagawa-Singer, M. (1995). Interpretation of symptom presentation and distress: A Southeast Asian refugee example. *Journal of Nervous and Mental Disease, 183*(10), 639–648.

Connolly, C. (2005). Health care costs, spending up: More in middle class could join ranks of the uninsured. *The Washington Post.* Retrieved from http://www.washingtonpost.com/wp-dyn/content/article/2005/06/20/AR2005062001169.html

Constantine, M. (2006). Racism in mental health and education settings: A brief overview. In

M. G. Constantine & D. W. Sue (Eds.), *Addressing racism* (pp. 3–14). Hoboken, NJ: Wiley.

Draguns, J. (2000). Psychopathology and ethnicity. In J. F. Aponte & J. Wohl (Eds.), *Psychological intervention and cultural diversity* (pp. 40–58). Needham Heights, MA: Allyn & Bacon.

Elias, M. (2009, May). Racism hurts kids' mental health. *USA Today.* Retrieved from http://www .usatoday.com/news/health/2009-05-05-race -depression_N.htm

Fletcher, M.A. (2008, October). 1 in 4 working families now low-wage, report finds. *The Washington Post.* Retrieved from http://www.washingtonpost .com/wp-dyn/content/article/2008/10/14/AR 2008101402646.html

Frank, J. D. (1968). The role of hope in psychotherapy. *International Journal of Psychiatry, 5,* 383–395.

Helms, J. (1984). Toward a theoretical explanation of the effects of race on counseling: A Black and White model. *The Counseling Psychologist, 12*(4), 153–165.

Helms, J. (1992). *A race is a nice thing to have.* Topeka, KS: Content Communication.

Helms, J. (1995). An update of Helms's White and people of color racial identity models. In J. G. Ponterotto, J. M. Casas, L.A. Suzuki, & C. M. Alexander (Eds.), *Handbook of multicultural counseling* (pp. 181–198). Thousand Oaks, CA: Sage.

Ho, C. K. (1990). An analysis of domestic violence in Asian American communities: A multicultural approach to counseling. *Women & Therapy, 9*(1–2), 129–150.

Horejsi, C., Craig, B. H., & Pablo, J. (1992). Reactions by Native American parents to child protection agencies: Cultural and community factors. *Child Welfare Journal, 71,* 329–342.

Hughes, M., & Demo, D. H. (1989). Self-perceptions of Black Americans: Self-esteem and personal efficacy. *American Journal of Sociology, 95,* 135–159.

Kessler, R. C., Chiu, W. T., Demler, O., & Walters, E. (2005). Prevalence, severity and comorbidity of 12-month DSM-IV disorders in the National Comorbidity Survey replication. *Archives of General Psychiatry, 62,* 693–713.

Krug, E. G., Dahlberg, L. L., Mercy, J. A., Zwi, A. B., & Lozano, R. (2002). *World report on violence and health.* Geneva, Switzerland: World Health Organization.

Lambert, M. J. (1992). The effectiveness of psychotherapy. In A. E. Bergin & S. L. Garfield (Eds.), *Handbook of psychotherapy and behavior change* (4th ed., pp. 143–189). New York, NY: Wiley.

Lambert, M. J. & Bergin, A. E. (1994). The effectiveness of psychotherapy. In A. E. Bergin & S. L. Garfield (Eds.), *Handbook of psychotherapy and behavior change* (4th ed., pp. 143–189). New York: Basic Books.

Lewis, T. (2003). *The growing gap between rich and poor.* Global Policy Forum. Retrieved from http:// www.globalpolicy.org/socecon/inequal/2003

Lopez-Bushnell, F. K., Tyer, P. A., & Futrell, M. (1992). Alcoholism and the Hispanic older adults. *Clinical Gerontologist, 11,* 123–130.

Mummolo, J. (2009, March). Girl's cries for help 'fell on deaf ears.' *The Washington Post.* Retrieved from http://www.washingtonpost.com/wp-dyn/content/ article/2009/03/08/AR2009030802194.html

Pedersen, P. B. (2000). *A handbook for developing multicultural awareness* (3rd ed.). Alexandria, VA: American Association for Counseling and Development.

Phillips, L., & Draguns, J. (1969). Some issues in intercultural research on psychopathology. In W. Caudill & T. Y. Lin (Eds.), *Mental health research in Asia and the Pacific* (pp. 21–32). Honolulu, HI: East-West Center Press.

Raval, H., & Smith, J. (2003). Therapists' experiences of working with language interpreters. *International Journal of Mental Health, 32*(2), 6–31.

Sartorius, N., Gulbinat, W., Harrison, G., Laska, E., & Siegel, C. (1996). Long-term follow-up of schizophrenia in 16 countries. *Social Psychiatry and Psychiatric Epidemiology, 31,* 249–258.

Snyder, C. R. (1994). *The psychology of hope: you can get there from there.* New York, NY: Free Press.

Steele, C. M., Spencer, S. J., & Aronson, J. (2002). Contending with group image: The psychology of stereotype and social identity threat. In M. Zanna (Ed.), *Advances in experimental social psychology* (Vol. 23, pp. 379–440). New York, NY: Academic Press.

Sue, D. W. (2003). *Overcoming our racism: The journey to liberation.* San Francisco, CA: Jossey-Bass.

Sue, S., Fujino, D., Hu, L., Takeuchi, D., & Zane, N. (1991). Community mental health services for ethnic minority groups: A test of cultural responsive hypothesis. *Journal of Consulting and Clinical Psychology, 59*(4), 533–540.

Triandis, H. C. (1994). *Culture and social behavior.* New York, NY: McGraw-Hill.

U.S. Census Bureau. (1999, September). *Poverty in the United States: Current population reports: consumer income.* Washington, DC: Author.

U.S. Census Bureau. (2002, July). *United States Census 2000.* Retrieved from http://www.census.gov/main/www/cen2000.html

U.S. Census Bureau. (2008a). *An older and more diverse nation by mid-century* [Press release]. Washington, DC: U.S. Department of Commerce. Retrieved from http://www.census.gov/Press-Release/www/releases/archives/population/012496.html

U.S. Census Bureau. (2008b). *Census Bureau projects U.S. population of 305.5 million on New Year's Day* [Press release]. Washington, D.C.: U.S. Department of Commerce. Retrieved from http://www.census.gov/Press-Release/www/releases/archives/population/012496.html

U.S. Department of Health and Human Services. (2001). *Mental health: Culture, race, and ethnicity.* A supplement to Mental health: A report of the Surgeon General. Rockville, MD: U.S. Department of Health and Human Services.

U.S. Department of Justice, Federal Bureau of Investigation. (2006). *Hate crime statistics 2005.* Washington, DC: Author.

5

MULTI-PHASE MODEL (MPM) OF PSYCHOTHERAPY, COUNSELING, HUMAN RIGHTS, AND SOCIAL JUSTICE

Be the change that you want to see in the world.

(Mahatma Gandhi)

Everybody can be great, because everybody can serve. You don't have to have a college degree to serve. You don't have to make your subject and your verb agree to serve. You don't have to know about Plato and Aristotle to serve. You don't have to know Einstein's theory of relativity to serve. You don't have to know the second theory of thermodynamics in physics to serve. You only need a heart full of grace, a soul generated by love, and you can be that servant.

(Martin Luther King Jr.)

WARM UP EXERCISE

1. *When you are talking about serious personal issues, do you prefer to speak to one person at a time or a few people at a time? What creates this preference for you?*

2. *Reflect on your own family experience growing up and today. How do you imagine this will affect you in working with families?*

(Continued)

(Continued)

3. Have you ever been in a completely new culture or known someone who described their experience being in a new culture? What are some of the first things you or others you knew had to do to adjust to the new culture?

4. Do you ever have discussions with anyone who has nothing to do with counseling and psychology? What is it like to get a different perspective and outlook on different issues and the world? Does it expand your horizon? If so, how?

This chapter presents a model of counseling and psychotherapy that emphasizes social justice and human rights. The model is called the Multi-Phase Model of Psychotherapy, Counseling, Human Rights, and Social Justice (MPM). The MPM is an extension of the Multi-Level Model (MLM) (Bemak & Chung, 2008; Bemak, Chung, & Pedersen, 2003; Chung, Bemak, & Kudo Grabosky, 2011) that was created specifically to work with refugees and immigrants. The MPM is more versatile and can be used as an intervention for any oppressed, disenfranchised, or marginalized population. In this chapter we will provide a discussion of the five different phases of the MPM and discuss how to apply the model to everyday counseling and psychotherapy.

The MPM is a psychoeducational model that incorporates affective, behavioral, and cognitive intervention and prevention strategies that are rooted in cultural foundations and relate to social and community process and change. Figure 5.1 illustrates the five phases of the MPM:

- Phase I: Mental Health Education
- Phase II: Group, Family, and Individual Psychotherapy
- Phase III: Cultural Empowerment
- Phase IV: Indigenous Healing
- Phase V: Social Justice and Human Rights

It is important to emphasize that there is no fixed sequence to implementing the MPM phases, so that they may be used concurrently or independently. Although there is an interrelationship among the five phases, each phase may be considered independent of the other phases, and each phase is essential for attaining the desired goals of psychotherapy and counseling. The psychologist or counselor may use a phase at any stage of the therapeutic process or use elements of a phase anytime throughout the counseling process. For example, although it is important to discuss Phase I (Mental Health Education) at the beginning of the session, this could be revisited at any period during counseling to ensure that the counselor or therapist's role is clear and the goals for counseling are unambiguous. The choice to use a particular phase or combination of phases of the MPM is based upon the assessment of the counselor or psychologist. Furthermore, it is important to note that the MPM is not a model that requires additional resources or funding.

Phase I—Mental Health Education

Phase I is focused on educating client(s) about the therapeutic encounter. Generally clients are not familiar with mental health services and do not have a clear understanding of what happens in counseling. This may be especially true for clients from non-Western cultures, where personal problems are not usually shared with people outside the family network. Also, professionals working with clients from a non-Western background may be more directive, active, and prescriptive in ordering assigned tasks or steps for treatment.

An essential element during Phase I is to establish a therapeutic alliance, which has been identified as critical for effective psychotherapy

Figure 5.1 Multi-Phase Model of Psychotherapy, Counseling, Human Rights, and Social Justice

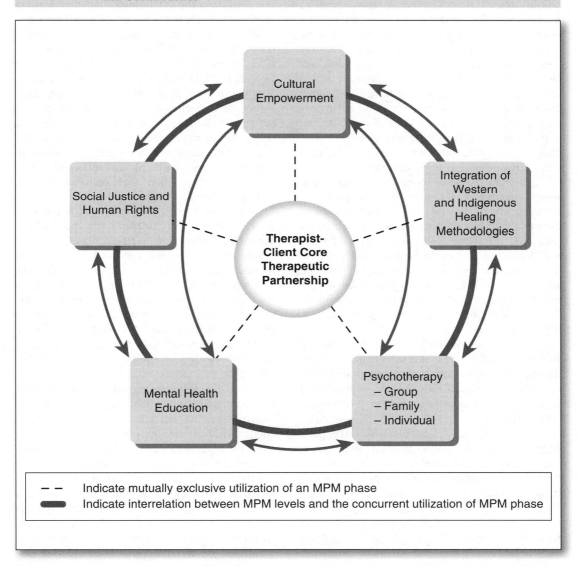

and counseling (Wohl, 2000); it accounts for 30% of therapeutic outcomes (Lambert & Bergin, 1994). This may be particularly salient for racial and ethnic groups in the United States who have exhibited low utilization of and premature dropout from Western traditional mental health services due to the lack of cultural sensitivity displayed by psychologists and counselors (Sue, Fujino, Hu, Takeuchi, & Zane, 1991; U.S. Department of Health and Human Services [U.S. HHS], 2001). Thus, a key in Phase I is working to develop trust and rapport while being particularly sensitive when working across cultures, without stereotyping or making assumptions about clients. We would extend this heightened awareness to include working with people who have been oppressed or experienced a violation of their human rights. In fact, non-Western clients may need more time to explore and discuss the issues (Root, 1998), and this need for extra time would also be relevant for clients who have experienced social injustices. Therefore, it would be important in Phase I of the MPM to discuss, define, and clarify the roles of the client and the psychologist or counselor and to explore and clarify culturally appropriate expectations.

An integral aspect of Phase I is a discussion of mental health basics. During this discussion, the mental health professional offers an orientation to the therapeutic encounter; discusses expectations about meeting times and the concepts of time, self-disclosure, and the sharing of personal feelings, thoughts, and events; explains the type and style of questioning that may be used during meetings; and talks about what happens during an intake session and the reasons for gathering personal information. It is also important for the psychologist or counselor to clearly describe the concept of confidentiality and to explain that she or he will have no communication regarding the client with any public officials or other people, except under the criteria outlined in the professional ethical standards.

For example, refugee populations who experienced political oppression in their home countries and have immigrated to a new country may be hesitant or fearful to answer personal questions or share personal information. They may have a personal, family, or community first-hand history of incarceration, physical or sexual abuse, and interrogation, and may view intake questions and counseling with great distrust. Similarly, individuals who have had negative encounters with law enforcement may perceive the questioning of helping professionals as being similar to interrogation by police and may be resistant to talking openly about personal problems or issues.

Furthermore, helping professionals must be very clear with clients that community members will not be privy to any information discussed during the counseling sessions. When discussing confidentiality, it is important that helping professionals share their view of what confidentiality means and also makes sure this is consistent with how the client defines confidentiality, since clients' definitions may differ from those of professionals. For example, in some cultures, confidentiality may mean that family members and/or close friends have access to the client's personal information. If this is the case, the counselor or psychotherapist must respect the client's definition and work with the client to establish a new, workable definition of confidentiality that the client feels comfortable with and agrees upon.

The issues of confidentiality and boundaries around what is confidential are particularly important for individuals who have experienced persecution or discrimination and are beginning to once again develop trust. Given concerns about confidentiality, if interpreters are used in the therapeutic encounter, it is important to discuss their role and commitment to maintaining privacy, especially since the interpreter and the client may be connected to the same larger cultural community, or similar communities, outside of the therapeutic milieu.

It is also helpful to describe different psychotherapeutic techniques that may be used during therapy in terms that are understandable to the client. For example, the counselor may explain using genograms to better understand one's family, the use of drawings and creative writing or journaling to depict deeper issues, or the use of therapeutic homework assignments to facilitate behavioral change. It is also important to discuss relationship boundaries while maintaining cross-cultural sensitivity and understanding that traditional Western professional boundaries may be inappropriate for many clients who come from non-Western backgrounds. For example, counselors and psychotherapists are taught to maintain clear professional boundaries with clients, and that the counseling relationship should not cross social boundaries. However, for some cultures, professional and social boundaries are not so clearly defined and in fact are blended into relationships.

The following example illustrates this point. A friend and colleague who is a psychiatrist in Brazil described how he practiced:

> My clients can call me anytime. If I decide they are having a serious problem I will go to their homes, sit in the living room, eat with them, and talk about the crisis. Sometimes I might even take off my shoes and sit with my feet up in their living rooms.

For individuals from collectivistic cultures that emphasize family and community and do not distinguish social and professional relationships as narrowly as do Western countries, there may be confusion about the "distance" and "coolness" of the Western psychologist or counselor who refuses social invitations to dinner or a social community event that is significant to individuals and their families or communities.

Medications also must be mentioned as part of Phase I. Educating clients about medication use is important, especially as it relates to their choices and the rights they have in relation to taking prescribed drugs. Confusion may arise about the types, numbers, and colors of medications; when the medications need to be taken; the need to continue with medication when they feel better; or their rights in deciding to take medication. Furthermore, it is important to provide clear explanations about the dangers of sharing medications with family, friends, and community members who report similar symptoms. For example, I (Rita) discovered within the Chinese community that some of the older community members were exchanging medications. In their daily interactions, the community members would compare health symptoms and share their medication with family members and friends whom they thought had symptoms or problems similar to their own. In sharing medications, community members thought they were being helpful and saving family and friends a visit to the doctor or mental health professional. Finally, an important point related to discussing medications during Phase I is discussing the potential danger in

taking a mixture of Western and traditional medications. A more detailed discussion on indigenous healing methodologies will be discussed in the section on Phase IV (Indigenous Healing).

Reviewing these parameters of the therapeutic relationship helps clients generate expectations for what will happen during sessions with the counselor or psychologist. This is extremely important, particularly for individuals who experience little control over their lives and have felt powerless at different times in their lives. Defining mutual expectations for the helping relationship reduces clients' anxiety and confusion about how to act and about what kind of behavior will be conducive to their receiving the help they want through counseling. Thus, Phase I provides information, as well as education and clarification, for the individual, group, or family about the process of psychotherapy and the mental health encounter.

It is important to identify that this process in Phase I is not just a one-way process, but just as importantly, a two-way process. Although psychologists and counselors are educating and outlining the parameters of the helping relationship, they are simultaneously gathering information about clients' belief systems about healing, their cultural perspectives on the origins of mental health problems, their cultural preferences for help-seeking, their treatment expectations, and their comfort with therapeutic techniques that will be applicable during other phases of the MPM. In turn, the client is acquiring an understanding of what happens in psychotherapy and counseling and assists in defining the parameters of the therapeutic relationship in a culturally relevant manner. For example, clients may not realize that discussion of their intimate problems in marriage is considered acceptable as a topic of conversation in counseling, while the psychotherapist may not realize that it is highly irregular in certain cultures to discuss interpersonal marital difficulties, such as sexuality, with someone outside the family. To present these topics as normative during Phase I in the MPM assists the client in reframing what is acceptable within the therapeutic relationship and helps the psychotherapist or counselor understand the difficulty and taboo associated with discussion on such a personal level.

Some clients may also have a history of distrust toward others and the world around them. Clients' experiences of being underrepresented, undervalued, or oppressed may manifest as resistance, anger, anxiety, and/or fear in psychotherapy or counseling. On an individual level, an example would be a woman who was raped and/or sexually abused and then felt maligned by the judicial system during the court trial of her rapist. She might carry strong reactions to men in general and doubts about the responsiveness and fairness of the courts. She might enter therapy highly distrustful and angry and deeply concerned about her own personal power within the therapeutic relationship. Subsequently other events in which she has less direct personal involvement may generate an equally strong emotional response.

Similarly, consider the history of slavery of African Americans, the genocide of Native Americans, the Nazi Holocaust, or the internment of Japanese Americans in the United States during World War II as just a handful of examples that contribute to strong historical intergenerational trauma, feelings and responses. On both personal and institutional levels, any one of these examples requires psychologists and counselors to understand the experience of being a member of a group of people who felt violated and oppressed, who carry the effects of intergenerational trauma from these historical sociopolitical events, and who believe that they as a group of people have not received fair treatment or justice. This is consistent with the importance of helping professionals' acknowledgment that racism, discrimination, and oppression are not relics of the past, but are also currently encountered by some individuals on a daily basis.

Therefore, it is essential that helping professionals fully comprehend the origin of clients' anger, fear, and resistance and strive to create a safe environment. Phase I is where the seeds of trust are planted. Clients' skepticism, suspicion, and reluctance must be understood as resulting from their experience and history of oppression and viewed within this larger context, rather than interpreted as individual psychopathology. In fact, we would suggest that these characteristics of mistrust may be construed as a survival strategy that helps clients to maintain mental health in the face of inequities. A culturally sensitive beginning in the therapeutic process, which includes explanations about how counseling works, may reduce client fears, anxiety, and mistrust.

Phase II—Group, Family, and Individual Psychotherapy and Counseling

Phase II is based on the application of traditional Western individual, group, and family therapy in a culturally responsive manner that focuses on and incorporates issues of social justice and human rights. As with any type of psychotherapy and counseling, the helping professional must first evaluate the problem and the client's needs. This evaluation informs the theoretical basis for psychotherapy and helps identify related intervention strategies that will be most suitable for the client in *that* moment in *that* situation. Underlying the assessment and subsequent therapeutic intervention in this phase of the MPM is its integration with Phases III (Cultural Empowerment), IV (Integration of Western and Indigenous Healing Methodologies), and V (Social Justice and Human Rights).

To employ culturally relevant techniques in Phase II that incorporate social justice and human rights, there must be an integration of theory, therapeutic processes, and models of prevention and intervention. Given the history or current conditions of oppression, discrimination, racism, sexism, and other "isms" that many clients encounter, it is essential to understand and consider the client's background as it impacts her or his psychological functioning. Ecological, historical, and sociopolitical factors may require vigilance about the contextual aspects of the person's life and a heightened awareness of how that affects the therapeutic relationship.

For some clients, daily survival may require maintaining psychological defenses and not adopting an open, vulnerable posture. Daily microaggressions such as invalidations, insults, or assaults dramatically impact psychological well-being (Sue, Bucceri, Lin, Nadal, & Torino, 2007). For example, due to the daily, ongoing microaggressions and racism they experience, some African Americans may exhibit "healthy or cultural paranoia" as a defense mechanism in coping with a potentially discriminatory situation (Jones, 1990; Ridley, 1995). This is part of the broader context that may be part of an African American client's life situation. When a client who exhibits "healthy paranoia" as a coping strategy enters into counseling, the client may perceive a psychologist's highly personal questions as dangerous, threatening, and/or inappropriate. Since psychotherapy requires openness and personal self-disclosure, trust must be built carefully while keeping in mind the client's worldview based on historical, sociopolitical, and life experiences.

Culturally sensitive interventions. It is critical that helping professionals are culturally competent and have the skills and ability to adapt, alter, modify, and change traditional Western techniques and interventions so that they are culturally responsive to and effective for clients and families from diverse groups. Intervention strategies are derived from an integration of cultural worldviews that incorporate cultural norms and practices into Western-based interventions. For some groups (e.g., Asians, Latina/os), talk therapy is not the natural means of resolving problems. Therefore it is essential that helping professionals understand the cultural values and worldviews of clients to employ culturally sensitive techniques.

One example of an alternative to talk therapy could be using a genogram that maps out family history and relationships. This may be especially relevant to someone who comes from a culture that highly values family (such as Asian, African, Latina/o, and Native American cultures). With people from cultures that believe that the spirit of those who have passed away remains present (e.g., Africans, Asians, and Native Americans),

another alternative to talk therapy may be effective: In this work, the presence of the spirit of the deceased may play an important role in psychotherapy; the perceptions and advice of the ancestors may be discussed within the counseling session through metaphors and symbolism.

A variety of culturally specific interventions have been found to be helpful to different ethnic and racial groups. Some examples of various culturally specific techniques are presented below (please note that this is not an exhaustive list):

- sweat lodges and sundance ceremonies with Native Americans (Herring, 1999)
- pouring of libations and calling on ancestors and/or historical figures for assistance with healing for African Americans (Parham, 1989)
- cottage industry therapy groups for low-income East Indians
- multiple-family therapy groups, the practice of *espiritismo* (spritism), *santeria,* and *cuaranderismo* with Puerto Ricans, Cubans, and Mexican Americans (Higginbotham, Trevino, & Ray, 1990; Koss-Chioino, 2000)
- cleansing rituals by Buddhist monks (Ito, Chung, & Kagawa-Singer, 1997)
- shamanic healing, herbal remedies, physical/bodily manipulation or exercises (e.g., acupuncture, moxibustion, massage, coining, and breathing exercises such as Tai Chi, Qigong) with some Asian cultures (Kleinman & Kleinman, 1985; Koss-Chioino, 2000; Muecke, 1983; Westermeyer, 1988).

Traditional Western interventions. There have been a number of recommendations for traditional Western therapeutic techniques that are effective in working across cultures and have relevance for social justice. For example, Zane and Sue (1991) found applicability of individual and family therapy to several culturally distinct groups. Cognitive-behavioral interventions have also been used successfully with refugees in assisting this group to better acclimate to the present by enhancing their capabilities to move beyond painful memories and experiences and reduce anxiety about the future (Beiser, 1987; Bemak & Greenberg, 1994; Egli, Shiota, Ben-Porath, & Butcher, 1991). This technique is also effective with individuals suffering from depression (Hollon & Beck, 2000) and those who have experienced sexual abuse, helping them reframe their experiences and learn more adaptive behaviors.

Specific ethnic groups have also found the cognitive-behavioral technique effective. For example, it has been identified to be helpful for Asian clients because of its compatibility with Buddhism (De Silva, 1985; Mikulas, 1981), helping clients to rethink about various problems within a Buddhist perspective. Others have found coherence between cognitive-behavioral therapy and the Latina/o culture (Arce & Torres-Matrullo, 1982; Comas-Diaz, 1985; Stumphauser & Davis, 1983), again redefining problem situations and changing behavior within the framework of Latina/o culture. Another source of effective interventions has been exposure techniques to reduce anxiety disorders (Beck, Sokol, Clark, Berfchick, & Wright, 1992; Krijn, Emmelkamp, Olafsson, & Biemond, 2004). Marriage and family therapy has also been shown to facilitate improvement in clients (Ho, 1987; McAdoo, 1993; McGoldrick, 1998), while feminist-oriented therapies have been found to be helpful for women (Bowman et al., 2001; Brown & Root, 1990).

Non-Western traditional interventions. Other therapeutic techniques are also incorporated into the MPM that move beyond more traditional Western interventions and have a bearing on mental health/social justice. For example, dreamwork can play a central role in culturally sensitive therapy (Bemak, 1989; Bemak & Timm, 1994; Szapocznik & Cohen, 1986). I (Fred) had a refugee client who was resistant to traditional psychotherapy and used dreamwork as a means to resolve his post-traumatic stress (Bemak & Timm, 1994). Through the use of dreamwork, the client was finally able to discuss difficult past events and his responses to them, eventually resolving his long-standing pain and fear about these events.

Storytelling and projective drawing have effectively assisted previously traumatized children to regain control over their lives (Pynoos & Eth, 1984), facilitating the expression of unconscious feelings and thoughts. Narrative therapy, in which individuals are able to reconstruct their stories, has been useful in a variety of different settings (Monk, Winslade, Crocket, & Epston, 1997). Play therapy has been used with many children and adolescents in numerous settings (Vargas & Koss-Chioino, 1992). A focus on moral development and strongly valued cultural traits such as honesty was found to be an effective intervention with Haitian refugees (Charles, 1986). Other techniques that may be employed in the MPM include gestalt, in which a counselor can have clients examine various parts of themselves as expressions of inner conflict; relaxation techniques, with which stress can be reduced through deep breathing or systematic desensitization through muscle relaxation; role-playing, in which clients can reenact past or anticipated situations, gaining new perspectives and insights; and psychodrama, which can be a helpful replaying of situations that have been highly stressful or anxiety producing for a client.

Group and family psychotherapy and counseling focus on social justice. A criticism of traditional Western psychotherapy is that individual work perpetuates the status quo and emphasizes changing the individual at the expense of the family, social network, or community. Given that 70% of the world's cultures and a majority of the ethnic groups in the United States are from collectivist cultures, we would strongly recommend group, family, and community work to foster interdependence in social and family networks (Morris & Silove, 1992; Rechtman, 1997) to promote social change. The movement away from individual counseling toward a more systemic approach that is rooted in social networks is fundamental to the MPM and its focus on human rights.

Within collectivistic cultures, the emphasis on the group and family is far more important than the emphasis on the individual. In many cultures that value interdependence, the contributions that an individual makes to meet the needs of and benefit the family and community are far more important than individual needs and goals. For example, an individual's choice of a career may be contingent on how it fits into the constellation of the family in terms of geography and possible employment that is close to where the family lives, ability to generate income support for the larger family, status of the position, ability of family to finance special training or university tuition, and so forth. Thus, the MPM emphasizes group counseling, family therapy, and community interventions as methodologies of choice for mental health work with people coming from collectivistic cultures that form the basis of society on kinship with the nuclear and extended family and community.

In providing group, family, or community interventions, it is essential that helping professionals have a clear understanding of and knowledge about the nature of social networks and systemic change within a cultural context; this will inform their determinations about who to include in broader socially based mental health interventions. The MPM includes an evaluation of the larger social network that incorporates grandparents, aunts, uncles, cousins, and others who are not biological family members but are identified by the client as part of the family, such as religious leaders, neighbors, friends, or distant relatives. Individuals who are not in the biological family but are considered family members may influence the family system and relevant groups that the family belongs to as well as the larger social community.

In many cases this combines members of the client's biological family, other people identified as family members, neighbors, community members, the local religious leader, local elder, and so forth (Bemak, Chung, & Pedersen, 2003). Once psychologists or counselors have determined who is in the social network—whether it be family, friends, or associates, it is crucial that they be aware of hierarchy and social patterns of communication, and that they appropriately address and acknowledge those who warrant greater respect by virtue of their role in the family or community. For example, if one enters a matriarchal culture where the female elder of the community warrants greater authority or respect than the male head of the household, it is important and respectful for the psychologist or counselor to addresses the female elder first.

Culture and diagnoses. When using the MPM, we strongly advise caution when employing Western-based frameworks of diagnoses (e.g., DSM, ICD). The Western assessment tools may not be appropriate or culturally sensitive, especially when focusing on mental health and human rights. In fact, specific diagnoses may perpetuate stigmatization of clients and the loss of human rights, and in many cases they are labels that clients carry for life.

We previously discussed cultural influences on the conceptualization of mental health problems that result in cultural expression or symptom manifestations that frequently fall into patterns that are outside of the discrete classifications of Western disorders. Even so, psychologists and counselors may try to force discrete categorizations that result in misdiagnoses and ineffective treatment (Chung & Kagawa-Singer, 1995; U.S. HHS, 2001). In fact, research has shown that misdiagnosis of psychiatric disorders of ethnic clients in the United States (Asians, Latina/os, and African Americans) has resulted from psychotherapists' lack of understanding or knowledge of the clients' cultural and/or linguistic differences (e.g., Baskin, Bluestone, & Nelson, 1981; Huertin-Roberts & Snowden, 1993), and therefore racial/ethnic stereotypes come into play in making diagnoses (U.S. HHS, 2001). Therefore, to diagnose accurately, mental health professionals must be knowledgeable about how their clients conceptualize mental illness and express their psychological distress. This requires an awareness of ethnocentric biases inherent in diagnostic categories (Chung & Kagawa-Singer, 1995) as well as personal stereotypes and prejudicial views.

An example of misdiagnosis can be seen through my (Fred's) experience in working with a Native American client on an Indian reservation in Wisconsin. The client was struggling with a decision about leaving the reservation and shared an experience where he had a vision of meeting an elderly man who had been deceased for 20 years. The elderly man had spent his entire life on the reservation and had been recognized as an important elder who, because of his wisdom and experience, provided guidance to many people on the reservation. The client explained how he initially thought that his encounter with the elderly man was a dream. Although the elderly man was shrouded in a veil of clouds, the client could still identify him and was somewhat frightened by the encounter. As the client went to say hello, the elderly man leaped nearly six feet into the air to the top of a boulder and pointed toward a large deer that was walking into the desert toward the reservation. The elderly man then told the client that he was not dreaming and the encounter was real. The client woke up very frightened and believed that the encounter was not a dream after all, but a true life event. Given the authenticity of his encounter, he decided that he must follow the deer and remain at the reservation.

It would have been easy for me or other helping professionals to think about this client as having delusions and therefore misdiagnose him, especially since the client did not believe that his experience was a dream, but rather considered it a real life experience—that he met a man who had died 20 years earlier. Instead, understanding the framework of his Native American culture and supporting him in his beliefs and experience was instrumental in assisting the client with a major life decision. Hearing the client's story became a window into understanding his expectations, cultural values, worldview, and cultural ways of making decisions. Bridging the divide between his and my conceptualization of mental health was central to an effective diagnosis and subsequent interventions. This has been pointed out by Kleinman (1980) and requires psychologists and counselors to fully explore the totality of the situation, from etiology, causes, and course of the problem to help-seeking behavior and treatment outcomes. This also incorporates understanding and acceptance of culturally unique manifestation and expression of symptoms, culturally preferred treatment, and cultural expectations that lead to cultural treatment outcomes.

Although progress has been made in incorporating cultural variables and more culturally sensitive and cross-culturally suitable categories in the psychiatric diagnosis disorders of the DSM (Fabrega, 1992; Mezzich, Fabrega, & Kleinman, 1992), the question still remains regarding the cultural competencies of helping professionals (e.g., Arredondo et al., 1996; Sue, Arredondo, & McDavis, 1992). Furthermore, Western psychologists and counselors must be aware of and acknowledge the influence of their own Eurocentric worldview and how their worldview may interfere with a culturally responsive diagnosis.

For example, African Americans have been diagnosed with schizophrenia more often than individuals in other groups, while Asian Americans have been diagnosed more often as having personality disorders as compared to those in other groups (Draguns, 2000). In both cases, the increased incidence of the specific disorder may reflect misdiagnoses based on culture and worldviews, given the racism experienced by some African Americans that may contribute to mistrust and paranoia, and the cultural viewpoint of many Asian Americans where family dependency is seen as a healthy aspect of life. Again, these examples emphasize how important it is that helping professionals be multiculturally competent when working across cultures.

Phase III—Cultural Empowerment

The MPM's Phase III provides another important dimension in the healing of clients. Cultural empowerment is a critical element in the therapeutic process, as it assists clients to acquire skills and abilities to master their world. Clients who present themselves to helping professionals may have pressing needs that relate to basic survival issues, such as finding employment or housing, knowing how to use public transportation to get to work, or knowing where to go if they become sick or to cash their welfare checks. For example, I (Rita) came across a refugee family who was living on a loaf of bread for two weeks while waiting for their welfare check. In fact, they had received their welfare check two weeks before, but didn't know about banks or how to cash a check. Their limited English led them to understand that the check could be directly exchanged in return for food at the local market. When their attempts to exchange the check for food failed, they were at a loss and thought the check was worthless. They didn't know what to do, so they just waited for the "real" check to arrive, rationing the bread among family members.

Unfair treatment and inequities are also issues that clients may encounter. They may be victims of racism, sexism, or ageism; may be unable to access human service systems; may encounter discriminatory landlords and housing practices; or may be unfairly fired from a job. These and countless other issues have far more immediacy for the client than delving into intrapsychic or interpersonal issues and require that the clients become empowered and more knowledgeable about their worlds. In fact, clients who are experiencing high levels of anxiety, depression, anger, frustration, or stress due to their inability to effectively understand and resolve problems and concerns in their social and community life may be far better off working on mastering their environment and developing appropriate responses, rather than working on deeper psychological reactions (e.g., anxiety, depression, anger, frustration, or stress) to the situation. Thus, psychologists and counselors can play a critical role in providing support, guidance, and information as partners in the therapeutic process.

Interdisciplinary collaboration: Working with multiple agencies. Since clients may become involved with multiple service systems, there may be a need for helping professionals to go beyond the constraints of traditional office walls to work with multiple agencies. To obtain a holistic picture of clients' lives, it is essential to have a comprehensive understanding of the types of agencies and systems that clients are interacting with and these agencies' respective impact on clients' lives. Agencies could include those for child protective services, social services, juvenile

services, housing, education, employment, health and public health, criminal justice, and/or medical services, to name a few. When the client is interacting with multiple agencies, it is necessary for the helping professional, with the client's permission, to also be a part of this network and share information.

An example of this was encountered by Rita regarding four immigrant women. Their English language skills were poor, and one of them was having problems with her eyes. To support each other, they decided that they would all go together to the optometrist for the exam. Although the client could not recite the alphabet, she and the others decided to memorize the eye chart in order to "pass" the exam. The lack of understanding that the eye exam was not a test that one needs to "pass" and that each of them needed to have their own exam and test results, required a helping professional to educate them about how the medical eye exam works, explaining the diagnostic nature of the exam and that they didn't need to "pass." The helping professional also had to explore with the client the best way to gain support from her friends.

Finally, this situation warranted communication between the helping professional and the optometrist to inform him that the patient had memorized the eye chart in order to produce "good" results. This networking with the optometrist was an important linkage for the client and was initiated by the helping professional. Helping the client understand the purpose of having an eye examination, the role that she had as a medical patient, and the part that her friends could play in supporting her were important in developing an understanding and sense of mastery over her world.

Another example of linking with other agencies to help develop cultural mastery was evident with an 18-year-old client who was having health problems and was diagnosed with hepatitis. He was told by a physician at a health clinic not to engage in "sexual activity" or have "physical contact" with anyone. The medical directive caused tremendous confusion and stress, since the client was unsure about what "physical contact" meant, how long he needed to avoid it, what this meant for marriage, and so forth. Using the MPM, it would be important for a helping professional to discuss the medical information with the client, support the client in finding out more, and talk about ways to integrate management of his hepatitis into his life. This may require supporting the client while he makes a phone call to the physician during counseling, role-playing conversations with his girlfriend, and so forth.

Thus, the MPM necessitates that the helping professional be attuned and highly sensitive to the full scope of the client's life and becomes knowledgeable about institutional and systemic forces that impact the client. It requires that helping professionals redefine their roles to expand beyond traditional "office-only" practice and offer case management type assistance, guidance, and resource information that will empower the client. It is important to note that this does not require additional time. Instead, cultural empowerment is an embedded core component of the therapeutic encounter that is included within regular meeting times and schedules.

Cultural system information guide and advocate. One way to think about the dimension of cultural empowerment is for the helping professional to assume responsibilities as a "cultural system information guide and advocate." In this capacity, the helping professional proactively assists the client with relevant information about how systems work, how to resolve problems the client encounters within those systems, and what subsequent new coping strategies are needed. This requires the helping professional to rethink how therapeutic time is spent, especially with the long-term goal of enabling the client to develop knowledge and skills to deal with systemic problems. The resultant mastery of these skills by the client creates successful experiences and cultural empowerment.

Integration of cultural empowerment and psychotherapy. It is important to reiterate that in Phase III, no extra time is spent with clients beyond the normal therapeutic sessions. Cultural empowerment is built into psychotherapy or counseling as an integral aspect of the work. For example, with the client's permission, making phone calls together, writing letters to agencies, calling other professionals to determine the status of services and acquire information, and similar activities become part of the therapeutic encounter and are redefined as valuable uses of time in therapy and counseling. Hence, the professional is undertaking multiple tasks that contribute to the mental health and psychological well-being of the client.

Thus, the psychologist or counselor is modeling successful skills in accessing and dealing with systems while at the same time assisting and teaching clients how to integrate existing skills with newly learned skills to effectively access resources within the larger community. It may be said that one aim of counseling during this phase is to eliminate stressors that are inhibiting clients, and this is done through empowering them to better understand systems and dynamics and then helping them to develop the requisite skills. This provides the clients with some degree of control over their lives and may instill hope. Obtaining the skills to navigate and access systems will also help to alleviate some of the symptoms of anxiety, frustration, and depression and the general feelings of helplessness and hopelessness. Establishing a basis for security and self-determination paves the way for further exploration of deeper psychological issues, reverting back to Phase II (Psychotherapy and Counseling).

Understanding and combating the "isms." Another important element in Phase III is developing skills to deal with the "isms," for example, ageism, ableism, racism, sexism, classism, and other forms of discrimination and oppression. As we discussed previously, a byproduct of the ethnocentric and egocentric values in Western individualistic countries is discrimination and racism (Pedersen, 2000), resulting in covert and overt discriminatory practices and behaviors. Prejudicial attitudes and acts are exacerbated during more difficult economic times and when political situations are heightened, such as when acts of hatred toward Arab Americans escalated during the war with Iraq. The lack of tolerance, understanding, and acceptance of clients who are not part of mainstream society—people who come from different racial, ethnic, or religious backgrounds; gays and lesbians; immigrants; the impoverished; and the physically and mentally challenged—may cause significant mental health problems and takes a toll on the psychological well-being of clients. This is substantiated by research that clearly documents the ill effects of racism on psychological well-being (e.g., Aponte & Wohl, 2000; Asamen & Berry, 1987; Hughes & Demo, 1989; Steele, 1998; Steele & Aronson, 2000) and correlates with the research on therapeutic outcomes that shows 40% of the outcome is attributed to factors outside the therapeutic session related to the client's environment and quality of life (Lambert & Bergin, 1994).

Therefore when using the MPM where mental health and social justice are intertwined, it is critical that helping professionals be attuned and highly sensitive to the difficulties and challenges facing clients that are related to their social and environmental conditions, and that helping professionals have an awareness and understanding of how these issues affect their clients' psychological well-being. To fully understand the multidimensional nature of how clients interact with their environment, it is important to underscore the need for psychologists and counselors to be aware of, acknowledge, understand, and accept their own prejudices, biases, and privilege.

An example of this would be a gay couple that comes for counseling to explore marriage, in a state with a law banning same-sex marriages. It would be essential for the psychologist who worked with these two individuals to evaluate his or her own values and beliefs about gay marriage and to understand the impact of the law on the clients. As the clients expressed their anger and frustration about the law and the difficulties they faced in mainstream society, it would be essential that the psychologist have a clear understanding of his or her own reactions to the issue as well as an understanding and acceptance of

the real barriers that exist for lesbian, gay, bisexual, transgender, or questioning (LGBTQ) populations. This self-understanding can help the psychologist to accept a client's worldview and life experiences and has great importance in the work toward social justice. For example, while working with the gay couple to contemplate marriage, the psychologist may simultaneously work with them to contemplate changing state and federal legislation and policy, or even work with the larger LGBTQ community to reach these goals, hence incorporating Phase V (Social Justice and Human Rights) of the MPM.

Phase IV—Integration of Western and Indigenous Healing Methodologies

The integration of indigenous healing methodologies and Western mental health practice constitutes Phase IV of the MPM. Generally, Western mental health has emphasized intrapsychic processes, neglecting the importance of social and cultural factors and the relevance of spiritual and supernatural forces that contribute to psychological well-being (Lefley, 1984). Helms and Cook (1999) describe the difference, stating, "Sources of etiology for Western mental health systems include biogenetic, psychosocial, and interactional factors, in contrast to the supernatural, interpersonal, and interactional factors in non-Western healing systems" (p. 255).

The World Health Organization (1992) recognized that an integration of Western mental health practice and indigenous healing actually results in more effective outcomes. This is consistent with the widespread use of alternative healing methodologies throughout the world. For example, it has been reported that approximately one third of the U.S. population, half of those in Europe, and more than three quarters of people worldwide regularly utilize some form of alternative or indigenous (non-Western) methods of healing (Micozzi, 1996), such as yoga, acupuncture, herbal medicine, aroma therapy, prayer, and so forth. Western and non-Western approaches to healing are becoming increasingly complementary as the fields of counseling and psychology give more attention to this area (Pedersen, 2000). Even so, Western helping professionals routinely discount indigenous practices. Including alternative healing practices requires an openness to and acceptance of non-Western, culturally bound forms of healing and an abandonment of beliefs that Western forms of healing are superior to other indigenous types of healing. Often, the rejection of or inability to be open to other cultural healing practices is due to a lack of knowledge and understanding about the worldviews of other cultures that is tied into a Eurocentric and ethnocentric perspective that reinforces the idea that Western beliefs and practices are the best and the only effective methods of healing.

To broaden knowledge and acceptance of other cultural practices, some universities have begun to include courses in indigenous healing. For example, a course in indigenous healing is now offered in the medical school at the prestigious Johns Hopkins University as well as at some other medical schools across the United States. Simultaneously, a small number of mental health training programs have begun to build in courses on indigenous healing, showing movement to incorporate traditional healing practices into Western training. Furthermore, there has been an increase in the literature on cultural competence and hence the integration of Western psychotherapy and traditional healing practices (e.g., Aponte & Wohl, 2000; Constantine, 2007; Constantine & Sue, 2005; Gielen, Fish, & Draguns, 2004; Pedersen, Draguns, Lonner, & Trimble, 2002).

An example of incorporating Western and traditional healing methodologies can be seen in the work I (Fred) did with troubled youth from Cambodia who had lost family members during the Pol Pot regime, which killed millions of people in Cambodia. The youth were grieving their losses and were deeply sad and regretful that the family members had not received a proper burial according to Buddhist tradition and custom. Psychotherapy could not heal this wound, so a partnership was formed with monks at a Buddhist temple, who conducted ceremonies to respectfully honor and bury the deceased relatives. These rituals were combined with individual and family therapy, thus combining cultural practices and traditional Western psychotherapy. This method of an integrated intervention contrasts with the sole use of traditional Western techniques that are rooted in psychodynamic theory and based on psychopathological constructs. Such techniques, we would suggest, are not grounded in addressing the human rights aspects of mental health.

When working with traditional healing, a word of caution is necessary. It is important to note that not all indigenous healers are legitimate, so Western practitioners must be mindful and determine authenticity before referring clients to them or collaborating with them. Establishing relationships with community, religious, and spiritual leaders will be helpful in exploring the type and method of preferred healing, as well as assessing the credibility of traditional healers. An example of this can be seen with a Somali client who had witnessed the murder of several of her family members by bandits before migrating to the United States. Not being able to get these events out of her mind, she was having increasing trouble sleeping, having nightmares, and losing concentration at work. Finally, in desperation, she went to see a counselor. The counselor had heard that within the Somali community there was an elderly man who practiced traditional medicine. With the permission of the client, the counselor contacted a local Somali community leader, who gave the counselor contact information about the traditional healer. The counselor and healer discussed the client's situation and determined that rituals to appease the spirits of the deceased family members would be very important in the client's treatment. Subsequently, the client participated in important ceremonies with the healer, reading passages from the Koran, burning incense, and eating special foods, while also continuing to see the counselor. The combination of healing practices helped this individual come to peace with the death of her family members.

Accessing communities. Actually accessing communities may be challenging. Some communities are not very open to outsiders. This requires that counselors and psychologists be creative about how to gain recognition and respect within a community. A first and most important way of achieving credibility is to respect the cultural attitudes, values, beliefs, and practices of the community and the individuals within that community. This requires an openness and genuine valuing of the community. One may also attend religious and community events as a way of establishing contact, as many national figures in the United States did after September 11th—they attended meetings and ceremonies at mosques and in Arab American communities. Other ways to better engage in a community may include something as simple as going to a community restaurant to try or enjoy the food, or even taking out food from a local restaurant on a regular basis and getting to know the owners of the establishment. It is also helpful for helping professionals to speak in local communities, explaining how therapy and counseling may contribute to healing. Regardless of how one reaches out, it is critical that it is done with honesty and authenticity, with an aim toward understanding and accepting another culture.

Types of traditional healing methodologies. Jerome Frank (1974) originally wrote about psychotherapy being effective within cultural groups that share a common understanding and mythology. Partially stemming from his work, there has been a greater acceptance in the mental health field of traditional healing. More recently, four approaches by indigenous healers have been identified: (1) physical treatments, (2) magic healing methods, (3) counseling, and (4) medications (Hiegel, 1994). These four approaches provide a basis of understanding for helping professionals to form "treatment partnerships" with indigenous healers. Religious and spiritual leaders may play an important part in indigenous healing, particularly when working with families and communities that have strong roots in religious or spiritual practices. Two examples of

treatment partnerships are presented below to illustrate the efficacy of this work.

First is the example of an Afghani family who had migrated to the United States seven years ago. The mother had lost two of her brothers and a cousin during the conflict with the Russians in Afghanistan. She had been a strong figure in the family but was growing increasingly lethargic and depressed and having nightmares about the "bombings." After problems in the family escalated, the family brought her to a mental health professional who had become reputable in the Afghani community. In the first counseling session, the psychotherapist learned that her client was very religious. From previous work, the psychotherapist already knew about religious and mental health practices in Afghanistan and knew about the importance of prayer, spiritual and religious leaders, and the practice of using specific verses of the Qur'an to cure certain illnesses.

The psychotherapist also knew that certain rituals such as *ta'wiz* (writing down special verses and wearing the writings on a necklace), *shuist* (soaking the written verses in water and later drinking the water in a special ritual), and *dudi* (burning written verses with incense and inhaling the smoke) are healing practices that are based on the will of Allah. Of great concern to the Afghanis were *Jinns*, or supernatural beings, as well as *nazar*, or the evil eye, which may cause illness and is important and related to dreams. Acknowledging that this cultural belief system and these healing practices were beyond her training and ability as a mental health practitioner, the psychotherapist made contact with the leader of a nearby mosque to form a treatment partnership. In this partnership, the therapist was able to ensure spiritual guidance and intervention for the family that was consistent with her ongoing work with the client.

A second example is the case of a Vietnamese woman who had been raped during the Vietnam War. I (Rita) learned that she was a devout Buddhist. So with her permission I contacted the local Buddhist temple and asked about healing rituals for rape. Although there was not a healing ritual developed for rape or sexual assault,

I explained to the monks how a number of Southeast Asian refugee women had been raped during the war. I also informed the monks that I have worked in other countries with Buddhist monks on this issue. The monks then discussed the feasibility of developing a healing ritual for the cleansing of rape and agreed that this would be both possible and helpful. This treatment partnership facilitated the development of new practices by the monks that helped balance the mental health work.

These two examples illustrate the need to be receptive to culture-bound practices and to develop treatment partnerships with indigenous healers. Helping professionals must be receptive to healers and community elders and cooperate with them during treatment (Chan, 1987; Hiegel, 1994). Equally important is the realization that clients may prefer indigenous methods to Western oriented psychotherapy, or a combination of Western with indigenous treatment techniques. In fact, a number of clients may use both methods concurrently without the knowledge of the psychotherapist or counselor (Chung & Lin, 1994).

Establishing true partnerships with traditional healers. The above examples demonstrate the importance of the partnerships that integrate Western and traditional healing practices through collaborative partnerships between psychologists and counselors and traditional healers in ethnic communities. For more than 20 years, there has been a call by a number of psychologists and counselors for cooperation between traditional healers and Western helping professionals (e.g., Bemak et al., 2003; Bemak & Chung, 2008; De La Cancela & Martinez, 1983; Delgado, 1977; Ishiyama, 1990; LaFromboise, 1988). Partnerships can be cultivated with community leaders, priests, monks, shamans, healers, and other significant community members. Community members play an important role in assisting psychologists and counselors in learning about clients' cultural background, help-seeking behaviors, and perspectives on mental health and healing, and they can provide other related cultural perspectives on health and

mental health issues. Significant community members also can assist helping professionals to educate the community regarding mental health and counseling practices, while the helping professional can honor and support centuries of traditional healing practices and cultural beliefs.

Important to remember in working with indigenous healers is that to be effective, the nature and quality of the relationship must be based on genuine mutual respect, trust, and understanding. This allows traditional healers to practice unencumbered by the Western practitioner's judgment while maintaining an open dialogue about their respective practices. It is important for Western-trained psychologists and counselors to remember that established traditional healers are respected and trusted within their communities, even though some of their behaviors may seem odd to the helping professional, such as the tendency for indigenous healers to boast about their ability and protect their image (Hiegel, 1994).

Furthermore, helping professionals' personal values should not get in the way in establishing partnerships with traditional healers. For example, eating or drinking certain foods such as monkey brains, intestines, testicles, snake or chicken blood, may be repugnant to Western culture, yet valued in certain cultures as a means of healing. Helping professionals must overcome their own distaste for these foods in order to support clients' participation in valuable healing rituals, since the ultimate aim of forming partnerships with traditional healers is to ensure that the client receive culturally responsive and effective treatment. A value free and judgment free openness to treatment partnerships with a genuine acknowledgment that both healing methodologies are beneficial is essential in aiming toward the same goal of mental health.

An interesting example can be seen with my (Rita's) experience working collaboratively with Buddhist monks. The monks, being strict Buddhists, were not permitted to have direct interaction with a woman on certain days, and on other days could interact with a woman only at certain hours of the day. Often, I would have to talk to a monk from behind a screen. At times it was frustrating, because the monks would make appointments to see me only at specific times that were allowed by their religion, sometimes inconvenient to my Western-paced work schedule. In this situation, personal issues about not being treated as a professional and being insulted as a woman could easily emerge and clash with my views on feminism. Although I did not have this view in these circumstances, if I had, it would have been detrimental to the treatment partnership, and in the long run it would have negatively impacted the client. Understanding, accepting, and being respectful of the Buddhist monks' practices was of utmost importance in this situation and allowed them to work together to help the client.

Preferences for treatment. Even though the MPM highly recommends that psychologists and counselors work collaboratively and in partnership with indigenous healers, a word of caution is in order about stereotyping clients' treatment preferences. Psychologists and counselors should not assume that all clients from non-Western cultures prefer traditional healing as their treatment of choice. The MPM advocates for an exploration of and openness to culturally applicable interventions that can be explored with clients and their social networks. Thus, it is necessary for helping professionals to explore and investigate the efficacy of traditional healing as an effective intervention given specific circumstances, cultural belief systems, and ascertained credibility of the traditional healer.

Phase V: Social Justice and Human Rights

As mentioned earlier, the MPM is based on the premise that counseling and psychotherapy are inextricably linked with social justice and human rights and provide a foundation for mental health interventions. We would suggest that extratherapeutic factors that have been found to account for 40% of therapeutic outcomes (Lambert & Bergin, 1994) would have a high correlation with social justice and human rights. More specifically, in the MPM, issues of equality, equal access, and human rights that include oppression, racism, discrimination, interpersonal violations, abuse, physical and psychological danger, the threat to one's livelihood, hunger, poverty, or violence would be significant in this 40% category related to positive outcomes. We believe that the MPM is unique in addressing the social justice and human rights issues that are inherent in these extratherapeutic factors.

The MPM shifts the view of mental health to emphasize social justice as a key component. This requires not only a philosophical shift but also a redefinition of one's role as a psychologist or counselor. Helping professionals must therefore be risk takers, take a proactive, leadership role, and assume a social advocacy position with regard to the client's personal, social, political, and ethical rights. Phase V assumes that social justice and human rights are inherent in one's psychological well-being and an integral component of the therapeutic relationship. This perspective has been supported in the literature (e.g., Aponte & Johnson, 2000; Asamen & Berry, 1987; Bemak, 1989; Chung & Bemak, 2007; Hughes & Demo, 1989; Toporek, Gerstein, Fouad, Roysircar, & Israel, 2007).

Based on this research, as cited previously, we believe that neglecting issues that violate clients' human rights is unconscionable and results in contributing to the perpetuation of those violations. Thus, the helping professionals must attend to more than psychodynamic and intrapsychic issues, and expand their work to include concerns such as personal safety; adequate food and clothing; access to appropriate and supportive social services; access to quality health and mental health care; financial support as needed for heating, electricity, and water; housing benefits; access to equal education; individual and institutional strategies to deal with discrimination and racism; unfair treatment; and access to other resources and opportunities available in the community and society. Issues such as these contribute to mental health problems that paradoxically may be reduced or eliminated once there is adequate attention to addressing human rights violations. Therefore it is important that psychologists and counselors incorporate social advocacy that is derived from an honoring of social justice and equity as an important value in mental health interventions.

Differences between the MPM and traditional models. It is important to highlight the difference between the predominant models of Western-based individual psychotherapy and the MPM. Individual psychotherapy helps clients to more effectively deal with their problems, looking at issues from an individualistic viewpoint that speaks to changing oneself. Although variations on this have taken form with group, family, and community intervention models, individual psychotherapy remains the prevalent means of intervention. In contrast, the MPM encompasses the individual as part of a larger ecological system and aims to work in partnership with individuals for personal, social, family, community, and institutional change. Put another way, rather than changing the individual to fit the system, the MPM advocates assisting individuals to change inequities in their lives so that they have the same rights, opportunities, and treatment as others. Therefore instead of changing the individual to fit the system, the MPM advocates for changing the system so that there is universal equality and equal rights. Fundamental in the MPM is the belief that social justice and human rights drive individual, group, family, community, and systemic changes.

An example of this can be seen when working with clients who face racial discrimination at the worksite. Traditional psychotherapy may assist these individuals in figuring out how to respond to the racist comments, ignore the perpetrators, take time out to "collect themselves" rather than getting angry, become more assertive in responding to comments, reframe their thinking about their reactions, and so forth. These strategies do not address the larger situation of the ongoing racism that is directed at the clients and possibly coworkers, nor does it attend to the larger problem that may be generalized to others at the worksite, even if the clients personally come to terms with how to handle the situation.

Using the MPM, psychologists and counselors would address coping strategies that would not only assist the individuals but also create larger institutional change. This may mean supporting the clients, through discussion and role-play, to speak to the human resources department, helping the clients figure out effective ways to discuss the problem with supervisors from a perspective that is broader than that of just their individual problems, talking with the clients about designing a constructive course of action with peers experiencing similar problems at the worksite, helping the clients construct means to educate the management and workers about cultural diversity and tolerance, or assisting the clients to develop strategies for approaching management to formulate policies and procedures that would address racism in the organization. These interventions are all along the lines of helping the clients to change a discriminatory environment rather than narrowing the focus to the client's own personal problems that resulted from a racist work setting.

Social justice, advocacy, and leadership. Phase V, similar to the other phases of the MPM, is not a discrete linear step in the model. Rather, Phase V becomes infused throughout Phases I, II, III, and IV, requiring that helping professionals be proactive risk takers while assuming a social advocacy role. This role should emphasize addressing violations of basic human rights that contribute to psychological problems for clients. In this paradigm, interventions are both proactive and active, rather than only reactive.

Given the statistics highlighted throughout this book regarding national and global social inequalities and injustices, we believe that psychologists and counselors can no longer deny, avoid, or ignore their potential as proactive change agents. If the aim of the profession is to assist individuals, families, and communities toward healthy, positive well-being, then the profession *must* move forward and not stay mired in past practices. To support social justice and human rights as integral to mental health and psychological well-being, it is important that psychotherapists and counselors also undertake more research and writing to disseminate information about the efficacy of mental health and social justice interventions.

An example of this can be seen in a study conducted by Chung and Kagawa-Singer (1995) on four different Southeast Asian refugee groups. The study examined cultural influences on the conceptualization, manifestation, and expression of mental illness. The researchers found that this population does not express mental illness in the same way as Western populations, and this finding has significant implications for diagnosis, use of the DSM and ICD, and subsequent treatment interventions for this population. If we generalize this to other culturally diverse groups and postulate that Western classification categories have cultural limitations, we may be doing an injustice to these groups by forcing them to fit into discrete Western diagnostic categories. As a result, diagnosis and treatment could prove to be ineffective and even harmful.

Social justice work can be infused in various levels of the MPM. Examples could be educating clients about their rights; assisting clients, their families, and their communities to fight for equal treatment and access to resources and opportunities; changing policy and legislation by writing to senators; participating in demonstrations; and educating helping professionals regarding inter- and intra-ethnic group differences to ensure they are aware of differences within and among specific ethnic categories, thus avoiding erroneous clustering and the assumption that all groups are the same within an ethnic category. In the process of doing social justice work, there is an implicit acknowledgment of the uniqueness of the multiple groups that compose a diverse culture, thus leading to small, middle, and large steps in social reform.

CONCLUSION

Many clients and their families have experienced or are experiencing social injustices. Although many clients are highly resilient,

there are many others who have more serious difficulties that are exacerbated by the violation of their human rights. Unfortunately the mental health world continues to perpetuate Western traditions based on individual treatment that ignore more complex and psychologically destructive social injustices. In this chapter, we described a model that combines mental health and social justice/human rights. The model is founded on the premise that the two cannot be separated and that a new paradigm of interventions must be developed to effectively work with both.

The Multi-Phase Model of Psychotherapy, Counseling, Human Rights, and Social Justice (MPM) is a five-phase cross-cultural intervention approach that integrates traditional Western-based counseling with nontraditional approaches. It is a model that is culturally responsive, incorporating indigenous healing methods, cultural empowerment, psychoeducational training, and social justice/human rights. The MPM takes into account historical perspectives, cultural belief systems, worldviews, social dynamics, family dynamics, community relationships, policies, politics, the economy, and experiences of racism, discrimination, and oppression to provide a holistic framework that conceptualizes a fluid and integrated strategy to meet the multifaceted needs of clients.

DISCUSSION QUESTIONS

1. Think of three different scenarios where the MPM model could be applied. Explain how you would use it in each scenario.

2. Think of your first session with a client:
   a. How would you explain confidentiality to a recent adult female immigrant from Somalia?
   b. How would you explain the same concept to a 10-year-old African American male who was referred to your office because of suspected domestic violence at home?

c. How would you handle the privacy and confidentiality issues in a group of veterans from the Afghanistan war who are suffering from PTSD?

d. Do you expect any particular reaction in each situation?

3. What has the MPM taught you about your strengths as a counselor and about the areas in which you need further development?

4. Describe a way that you can show cultural sensitivity when working with a client whose worldview is different from yours.

5. Which "ism" do you think will be the most difficult for you to work with and why?

6. Julia, aged 20, is a new client who is in a new marriage. Although Julia describes herself as very much in love with her husband, she is feeling stifled and "shut down" in her new marriage. In your first session, Julia brings up issues she has heard about, including women's rights, pregnancy, STDs and HIV. How would you discuss these issues with Julia? What approach would you take?

7. Are there interventions and techniques for group, family, and individual psychotherapy that you have learned that go beyond talk therapy? What other strategies could you imagine might work with an individual, group, or family where talk therapy is not working very well?

8. Using the MPM model, what would you do in the following situation? An Iraqi family migrated to the United States four years ago. Dad, mom, and two children are waiting to get their asylum granted. Two other children were born in the United States. While they wait for the final decision, the family has been living off of their savings and wages from short-term, temporary unskilled jobs. Due to difficulties in the marriage and a situation of domestic violence, one of the children was removed from the house due to medical neglect. The family does not have health insurance and the parents didn't want to spend the last of their savings on what they thought was a cold and a fever. When they finally took the child to emergency services, the child was dehydrated and convulsing. Given the severity of the child's illness, the family was assigned to the family preservation unit in their county and assigned a mental health worker. The mental health worker's job was to assess parenting practices and determine whether the other children should be removed. Respond to the following questions as if you were the mental health worker applying the MPM model.

• How would you apply the different phases of the model?

• How would you define your role in the case?

• What are some of the skills and knowledge you would need to use?

• What are some of the social challenges you would face?

• What would be some of your fears and concerns?

REFERENCES

Aponte, J., & Johnson, L. R. (2000). The impact of culture on intervention and treatment of ethnic populations. In J. Aponte & J. Wohl (Eds.), *Psychological intervention and cultural diversity* (pp. 18–39). Needham Heights, MA: Allyn & Bacon.

Aponte, J., & Wohl, J. (2000). *Psychological intervention and cultural diversity.* Needham Heights, MA: Allyn & Bacon.

Arce, A., & Torres-Matrullo, C. (1982). Application of cognitive behavioral techniques in the treatment of Hispanic patients. *Psychiatric Quarterly, 54,* 230–236.

Arredondo, P., Toporek, R., Brown, S. P., Jones, J., Locke, D. C., Sanchez, J., & Stadler, H. (1996). Operationalization of the multicultural counseling competencies. *Journal of Multicultural Counseling and Development, 24,* 42–78.

Asamen, J. K., & Berry, G. L. (1987). Self-concept, alienation, and perceived prejudice: Implications for counseling Asian Americans. *Journal of Multicultural Counseling and Development, 15,* 146–160.

Baskin, D., Bluestone, H., & Nelson, M. (1981). Mental illness in minority women. *Journal of Clinical Psychology, 37*(3), 491–498.

Beck, A. T., Sokol, L., Clark, D. A., Berfchick, R., & Wright, F. (1992). A crossover study of focused cognitive therapy for panic disorder. *American Journal of Psychiatry, 149*(6), 778–783.

Beiser, M. (1987). Changing time perspective and mental health among Southeast Asian refugees. *Culture, Medicine, and Psychiatry, 11,* 437–464.

Bemak, F. (1989). Cross-cultural family therapy with Southeast Asian refugees. *Journal of Strategic and Systemic Therapies, 8,* 22–27.

Bemak, F., & Chung, R. C-Y. (2008). Counseling refugees and migrants. In P. B. Pedersen, J. G. Draguns, W. J. Lonner, & J. E. Trimble (Eds.), *Counseling across cultures* (6th ed., pp. 325–340). Thousand Oaks, CA: Sage.

Bemak, F., Chung, R. C.-Y., & Pedersen, P. B. (2003). *Counseling refugees: A psychological approach to innovative multicultural interventions.* Westport, CT: Greenwood Press.

Bemak, F., & Greenberg, B. (1994). Southeast Asian refugee adolescents: Implications for counseling. *Journal of Multicultural Counseling and Development, 22*(4), 115–124.

Bemak, F., & Timm, J. (1994). Case study of an adolescent Cambodian refugee: A clinical, developmental and cultural perspective. *International Journal of the Advancement of Counseling, 17,* 47–58.

Bowman, S. L., Rasheed, S., Ferris, J., Thompson, D. A., McRae, M., & Weitzman, L. (2001). Interface of feminism and multiculturalism: Where are the women of color? In J. G. Ponterotto, J. M. Casas, L. A. Suzuki, & C. M. Alexander (Eds.), *Handbook of multicultural counseling* (2nd ed., pp. 779–798). Thousand Oaks, CA: Sage.

Brown, L. S., & Root, M. P. P. (Eds.). (1990). *Diversity and complexity in feminist therapy.* New York, NY: Haworth.

Chan, F. (1987, April). *Survivors of the killing fields.* Paper presented at the Western Psychological Association Convention, Long Beach, CA.

Charles, C. (1986). Mental health services for Haitians. In H. P. Lefley & P. B. Pedersen (Eds.), *Cross-cultural training for mental health professionals* (pp. 183–198). Springfield, IL: Charles C Thomas.

Chung, R. C-Y., & Bemak, F. (2007). Immigrant and refugee populations. In M. G. Constantine (Ed.), *Clinical practice with people of color: A guide to becoming culturally competent* (pp. 125–142). New York, NY: Teachers College Press.

Chung, R. C-Y., Bemak, F., & Kudo Grabosky, T. (2011). Multicultural-social justice leadership strategies: Counseling and advocacy with immigrants. *Journal of Social Action in Psychology and Counseling, 3,* 86–102.

Chung, R. C.-Y., & Kagawa-Singer, M. (1995). Interpretation of symptom presentation and distress: A Southeast Asian refugee example. *Journal of Nervous and Mental Disease, 183*(10), 639–648.

Chung, R. C-Y., & Lin, K. M. (1994). Helpseeking behavior among Southeast Asian refugees. *Journal of Community Psychology, 22,* 109–120.

Comas-Diaz, L. (1985). Cognitive and behavioral group therapy with Puerto Rican women: A comparison of group themes. *Hispanic Journal of Behavioral Sciences, 7,* 273–283.

Constantine, M. G. (Ed.), (2007). *Clinical practice with people of color: A guide to becoming culturally competent.* New York, NY: Teachers College Press.

Constantine, M. G., & Sue, D. W. (2005). *Strategies for building multicultural competence in mental health and educational settings.* Hoboken, NJ: Wiley.

De La Cancela, V., & Martinez, I. Z. (1983). An analysis of culturalism in Latino mental health: Folk medicine as a case in point. *Hispanic Journal of Behavioral Sciences, 5*(3), 251–274.

Delgado, M. (1977). Puerto Rican spiritualism and the social work profession. *Social Casework, 58,* 451–458.

De Silva, P. (1985). Buddhism and modern behavioral strategies for the control of unwanted intrusive cognitions. *The Psychological Record, 35,* 437–443.

Draguns, J. (2000). Psychopathology and ethnicity. In J. Aponte & J. Wohl (Eds.), *Psychological intervention and cultural diversity* (pp. 40–58). Needham Heights, MA: Allyn & Bacon.

Egli, A., Shiota, N., Ben-Porath, Y., & Butcher, J. (1991). Psychological interventions. In J. Westermeyer, C. Williams, & A. Nguyen (Eds.), *Mental health services for refugees* (pp. 157–188). Rockville, MD: U.S. Department of Health and Human Services.

Fabrega, H., Jr. (1992). Diagnosis interminable: Toward a culturally sensitive DSM-IV. *Journal of Nervous and Mental Disease, 180*, 5–7.

Frank, J. D. (1974). *Persuasion and healing: A comparative study of psychotherapy.* New York, NY: Schocken Books.

Gielen, U. P., Fish, J. M., & Draguns, J. G. (Eds.). (2004). *Handbook of culture, therapy, and healing.* Mahwah, NJ: Lawrence Erlbaum.

Helms, J. E., & Cook, D. (1999). *Using race and culture in counseling and psychotherapy: Theory and practice.* Boston, MA: Allyn & Bacon.

Herring, R. D. (1999). *Counseling with Native American Indians and Alaska Natives: Strategies for helping professionals.* Thousand Oaks, CA: Sage.

Hiegel, J. P. (1994). Use of indigenous concepts and healers in the care of refugees: Some experiences from the Thai border camps. In A. J. Marsella, T. Bornemann, S. Ekblad, & J. Orley (Eds.), *Amidst peril and pain: The mental health and well-being of the world's refugees* (pp. 293–310). Washington, DC: American Psychological Association.

Higginbotham, J. C., Trevino, F. M., & Ray, L. A. (1990). Utilization of curanderos by Mexican Americans: Prevalence and predictor findings from HANES 1982–1984. *American Journal of Public Health, 80*(Suppl.), 32–35.

Ho, M. K. (1987). *Family therapy with ethnic minorities.* Newbury Park, CA: Sage.

Hollon, S. D., & Beck, A. T. (2000). Cognitive therapy. In A. E. Kazdin (Ed.), *Encyclopedia of psychology* (Vol. 2, pp. 169–172). Washington, DC: American Psychological Association, and London, UK: Oxford University Press.

Huertin-Roberts, S., & Snowden, L. (1993, December). *Comparison of ethnographic descriptors of depression and epidemiological catchment area data for African Americans.* Paper presented at the 18th annual American Anthropology Association Meeting, Washington, DC.

Hughes, M., & Demo, D. H. (1989). Self-perceptions of Black Americans: Self-esteem and personal efficacy. *American Journal of Sociology, 95,* 135–159.

Ishiyama, F. (1990). Meaningful life therapy: Use of Morita therapy principles in treating patients with cancer and intractable diseases. *International Bulletin of Morita Therapy, 3*(2), 77–84.

Ito, K. L., Chung, R. C-Y., & Kagawa-Singer, M. (1997). Asian/Pacific American women and cultural diversity: Studies of the traumas of cancer and war. In S. B. Ruzek, V. Olesen, & A. Clarke (Eds.), *Women's health: Complexities and differences* (pp. 300–328). Columbus: Ohio State University Press.

Jones, N. (1990). Black/White issues in psychotherapy. *Journal of Social Behavior and Personality, 5,* 305–322.

Kleinman, A. (1980). *Patients and healers in the context of culture.* Berkeley: University of California Press.

Kleinman, A., & Kleinman, J. (1985). Somatization: The interconnections in Chinese society among culture, depressive experiences, and the meaning of pain. In A. Kleinman & B. Good (Eds.), *Culture and depression: Studies in the anthropology and cross-cultural psychiatry of affect and disorder* (pp. 429–490). Berkeley: University of California Press.

Koss-Chioino, J. D. (2000). Traditional and folk approaches among ethnic minorities. In J. Aponte & J. Wohl (Eds.), *Psychological intervention and cultural diversity* (pp. 149–166). Needham Heights, MA: Allyn & Bacon.

Krijn, M., Emmelkamp, P. M. G., Olafsson R. P., & Biemond, R. (2004). Virtual reality exposure therapy of anxiety disorders: A review. *Clinical Psychology Review 24*(3), 259–281.

LaFromboise, T. D. (1988). American Indian mental health policy. *American Psychologist, 43,* 388–397.

Lambert, M. J., & Bergin, A. E. (1994). The effectiveness of psychotherapy. In A. E. Bergin & S. L. Garfield (Eds.), *Handbook of psychotherapy and behavior change* (4th ed., pp. 143–189). New York, NY: Wiley.

Lefley, H. P. (1984). Delivering mental health services across cultures. In P. B. Pedersen, N. Sartorius, & A. J. Marsella (Eds.), *Mental health services: The cross-cultural context* (pp. 135–177). Beverly Hills, CA: Sage.

McAdoo, P. H. (1993). *Family ethnicity: Strength in diversity.* Newbury Park, CA: Sage.

McGoldrick, M. (1998). *Re-Visioning family therapy: Race, culture, and gender in clinical practice.* New York, NY: Guilford Press.

Mezzich, J. E., Fabrega, H., & Kleinman, A. (1992). Cultural validity and DSM-IV. *Journal of Nervous and Mental Disease, 180,* 4.

Micozzi, M. S. (1996). *Fundamentals of complementary and alternative medicine.* New York, NY: Churchill Livingstone.

Mikulas, W. (1981). Buddhism and behavior modification. *The Psychological Record, 31,* 331–342.

Monk, G., Winslade, J., Crocket, K., & Epston, D. (Eds.). (1997). *Narrative therapy in practice: The archaeology of hope.* San Francisco, CA: Jossey-Bass.

Morris, P., & Silove, D. (1992). Cultural influences in psychotherapy with refugee survivors of torture and trauma. *Hospital & Community Psychiatry, 43*(8), 820–824.

Muecke, M.A. (1983). In search of healers. Southeast Asian refugees in the American healthcare system. *Cross-Cultural Medicine, 139*(6), 835–840.

Parham, T. (1989). Cycles of psychological nigrescence. *The Counseling Psychologist, 17*(2), 187–226.

Pederson, P. B. (2000). *A handbook for developing multicultural awareness* (3rd ed.). Alexandria, VA: American Counseling Association.

Pedersen, P. B., Draguns, J. G., Lonner, W. J., & Trimble, J. E. (Eds.). (2002). *Counseling across cultures* (6th ed.). Thousand Oaks, CA: Sage.

Pynoos, R., & Eth, S. (1984). Children traumatized by witnessing acts of personal violence: Homicide, rape or suicide behavior. In S. Eth & R. Pynoos (Eds.), *Post-traumatic stress disorder in children* (pp. 17–44). Washington, DC: American Psychiatric Press.

Rechtman, R. (1997). Transcultural psychotherapy with Cambodian refugees in Paris. *Transcultural Psychiatry, 34*(3), 359–375.

Ridley, C. R. (1995). *Overcoming unintentional racism in counseling and therapy: A practitioner's guide to intentional intervention.* Thousand Oaks, CA: Sage.

Root, M. M. (1998). Facilitating psychotherapy with Asian American clients. In D. R. Atkinson, G. Morten, & D. W. Sue (Eds.), *Counseling American minorities* (5th ed, pp. 214–234). New York, NY: McGraw-Hill.

Steele, C. M. (1998). Stereotyping and its threat are real. *American Psychologist, 53*(6), 680–681.

Steele, C. M., & Aronson, J. (2000). Stereotype threat and the intellectual test performance of African Americans. In C. Stangor (Ed.). *Stereotypes and prejudice: Essential readings. Key readings in social psychology* (pp. 369–389). New York, NY: Psychology Press.

Stumphauser, J., & Davis, J. (1983). Training Mexican-American mental health personnel in behavior therapy. *Journal of Behavior Therapy and Experimental Psychiatry, 14,* 215–217.

Sue, D., Arredondo, P., & McDavis, R. (1992). Multicultural counseling competencies and standards: A call to the profession. *Journal of Multicultural Counseling and Development, 20,* 64–88.

Sue, D. W., Bucceri, J., Lin, A. I., Nadal, K. L., & Torino, G. C. (2007). Racial microaggressions and the Asian American experience. *Cultural Diversity and Ethnic Minority Psychology, 13,* 72–81.

Sue, S., Fujino, D., Hu, L., Takeuchi, D., & Zane, N. (1991). Community mental health services for ethnic minority groups: A test of cultural responsive hypothesis. *Journal of Consulting and Clinical Psychology, 59*(4), 533–540.

Szapocznik, J., & Cohen, R. E. (1986). Mental health care for rapidly changing environments: Emergency relief to unaccompanied youths of the 1980 Cuba refugee wave. In C. L. Williams & J. Westermeyer (Eds.), *Refugee mental health in resettlement countries* (pp. 141–156). New York, NY: Hemisphere.

Toporek, R. L., Gerstein, L. H., Fouad, N. A., Roysircar, G., & Israel, T. (2007). *Handbook for social justice in counseling psychology.* Thousand Oaks, CA: Sage.

U.S. Department of Health and Human Services. (2001). *Mental health: Culture, race, and ethnicity.* A supplement to *Mental health: A report of the surgeon general.* Rockville, MD: Author.

Vargas, L. A., & Koss-Chioino, J. D. (Eds.). (1992). *Working with culture: Psychotherapeutic interventions with ethnic minority children and adolescents.* San Francisco, CA: Jossey-Bass.

Westermeyer, J. (1988). Folk medicine in Laos: A comparison between two ethnic groups. *Social Science & Medicine, 27,* 769–778.

Wohl, J. (2000). Psychotherapy and cultural diversity. In J. Aponte & J. Wohl (Eds.), *Psychological intervention and cultural diversity* (pp. 75–91). Needham Heights, MA: Allyn & Bacon.

World Health Organization. (1992). *Refugee mental health: Draft manual for field testing.* Geneva, Switzerland: Author.

Zane, N., & Sue, S. (1991). Culturally responsive mental health services for Asian Americans: Treatment and training issues. In H. Myers, P. Wohlford, P. Guzman, & R. Echemendia (Eds.), *Ethnic minority perspectives on clinical training and services in psychology* (pp. 49–58). Washington, DC: American Psychological Association.

PART III

Social Justice Journeys and Personal Applications

6

Journey of an Asian Woman Human Rights and Social Action Warrior

Rita Chi-Ying Chung

Every great dream begins with a dreamer. Always remember, you have within you the strength, the patience, and the passion to reach for the stars to change the world.

(Harriet Tubman)

The time is always right to do what is right.

(Martin Luther King Jr.)

Why Human Rights and Social Action and Not a Doctor?

I was once told by a White male friend that I had three strikes against me: 1) being an Asian, 2) being female and 3) growing up in a British colony. I grew up in a traditional Chinese family where the sole ambition for girls was to get married into a respectful family. Girls getting an education were not viewed as a top priority, and if you were going to get an education then you should be doing a degree in law, medicine, or engineering. It was difficult for my parents to understand why I did a degree in psychology since compared to a doctor,

---

This chapter is reprinted from "Reflections of an Asian woman human rights and social action warrior" by Rita Chi-Ying Chung, 2009, *Journal for Social Action in Counseling and Psychology, 2*(1), 36–43. Reprinted with permission.

a psychologist has lower status and receives significantly less income. Ironically, it was the values that were instilled by my parents that led me into psychology, human rights, social justice, and social action.

I did not realize that my social injustice lesson came at such an early age until recently. I was watching a television show where someone was doing an exercise about earliest memories. At that time I thought, "What a great exercise." So I began to think about my earliest memory. My earliest memory was a wonderful memory of holding my grandfather's hand and only being able to see his knee as I was learning how to walk. That warm memory suddenly shifted to confusion and pain. As we walked to the door of our family's fruit shop I saw my parents and aunties and uncles serving the White customers. I was probably around 18 months and did not understand the interaction between my family members and the customers. But one thing was clear, even at 18 months, I was aware that the demeaning, sniggering, patronizing, and belittling behavior exhibited by the White customers to my family were painful to witness. This was my first memory! Unfortunately, it would not be my last memory of racism and oppression.

From that time until now my family and I have had numerous experiences of racism, discrimination, and oppression. For example, my father, as a young adult, was denied entry in a movie theatre since the sign outside stated: *no dogs or Chinese,* or the time when my sister was told that she would not be the valedictorian. The school principal harshly told my sister: *"We all know that you're the best student in the school, but we can't give this status to a Chinese."* The repeated messages of being inferior to White people and not even seen as being part of the human race were strongly imprinted in my mind. I still have vivid memories of being 13 years old and my history teacher lecturing to our class about World War II. Being the only student of color in the class I was tense throughout the class, knowing fully that there would be discussion about the Japanese participation in World War II. My main concern was that the White students

would think that I was Japanese. Well that was the least of my concerns. When the history teacher asked the class*: "Why do you think Chinese are yellow?"* I knew immediately that this was not going to be a positive response. The history teacher then proudly announced to the class that: *"During World War II the Chinese men did not want their women and girls to be raped, so they put them in the barrels when people would urinate in and hence they became yellow."* These countless stories of racism and oppression you may already be familiar with since these are the experiences of many people of color and have been told in various outlets such as in movies, plays, books, narratives, poems, songs, dance, etc.

Despite these injustices, my parents who were both unaccompanied refugee minors in a British colony based on their experiences of World War II, have instilled in my siblings and me the core values of being humble, always helping those who are less fortunate than you, treating everyone respectfully regardless of race, ethnicity, culture, socioeconomic status, disability age, religion, etc., and not be judgmental, selfish, arrogant, or egocentric. Coming from a Confucius and Buddhist background we were taught the yin-yang approach to social injustices, where we were educated to be open, empathic, humble, and learn the art of forgiveness. We learned not to complain about being ridiculed or about the discrimination, inequalities, or unfair treatment that we experienced. Some may interpret this as passive acceptance, but the Asian approach, which I did not understand until I was older, is that from acceptance comes harmony, balance, and energy to strategize on how to effectively combat these injustices.

Being an immigrant and living in a migrant community I became a cultural and language broker for newly arrived Chinese immigrants and Southeast Asian refugees. Not surprisingly, my personal experiences led me to help my community with the aim to minimize racism, discrimination, and oppression so that the next generation would not have to endure such injustices. To understand more about my experiences and those of my family and community I decided to do a degree in psychology. And through psychological concepts, theories, and models of racism, hatred, prejudice, discrimination, stereotypes, forgiveness, liberation psychology, and restorative justice, it gave me the tools, skills, and courage to combat human rights violations and social injustices. My experiences define who I am, what I stand for, and what I am willing to fight for.

Since I was a child I fought for human rights and social justice so it naturally evolved into my professional work as a psychologist. My name is Chi-Ying, literally translated as bestowed from heaven courage: she who courageously endures nature's hardships by harmonizing with her environment (Aria & Gon, 1992). It is my karma to have experienced and endured racism, discrimination, and oppression and will continue to do so. But it is also my karma to learn from my experiences and to move out of my traditional Chinese woman's role to take a leadership role and proactively combat human rights violations and social injustices. And it is my karma to weave my Asian cultural values and teachings into social action, blending the yin and yang of knowledge and action. I do not have special skills nor am I different than other people, all I have is my passion and commitment to fight against the injustices and human rights violations I encounter, for I cannot and will not be silent about these injustices. Below is my humble story of my lessons learned as an Asian woman fighting for rights and fair treatment for *all* people.

Eight Key Lessons Learned as an Asian Woman Social Justice Warrior

Patience, Perseverance, Tenacity, Creativity, Flexibility, Compassion, Forgiveness and Hope: these are the eight key lessons I have learned in doing social justice and human rights work. The successful outcome of social justice work does not necessarily happen within days, weeks, or months. This may take years. I truly believe in the *planting seed* analogy. Part of social action work is sometimes about planting seeds. I have learned to be patient and trust that what I am doing will be effective and will lead to change. Change that I may never witness. Instead of dwelling on whether I can make a difference, I trust and have faith that I can make a difference. For example, I am endlessly surprised and humbled by emails, cards, or letters I receive from students and community members about the impact of our interactions and the change that has developed as a result of their contact with me. Since the eight key points have impacted my social justice work, below I will share examples of how each of these eight critical lessons affected me personally and professionally.

Patience, Perseverance, and Tenacity

No one said that social justice work is easy. Change is hard for most people. The Chinese word for crisis translates into *danger and opportunity* which describes the difficulty and essence of change for people and systems. Change represents a sense of fear and danger. Danger and fear of the unknown. Therefore, to do social action work requires patience with perseverance and tenacity. One cannot give up fighting against social injustices. It is all too easy to give up. When I feel that I do not have the energy or time to do social justice work I am reminded of the people I met after Cyclone Nargis in Myanmar (Burma) in May 2008. The young man I worked with who lost his entire family or the young boy who told me that while he was looking for his family member he began counting the dead bodies and gave up after he counted 200. Both of them, even with their recent experience of family members dying and total destruction of their entire village, volunteered at a local INGO (International Nongovernmental Organization) to help protect orphaned minors who have lost or were separated from their families as a result of Cyclone Nargis. The courage, strength and resilience they displayed provide me with the strength to persevere, be tenacious, and patient when fighting for social justice and human rights.

Creativity and Flexibility

Thinking out of the box and being creative and flexible is another lesson I have learned. Working with refugee families and trying to educate the host community and accessing services for this population is a challenge. Going through traditional mainstream channels does not necessarily result in positive outcomes. So, there is a need to think creatively on how to ensure that this population receives fair treatment and equal access to resources and opportunities. For example, after spending numerous hours trying to educate social services, health and mental health professionals, teachers, and social service providers about culturally responsive practices for refugees I realized that I was not getting anywhere. No-one was willing to listen. They wanted to just quickly fix the problem. They believed that refugees were adjusting well to their resettlement country since newspaper articles showed pictures of refugees wearing Western clothes, and standing outside their new homes.

Frustrated with this myth, which partly was created and reinforced by the media, and the lack of understanding, awareness and willingness by education, social, health and mental health professionals to be culturally responsive, I decided to use the same source that created this misperception to fight against the erroneous view. I decided to use the media as a tool towards social action. Looking through the major newspapers I identified a journalist who appeared to be aware of the postmigration challenges of refugees. I made contact with the journalist and asked if he was willing to write a more accurate account of the postmigration challenges of refugees. After some negotiations the journalist agreed to write the story. We (the refugee community, the journalist, and myself) collectively agreed that the journalist would write a series of articles over a period of several months, since one article would not be enough to create the desired impact. The articles would focus not only on the challenges, but also on the strength and resilience of this population and the contributions refugees were making in their communities. As the result of the newspaper articles I was approached by the Department of Health, Education, and Social Services to conduct a series of workshops and training to health and mental health professionals, social services, and other care providers regarding culturally responsive services for refugees.

Another situation presented itself that also required being creative. The Asian refugees and immigrants that I worked with had a traditional approach to health and mental health. Coining has been used as a method of healing. Coining is the use of a coin to rub on the person's body, resulting in marks or bruises on the person's body. These marks have been misinterpreted by mainstream Western health and mental health and educational professionals as signs of abuse. I had been asked numerous times by the Asian community to assist in situations where a child had been removed from their parent's home because teachers mistakenly identified the marks of coining as physical abuse or physicians seeing coining marks on an elderly person and labeled it as elderly abuse.

As a result of constant education of service and care providers about coining, I thought an effective way of reaching a larger group of people would be to produce a video on coining. Not having any funds or skills to produce the video I called video production companies found in the yellow pages and asked if they would be willing to provide their services for free. Eventually, I was able to convince a company to produce the video free of cost, and worked in collaboration with the refugee community and the video company to produce a 15 minute video on coining that was distributed to schools, hospitals, child protective services, public health services, social services, law enforcement, teacher education, health and mental health university training programs. The aim of the video was to educate service and care providers about the cultural healing method to prevent the misinterpretation of this traditional healing technique as abuse (details of this situation are described in Case Study 3 below).

Compassion and Forgiveness

A difficult lesson for me in human rights violations and social injustices is to have compassion and forgiveness for social injustice perpetrators. I have learned from the survivors of injustices and human rights violations the difficult, yet valuable lesson of forgiveness and compassion. It is not for me to judge others, but to understand the behaviors and motivation in why and how people participate and engage in injustices. If the survivors I worked with can forgive and have compassion for their perpetrators then I as a social justice psychologist and counselor also need to have those qualities. Working with survivors of torture or women who have experienced multiple rape and sexual abuse and yet have the ability to forgive has been an invaluable lesson in forgiveness, true kindness, and an authentic sense of humanity. Therefore, I too as a social justice counselor and psychologist must embrace the value for forgiveness and compassion for everyone.

Hope

A major lesson I have learned is the degree of hope individuals have, as well as the need for psychologists and counselors to instill hope in individuals. Time and time again working with refugees who have survived genocide, and the atrocities and traumas of war, human trafficking survivors or individuals, families, and communities who have survived natural disasters, such as, the Tsunami, Cyclone Nargis, Hurricane Katrina or the Wildfires in San Diego I am always surprised and humbled by the degree of hope and resiliency of survivors of social injustice. For example, driving up to the Indian reservation in San Diego when a large portion of the reservation was totally destroyed by the 2007 wildfires, there was a painted sign at the entry of the reservation saying: *We Believe in Miracles.* The same degree of hope was also witnessed in Mississippi after Hurricane Katrina. Driving to areas most severely hit by Hurricane Katrina I saw signs on the road that said: *Together, We will rebuild our community, Together, We will support each other, Together, We will lead the way.*

Outcome research attributes hope to 15% of successful counseling. Having witnessed the degree of hope in those who have survived natural disasters,

war and other oppressions I would say hope is at least 65% of successful outcome. Contributing to hope and resiliency it is critical for the counselors and psychologists who are doing social action work to have hope in their clients, their families and communities, as well as the ability to instill hope.

INCORPORATING THE EIGHT LESSONS LEARNED INTO CURRENT SOCIAL JUSTICE ACTION

Current International Social Justice Action

Currently, I am working with survivors of human trafficking in Asia. This involves girls who have been trafficked into the commercial sex industry. This work also includes looking at child protection issues. Working with human trafficking survivors promotes the same themes of resiliency, strength, hope, and forgiveness. I had the privilege to be asked by an INGO to work on prevention of child trafficking and child protection. For the past three years I have worked in urban cities and rural villages in Myanmar (Burma) where there are minimal resources. Sometimes, I am in villages without electricity, running water, and bathrooms, etc. In these villages the people have never seen anyone who is not Burmese. The living conditions are primitive. People sleep on mats on the wooden floor. Some huts just have a roof and no walls or doors. Not being a fan of camping, this experience has led me to put aside my personal comforts in life and focus on the purpose of my work.

I have been holding meetings with the villagers that consist of 100 to 400 people on issues of trafficking and child protection. For some villagers this is the first time they have heard of these concepts, although human trafficking and child abuse and violence are widespread. Patience, perseverance, tenacity, flexibility, and creativity are needed in educating illiterate people, who are living in constant and extreme high poverty, who are living on the edge of civilization, and who are regularly beating and selling their children. The

INGO has taught the children to use political theatre as a way of bringing awareness and education to their parents and members of the villages. As the children acted out their experiences to the entire village there are always many tears and emotions. This is the first time children have voiced to their parents, elders, and members of the village, their experiences of violence, trafficking, and abuse. Utilizing my cross-cultural skills in communication, group dynamics and group process I am working in collaboration with the children and village members about furthering awareness and prevention and intervention of child trafficking, child labor, and violence.

The following is an example of the powerful result of the children doing social justice theatre to educate their parents and village members. After the children perform their social justice theatre, we (the children, village members, INGO staff, and myself) sit on the ground for hours as I facilitate brainstorming of how parents could stop beating their children. Mothers are sitting around crying since they did not realize the effects of their beatings had on their children. We all talk and share what could parents do positively if their children are naughty. Children share their ideas with their parents about what they believe could be effective discipline and give suggestions on how parents could interact with them if they are naughty without beatings. Leaving the village there were promises of child protection rather than child neglect and abuse. This all takes patience and the results are not necessarily immediate. After a period of time, going back to the village, a mother who had not realized the effects of beating on her child, told me in front of the entire village: "*I no longer beat my child 5 times a day, I only beat him 3 times a day.*" For the child, the mother, and the villagers that was progress. Both mother and child have hope that things will be different. The child forgives the mother on all the previous severe beatings he endured and now promises that he would try to be a good child. This was a lesson for the entire village.

The mother is now talking to other parents about alternative ways of releasing anger and frustration and not beating their children. There is collective hope, collective forgiveness in the village,

children in the village are given a voice, both adults and children know the CRC (U.N. Child Rights Convention) and there is a collective genuine intention on implementing the CRC at the village level. A child protection committee was formed in the village that consists of elders, village members, and children to ensure that the CRC is upheld. This is just one example of how change can occur on individual, family, and community levels as an outcome of social action. On a systematic level, in collaboration with the INGO we held meetings with village leaders, spiritual leaders, township authorities, the local police, and the Myanmar social welfare and health officers on prevention of child trafficking and child protection.

Current National Social Action Work

In the U.S., I have designed and teach a Master's Level course on social justice. This is a course taken by all the graduate students in the Master's program. This course is designed as a "hands-on" course. Each semester students are assigned social justice projects. These projects range from developing and implementing a tunnel of oppression on the university campus, working with the American Counseling Association Public Policy and Legislation Committee, developing a school counselor's gang prevention manual for the American School Counseling Association, collecting clothes for homeless shelters, food for food banks, collecting and making care packages for the troops in Iraqi, and working in a variety of nonprofit community agencies on various social issues. Some examples include developing and assisting in a national conference on torture survivors, helping with an international conference on unaccompanied minors and vulnerable children, working with the refugee elderly populations, creating a job fair for immigrants which includes resume writing, interview skills and career counseling, and developing a community resource booklet for immigrants.

Also working with my colleague Dr. Fred Bemak who established the *Counselors Without*

Borders I have had the opportunity to co-lead and supervise groups of students in doing post-disaster work, such as working with survivors of Hurricane Katrina and working on the Indian Reservations and Latino/a migrant communities after the San Diego Wildfires. Through working with the *Counselors Without Borders* and the Social Justice course the aim is to instill in the next generation of counselors and psychologists a multicultural social justice action approach in their work.

Importance of Disseminating Social Action Work

It is also critical that as social action counselors and psychologists we disseminate our work through various types of scholarship from professional journal articles, books, videos, community newsletters, as well as to give presentations both in professional organizations and community venues, such as in nonprofit organizations, churches, schools, etc. It is important that the work we do is shared with our colleagues, government and state officials, policymakers, other professionals and the public. Part of doing social justice and human rights work is to educate. With the age of technology our work can be disseminated in a variety of sources. I have had the opportunity to give numerous local, national and international presentations, and published extensively about my work. Through my publications and presentations I have had the fortune of receiving many invitations, such as being invited to do a presentation at the United Nations (U.N.) in New York on trafficking of Asian girls into commercial sex, and being invited by the American Psychological Association to participate in the APA Expert Summit on Immigration and the APA training video on working with immigrants. As a result of the U.N. presentation I was asked to publish my presentation in a professional journal, as well as, I was offered a book contract on the same topic. This "snowballing" of social justice action work frequently happens when anyone of us is engaged in this type of social justice projects.

The work that I have done with the trafficking survivors and child protection has made me again rethink the Western theories, models, and interventions. For example, I am now currently writing a manuscript on the theories of human growth and development and moral development from the perspectives of those living in constant extreme poverty. The Western concept of choice is another topic that I have presented on and am currently writing about with regards to trafficking survivors. It is critical we view social action as not only action with individuals, in the community or changing systems, but also action in terms of education by disseminating the work one does through presentations and scholarship.

In summary, these are just some of the examples of the change I am trying to create in our field of psychology and counseling as we educate the next generation of multicultural social justice psychologists and counselors. I hope my narrative has provided ideas for you about how to move social justice and human rights knowledge to action. I pass on to you the eight key valuable lessons I have learned from social action work: Patience, Perseverance, Tenacity, Creativity, Flexibility, Compassion, Forgiveness and Hope, and wish you well on your social action journey. Below are three additional case study examples of integration social justice work in our field.

Case Study One: Gambling

Mrs. K. is a Bosnian refugee who was concerned about her husband's gambling. The gambling first began as a Saturday night activity and now has become a daily evening event. She was ashamed and embarrassed to share this concern in her group counseling meetings. As the situation progressively became worse, she could no longer keep silent, especially with the increasing number of occasions when there was no money to buy food or pay the rent. Mrs. K. was concerned that the family would be homeless and her children would go hungry if her husband continued to gamble.

When she confronted her husband about his gambling, he denied that there was a problem and claimed that since he worked long hours as a taxi driver, he was entitled to have some relaxation time. When Mrs. K. shared her concerns with the group (in which I was the group facilitator), other Bosnian refugee women reluctantly talked about their similar concerns with their husbands' gambling. It became obvious that this was not an isolated situation and that other men in the community spent many hours gambling as a way to relieve stress, although at the same they time put their families at risk when they lost their weekly earnings.

The problem became a collective concern. I asked the group how to best address the situation. It was clear that talking individually with their husbands did not work. They brainstormed several ways to deal with the issue. Since men have more authority over women in Bosnian culture, the group decided that the most effective approach would be to address the situation as a community concern. This meant involving other Bosnian women and their families as well as enlisting the assistance of community leaders. I suggested that group members role-play different strategies aimed at securing a buy-in from community members and leaders to address the larger problem of gambling in the community, rather than just individual gamblers.

The group arranged for community leaders to be at one of the gambling evenings, which was held in someone's house. Community members agreed in advance to take care of the children, so that the women from the group could be present and confront their husbands about the gambling. In collaboration with community leaders, I facilitated the discussion and ensured that everyone had a chance to voice her or his opinion and respond to the situation. I was also able to educate the community about the consequences of perpetual gambling on individuals, families, and the larger community. The situation evolved into a town hall meeting with the involvement of many members of the community. Since the word spread in the community that there would be a community meeting about gambling, other people who were concerned about friends' and relatives' gambling habits showed up at the house to participate in the discussion. The community meeting addressed methods of dealing with stress other than gambling and provided a situation that empowered the women to speak out and take action.

This situation provides an example of refugee women being empowered to challenge their husbands' behavior in a culturally sensitive manner, and it also demonstrates how collaboration between counselors or psychologists and community leaders can change the focus of a problem from one individual to the larger community, with an emphasis on systemic change.

Case Study Two: Domestic Violence

Mrs. L. is a Somali Bantu refugee who had physical signs of domestic violence but was reluctant to talk about it. She said that her husband was under a lot of stress, working long hours to support the family, which included Mrs. L., six children, and his mother. Due to his lack of English proficiency and education, Mr. L., in his forties, was forced to take menial jobs; he worked as a dishwasher during the day and at several janitorial jobs in the evenings. Mr. L. was tortured during the war in his home country and had witnessed the brutal murder of almost his entire village. He had had difficulty sleeping since he arrived in the United States.

Mr. L. had been becoming increasingly angry and had started hitting his wife. Mrs. L. described the hitting as "being related to his frustrations in trying to earn enough money to buy food and pay the bills." She added, "He never hit me when we were living in Somalia." One evening when there was a violent argument, the neighbors heard Mrs. L. screaming and crying, and they called the police. No arrests were made. A social worker visited the family the next day when Mr. L. was away at work. The social worker told Mrs. L. that she should take the children and go to a domestic violence shelter. Mrs. L. was hesitant to go to the shelter; she expressed her concerns about her husband's anger and the consequences of being alienated from the community if she left her husband. The social worker explained to Mrs. L. that she and the children would be safe at the shelter and that her husband would not find her. Mrs. L. was resistant and again expressed her concerns; she told the social worker that in her culture, these issues should be kept within the family and community. The social worker, believing that the shelter was the best option for Mrs. L. and her children, insisted on her leaving, and took the children and Mrs. L. to the shelter.

After witnessing the social worker forcefully taking Mrs. L. and the children away, Mr. L.'s mother, who also lived in the house, asked a friend to call me for assistance. I had already established credibility and was known in the Somali community; I was asked to be involved due to my previous work with the community. The mother did not understand what was going on and associated the action of the social worker with her war experiences in Somalia, where militias would come into the village, take family members, and disappear; the villagers never saw their family members again. I knew the social service system and was able to locate Mrs. L. It was clear from talking to the Mrs. L. that she did not want to be at the shelter, even though staff were strongly encouraging her to stay. Mrs. L. complied, because in her war experience, to resist authority figures could result in death for her and the children.

My first social justice intervention was to educate Mrs. L. about her right to leave the shelter if she wanted to, and I educated the staff at the shelter of the cultural consequences for Mrs. L. if she remained in the shelter. The education of Mrs. L. and the shelter staff was the first step in promoting social justice. I then asked Mrs. L. what would be the most effective approach in addressing the domestic violence. Mrs. L. had not discussed the domestic violence with her mother in-law because she was ashamed, even though her mother in-law suspected physical violence. But now Mrs. L. decided that the situation was getting out of control and felt that her mother in-law could intervene effectively, since in Somali culture there is a lifelong respect for parents. Also, family stability and unity is viewed as an important aspect of the culture. With my support and in my presence, Mrs. L. spoke to her mother in-law, who agreed with her that the violence had to stop and agreed to speak to her son.

I also spoke with community elders. Given the elders' stature and respect in the community, many family conflicts are managed through arbitration by them. In partnership with community elders, I established and facilitated ongoing community forums that focused on family unity and stability, which is a culturally sanctioned method for discussing sensitive issues such as domestic violence. Community support groups were also organized. Furthermore, I provided workshops for domestic violence workers, social services providers, and other helping professionals, such as social workers, counselors, psychologists, public health nurses, and so forth, on providing culturally sensitive services when working with refugee populations about domestic violence issues. Thus, there was a social justice intervention on multiple levels—including the family, the community, and mainstream helping professionals—that promoted social justice and worked to prevent human rights violations.

Case Study Three: Traditional Healing Practices

Child Protective Services (CPS) took two Cambodian refugee children into custody after their U.S. teachers reported that they had been abused. The police and CPS staff came to the family's house. There was a communication problem, since neither parent could speak English. The parents could not understand what was going on and were fearful as they watched their two children being taken away. Soon after, a community leader contacted me requesting my help. I had worked with the Cambodian refugee population for many years and had established credibility in the community. I was asked to intervene on behalf of the parents and community. Having a good relationship with CPS and law enforcement, I was allowed to see the children. My assessment was that the bruises on the children's backs were not from abuse but rather from *coining,* which is a traditional Cambodian healing method for physical illness.

I talked to the worried parents and told them of the misunderstanding. The parents asked me to accompany them to talk to the CPS staff and school officials to try to educate them about *coining* and how it can be mistaken for abuse. But neither the school nor CPS believed our explanation;

they continued to be convinced that the bruises on the children's backs were evidence of abuse. I was highly concerned with the mistrust and misinterpretation and decided that the most effective way to address this situation was to mobilize various professionals in the community who were familiar with *coining*. I compiled documentation from research findings showing that *coining* is a cultural healing method. I also solicited letters of support from local and national physicians, community leaders, health and mental health professionals, and public health professionals who were familiar with *coining*.

Despite this documentation, CPS refused to release the children. In response, in conjunction with a Cambodian community leader, we contacted a lawyer who did pro bono work and a journalist working for a national newspaper. The journalist interviewed the parents via a translator, talked with health and mental health professionals about *coining*, and wrote a lead article for the newspaper. Simultaneously a court hearing was scheduled, and after being satisfied that children's bruises were not the result of abuse, the judge told CPS to release the children to their parents.

To ensure that this situation did not reoccur, the community decided that an educational video would be made and distributed. I contacted film companies and asked if they could make the video at a reduced fee. Having read the article in the newspaper, a film company agreed to make the video and copies for distribution free of charge. I worked in partnership with the community to make a 15-minute video to educate teachers, health professionals, CPS, law enforcement, and other service providers about *coining* and its potential

for misinterpretation. The video included medical experts and community and spiritual leaders describing the longstanding tradition of *coining*, as well as teachers talking about their experience with coining and how it could be mistaken as abuse. The video also showed a child being coined by a community member. Community members were involved in the video explaining the *coining* process and how its patterns of bruising differ from those of child abuse and other forms of violence. The video was used for training in community agencies and by local universities in their medical, social work, counseling, psychology, and teacher training programs.

In addition, with the assistance of a local nonprofit agency, I developed lists of culturally sensitive health and mental health professionals, bilingual and bicultural translators, and other relevant resources within the area. The lists were translated into Khmer and other languages and distributed to community members.

This case study is an example of using multiple strategies in social justice work. It illustrates the importance of working in partnership with individual clients, families, and communities. It is within this collective involvement that workers for human rights and social justice can effectively address prevention and intervention from a holistic and ecological standpoint.

REFERENCE

Aria, B., & Gon, R. E. (1992). *The spirit of the Chinese character: Gifts from the heart*. San Francisco, CA: Chronicle Books.

7

THE ROOTS OF SOCIAL JUSTICE: THE PERSONAL JOURNEY OF A HUMAN RIGHTS ADVOCATE

Fred Bemak

Injustice anywhere is a threat to justice everywhere.

(Martin Luther King Jr.)

A 'No' uttered from the deepest conviction is better than a 'Yes' merely uttered to please, or worse, to avoid trouble.

(Mahatma Gandhi)

A small body of determined spirits fired by an unquenchable faith in their mission can alter the course of history.

(Mahatma Gandhi)

When I reflect on my lifetime work in social justice I realize that the values and sense of action were simply part of my life from a young age. Although social justice was not the term that was used to characterize my earlier life, it was the essence of the values that I had been brought up with and espoused in my family. My grandfather, an immigrant from Russia, had been a union organizer, fighting for worker's rights. Interestingly, he

This chapter is reprinted from "The roots of social justice: The personal journey of a human rights advocate" by Fred Bemak, 2009, *Journal for Social Action in Counseling and Psychology, 2*(1), 36–43. Reprinted with permission.

maintained the values of concern and fairness for workers, even when he later became a manager and owned his own shoe factories. His beliefs and tenacity about fairness, equity, rights, human dignity, and privilege remained the heartbeat of my family ethos.

Along with my grandfather's core beliefs were my parents, who were young and rebellious. We learned not to care about material goods, enjoyed protest singers such as Pete Seeger, and learned about how to question things that did not make sense. One early experience where there was a clash with these values was in my 6th grade class. I was in the only advanced 6th grade class in the school. All the students in the advanced class knew we were different than other 6th graders and received constant messages that we were being primed for successful futures. It was clear to the entire school that those in the advanced class were identified as future leaders and were being given special treatment, special course-work, and special attention. Interestingly the teacher selected to teach us was a devout and overly zealous former marine officer, who saw very little beyond his U.S. military view of the world and U.S. philosophical, scientific, and military domination. An example of his worldview was his selection for the advanced class annual field trip. Rather than visit a famous museum, historical sites, fascinating work environments, or attend a cultural event (all of which were within 1 hour of our school) he chose to visit the U.S. Naval Academy in Annapolis, Maryland, which was a 10 hour roundtrip journey.

Already at the young age of 11 I had been reading and thinking about the merits of socialism and communism that might be helpful to those less fortunate in U.S. society and had already identified my favorite magazine as *National Geographic* and one of my favorite books as a Time/Life Book on *World Religions*, both of which provided a fascinating exposure to other cultures and diverse viewpoints. In class one day our 6th grade teacher was once again berating cultures, religions, and political thinking and identified differences from predominant U.S. values as "horrible, bad, and evil." Reflecting about my readings and discussions at home with my parents and thinking about my grandfather's Russian background, I raised my hand and shared a different point of view about other cultures. Questioning my teacher resulted in difficulties for me for the remainder of the school year. Despite being popular and having many friends, my teacher from that point on clearly felt that I would not make a "good marine" and should not be part of the club. The sense of devaluation and criticism did little to diminish my wonderful social network or critical thinking, laying a foundation for continued reflection, an even greater conviction for not taking statement as fact, and questioning that which did not make sense.

This 6th grade experience set the tone. Several years later in 11th grade I found myself in the midst of a controversy in my high school. All my classmates were complaining about the lunchroom food. While I was eating horribly tasting food filled with sugar and starch, I was also learning about leaders and heroes such as Martin Luther King Jr., Mahatma Gandhi, and John F. Kennedy, who were fighting for civil rights and human rights. They were standing up to make a difference in worlds much larger than my high school. To top it off, astronauts had reached the moon so anything seemed possible. Leaders, change, rights, justice—all of these concepts were swirling around in my 16 year old mind giving me a glimpse of higher mountains and the possibility of dreams actually coming true! With this in mind, and facing the daily dread of lunch with my classmates, I organized the first sit-in my high school to protest the lunch food.

Amazingly I couldn't find one classmate who disagreed that we were eating horrible tasteless food and that "yes, we should do something about it!" Many of my peers joined in the protest, sitting in the high school campus courtyard refusing to go to class, testing the parameters of possibilities, and flexing our muscles to see if we might also be able to change the world. Very quickly an irate school administration squashed our protest, ordered students back to class under the threat of suspension, singled out the ring leaders (two others and me), called my parents, and angrily brought me to the office. With a serious threat of high school suspension hanging over my head, a new awareness about personal commitment to one's strongly felt beliefs and convictions, a sense of isolation (yes, my classmates all scurried back to class while I remained protesting), an evolving understanding about power in action, a new level of experiencing some of the *ins and outs* of leadership, and the accompanying knowledge that the cafeteria food was still in fact horrible, I began to more clearly define what I believed in, what I stood for, and who I was as a person. As my classmates complained about their impotence and lack of ability to change things I was formulating my own path and sense of self as it related to fighting for equal rights, fairness, equity, and social justice.

Thus, my social justice march crystallized at the age of 16 with bad food and autocratic administrators, as I began to learn lessons about social change, equality, equal rights, dignity, tolerance, and human rights. It is no surprise that I soon became involved in civil rights, working with African American youth and families in Roxbury, Massachusetts during the late 1960s as a university student. My work in Roxbury accompanied protesting against civil rights violations and the Vietnam War, a personal refusal to fight in an unjust war in Vietnam, and working as a summer counselor at the University of Massachusetts, Amherst, Upward Bound Program, which was a project that was part of JFK's national *War on Poverty*. Upward Bound was a fertile ground to live and breathe interracial understanding and tolerance and figure out how to create an intensive 8–10 week summer cross-cultural community residential program with low income academically failing Black, Hispanic, and White high school students, many of whom had never been in contact with people from other races or ethnicities. We were a microcosm community struggling with interracial tensions, Black Power, migrant Hispanic communities, English as a Second Language, the devastating effects of poverty, and generations of racism and discrimination as we worked daily with the struggles of the youth and staff in the program and our community's trials and tribulations.

After receiving my undergraduate degree I was invited to work full time in the Upward Bound Program, expanding the student focus of my summer counseling job to working with the families, communities, and schools, where on a daily basis I encountered issues of poverty, injustice, discrimination, and racism. Simultaneously I attended graduate school at the University of Massachusetts, Amherst, where I tried to meld the world of higher education with the daily realities of the Upward Bound experience. The merging of work life and graduate student life was fascinating. One day I would find myself in Washington D.C. in meetings on Capitol Hill to negotiate budget and project parameters or in the University President's office talking about the program achievements and community initiatives. The next day I would be at a local community center in the inner city with Upward Bound students and their parents and grandparents to discuss advocacy strategies for their children at the local high school when they were denied services, resources, or enrollment access to college bound classes. In the middle of days like this, I would attend classes where many of my classmates had neither experience nor knowledge about the real workings of social justice, human rights, human dignity, multiculturalism, racism, or oppression.

Five years into this experience at the age of 26 I found myself as the youngest Upward Bound Project Director in the country with an earned doctoral degree. The Upward Bound experience set the stage for my life's work. Moving between high level national and state policy and budget meetings to grass roots organizing and community work became a necessary and critical skill to promote social change and the values of social justice that were now part of my being. Understanding differences, the pain and anger associated with injustice, the firm conviction to take risks, and the growing skills as a leader and advocate, were all formed during my years in Upward Bound. This experience was enriched by other major personal and professional journeys such as leaving Upward Bound and spending one year with a backpack traveling on local buses and trains in developing countries around the world, which helped me gain a far deeper appreciation of cultural differences and a much broader worldview. Other experiences followed where I carried the same convictions and values such as directing a national mental health pilot community-based project for deinstitutionalized youth, assuming the position as the Clinical

Director for a National Institute of Mental Health funded consortium providing national consultation and training to a wide variety of community-based programs, and receiving several significant cross-cultural international awards to undertake research and scholarship in other countries (Fulbright Scholar in Brazil, International Exchange of Experts Research Fellow in India, Kellogg Foundation International Leadership and Development for 2½ years throughout Latin America and the Caribbean).

These experiences helped solidify a long term commitment for my life's social justice work. I have done consultation and training throughout the United States as well as worked in 34 countries focused on issues of social justice. My research and scholarship continues to focus on social justice and human rights related to youth and families at-risk and has been both throughout the U.S. and internationally. The key focus of my research has been an intersection in the areas of social justice and human rights, cross-cultural mental health, poverty, human trafficking, refugees, academic achievement and equity for all students, homelessness, separated and vulnerable children, immigrants, streetchildren, child soldiers and post-disaster mental health.

It remains somewhat unclear how this happens but at any given time in my career there are multiple activities on my plate, all related to my work which is rooted in social justice. Each of us must find our own style and pace, and I have always felt comfortable to have multiple activities going on at one time. In hopes that it might be helpful for you in crafting out your own social justice journey and commitment, please allow me to describe what is going on for me currently in terms of my social justice work. I should also add, before sharing what I am doing at this moment, that this is fairly standard for the pace I typically maintain as a professional, and that as a Full Professor who has been tenured for many years, I could easily choose not to do any of this work. It is also striking to me that I rarely seek out these activities any longer, but more often they come in the form of invitations or requests. I imagine that the bottom line is the passion and commitment to change and improving the human condition rather than any other extrinsic reward, which has been a fairly constant theme during my career, and in my opinion, has some relationship to the continued stream of invitations and opportunities. My firm conviction and belief is that this also relates to your work, that as you pursue social justice for the work itself, that opportunities expand and snowball so that you are able to contribute more and help with changes that are beneficial on multiple levels.

That being said, here is what is happening at the moment in my social justice work. As I write I am preparing for two invited and funded international projects and exploring a third international project. One is to Costa Rica to help set up a collaborative project to work on the prevention of child trafficking since Costa Rica is a major international hub for child trafficking and commercial sex work and to provide the first phase of a sequence of ongoing training sessions for mental health workers after the January earthquake. The second international trip is to do consultation work with a large international non-governmental organization based in Asia. I was invited to lead a team to evaluate cross-border child trafficking programs in six Asian countries. In a few weeks I will be traveling to Thailand, China, and Cambodia, while the other evaluators will spend time in Myanmar, Vietnam, and Laos. We will look at the success of the six nation cross-border programs, make recommendations for program improvement, and recommend national and international policy changes that may be helpful to develop more effective programming. Similar to other work I have done in the past and my roots with Upward Bound, I will spend time in meetings with high level government and agency officials as well as meeting with villagers and children in very remote villages (sometimes accessible only by motorcycle or boat) interviewing children and families. A third international social justice activity is to provide psychosocial training and support for staff in Uganda working with child soldiers.

Along with these international activities, I have always maintained a balance with national projects, being committed to helping in the U.S. as well. At the current time a colleague and I are in discussions with Washington D.C. Public

Schools to develop a pilot project based on a group counseling model I co-developed to provide interventions with the 20% of students in the school system who are at the highest levels of failing. Simultaneously I was called by a major national educational association to be a speaker at their national conference about models and strategies for school counseling and academic success. The association and I are jointly surveying school counseling programs from across the country to determine what school counseling district wide programs are doing and what needs to change, to try and determine next steps in promoting school counseling having a key role in academic achievement. To complement this work, along with a co-author, I am in the final stages of completing a book on social justice and in various stages of writing several articles about how to infuse social justice work in various aspects of mental health.

In summary, I truly enjoy my professional life. It is no longer work, but a melding of social justice work and life. Days unfold that provide an avenue for my commitment and passion to social justice and social change that will be a small part in trying to help and improve our world. I would like to leave you with a small story that had significant impact on my social justice work that may have some relevance for you. It is a story that I often come back to when thinking about what we each can do and how each of us can contribute to social justice work. Earlier on in my career I was working in Nicaragua providing consultation to the Ministry of Health. This was after the civil war in Nicaragua and as always happens, there were many orphans as a result of the war. I was sitting with the national Minister of Health and Director of Mental Health and discussing staffing structures that would be most helpful in meeting the needs for the orphaned children. It was quite an experience feeling like I was having a national impact and helping to craft a national strategy. The very next day staff from the major mental health hospital wanted to take me out to a distant village to observe the success in aftercare program to meet a former inpatient client. We drove to a remote area to meet the former client. Our drive took us on smaller and smaller roads until we finally stopped at the edge

of a jungle. Leaving the car we began walking, through banana groves, through rice fields, past small shacks and over muddy rivers. As we walked I remember vividly thinking that I was truly in a remote corner of the world and surely near the "end of the earth." When we finally arrived at a small village I met a former client and his family. He had been given a scissors and comb, taught how to cut hair while in the mental health institution. Upon returning to his community he set up a small salon practice with the help of an old weather-beaten chair and broken mirror under an old tree that provided a little shade. As I spoke to him, his family, and the villagers who quickly gathered, the encounter quickly turned into a family therapy/community intervention session. As our time ended, the former client and his family expressed tremendous gratitude for our discussion and talked about how much better they felt after our meeting. It was at that moment that I had a profound realization—it truly did not matter if I was speaking with the Minister of Health to develop an entire national system, or helping one single person living in the jungle at the "end of the world." The experiences, the work, the emphasis on social justice were exactly the same—one person or an entire country. Whatever and wherever we have the capacity to help is exactly where we need to be. This lesson was a lesson well learned—at this point in my career it is fine if I am in a corner speaking with an individual in need of social justice support, help, and assistance, or working with a national government to recommend policy change about major global social justice issues. Social justice is social justice is social justice and each of us has a part to play. Peace be with you.

Below are three case study examples of my social justice work.

Case Study One

The first case study illustrates the use of empowerment groups in educational settings directly with students. Over the years, beginning with my Upward Bound days working with inner city youth identified as being at risk, I have conducted multitudes of groups using the Empowerment Groups for Academic Success Approach (EGAS). (For a comprehensive description of the EGAS approach, see Bemak, Chung, & Sirosky-Sabdo, 2005.) I chose this case study to use as an example since it recently took place in a suburban Washington, D.C. area high school. The project was funded through a grant and conducted in collaboration with one of my doctoral students, who was working as a high school counselor while finishing his dissertation. During the third month of school, we asked the 10th grade teachers to identify students at the highest risk of failure. At their two separate 10th grade team meetings, each teaching team identified 15 students who were regularly absent from school, not turning in homework, and receiving failing grades.

Out of these 30 students, we randomly chose 8 from each group, for a total of 16 students. The final 16 students were from culturally diverse backgrounds; they included African Americans, Latina/os (both U.S. born and foreign born), Asians, and Whites. We prescreened each of the 16 students and invited them to join a 12-week group counseling session to discuss the problems they were having in school that related to their poor performance. All 16 willingly agreed to try the group counseling intervention and participate. They were placed randomly into two separate groups. Following the EGAS approach, the groups focused on problems identified by the students, with a goal of resolving the difficult personal and interpersonal issues they brought up. The group intervention served as a means of improving academic performance by providing support for students who were at high risk for failure. The goal for the group—that is, academic success—was clearly explained to group participants. The format of the group was also presented which involved the group members clearly setting the agenda, direction, and content of the group discussions.

At first, members of both groups were skeptical—"Can we really talk about what we want?" "Are you going to lecture us about failing, doing our homework, and studying?" "Do we really have a say about what happens here?" As the groups began to explore parameters of what was allowed and to see that they were, in fact, really free to talk about things other than academics, they began to feel safe and secure in the group. The school counselor and I, facilitating the groups, addressed deeper underlying issues and problems that both groups eagerly began to explore. In fact, both groups spoke about the group being the only place where they could discuss problems with parents, sex, pressures about substance abuse, peer pressure, family problems, and so forth. And not only were they discussing these issues for the first time in a serious way, they were helping each other figure out how to manage and cope with very difficult and confusing situations.

Interestingly, about seven weeks into the group experience, the school principal decided that given upcoming state tests, all extracurricular activities, including meetings of the two groups, would be suspended and turned into study halls. When this edict was presented to the groups, the students were outraged. "How can they do this to us?" "This is unfair, they can't do this!" "This group can't stop—it is the best thing all week." "This group is helping us in our schoolwork—they can't stop this!" When pushed about why they wanted the group meetings to continue, they vehemently argued that the meetings were places where they could "open up" and "really talk to each other." All 16 students forcefully declared that they felt better and were doing better because of their groups.

At that point I intentionally challenged the students about the goals of the group and their academic performance. "How can the principal make an exception if your grades aren't improving? If you're not trying harder? If your test scores aren't improving? If you're not handing in your assignments? What would you say if you were the principal?" Well, this started a flurry of very strong reactions by all of the students in both groups. "We are improving!" "Our grades have gone up—ask the teachers!" "Ever since this group started meeting, we have been doing much better!" Having checked school records and teacher progress reports, we knew that in fact only one student continued to have the same level of academic difficulty as before. When she shared this, her group strongly confronted her, pleading and cajoling her to work harder "or else the group can't continue." She actually agreed to try much harder (and in fact for the next several sessions brought her homework to the group).

It is important to note that this was the first time that there was a serious and concentrated conversation about grades and academic performance in the groups and that the students were fighting with the school counselor and me to maintain the groups! Having reviewed their academic progress reports, we knew that they had in fact improved in their classes. Subsequently we suggested to each group that they advocate for themselves and write the principal a letter explaining why their group meetings should continue. The experience of advocating for something they believed in and constructively challenging a figure of authority was new for them. All 16 group members eagerly wrote letters to the principal. Within a day, the principal agreed to let the two groups continue, while every other school activity was forced into study halls to prepare for exams.

Participation in a group experience where they felt ownership was new and revolutionary for every one of the students. Students also had an opportunity to advocate for something they believed in that was important to them, that is, the continuation of the group. Their advocacy was a success, their grades and attendance dramatically improved, and their sense of confidence and empowerment grew significantly and changed who they were and how they were as students and people.

Case Study Two

The second case study involves the work I have been doing in northern Uganda for the past few years. Because of more than two decades of civil war, many families there have been destroyed through murder, death, torture, abduction, poverty, and rape. Many children of these families are highly vulnerable because they have been orphaned, infected with HIV/AIDS, abducted to serve as child soldiers, or become child mothers. My work there has been with an international nongovernmental organization (NGO) that works with highly vulnerable adolescents to support their returning to school and succeeding academically. The

problem the NGO has faced, similar to problems in postconflict regions throughout the world, is that many of the youth have been so highly traumatized that despite their best intentions and efforts to succeed at school, they are unable to concentrate or study because of the conditions of their lives, memories of the past, and subsequent mental health problems.

The social justice counseling work in Uganda has involved consulting and training for the NGO staff about basic psychosocial interventions and assessment related to trauma and post-traumatic stress disorder (PTSD). The work has included extensive visits to villages, towns, schools, and sometimes prisons throughout the northern region of Uganda to meet with children and their families and help them come to terms with their very difficult current life circumstances and horrible experiences from the war period. In every encounter, NGO staff are with me, so their training includes observing me as I model counseling interventions. At a later time, I observe NGO staff in counseling encounters with the children and their families, and I follow this with individual and group supervision. Examples of the types of traumatized individuals I have encountered during this work include abducted child soldiers who have been forced to kill and rape others; children who have witnessed the rape or murder of a parent, family member, or neighbors; single teenage mothers; children who have discovered they are HIV positive; children who are responsible for younger siblings; and children who have experienced or are experiencing reccurring nightmares, intrusive memories and thoughts, loss of a parent, homelessness, delinquency, poverty, and/or a deep-rooted fear and distrust of others. Many of these issues have resulted in depression, serious problems in school, and a lack of hope for the future. The purpose of my work with NGO staff has been to assist them in working with the youths' trauma, pain, fear, and anger and gain an understanding about how to reach and touch the children so that they can heal and subsequently succeed in school.

The emphasis on the ecological context of the individual is essential in this work (Conyne & Bemak, 2004) and includes attention to factors such as poverty, trauma, vulnerability, discrimination, sexism, violence, educational policies, and so forth. To ignore significant contributing influences that impact a client's school life, academic performance, and prospects for a better life can be a major obstacle to helping them have a meaningful future. In my work, I continually consider it imperative that counselors, psychologists, and social workers pay close attention to social, political, and economic realities of students and their life situations and address these as critical elements in the counseling. For us to ignore the impact of inherent power structures that contribute to clients' academic difficulties is to participate in the insidious cycle of low performance and failure for the students of Uganda and all other nations.

Case Study Three

The third case study focuses on the work I did in Haiti following the devastating earthquake in 2010. The work was based on the disaster cross-cultural counseling model (DCCC). (For a comprehensive description of the DCCC model, see Bemak & Chung, 2011.) The earthquake affected the entire country, destroying buildings, killing and injuring hundreds of thousands of people, and leaving well over one million people homeless.

Following the earthquake, there was a tremendous need for psychosocial support focused on working with trauma and PTSD. An international NGO was familiar with the work of Counselors Without Borders (CWB), an organization that I had founded in 2005 to respond to Hurricane Katrina that later expanded to address other national and international crises. Soon after the earthquake, I began discussions about having CWB provide training for school personnel and mental health community-based professionals in Haiti, and I received funding to take a CWB team there three months after the earthquake. (The team included the other author of this book as well as myself.)

We began our training in a Port-au-Prince school, where only a portion of the school buildings remained standing. Invited to the training were directors from eight schools around the capital city, and numerous school administrators. Since there are not mental health professionals in the schools in Haiti, it was common practice for the administrators to provide counseling for students. The training reviewed how to provide psychosocial support for traumatized students, parents, and staff and helped design a plan of intervention. Simultaneously, as frequently happens in postdisaster situations, we also helped administrators cope with their own trauma. The two day training was followed by direct counseling interventions by the team for the next few days. While they were doing these interventions, they were being shadowed by school administrators, who observed how to implement the DCCC model. The direct counseling was done with students (individuals, families, and groups), parents (individuals, families, and groups), and staff (individuals and groups). Following the direct counseling interventions, CWB staff met with school administrators to provide supervision and consultation.

Similar training was done at other community sites with psychologists and social workers who, although they were trained in their respective disciplines, did not have any knowledge of or skills for working in a postdisaster situation. All of the training and counseling was done within a culturally responsive social justice framework, taking into account reactions to the anger and frustration at the lack of political response to the disaster, the economic concerns that were raised, apprehension about housing and medical care, cultural beliefs and practices about healing, and interest in advocating for better, more responsive services and support.

REFERENCES

Bemak, F., & Chung, R. C-Y. (2011). Social justice group work and group supervision in post-disaster situations. *Journal for Specialists in Group Work, 36*(1), 3–21.

Bemak, F., Chung, R. C-Y., & Sirosky-Sabdo, L. A. (2005). Empowerment groups for academic success (EGAS): An innovative approach to prevent high school failure for at-risk urban African American girls. *Professional School Counseling, 8,* 377–389.

Conyne, R., & Bemak, F. (2004). Teaching group work from an ecological perspective. *Journal for Specialists in Group Work, 29,* 7–18.

8

SOCIAL JUSTICE REFLECTIONS OF GRADUATE STUDENTS

This chapter consists of students' reflections about their experiences in the George Mason University (GMU) Counseling and Development Program, which has a core mission of training future multicultural social justice counselors. Students were asked to reflect on their experiences in their graduate studies and to focus on pivotal and poignant moments in their training. Although social justice issues are emphasized and intensely explored from the introductory first class and included in every course in the program, students' awareness and insight related to social justice and multiculturalism most often peaks during two classes, the Multicultural Counseling class and the Counseling and Social Justice class; the latter is the only required social justice course in a graduate counseling or psychology program to our knowledge. Therefore we have asked students to reflect on this pivotal moment in their training, tapping into their experiences in either one of these classes. The student reflections are deeply personal and provide examples of students' life changes, the risks they have taken, and the courage they have had to speak out and act on

social injustices as these injustices relate to their personal and professional development.

I SEE YOU BLACK GIRL—BUT I DARE TO SPEAK AND CHALLENGE

Reston Bell

I was born with two marks against me. My name is Reston Bell and I . . . am . . . a Black . . . woman. This is the foundation upon which this course (Multicultural Counseling) reflection stands. What made me feel safe enough to share? What prompted me to take the next step? What words can be imparted to give people the courage to speak up? These are all very good questions that I will do my best to provide real and occasionally raw responses to. As you read this piece, I ask that you do so with an open mind, knowing that my expressions, sentiment and pain are not yours or mine alone to bear. Reality is . . . the blemishes of racism and racial discord that are perpetuated through our hesitant honesty and collective silence; these are a shared responsibility. And so, upon these pages I will seek to write truth.

What Prompted Me to Take the Next Step?

Before enrolling in this course, I was forced to ask myself, "Reston, do you really want to take down the protective wall that you have built painful brick by painful brick?" Though uncertain of the answer, I enrolled and seriously doubt that I will ever be the same. For me, it has all been worth the occasional sleepless nights, the irritability, and the hurtful remembrance of difficult events. The greatest challenge of this course, Multicultural Counseling, concerned my struggle to unlearn the defense mechanisms that I was socialized to develop. The challenges associated with unlearning these crippling yet protective mechanisms went/go (it is a process) hand in hand with my fear that I would be unable to do so. This relearning process was especially difficult because despite foolishly trying, I could not figure out how far back these learned responses went. Reading, writing, and arithmetic were not accompanied by the subject of self-hatred, but I learned it. In one of our assignments I wrote, "I cannot say that I remember being taught how to internalize mistreatment and direct the resulting hate inward, all the while never addressing my aggressors. No, my social education was much more subtle than this, and for this fact my relearning has to be that much swifter." After careful reconsideration, I know this to be untrue.

Finding the Courage to Speak

Like countless others, the messages that I received were far from subtle and knew no limits. When I cut off my relaxed hair and went natural, a 70-year-old African American woman asked, "What, you think you have good hair or something?" The message was disheartening. When I straightened my hair after wearing it in its natural curly state for a year and a professor from one of my former programs remarked, "You look so professional with your hair like that," I was hurt, because in my natural state, I know that my professionalism will always be smoke and mirrors to some message. When I shared my educational aspirations with my high school guidance counselor and he stated, "That's nice, but I think you should be realistic," I was pissed because he said it and infuriated because parts of me wanted to believe it, message. It is being told "job well done" on a completed assignment, when the product reflects nothing more than a mediocre effort with the implication being, you expect very little from me, or even worse, you are not sincerely concerned with whether or not I am successful in my learning process, message. When my English teacher never called on me, yet labeled me disinterested and unprepared, it conveyed a certain message. When I returned from the 2009 inauguration and found my front yard littered with headlines from the morning's newspaper, I found a message in that. When some say "you talk like a white girl," or others note "you are so articulate," is speaking like a "white girl" a compliment? Am I articulate, or am I articulate for a "black girl"? Another message. A pastor during last year's revival preached, "It's not what's on the resume that I praise Him for. No, I praise Him for everything that happened between those lines." In this same way, it is not necessarily the intent or the words exchanged, but their message, what lies between the lines that stings, pervades, and paralyzes our progression.

Development and strengthening of openness and patience is underway. Over and over again, one of our readings stressed the difficulty of coming to terms with what it means to be White in our country. As an African American woman, my understanding of what it means to be White generates what I would call envy. I am envious of the fact that Whites have to work so hard to determine what it means to be White and its implications. Minorities do not have this luxury, and it is upsetting. I wish that I could walk into a room and not feel the hush that comes over it. But, like most minorities, I have never had the opportunity to forget who I am and what that means in the dominant culture. Lest I forget, my skin always tells on me, and the world, like a taunting child, pulls me in for a hug and quietly whispers in my ear, "I see you Black girl." At least this is how I feel, always with the give and take. I climb, but can only climb so high before I am reminded.

Previously, I made efforts to cross ethnic/color lines with the intent to remain until comfortable. However, through taking the Multicultural Counseling course, I realize that the impact of such efforts has always been limited to me. What good is it for a man to reach the top of a mountain and have no one with whom to share the moment? This class revamped my outlook. For many years I fought to climb this mountain all by myself, believing that tolerance was a personal journey. While there is some truth to this fact, in the same way war never really leads to peace; isolation never really leads to widespread acceptance. And so, I along with many of my classmates took the frightful plunge into the abyss that is the harsh yet real reality that accompanies honest racial discourse. Consequently, things I used to notice and "overcome"/internalize are now up for discussion.

For those valiant professors who are planning to facilitate this course, I commend you for taking a step towards teaching tolerance that many in your position will never care to take. I want for you to know that it will not be an easy task, as truth is the hardest lesson to teach, but the easiest to resist. I think it was Dr. Chung's fearlessness when it came to speaking candidly that allowed students to feel as though our classroom was a safe place for honesty, even when their opinions dissented from the group's. Push your students to eat, sleep, and drink multiculturalism. Show your students that it is more than letters on a page or words exchanged between classmates. Teach them that it is wasteful to leave words bouncing around the four walls of your classroom. Teach them that their real work begins when they leave your classroom and come into contact with the world. With my fellow students I share simple words.

Dare to listen; be validated, wrong, hurt, challenged, and honest; but almost most importantly, dare to speak, dare to be heard!

ADDICTION TO WHITE PRIVILEGE

Elizabeth Davis

I am a 27-year-old Caucasian female and I have lived in the same southeastern state all my life. In recent years I became engaged and then married to my husband and relocated from the northern suburbs to the southern rural farm land of Virginia. I grew up going to school with quite a diverse group of peers and now live and work amongst majority Caucasians. However, I do visit my hometown quite often as I am a graduate student completing the last year of my master's degree in school counseling at GMU. Even though I grew up with peers of different cultures and nationalities, I never considered how little concern I had for multicultural issues and how they could have affected my peers until I took the Multicultural Counseling class.

I have to be completely honest and admit that Multicultural Counseling was not a course I was looking forward to taking. I was afraid and embarrassed to begin an open and honest discussion about a topic I was always taught was taboo, race. In my family there are four things you just don't talk about: money, religion, politics, and race. My fear of discussing race was so severe that if asked to identify a person of color in a crowd, I would have rather described that person by the color of the shirt than the color of the skin.

During Multicultural Counseling, I went through a myriad of emotions from fear and anger to guilt, then confusion and finally confidence. Yet, I never experienced these emotions alone. I strongly suggest having allies in the journey to becoming more culturally competent, because otherwise it can be a lonely road. At first I was afraid to speak honestly with my classmates but many of them have become strong allies in my journey. In fact if it were not for the encouragement and kind words of one of my classmates, I don't think I would be the person I am today.

I believe my turning point came after reading *A Race is a Nice Thing to Have: A Guide to Being a White Person or Understanding the White Persons in Your Life* (Helms, 2008). We were required to write an honest reflection on this reading. At the time I had a friend who was struggling with substance abuse. Experiencing this struggle and reading this book compelled me to write about the correlation between the feeling of superiority that is provided via racism and the high that is provided by narcotics. Like narcotics, racism is the poison that one seeks out to feel content. However, just like one must work to become sober, a Caucasian individual like myself must constantly work to develop a healthy White racial identity. Reading Helms's guide made me discover my addiction to White privilege. It also made me explore the rewards of establishing a healthy White identity in order to combat racism, albeit with some discomfort along the way. Just as a drug addict has to go through withdrawals from narcotics, I had to experience withdrawal from the high superiority gave me. Just as addicts writhe about in pain as they detoxify, I had to get used to the anguish I felt about my own race and other racial groups while on my journey to becoming a more racially competent counselor. One of the hardest parts for me to read aloud was the recollection of previous racist views. As I read my candid reflection aloud to my class, I could feel myself trembling, the hot tears of embarrassment upon my face and what seemed like a lifetime of repressed viewpoints all coming pouring out. After this experience, I felt as though the emotional barriers were lifted, and I was free to further explore myself.

There were a few factors that contributed to my success in this Multicultural Counseling course. First, as I mentioned previously I had support from classmates, our professor, and my family. One tool I believe was useful in helping my classmates and me share was Blackboard. Blackboard provided a cyber-support group, and it allowed us to share honestly without being judged in person. Second, the reading materials and assignments that we were given allowed us to view others' struggles with racism and explore our own struggles.

Through this course I was able to learn that it is not only okay to talk about racial issues, it is absolutely necessary. Completing Multicultural Counseling has helped me to better understand and empathize with clients of color. This course has also empowered me to speak out against racism. This was no easy task, and my journey is far from over.

BEEN THERE, DONE THAT: I THOUGHT THERE WAS NOTHING MORE TO LEARN

Jan Weng

I graduated with a master's in counseling in 2006. During my academic career, there have been two courses that stand out in providing the culmination of my training in social justice and multiculturalism and impacted me the most: Counseling and Social Justice, and Multicultural Counseling. I suspect there are several other reasons why this is, but the main reason in my mind is the courses' relevancy to my life and my life's work, which is counseling.

I am a 54-year-old, Black male with a birth-defected left arm. I am also an addict who has been in recovery for almost 18 years. Further, I have been a substance abuse counselor for almost 27 years. You may ask, "How can someone have more years as a substance abuse counselor than he has as a recovering person?" It is important to consider this question, as a part of who I am, and from where I came professionally . . . and also to note that my story is not unique. My life experience is key to why these two courses have been so influential in my development as a person and as a counselor. Growing up, I did not like myself much, and as result, I behaved in ways that caused me to feel worse about myself, and in turn, exhibit even worse behavior. I was caught up in a destructive cycle of low self-esteem, addiction, crime, and punishment. In 1975, I was offered treatment instead of prison, and of course I took treatment.

Near the end of my treatment, I was offered a job, as a counselor, in the very same program

I was being treated in. Although I did more administrative work than clinical, at the time, I was among the ranks of a new breed of counselor that was becoming more prevalent, especially in substance abuse treatment: the peer counselor or recovering counselor. This "new" professional became popular, I believe, for two reasons: 1) The labor was cheap, and 2) these recovering addicts had firsthand experience of active addiction and recovery from addiction. So who else could better provide a road map from active addiction to recovery than one who has walked the road himself?

Although I ultimately received training in the therapeutic community model of treatment and in counseling techniques, it was minimal by comparison to what was needed. Most substance abuse counselors were not exposed to the rigors of counseling theory and ethics. If you did not seek formal training on your own, you did not receive it. Hence I struggled persistently with reacting, rather than responding, to clients and their needs. I had no clue about issues such as transference/countertransference, and for the most part I, like many other peer counselors, "flew by the seat of my pants!" In hindsight, I suspect that I harmed some clients out of ignorance, but I find consolation in the belief that I maintained a genuine desire to be helpful to another human being. It always seemed easier for me to care for another than it was to care for me. I learned a lot in those many years of counseling: I developed an understanding of theory and practice that sustained me in what became my career.

Prior to coming to GMU, I was convinced that there was not much more I could learn: I was cocky about my expertise and came to classes with a know-it-all attitude, yet I felt inadequate as a student, and hence I resisted academics even more! When I think of the Multicultural Counseling and Counseling and Social Justice courses I participated in, under Dr. Chung's facilitation, I think of them as a combined experience, rather than as two separate courses. The Multicultural Counseling course was a safe place to talk: Dr. Chung insisted upon it; she led by example by supporting those who took positive emotional risks and by taking emotional risks herself. I took a risk, expressing what it felt like to be a Black man in the United States, and further a Black man with a physical handicap.

Through that discussion I was able to process the countertransference I experienced when counseling White middle class families. For years I had struggled with that discomfort, and never once brought it up or discussed it with anyone. I never heard the term "White privilege" prior to the course. Instantly, I understood a major source of my insecurity and inadequacy. In a reaction paper I wrote, I was able to report that the discussions about racism, for the first time in my experience, felt hopeful and genuine in the search for remedy and understanding. Also, it was evident that such discussions were brought to larger forums, that is, I took much of what I learned back to my own workplace and applied it in my own supervision, as well as with those employees I supervise. Reading Helms's book gave me a clear direction in conceptualizing the various degrees of racism that I encounter in my routine interactions with White people and people of color. It's still amazing to me how this class helped me process my own "Whiteness" as a Black man, especially in terms of my interaction with other Black people, particularly Black people from low income areas.

Counseling and Social Justice was a continuation of Multicultural Counseling. It began with Dr. Chung's contract for safety, in the class and in our discussions. Many of the students in this class had been in the previous one as well, so the relationships carried over. The most significant process that I remember about this class involved the character portrayals. Each student was required to portray a character of a different gender, class, race, and ethnic group from their own. Each character had an issue that the students had to discuss and advocate for. Dr. Chung assigned each student a character that was most unlike that student. I was assigned a White, middle class housewife in her 30s with two children. Her husband was abusive but worked hard, made a lot of money, and paid the bills. Throughout the semester, we referred to the various characters and their issues as they pertained to the elements of social justice, such as advocacy, empowerment, etc.

Traditional counseling postulated that the problem was within the client, and that there was where the work needed to take place, and that society was basically too big to affect in any way. Social justice counseling validates clients' experiences. I learned a concrete way of understanding client-centered therapy and the notion of collaboration. The strength-based approach has also been made clear to me in our discussion of pathologically based treatments, which is the style I "grew up" under: Pointing out what's wrong and "telling" the client how to "fix it."

These are just some of the examples of how these two courses have impacted my view of counseling. I sincerely have had a paradigm shift as a direct result of my coursework at GMU, and specifically the curriculums of Multicultural Counseling and Counseling and Social Justice. These are two very effective processes that address the area of focus most needed at this time: the counselor's process in establishing a therapeutic relationship with his clients, particularly as it relates to that counselor's own issues regarding gender, race, class, ethnicity, religion, sexual orientation, etc. Ultimately we are tasked to serve our clients not by insisting on what we think they need, but by empowering, guiding, and coaching them in the direction they envision for themselves, ultimately.

WHITE DENIAL: I'M NOT WHITE, I'M JEWISH

Katherine Golkow

Reflecting back upon my experience in my Multicultural Counseling class, I am struck by the extreme challenges that class presented for me. The topic that I struggled with the most was coming to terms with White privilege. Though I found much of the material hard to swallow, the thought of joining the ranks of the many counselors who are not trained to be multiculturally competent was far more alarming and prompted me to press on.

Before beginning my Multicultural Counseling class, I had never even heard of the term *White privilege*. In fact, I hardly considered myself White; the running joke in my household was to check "Other" on race questionnaires and write in "Ashkenazic," which is the Jewish ethnicity of my family. The idea that being Jewish separated me from the rest of the White population was something that had been emphasized for me my whole life; I learned about Jewish people suffering throughout history, that many people today still hold anti-Semitic ideologies, and that even though I had the same skin color as other White people, I was really different than them. I was in "White denial," where I fully embraced the idea that I wasn't "really" White; I was Jewish.

The classroom exercise that really hit home with me was a White privilege questionnaire where we checked off ways in which we had benefited from White privilege; I felt shocked as I checked off each and every item. This realization set off a series of strong emotions within me. After denying my "White-ness" for so long, I felt angry and confused. My anger was deep, and was aimed both outward and inward. I was angry with my family for raising me with blinders on toward my White privilege, I was angry with society for being content to perpetuate White privilege, and I was angry with myself for having lived in blissful ignorance for so long. I became angry with friends, family, and even strangers for being as blind as I had been and continuing to choose to do nothing about it. All this anger sparked confusion. My worldview up until that point had just been proven wrong, and I didn't know what to do next. I had a new viewpoint, a lot of anger, and was left with the question: what now?

At this point, several aspects of my Multicultural Counseling class became key in helping me move forward, specifically, the emphasis put on sharing and processing. The professor encouraged us and challenged us to share our reactions to the class material and created a safe environment for expression. I benefited from being able to process my anger and confusion, just as I benefited from hearing other students do the same.

It is important to note that while the emphasis on sharing and processing was very helpful to me in many ways, it also presented a challenge. It took several weeks for me to be comfortable enough to open up about painful topics and air my own experiences and biases to the class. However, once I did it, I felt a powerful surge of emotion and empowerment. It was empowering because when you don't discuss your own racism, it owns you, but when you identify it and expose it, then you own it, and that's when you are able to make a positive change for the future. I believe that all Multicultural Counseling classes should include students reflecting on their own biases, however painful and difficult it may be, because without acknowledging that we all have biases and identifying what those biases are, counselors can cause harm to their clients by unknowingly projecting these biases onto them.

The assigned readings for our class also helped me progress beyond my upset emotions. Reading *One Struggle Through Individualism: Toward an Antiracist White Identity* (Croteau, 1999) was incredibly helpful to me. Like Croteau, I identified with a minority group in a collectivist sense without analyzing my role as a White person; I embraced the "we" of being a Jewish woman and hadn't until recently tried to understand what it means to be White. Croteau's insight on his identity as a homosexual man creating a "window" through which to view his identity as a White man was very intriguing to me. His journey helped me realize that being White didn't disqualify me from having an identity as a Jewish woman. In fact, my identity as a Jewish woman could be used as a way to view my identity as a White woman as well. Another reading that helped me move beyond my anger and continue to develop an identity as a White person was the book *A Race is a Nice Thing to Have* (Helms, 2008). This book helped map out a journey to a healthy White identity and made me realize where I was in that journey and where I had to go next.

Learning about White privilege and moving past anger and confusion to acceptance of my identity as a White woman was a life-changing experience. I felt like a blindfold had been removed; suddenly I could see the effects of White privilege not only in my own life, but in society as a whole. It is imperative that all counselors take the time to not only learn about White privilege on an academic level, but process it on a deeper level and as it relates to their own lives. I believe that only then will they be able to see how their clients benefit from White privilege or suffer under racism. It is my hope that my reflections on my experience in my Multicultural Counseling class will help other students who are struggling to feel like they are not alone, and will provide counselor educators with understanding of how to best help their students.

Living in the Shoes of Another Person: Social Injustice and Advocacy Come Alive

Rodolfo E. Marenco

My name is Suzanne Johnson. I am a 16-year-old White female in my last year of high school. Yes I am a senior. Big deal! The truth is that being a senior doesn't mean much to me, except perhaps for the fact that at least when I finish high school, my nightmare will be over. Yes, high school has been a nightmare for me. As a matter of fact, I think that my entire school experience has been a nightmare, a lie. I am tired of showing to others something I am not. I feel disgusted with myself, not for being a lesbian, but because I have kept it to myself all my life. I am tired of living the life of a heterosexual girl. I am tired of pretending I like guys. I wish I could just tell everyone the truth about me without having to worry about their rejection, without having to worry about losing my friends, my lifestyle, and even my parents. Sometimes I wish I would just finish it all for good. Yes, I have thought about ending my life on some occasions. I wonder why I had to be born in a world where my kind is not accepted by others. I wonder why it had to be me.

Ever since I was a child, I always felt I was different from other girls. In those days I didn't know I was a lesbian or what a lesbian was, but I knew enough about how girls were supposed to behave and feel to know that I needed to keep my feelings to myself. For this reason, I have always felt alone, isolated in my own world of who I really am. As I grew up in the safety of my upper-middle-class family, home never felt safe for me. Both my father and my mother are very conservative, and on occasion I have heard them disapprove of gay and lesbian people when these people appear in the media. My father travels a lot in his job. He is in the military and his job requires him to travel to different bases around the country very often. Being in the military, he has been trained to dislike those like me. My mom, on the other hand, is too busy to care about me. She lives in her own world of friends and shopping, spending the money my father makes. Besides, I think she is dealing with loneliness issues of her own by being married to a military man who is never home. I think that she is having an affair. No, I can't seek guidance from my parents, they would probably disown me if they knew they had a daughter who likes other girls. They would be ashamed of me. My worst fear is that they will someday find out. I can't even imagine what they will do. Would they throw me out of my home? I can't take that risk and cause them that much disappointment.

I have always been alone in my quest to find information about those like me. I am not friends with any lesbians in my school or in my neighborhood. All my friends are heterosexual, or at least act that way. Being the captain of the soccer team has made me very popular among my peers. I guess many would like to be in my shoes and have as many friends as I have, but if only they knew. I even have a boyfriend in my effort to hide and conceal that I am lesbian. He even thinks that I am attracted to him, but I feel disgusted when he gets near me. The only way I can stand being with him is by drinking alcohol when I spend time with him, usually on Friday evenings after the football games.

This kind of life has to stop. I can't go through life always looking at myself through the eyes of others, measuring my soul by the tape of a world that looks in on me. I am tired of lying. Yes, silence is a form of lying. I can't go through life making excuses for those around me who do not accept those like me, or worrying over the reputation of those who decide to stick around me when I do decide to come out. I have the right to be a lesbian

without receiving a cold shoulder and rejection. Until that day when I decide to come out, being a lesbian will continue to be lonely. On many occasions I have had to just sit there, listening to stereotypic comments about lesbians, without the courage to say anything for myself out of fear, just listening to the jokes. It is painful to sit and watch while my friends, classmates, and peers tell lesbian jokes right in front of me.

Imagine that this was your life, that you were this girl you are reading about, and that you had been living this life without any guidance, with fear, without hope. This is what I had to do as an assignment for my Counseling and Social class at GMU. The character you just read about, Suzanne Johnson, is not real. She was a product of my imagination who came to exist due to a class assignment to create a character adaptation. My assignment was to create and assume the character of a 16-year-old high school White female whose life experiences were like those you just read about.

The assignment proved to be more challenging than anyone can imagine, because not only was I being required to open up to different experiences from my own and to accept those who are very different from me, but I was also being forced to understand someone whose worldview I could not even begin to comprehend by trying to see the world from her own perspective, not mine. So the question posed by this assignment was whether I, a Hispanic man who has raised his two teenage children to be heterosexual themselves, would be able to comprehend the worldview of a person so different from me and everything I am familiar with.

No, creating Suzanne Johnson's character was not an easy task, for when I created her, I was 37 years old, a Hispanic married heterosexual male, father of a 16-year-old boy and a 12-year-old girl. Before this assignment, I had never read any literature about, nor had I ever had any real friendships with, any members of the Lesbian, Gay, Bisexual or Transgender (LGBT) population. In addition to my ignorance on the topic, my ethnic culture and military background worked against me for this assignment. I was raised in El Salvador until I was 19, and after moving to the United States and spending five years in California, I moved to Virginia and joined the U.S. Army, where I served as an enlisted soldier for over nine years. Nevertheless, thanks to the guidance of my professor in the program and to the literature that is available on the topic, Suzanne Johnson came to be. And even though she doesn't exist, she is very real as she exists in those who are like her, and who like her have to cope with people who don't accept them, people who judge them, people like us.

Imagine living in a world where you are not accepted by those around you. Imagine living in constant fear of everyone around you, especially those closest to you: your classmates, your friends, your coworkers, your employer, your parents, your siblings, your spouse, all of the people who are meaningful to you and even those who are not. Imagine living in a constant struggle to be someone you are not, trying not to be who you are, and hiding your true self even from yourself. Imagine the disgust of doing things you despise, and giving up doing things you would love to do. Imagine that one day you decide to confront everyone, and as you reveal the true self you have been hiding from everyone for all of your life, you find yourself not only alone and rejected, but also becoming a target for judgment, hate, violence, social isolation, and social injustice. Would you be strong enough to remain truthful to yourself, or would you give in to social pressures? For me, this assignment was the first time I was forced to ask myself these questions.

The GMU program infused multiculturalism and social justice in all the courses. I not only received training in counseling techniques, but in addition, I got to explore how social justice and multiculturalism played a role and influenced the topics covered and discussed in the classroom and in our class assignments. On a personal level, what this meant for me as a Hispanic was that as I learned new subjects in the classroom, it was within a context where my classmates and I became aware of how our different cultures and individual ethnic identities played a role and were affected by the topics we were learning. In other words, not only did we learn the topics required by the counseling program, but in addition, we also learned how multiculturalism and social justice affect not only our clients, but also our classmates and ourselves. Nowhere did this become truer than in the Counseling and Social Justice and Multicultural Counseling classes.

I am a Hispanic heterosexual male with a worldview typical of Latinos. Machismo is in my veins, and as a result, so is prejudice against LGBT people. At age 37, after having spent the first 19 years of my life in my native country, I was as homophobic as I could be. The interesting thing is that I was not aware of my homophobia. As a counseling student, I have always tried to understand and accept those around me, and before being confronted with my biases by the Counseling and Social Justice class and by the other classes taught in our program with a multicultural focus, I was sure that I had no problem accepting LGBT people. Thankfully, one thing that the GMU counseling program helped me to realize was that acceptance and tolerance are not enough when working with LGBT clients. If we are ever to become effective counselors with them, we not only have to explore our own biases and prejudice against them, but also, we must understand their worldview. This last item is where I've had the most difficulty while in the program. The only reason I have been able to become aware of my ignorance when dealing with LGBT people and with any other population from a culture different from my own has been because of the assignments in my graduate program, the readings required by the program, and most important, the guidance from professors who have made it a point to deliver their material with social justice and multiculturalism in mind.

I can't emphasize enough the importance of training counselors to become multiculturally competent, and to understand the social injustice issues their clients have to face daily everywhere—at work, at home, on the streets, when relaxing while watching television, when going out for dinner to a restaurant, etc. The counseling profession owes it to clients to stop ignoring the issues that affect those very mental health issues we are trying to help our clients to resolve. These days, no longer can we call ourselves professional counselors and psychologists if we choose to live in denial to social justice issues that affect our clients. These days the majority no longer has absolute power over the minorities, because the counseling profession is full of minority people who will no longer let issues such as White privilege or discrimination due to gender, class, ethnicity, color of skin, or sexual preference go unchallenged. It is time for the profession to be accountable and to lead the mental health profession out of ignorance and social correctness. We owe it to our clients, and most important of all, we owe to ourselves and to those we love, to push for mental health advocacy and awareness. No longer can we be keepers and enforcers of the status quo and call ourselves helpers in the profession. Our ignorance hurts us, it hurts our clients, and it hurts the mental health profession.

Programs like the one offered at George Mason University are gold to the mental health profession. The leadership this program has shown by freeing us counselors from the chains of social correctness and denial are going to create change in our profession, I have no doubt. This is because, just like me, there are many of my classmates who feel like I do, and who have been moved and motivated by our professors to be more than what social injustice allows us to be with our clients. We have been challenged and we are reacting by becoming carriers of change in the profession, change that will benefit our clients, not only those who follow society's expectations, but all of our clients, including those that society tries to ignore.

THE COURAGE TO UNEARTH WHAT I HAVE BURIED

Candace Fleming

As an African American woman, I was a little apprehensive about taking our Multicultural Counseling class. I was very reluctant to open up and share my experiences with racism with the class. I did not want painful memories and experiences that I have long since buried to resurface again. I did not want to feel vulnerable and most importantly I did not want to take down the walls that I have spent so much of my life building in order to protect myself from the pain and reality of racism. Ironically, what I discovered was that it was more painful for me to remain silent. I began to share my experiences with my classmates to prevent myself from internalizing them. It was my form of self care. I thought of my ancestors and all the obstacles they had overcome. To remain silent to some extent would be to deny their accomplishments and legacy. I also spoke up for my children. I am raising them to be proud of who they are. I could not look them in the eye if I remained silent. So I began to share. The opinions of others in my class were not my concern. My main concern was not succumbing to the evils of racism and not allowing it to penetrate and crush my spirit.

During the course of the semester, I became more comfortable sharing my experiences with racism with the class. In some ways it was very therapeutic for me. Some of the readings for this class validated my experiences. However, there was still something inside, warning me not to go any farther. It was not the pain and emotions that I feared, but the weakening of my coping skills and defense mechanisms that I developed over the years to help me function and cope with racism on a daily basis. I was afraid that if I truly allowed myself to explore and feel the reality and pain of racism, I would crumble and lose the ability to function and survive. This was my true fear. I could not afford to let this happen because I have children to raise and I have to remain strong and mentally tough in order to raise them to be strong, well-adjusted individuals.

This class had a significant impact on me. It was a very emotional experience. In the beginning I experienced a lot of anger and bitterness. I felt frustrated, vulnerable, defeated, and hopeless. Then, towards the end of the semester I began to feel inspired, validated, and a bit hopeful.

The most profound moment for me came at the beginning of the semester when Dr. Chung showed us a list of names. I did not recognize the names on the first list; however, I did recognize some of the names on the second list. The lists contained the names of individuals who had been reported missing. The first list was composed of missing minority individuals. At that moment, I realized that if my children were missing they would be on the first list, the list of names that no one has heard of or recognized. The ugliness and cruelty of racism became so apparent at that moment. Because of my children's brown skin, very little media attention would be given if they were missing. It was devastating to realize that the people I love and adore the most are not valued at all in this society.

I cried after that class. The thought still lingers in the back of my mind. When I shared this with the class, Dr. Chung replied by saying, then we (the people in this class) will help you look for your children. I believe that most of my classmates would help me if such a terrible thing were to happen, but what an awful thought.

There were times during the semester I felt I was regressing instead of progressing. I felt myself growing angry, bitter, resentful, and suspicious. After hearing some of my classmates describe the racist comments and beliefs of their parents and other relatives, I became discouraged and felt hopeless. Most of my classmates were younger than I, and to hear some of the thoughts and beliefs that were expressed by their families was painful and depressing. As a result, I became somewhat suspicious of some of my White friends and their families. I could not help but wonder what they say when I am not around. Do they have similar thoughts or feelings about me and my family?

Sharing my experiences with the class was difficult at times. I sometimes felt like an animal at the zoo. People like to visit the zoo so they can see and observe the animals, knowing that it is not a good environment for them to be in. They know it is not in the best interest of the animal to live in the zoo, but still they look and stare, then walk by. The animal is kept there, on display for the benefit or entertainment of others. I felt some of my classmates did the same thing with me. They were interested in getting a glimpse of what it is like for a minority to live in a racist society, but they were just walking by.

I have always been aware of racism and discrimination. It has just been part of my life experience. However, this class has forced me to really examine the impact and effects of racism, and accept that it is real. I can no longer just think, assume, or suspect that I have experienced it; I now know I have. For example, when I experience racism I sometimes try to convince myself that racism is not the reason the person in the store ignored me or was rude to me. Sometimes, I may justify an incident by telling myself that the individual was just having a bad day, or that is how the individual interacts with everyone, all the while knowing what was really happening. This class has taught me that my gut is usually right.

In some ways living in such a racist society is insanity. Being despised and hated because of your race is absurd. Yet, most minorities manage to persevere and are quite successful at coping with the insanity.

The challenge ahead of me is remaining strong and not allowing myself to be discouraged by others. Racism is painful and unfortunately it is a part of my life. I have to continue to work hard and not let it hinder or deter me from attaining my goals and dreams. I have to make sure that I do not let it ever get the best of me, or my children.

My heart is heavy right now as I write this. Racism and discrimination are tremendous burdens. However, I take comfort in knowing that I am strong and I am not afraid to stand up for myself or my family. I know I will be a great advocate for others who may need my help one day and this is what will keep me going. I will continue to move forward.

RECOMMENDATIONS

I encourage students taking a Multicultural Counseling course to be open to the experience. I encourage them to share their experiences no matter how sad or unpleasant they may be. There is always something to be learned from others' experiences. You never know how your story could impact and help someone else. There is also something very therapeutic and freeing about sharing.

There is nothing more powerful than witnessing the growth that someone achieves after sharing a painful story or experience that they kept hidden because they were ashamed or embarrassed. We have to share these experiences. Keeping them buried or hidden is one way racism is able to continue to fester in our society.

It may be difficult at times to listen to others share their experiences, but keep an open mind and try not to let it affect you personally. Let your classmates know that it is okay to discuss discrimination and racism. Participate and try to work through it. As my professor would often say, "Trust the process."

We are all affected by racism, some more directly than others, but it impacts us all. In order to be truly competent and effective counselors we must examine how we have been influenced by certain messages in society. We have to go there. Actively participating in a Multicultural Counseling class can help us explore and confront our biases, thus enabling us to better serve our future clients.

The Journey from Unawareness to Social Justice Advocate

Brad J. Pabian

I am a 31-year-old Caucasian male and I grew up in Long Island, New York in a mostly White, upper-middle-class neighborhood. I attended primary school with little to no contact with people from other races and cultures. I never really socialized with friends outside of my culture and race, nor did I have any desire to have friends from diverse backgrounds. All of my parents' friends were White; all of their friends' friends were White, and all of my friends were White. Basically, I had a very narrow worldview. The thing about having a narrow or ignorant worldview is that you lack knowledge of and are unaware that you even have a narrow worldview until something happens to change that view. Being aware of our own worldviews and those of clients is what the

GMU Counseling Program and the course on Counseling and Social Justice are all about.

I attended an almost all White liberal arts college in rural Pennsylvania. In fact, only when I studied abroad during my last year of college did I really begin to open my eyes to the world around. It was in Spain that I first realized and experienced what it was like to be an outsider, someone from another race and culture, someone who was different. I was "the minority" in Spain. I was an American in a foreign land and received lots of stares and even dirty looks. I remember thinking to myself, "Why are you staring at me? I don't deserve this. I'm not so different than you are." It was then that I began to realize, on a small scale, just how narrow my worldview had been for the first 20 years of my life and how prevalent oppressive forces and prejudices are in the world.

Taking Counseling and Social Justice really solidified for me how important it is for counselors to be aware of social justice issues and prejudices and to be advocates for clients. I never really thought of my role as a counselor as being one who pleads for the cause of another person until I came to GMU. I used to think my job was to help our clients mentally and emotionally, and that if social injustices were involved in their problems, then there was a limited amount I could do and basically clients would have to deal with it on their own terms. What GMU's mission statement describes and infuses into classes is that if social justices are not taken into account when doing counseling with clients, a whole piece is missing from the relationship and really limits our capacities to help them.

One assignment for our Counseling and Social Justice class was a character adaptation. The assignment entailed "becoming" our characters. The purpose was to get into the minds of people who have been oppressed. For my project I did extensive research on human trafficking. My character was a 24-year-old female from Indonesia who was trafficked to the United States. She was promised good pay and a place to stay working as a maid, but in the end, it was just a rouse to exploit someone who was underemployed in Indonesia.

I didn't really begin to "become" my character until I had gathered all of the data and started writing as if I were Muka, the trafficking victim. Muka's dream opportunity to work in the U.S. ended up being a complete farce. I didn't know what I would have done if I had been in her place. I began to imagine how exciting it must have been for someone from another country to come into the U.S. and find opportunity and freedom, and how depressing it must have been later to find herself exploited and manipulated. At this point, I began to remember my own excitement at the opportunity to live and attend school in another country and the prejudices I endured in Spain. I know that my experience in Spain was small compared to the horrors of being trafficked and deceived, but with my narrow worldview, it was all the personal experience that I had to utilize to try to "become" my character.

As I write this paper, I am aware of the angry and frustrated feelings inside me that probably are similar to those felt by a lot of people now in the U.S. who have been enslaved by human traffickers, and I believe this was the purpose of the assignment. I learned that, on some level, I needed to be aware of my own worldviews in order to help clients with their own personal worldviews and social justice issues. In my case, I needed to develop this ability better. I understand now that it is a part of our jobs to advocate for clients who have been oppressed. The Counseling and Social Justice class really mobilized in me a passion, a drive, to become more active in preserving the rights of clients, and to incorporate social justice and advocacy into my counseling practice. The class helped define a holistic approach to counseling that treats the entire client and enables us to empower clients to eventually advocate for themselves.

GMU'S counseling program has instilled in me the drive to affect systems. I attended another master's program before GMU, and it was good, but it did not mobilize me to become an advocate, or empower me to make an effort to change the oppressive forces of the dominant culture here in the U.S. The program really empowered us as counselors to be active participants, not just bystanders in making change. In addition, they taught us to have awareness that our worldview is not the only one and that "becoming" our clients

will make our abilities to bring about change even more powerful and enduring. The program made me feel like I could make a difference, but that it was up to me as to how small or how large I wanted to make it.

I Am an Advocacy Addict

Hollie M. Jones

When I decided to become a school counselor, I never considered the idea of self-reflecting on my own personal biases and how that would completely change my life. I grew up in a small town in Southern Virginia where everyone was either Black or White and things were kept very simple. I moved to Northern Virginia in 2006 where I began my own life as a 22-year-old female. I submerged myself in the diversity of the new area and enjoyed meeting people who were nothing at all like myself. Multicultural Counseling was a class that changed my entire life. I began my graduate program viewing the world with blinders on, and after reflecting on myself as a White female during the Multicultural Counseling course, I realized that I had been terribly blind.

Before the class, I had learned about process from my group counseling class, and I had learned that in order to be successful in group counseling, one had to trust the process of counseling. That never registered with me until I entered the Multicultural Counseling class. I remember sitting in my kitchen reading *A Race is a Nice Thing to Have* (Helms, 2008) which had been assigned in the class. I cried and allowed myself to fill up with anger, guilt, embarrassment, and shame. All I could see during the reading was my father, my grandparents, my mother, and all of those who played a role in my life growing up. I had been raised in a home that viewed the world through a very racist lens.

My sister had always dated African American men, and being the older of the two, I always felt it to be my job to help her hide this from our father. Every time the issue was brought up for his approval, it was quickly shot down with an argument filled with disgrace and shame towards my sister. How could she possibly date a Black guy and go against her family's beliefs? I used this, along with support from my classmates and Dr. Chung, to find the courage to speak out to my father about the issue of racism in our family. I became obsessed with educating him on social justice issues and would continuously call to talk to my mother or invite them up to attend a cultural experience I was attending in Northern Virginia. At first, they didn't hear me and were shocked that this was something I was "learning" at graduate school. My grandparents were also very appalled that this was my own developed view on social interaction. I was beginning to form my own values and beliefs, and for my family, it was a bit disappointing to see that my culture was developing into something very different from their own.

For the first time in my life, I realized that I was White. I understood that I was privileged in a way that others would never experience due to being persons of color. I too, had a color, and along with the color, White, came privilege. I realized how others of color viewed me as a blonde, White female and reflected on how I was then going to use this identity to connect to others. White privilege and race are not discussed because it makes people uncomfortable and defensive. My family spent some time being very uncomfortable, but soon realized that I was addicted to advocating and they had no other choice but to hear me.

Fighting through the guilt and shame, and then finding the courage to confront my family, affirmed for me that change happens over time and that even if I am only planting seeds with them now, over time they will listen. I had started the program in a committed five-year relationship, and after taking the Multicultural Counseling class, I realized that as a White female who had developed such passion for social justice work, I also needed a partner in life who supported my views. My relationship ended six months after taking the course due to the differences in values and beliefs we had about life. I felt almost renewed and ready to begin my journey the way I envisioned it to be. I had nothing holding me back and had developed a strong support system of family and colleagues who were ready to listen and support my desire for advocating.

We choose not to see the ugly, unjust issues in life when we are living in the skins of White privileged beings. One of our privileges is that we don't have to look; we don't have to live it. Past generations of those who held White privilege often abused the power they had and continued to feed into discrimination. I've learned that because I am a White female, people listen to me and will eventually hear me when I passionately advocate for students and those of color in any social injustices that may arise. I have a voice and the ability to speak up. My entire purpose in life changed after taking this Multicultural Counseling class. I processed feelings of guilt, shame, selfishness, courage, anger, frustration, and determination. My family has taught me a lot. I have learned that it's tough to talk about the ugly that's hidden under the rug so that the public doesn't know you're quietly racist, but it will bring a new realization to family members, and an overall sense of respect will develop.

I am a 5'0", blonde, White, privileged female and I have voice that I have chosen to use to speak out against social injustices. I would hope that those who read this reflection can relate and be willing to admit to their own views or biases and know that it's ok to remove your blinders and really take a look at your own color. The question next is, what are you going to do now that you can finally see?

I would suggest processing on your own to begin. Take that time out to cry, weep, and feel ashamed—ashamed that you weren't able to see until now. Admit to yourself that any biases you may have or that your family may have are ok. Give yourself permission to speak, because we may only be able to become who we allow ourselves to be. If we choose to look away and not speak out when discrimination occurs, then no matter what our values, we then still become the oppressor. Find courage through your classmates, your family, and professors. Living with White privilege is something many will never understand, but with this dispensation we can educate others about what it truly means to be living in our world as a White person of privilege. People who feel safe will be willing to disclose more. Connect to your colleagues, trust in them, and rely on them to help support you through this process. This is the process you must trust in order to successfully develop a true sense of multicultural awareness.

Students of color should also know that being angry and filled with hate towards the White person is also ok. Give yourself permission to be angry. Your challenge will be moving out of anger and into trust towards your fellow White colleagues and peers. I would suggest being as open as you are able to allow yourself to be. Our world has chosen to continue unjust actions that just look different than they may have years ago. Oppression occurs every day in every occupation, school, and life experience. We can all play a role in highlighting these actions and educating others on how a just system is something we all need to be advocating for.

It begins with discussion, communicating, and talking about the pain we all have that racial differences have created. There is a lot of hurt in the world caused by discrimination and transgenerational trauma for all cultures. For those living in a White privileged world like I am, we can all address this hurt if we simply find the courage to admit to what we've chosen not to see until now. Once you've found that courage to admit to these prejudices and then speak out to those in your life, you will begin to feel empowered, strong, and ready to speak out about issues you never even thought would be part of your life.

EMBRACING MY CULTURAL HERITAGE AND BEING A SOCIAL JUSTICE AGENT: A POSITIVE BUT LESS PLEASANT JOURNEY

Diana P. Ortiz

My name is Diana *(De-a-nna)* and I am Latina; I am part of the largest minority group in the United States. I am also a doctoral student in the counselor education program at GMU, where I also completed my master's degree.

Through the past years, I have taken the task of being thoughtful and have translated thoughts and good intentions into actions. It did not happen instantaneously, and the master's and doctoral programs at GMU had a lot to do with my growth; every class and each of the projects in it have provided a new opportunity to reaffirm some of my beliefs, challenge myself, and give me a new chance to grow. Through the next few pages, I will describe some critical moments of what has been one of the most positive experiences in my life. Warning: I said positive, but not *pleasant!*

I choose to be genuine in my reflections, as I share my journey with you, the reader. This expedition has been full of ups and downs, mysteries and revelations, pain and healing, tears and laughs. The passion for the work I do as a mental health professional and my advocacy work for the underserved population has helped me remain clear on my purpose to continue in this never-ending journey.

A Cultural Shock

I was born and raised in Colombia, and a few years ago I embarked in this multicultural and social justice journey. Six years ago, I landed in New York City after being recruited by a social service agency. For a new professional, the option was attractive; the agency offered me housing, transportation, and a decent salary (compared to the Colombian standards, not the U.S.). In exchange, the agency had a fully trained bilingual professional for cheap labor. Of course, I did not realize the last part at first! Nonetheless, this experience could very well have been the beginning of a long process that clearly enhanced my awareness and interest in becoming an advocate and an agent of change.

At that point, I was changing without knowing it; externally, I was being bombarded by attitudes, messages, ads, and tons of information that did not make sense to me. It didn't take too much to realize I was not feeling comfortable in my skin. I could not understand why I was *classified* as a minority. Once I landed in this country, I was no longer a *mestiza*, part of a big majority, with privileges and commodities. I was automatically a *Latina*, a woman of color, a minority. That was a tremendous shock, and my life is divided into before and after this experience. I thought I knew what racism was. I thought I was competent working with different ethnicities in my country, so I thought I could translate those experiences into my work in the U.S. I thought I was a social justice advocate because I worked with those underserved. Clearly, I did not know much about the tough realities in the U.S.

Let me be clear, in my country we have had many struggles; however, I would lie if I said I understood then—before I came to this country—what I understand now. Experiencing in my own skin what it means to be a minority, a person of color, provided me the opportunity to look internally and make decisions as to where I wanted to stand in this world. The first two years in the U.S. were very difficult; I was uncomfortable having to select the Latina/Hispanic checkbox. I was mortified with the idea of being associated with a group of people who seemed so distant from my culture, from who I was. At least, that's what I thought. It took some tough experiences to open my eyes and finally put words to the strong feelings that kept coming back. It has been a long process.

I did not like being associated with the sexy Latina stereotype (exotic, strong accent, great curves). I am proud of the beauty of our women, but as Latinas, we have much more to offer and be recognized for. We are worthy because of who we are, and not only for the curves we carry, the size of our bras, or the way we move our hips on the dance floor. I was not happy with the idea of people judging me for the way I look or for the accent I have. So, although I was not part of the problem, I could be part of the solution. I wanted to be proactive and change what was not helping me as a woman of color and help others in similar situations. At that point in my life, I could choose to live the struggles and try to adjust to them, or be part of the change. I was inclined to combat the fear and be active in challenging the status quo of what needed to be different. I needed more tools, though.

A Turning Point: Going To Grad School

After a year of being a foreigner, an immigrant working in this country, I felt like I only had a hammer and a screwdriver in my toolbox, and I was missing the rest of my tools. Although I felt inspired by each of the families I worked with, I also felt sad and confused. I told my supervisor I was applying to grad school, and I wanted to have a letter of recommendation from him; he looked at me and smiled. Then, he proceeded to explain how expensive and difficult my goal was. He said to me, "I know you are bright, but you are poor. Besides, you are a terrible writer. . . . Are you sure about this? Don't you have to go to Colombia anyway?" It has been more than five years since that conversation, and I still carry the stigma that I am not a good writer. It doesn't hurt anymore, but it is a constant reminder of my long path to where I am now.

Before coming to the program at GMU, I was very naïve about my racial and ethnic identity. I knew little about the subtle, and not so subtle, messages in my supervisor's words. I did not feel good that day, but I am glad that a stronger force kept me going. The constant racial microaggressions we experience every day, those *little* moments make us doubt whether we are overreacting, misinterpreting, or misunderstanding part of the message. Those moments are hard to swallow and ignore; they are so subtle and emotionally draining at the same time.

Embracing myself. At the time I started the first semester of my master's program, I was trying very hard to hide my accent. I tried to *blend,* to talk fast, and put a lot of emphasis on the way I looked and the image I wanted to show. My professors saw what I could not see at that time. They challenged me. They helped me process some of the raw feelings I still had. I finally was able to connect what I thought with what I felt. The program at GMU lives and breathes its five core components: multiculturalism, social justice, international reach, leadership, and advocacy. No matter how difficult the classes were,

I finally felt at *home*. It felt safe to be vulnerable and learn with all my senses.

Graduate school changed me not only professionally, but personally. I experienced a profound change; I wish all of us could have that privilege. I confronted my biases and prejudice. I cried and saw myself in the mirror differently; I learned and forgot. I thrived and became a better version of myself. I was aware of new realities, so I could sharpen my skills and open my mind and my soul to new knowledge. A commitment to change and take action is what ultimately makes me a different person today. I remember being seated in the multicultural and social justice classes in the master's program feeling happy to finally understand concepts such as *transgenerational trauma* and *internalized racism*. I felt more confident with my new skills and knowledge. By seeing myself in a better place, I could honestly and genuinely help others who had embarked on such a journey.

My acculturation process would have never been the same if I had not had the space and opportunity to reflect back, read, validate my experiences, and find new meanings for my emotions. Through those classes, I was able to make a conscious decision about taking an active role to transform today's reality for a more just and fair world. I was challenged by the readings, by the class discussions, by the reflections papers, and by projects I had to develop. With so many valuable hands-on experiences, it seems almost impossible not to learn!

In my Counseling and Social Justice class I learned about how numbers translate into issues, and issues into opportunities to act. I learned that no matter how good my intentions are, if I don't do something about them, nothing will change. I learned that change is active, it happens everyday, and I needed to have the guts to live a life worth living. I challenged my classmates, and my classmates taught me to be tough without losing my vulnerable side. I learned so much that I had more questions than answers. I knew I needed to learn more.

I decided to pursue a doctoral degree because I wanted to support and facilitate this process for other counselors in training. I have a mission for life to educate others in what human suffering looks like. I have a purpose in life to inspire future counselors and educators to challenge themselves. I want to cross borders and show young boys and girls that no matter what their skin color looks like, how tall or short they are, how *thick* their accents are, they can and should have the same opportunities as the majority. It is my promise to you and to me.

A New Self: Transformation Through Activism and Social Change

As a result of my graduate training, I embrace my cultural heritage and continue to learn about my community, my values, and my beliefs. I think of myself as a woman of color, a strong Latina, an immigrant, a daughter, a wife, a sister, a friend, a counselor, a neighbor, a leader, a voice, and a role model for other young Latinas who are straddling two worlds. I believe everyone should have the same access to opportunities. I envision a time in which I will not be the only Latina in a doctoral class or at a leadership meeting at a county office. I don't want to be the *exception to the rule*. I envision a time where I don't have to prove what I know once people identify my accent.

I decided to pursue a doctoral degree so I could have more sophisticated tools to combat injustice and transform archaic and unbalanced systems. Research helps me demonstrate what we want to change and how to do so. Leadership roles give me the opportunity to be effective and influence change. My day is full of different tasks and things to do, and I am happy to be exhausted at the end of the day. I don't want to miss an opportunity to *be* the change, to be where I need to be for my community and future generations.

One of the best things I have learned in my education is that I choose to be where I am, and with my choices I feel responsible for the privilege that comes with opportunities. I am thankful I am not the only one in this fight, and I surround myself with strong peers, and my support network is a safe place where I can recharge my energy to keep going. I have learned fear and inspiration can coexist at times. I have been fearful to continue seeing the injustice around me, and the fear translates into passion and energy to fight harder. I am no longer insulted by being classified as Latina; I am humble, honored, and willing to embrace my new identity in order to speak out for my fellow women and men of color whose voices are constantly unheard. I keep having experiences that are not pleasant, but they certainly are positive. They become reasons to continue thriving.

I dare you to dream of a better world. I dare you to embrace your cause and do something about it.

REFERENCES

Croteau, J. M. (1999). One struggle through individualism: Toward an antiracist White racial identity. *Journal of Counseling & Development, 77*, 30–31.

Helms, J. E. (2008). *A race is a nice thing to have: A guide to being a white person or understanding the white persons in your life* (2nd ed.). Hanover, MA: Microtraining.

PART IV

CRITICAL SOCIAL JUSTICE TOOLS

9

THE CRITICAL INTERSECTION OF SOCIAL CHANGE AND SOCIAL JUSTICE

It is not the strongest of the species that survive, nor the most intelligent,
but the one most responsive to change.

(Author unknown)

If you want to make enemies, try to change something.

(Woodrow Wilson)

Change is the law of life and those who look only to the past or
present are certain to miss the future.

(John F. Kennedy)

WARM UP EXERCISE

1. *Try to recall a time when you personally changed. What prompted you to decide to change?*

2. *What were the barriers that you faced in making the change happen?*

3. *Did the change occur as you hoped, or were there difficulties along the way?*

4. *What are some of the things that you want to change now? What is holding you back?*

5. *Have you observed or heard about people who are not able to express their personal rights? If so, what have you seen these individuals or groups try to do to transform that situation and gain their rights? What happened?*

6. *Consider what process means and all that goes into the saying, "Change is a process."*

Working on social justice and human rights issues involves a variety of components: social change, advocacy, leadership, and empowerment. To be an effective change agent, it is necessary to possess the skills of leadership, advocacy, and empowerment. Since social change is at the very essence of social justice work, it is necessary to understand the theories and models of change. This chapter will describe models of social change and their relationship to social justice and human rights. The chapter will help you understand the multidimensionality of social change, gain an understanding about the relationship between social change and social justice and human rights, and offer insights about how to be an effective change agent.

The Relationship Between Social Justice and Social Change

All of us working in the field of psychology and counseling are change agents. The goal of our work, whether it is with one client, groups, families, or larger communities, is to promote healthy positive change. Traditionally the emphasis of psychotherapy was on changing the individual. Incorporating social justice and human rights into counseling and psychotherapy broadens the dimensions and scope of change to include groups, families, and systems. Underlying the inclusion of systemic change is the assumption that mental health work is not driven by individual psychopathology and that the individual is not always at fault. Essentially, it is viewing the individual in the context of social, political, economic, historical, cultural, and environmental issues, and inherent in this view is the implication that the larger system must change. Embedded in and central to larger systemic change are social justice and human rights.

The emphasis on social justice is based on the assumption that individual circumstances, particularly those related to empowerment, equity, fairness, and justice, are influenced by external factors and subsequently not solely within the individual's control. Given the presumption that the problems of the individual are largely created by and from the community and society at large, interventions are needed that address the context of the individual's problems. For example, I (Fred) was once asked to consult in a public school to address mental health issues with an entire ninth grade class. This happened after numerous seventh graders came to the counselors and psychologists complaining about being bullied, discriminated against, and harassed by the ninth graders. Rather than attend to one after another of the seventh grade students, after consultation with the school, I decided to generate an intervention with the entire ninth grade and work on broader issues of safety, bullying, and fairness that affected the entire middle school. This is a good example of moving away from individual psychotherapy that would emphasize counseling with the more than 30 seventh graders who were having mental health problems as a result of the actions of the ninth graders. Instead, the focus was on changing the larger system that was steeped in racism, intolerance, and bullying.

Hence social justice and human rights work is closely intertwined with social change. This is in contrast to general change models (i.e., individuals changing personal behaviors, such as overeating, drinking too much, or smoking). We would define social change to include the changing or altering of systems (such as institutions and organizations) and structures (such as laws, policies, procedures, social roles, and functions) that hinder, obstruct, block, impede, and interfere with positive and optimal growth, development, opportunities, and physical and psychological well-being for *all* individuals, families, groups, and communities.

Social change can occur on individual, organizational, community, and societal levels. Even so, we would suggest that regardless of the level at which the change occurs, when counseling toward social justice, the impact of the change ultimately affects multiple levels (i.e., individuals and their families, groups, and communities). Mental health social justice work is therefore how we, as helping professionals, proactively, consciously, and intentionally contribute to social change. The aim of our counseling in social justice work is to propel social change that will intervene in and eliminate, reduce, or prevent existing and potential inequalities, "isms," unfair treatment, and disproportionate distribution of and access to wealth, resources, and opportunities. Understanding social change and the components of change—its process, effects, and impact—is essential for counselors and psychologists.

Change Is Not Easy

> *We would rather be ruined than changed; we would rather die in our dread than climb the cross of the moment and let our illusions die.*

>   (W. H. Auden)

> *Those who expect moments of change to be comfortable and free of conflict have not learned their history.*

>   (Joan Wallach Scott)

Change is everywhere. As counselors and psychologists, we live, breathe, and support change. Our world is filled with a constant bombardment of change. We continually hear media sound bites, view through the Internet the up-to-the-minute details of a community in protest in remote areas of China or Colombia, watch technological advances of yesterday become old today, and experience the rapid obsolescence of our state-of-the-art cell phones and computers. We have access through TV and the Internet to views of disasters around the world as they happen, we get front row seats to watch wars and conflicts "live" from our living room chairs, and we watch concerts from around the world that are directed to benefit social issues such as HIV/AIDS, global warming, or global poverty. For us as counselors and psychologists, these issues come into play both through the world we live and work in and our clients' worldviews.

Despite the fact that change is everywhere and the counseling and mental health professions

are aimed at positive change, change remains difficult for many people. Personal and social transformation presents a dilemma: Do we stay the same course or modify the course? The translation for the Chinese character for the word *crisis* clearly depicts the predicament of change. The two characters that make up the word *crisis* in Chinese are literally translated to mean *danger* and *opportunity.* Change can be an opportunity, a chance to transform, grow, and develop. At the same time, change can be dangerous, scary, and fearful, since it alters how one is and how one does things. Consequently change is both exciting and anxiety producing. It should be noted that the mixed reaction to change happens with both major changes, such as stopping a personal addiction, and more minor changes, such as modifying a pattern of interaction with a loved one or losing a small amount of weight. Depending on the degree of change, there is an accompanying degree of discomfort, anxiety, frustration, and distress, which may provoke fear, uncertainty, tension, and insecurity.

To fully understand personal and social change and its relationship to social justice, we would like to continue by describing psychological change and discussing the principles of social change. A brief summary of community social change models will be presented. To help illuminate these concepts, we will also examine how to infuse issues of change into social justice work through a discussion of the role of systems in social change, and the part that power and resistance play in promoting social change. Recommendations about social change will conclude the chapter.

THE PSYCHOLOGY OF CHANGE

The research has shown that counselors and psychologists do in fact create change (Lambert, Shapiro, & Bergin, 1986; Smith, Glass, & Miller, 1980). Interestingly, it has also been found that the kind of growth that results from psychotherapy and counseling can also result from other mechanisms outside of therapy (Hubble, Duncan, &

Miller, 1999). Prochaska and his colleagues (Prochaska, 1999; Prochaska & DiClemente, 1982; Prochaska, DiClemente, & Norcross, 1992; Prochaska, Norcross, & DiClemente, 1994) found that individuals use the same change strategies in therapy that they use in solving other life problems. For example, if I am trying to exercise more, I would apply the same tactics in my personal efforts to exercise as I would in counseling, where I am attempting to change the interaction patterns I have with my brother or sister. This presents interesting findings, illustrating that individuals have the potential to independently change without the assistance of psychotherapy (Norcross & Prochaska, 1986a, 1986b).

In an attempt to explain how people change, regardless of whether or not it is with professional help, Prochaska and DiClemente (1992) developed the transtheoretical model (TTM) of change. The TTM is one of the more comprehensive models of change in the field of psychotherapy and counseling, and it provides an explanation about the various stages of change. Research about the TTM has revealed that it is a viable model in settings ranging from outpatient therapy to self-change (e.g., DiClemente & Hughes, 1990; DiClemente & Prochaska, 1985; DiClemente, Prochaska, & Gillbertini, 1985; Lam, McMahon, Priddy, & Gehred-Schultz, 1988; McConnaughy, DiClemente, Prochaska, & Velicer, 1989; Prochaska & DiClemente, 1992). The TTM consists of five stages of change: precontemplation, contemplation, preparation, action, and maintenance (see Figure 9.1). We believe it is a critical basis for psychologists and counselors to understand and use as a springboard to social justice and human rights work, so we will explain the stages in more depth below.

The first stage, precontemplation, has been described as one of the most difficult (Brogan, Prochaska, & Prochaska, 1999). Individuals in this stage have no intention of changing. Many are unaware of their problem or even the need to change. Clients in this stage are typically in therapy because there is pressure by others (such as a partner, spouse, or family members) and may exhibit change that coincides with external pressure. So if my family wants me to stop eating

fried food because of my high cholesterol, then I may cut back when family members are around. When I am alone, however, I may continue to eat fried food, since I really don't believe this change is necessary. Thus, once the pressure is diminished, people quickly return to their old ways. During this stage, change is cursory and not sustained.

The contemplation stage finds individuals a little further along, with awareness of and a commitment to overcome existing problems. Thus, the person eating fried food now realizes that his or her cholesterol level is high and that it could lead to a heart attack. Despite this awareness and a promise to change, there is still not a commitment to take action (Prochaska, DiClemente, & Norcross, 1992). The person knows what needs to be done but is thinking about it rather than doing something. For example, we know that exercise is good for us, and we may seriously think about doing some type of physical exercise. We can contemplate doing exercise for many months or even years, but not actually take the steps to go to the gym. A danger in this stage is that individuals may become stuck.

In the third stage, the preparation stage, there is a combination of intention and behavior. Individuals in this stage intend to take action soon, and often have unsuccessfully tried to change in the past. Such a person may think, "I want to stop eating fried food," or "I want to exercise," but not yet have actually stopped eating fried food or started exercising. In this stage, there may be small behavioral changes, but an effective overall change has not yet taken root. When one is in the preparation stage, there is the intention to take action in the near future. So in this stage, I may have purchased a steamer to cook my food as an alternative to fried food, or purchased workout clothes in preparation for exercise that I will begin at some point. Prochaska et al. (1992) call this the early action stage.

The fourth stage, action, differs from the preparation stage, since individuals actually take steps to address their problems. I am now cooking with my steamer and going to the gym three times a week. This stage is characterized by overt behavioral changes and requires considerable

Figure 9.1 Transtheoretical Model (TTM) of Change

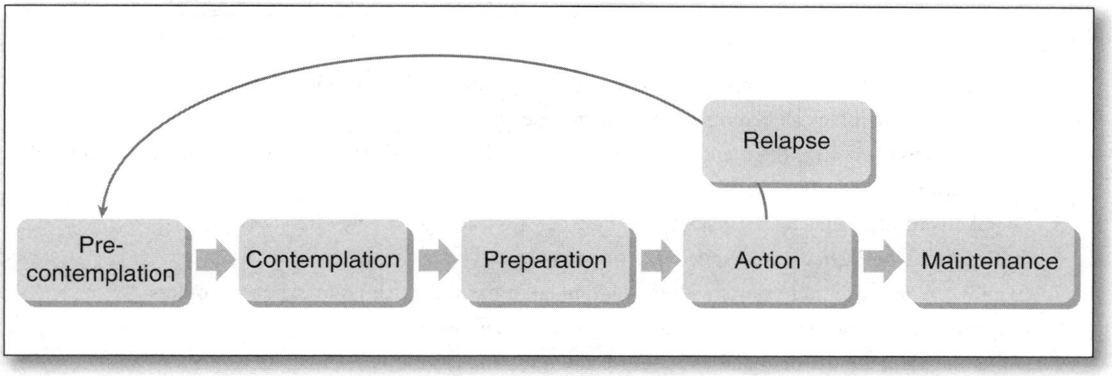

Source: Prochaska & DiClemente (1982).

commitment of time and energy. Individuals in this stage talk about "working hard to change" and "actually doing something about the problem." This stage should not be confused with the actual change, which requires movement to the last stage to be considered complete in this model. According to Prochaska et al. (1992), the hallmarks of the action stage are the modification of the target behavior to an acceptable criterion and significant overt efforts to change. Finally, one is actually "doing it."

Maintenance is the final stage, in which individuals work to sustain the gains attained during the action stage. This stage may be viewed as static; however, this phase is just as important as the action stage, because it is a continuation and maintenance of change. Not only have I begun going to the gym to work out, but I am continuing to do so. Preserving changes can be lifelong work, and can be seen in the efforts of individuals dealing with addictive behaviors. The hallmark of this stage is stabilizing and maintaining behavioral change that avoids and prevents relapse.

Individuals who reach the final stage and then relapse will wind up at the beginning stage once again, necessitating repeating the change process through all of the five stages. So, if I revert back to eating French fries and fried dough after cooking with my steamer for six months and completely avoiding any fried foods, when I try again in my eighth month to go back to the steamer, I will begin back again at the precontemplation and contemplation stages, considering again whether or not it makes sense to change. Thus, the process of change once again begins from the start. These five stages are important to keep in mind as we move into a discussion about the principles of social change in the next section.

PRINCIPLES OF SOCIAL CHANGE

Now that we have discussed how people change, we would like to broaden this change model to include the broader sphere of social change. Moving from individual to social change provides important building blocks and a foundation for social justice work. In the next section we examine some of the basic principles of social change adapted from Homan (2008). It is important to note that the list of principles is not exhaustive, but highlights fundamental beliefs that we think are essential for counselors and psychologists doing social justice and human rights counseling (see Table 9.1). In addition, although there are ideas that overlap some of the principles, we feel it is important to address each principle separately to present the full scope.

Table 9.1   Principles of Change

Description

1. Critical link—healthy environments lead to psychologically healthy people.
2. Social change involves an ecological systems perspective.
3. To constructively change the social environment, mental health professionals must plan and be intentional.
4. Social justice is not arbitrary.
5. Social change demands taking risks to use new behavior and go in new directions.
6. Critical to social justice work is the issue of power.
7. Even when empowerment starts with the individual, it has the potential to expand to others.
8. Empowerment means partnerships, not therapeutic imperialism.
9. Build on existing individual and community strengths and assets.
10. Identify and respect cultural diversity.
11. Change requires awareness, understanding, and appreciation of sociopolitical, historical, psychological, cultural, and ecological perspectives.
12. Change is a process, not a quick fix.
13. Change can come in small or large quantities.
14. There is a difference between planning change, on the one hand, and implementing change and action, on the other.
15. Promoting social justice through social change is not about ego; it is about working toward a larger cause.
16. Effective social change agents combine learning and teaching.

Fundamental Beliefs and Principles of Change

1) The critical link—healthy environments lead to psychologically healthy people. Our environments shape us. A healthy and safe environment correlates with psychological well-being and mental health. In contrast, an unsafe, depressed, or distressed community is more likely to create distress (Homan, 2008). It is important that counselors and psychologists doing social justice work understand this correlation and how it impacts counseling interventions. Clearly addressing and promoting community change, either with the client's own exploration of advocacy or directly with the surrounding community, has significant implications in fostering healthy and safe communities that value individuals, families, and the community as a whole. As social justice counselors and psychologists, we independently and collaboratively challenge circumstances that do not promote equity, fairness, and equality.

2) Social change involves an ecological systems perspective. Since individuals do not live in total isolation, it is critical that we examine the issues from a holistic macro perspective. An example is legislation regarding gay marriage. Even though this is an individual issue, it can affect a neighborhood; it can also affect a city, a state, or the country. (See Table 9.2 for an example of how this might occur.) Other examples are the shootings at Columbine High School and Virginia Tech that generated discussion about gun violence and legislation not only within those particular communities and states but also at the federal level. With globalization, addressing issues on multiple levels is critical—what is happening in the United States today impacts other parts of the world.

An ecological approach (Bemak & Conyne, 2004) involves looking at problems from a larger systemic perspective. There is an inherent relationship between various subsystems and the larger system. Changing any level or part of the larger system will therefore affect the entire ecosystem. For example, if a woman continually hears sexually inappropriate remarks directed to her at work, there may be an impact on her mental and subsequently physical health. Her work productivity may diminish, and her personal relationships may suffer. In fact, when looking further into the problem, one might find a number of other women at the same worksite experiencing the same problems. To adequately address this problem, a counselor or psychologist doing social justice work would not only discuss with the individual how to better cope with her situation, but also respond to the sexism and discrimination in her environment. Looking at the situation from an ecological macro standpoint, one would need to strategize with the client or clients about how to advocate within the system. If the professional was employed at the worksite, it would be important to address the larger scope of the issue (e.g., sexism, discrimination, and harassment) that is inherently a part of the

workplace and affects numbers of women. Therefore, it is critical that the issue be examined from a holistic perspective.

3) **To constructively change the social environment, mental health professionals must plan and be intentional.** Social justice work, by nature, changes the status quo. When we aim to transform and improve on current conditions, we must be deliberate and intentional. The result of such intentionality is to interrupt the status quo that reinforces and maintains social inequalities and unfair treatment. As we anticipate resistance and understand process, we develop plans of action to address expected hesitation. For example, if a counseling center were trying to shift to incorporate more group counseling, it could be predicted that the center's professionals who are more comfortable doing individual counseling will resist the change. Planning ahead, an employee might think of responding to this proposal with the notion that the center's psychologists and counselors could self-select to increase the amount of group counseling they do, rather than having to change their practice as a mandated clinical requirement.

Table 9.2 How an Individual Issue Can Affect a Larger Community

Uniting American Families Act (UAFA)

The Uniting American Families Act (UAFA) could turn lives around for gay and lesbian Americans who have foreign-born partners. The UAFA could make it possible for heterosexual and homosexual Americans and permanent residents to sponsor their partners in order for them to obtain legal residency here in the United States. The bill was introduced in the Senate and in the House, and if it passes, it would add "permanent partnership" after the words "spouse" and "marriage" in certain sections of the Immigration and Nationality Act. The couple would have shared financial responsibilities, and neither partner could be married to or in a "permanent partnership" with anybody else.

    The proposal defines "permanent partnership" as a "committed intimate relationship in which both parties intend a lifelong commitment." If any fraudulent activity occurs, the fines incurred would be the same as those for fake marriages: Couples can face up to five years in prison and a $250,000 fine. As of now, there are approximately 35,000 binational, same-sex couples in the United States. If this new legislation is extended to gays and lesbians, then couples would not have to turn to illegal marriages or exiling themselves from this country to be with their partners.

Source: "Separation anxiety" (2009).

4) Social justice is not arbitrary. There is a need to focus on an unambiguous gripping issue that violates human rights. The actual violation of human rights must be clear to parties involved. Clarity about particular injustices helps unify those involved and solidifies direction and goals. Educating clients or others about social injustices is an important aspect of our mental health work.

5) Social change demands taking risks to use new behaviors and go in new directions. Social change requires that one move away from old ways of thinking and doing things. New directions and new behaviors are integral to facilitating social justice. A counselor or psychologist must aid individuals, families, groups, and communities to develop new approaches as they tackle the new problems. Contemplating new behaviors is linked to the transtheoretical model (TTM) for change that was discussed in the last section and requires the individual to go through its respective stages. Finding new ways involves the ability, courage, and vision to be a risk taker as well as an ability to openly explore new directions with clients and others.

6) Critical to social justice work is the issue of power. It has long been understood that those who hold the power and consciously and unconsciously define the structure, norms, and dynamics within a social context are reluctant to let go. To confront or challenge the status quo means to challenge an existing power base. This reality is often juxtaposed against negative connotations for the meaning of "power" within the realm of counseling and psychology, whereby power may be associated with the negative elements of authority, domination, force, and coercion. Yet power is a critical tool in social change and social justice, and within the framework of social justice work, it has a positive subtext. Considering power within the context of social justice and social change relates to using power to be proactive. It means using power to positively act on ideas and to challenge power blocks that inhibit or suppress equity and justice. In fact, power is an essential ingredient for social change and a tool that mental health professionals must become comfortable using as they challenge and advocate for social justice.

A culturally insensitive clinician named Stephen provides an example. Stephen was working in a residential treatment program for youth. Although he was liked by staff, Stephen harmed the youth by ignoring and excusing problem behaviors such as drinking or using marijuana. Rather than confronting his young clients about the behavior, Stephen made private "deals" with the adolescents that he would not report them if they behaved well when he was around. In preparing to confront Stephen, it was important to know who his supporters were, what his power base was, and who would side with the ideas of treatment integrity and consequences for problem behaviors rather than support a friend. It was determined that the associate director of the program would be highly supportive of treatment integrity and was a clear power base, so this person was the first point of contact in eventually having Stephen removed from his position. An in-depth discussion of power and social justice work will be presented in Chapter 10.

7) Even when empowerment starts with the individual, it has the potential in social justice work to expand to others. Empowerment may start with one individual with whom we are counseling. Counseling may be helping clients gain confidence, take action, challenge inequities, or fight for equal treatment. Yet, even when working directly with an individual, we are working within the ecological context that was discussed above. Our belief is that empowerment does not happen in isolation, separate and detached from others in the client's life, but rather impacts others in that person's world. Social networks are part of a client's life, so that as clients become empowered, they also generate change in their surrounding environments. When one person begins to speak out and question inequalities and discrimination in the community, this has the potential to quickly lead to others joining.

8) Empowerment means partnership, not therapeutic imperialism. When we are working with clients, we are creating an equal partnership as we do social justice counseling. We are not the experts who are telling clients what to do; we are not controlling therapeutic sessions and setting up a codependent relationship; we do not assume roles of therapeutic imperialists. Rather we are fostering a therapeutic partnership that aims for advocacy and social change.

9) **Build on existing individual and community strengths and assets.** Change agents must be able to identify what strengths and resources already exist both within the individual and in the community. Capitalizing and building on these resources provides a good starting point for promoting social change. Knowing that a client has leadership qualities and experiences or community organizing skills helps the counselor or psychologist acknowledge and build on those skills to promote positive social change. Acknowledging existing strengths is instrumental in helping individuals and communities recognize what they already do and strategies that can be useful in addressing social inequities.

10) **Identify and respect cultural diversity.** Effective social change requires a clear and solid understanding of multicultural competencies. Our communities are composed of people from different racial, ethnic, and cultural backgrounds. The diversity within our communities and societies calls for us to be multiculturally competent as counselors and psychologists. We must be aware of, understand, appreciate, and honor different cultural perspectives and worldviews, as well as culturally dissimilar values, means of resolving problems, senses of time, negotiation and communication styles, and so on. We know that multiculturalism has the potential to generate a tremendous richness and openness and is conducive to social justice work.

An example is our experience when we brought a mental health team to work on an Indian reservation in California after the 2007 San Diego wildfires. We had heard about the tremendous destruction there and that there was a great need for culturally responsive mental health support. Having previously worked on reservations, we respectfully approached the Tribal Council to ask for permission to work on the reservation. The meeting with the Tribal Council consisted of a few hours of discussion, getting to know one another, seeing if our goals were in line, and an unspoken testing by the Tribal Council to see if we were truly respectful of the Indian culture and ways, and whether or not the mental health support we were proposing would fit into that cultural framework.

11) **Change requires awareness, understanding, and appreciation of the sociopolitical, historical, psychological, cultural, and ecological perspectives.** A critical element of being multiculturally competent is to be aware of, acknowledge, understand, and appreciate the sociopsychopolitical and historical perspectives of social justice issues within the individual's cultural background. Particular groups have experienced and continue to experience racism and discrimination on individual, community, and societal levels. For counselors and psychologists to truly understand the social injustices experienced by our clients, we need to incorporate not only the cultural but also the sociopsychopolitical, historical, and ecological perspectives.

12) **Change is a process, not a quick fix.** In a society where we value quick solutions and sound bites, we are often too impatient to allow the process of change to unfold. As counselors and mental health professionals working toward social justice, it is essential that we become comfortable with allowing the process to run its course. Social justice work cannot be superficial; it must take root and grow over time. Homan (2008) identified seven phases in the community change process, which are as follows:

1. **Introduction phase** is when the problem is recognized.

2. **Initial action phase** is a time when information is gathered and allies are identified.

3. **Emergence of leadership and structure phase** involves a leader emerging while the group simultaneously begins to take shape.

4. **Letdown phase** is when there is some deflation; there is a clear demarcation of those who

are committed to change and those who are not as interested in the "real" work that needs to take place.

5. **Recommitment, new task, and new members phase** constitutes a time when the group reconfigures; the direction is further defined as leaders become more solidified in their roles and remotivate the group.

6. **Sustained action phase** involves a deepening of the group's work and expansion to take on new challenges.

7. **Growth, decline, or termination phase** is the final phase, when the group is either going through the first six phases more expediently as it moves to fulfill the goal for social change, or it is beginning to end based on meeting or not meeting its goals.

13) **Change can come in small or large quantities.** Social change does not always imply major changes. Sometimes there are small changes that are part of a fabric of a longer term change process. Regardless of whether the changes are small or large, there is a disruption of the equilibrium and subsequent impact on individuals as well as in the larger community of that person.

It is important to not underestimate small changes. Taking "baby steps" to initiate and contribute to the process of change leads to changing the more complex and larger issues. For example, having an informal talk with colleagues, friends, or family members challenging their homophobic attitudes or attitudes toward the homeless may begin a longer-term process of changing their values and behavior and result in them questioning others' values. It is the planting of "social justice seeds" with ramifications that are not always immediately evident. After all, the civil rights movement did not happen overnight. It is critical that psychologists and counselors recognize, accept, and acknowledge small changes that can contribute and lead to a larger change.

14) **There is a difference between planning and implementing change.** There are significant differences between planning change and actually implementing change, and different

skills needed. It is important that counselors and psychologists recognize the distinctive skills for each.

15) **Promoting social justice through social change is not about ego; it is about working toward a larger cause.** When we are working to promote social justice, it is important to keep in mind that we are working toward a larger goal. In some ways, promoters of social justice changes can be seen as servants to a larger cause, working in partnership *with* people to promote justice. This means that during each phase of change, the input, suggestions, and ideas of clients, stakeholders, and community members are important, and we, as counselors and psychologists, receive others as social justice collaborative partners.

16) **Effective change agents combine learning and teaching.** A number of years ago, I (Fred) was working with street children in Brazil. The children were under the threat of attack from vigilante groups who were murdering them in an effort to "clean up the cities." My experience doing research with the children and in part attempting to address this murder of innocents was profound, since I learned as much from them as they from me. In fact, I eventually wrote an article about what I called *street researchers* becoming students of the street children (Bemak, 1996).

It is our belief that this concept carries over to the social justice and social change work that we do as mental health professionals. Our roles are transformed; we are no longer *only* the healer or helper or teacher; we are also students. It is important that we learn from the individuals and communities with whom we work and are ready and willing to abandon an unwavering role as the authority or expert. After all, it is those who are living with the social injustice who are the experts.

In summary, social justice work is about change, whether it is on an individual, community, or societal level. Social justice change is critical to ensure that *all* individuals, their families, and their communities have the opportunity for optimal psychological and physical growth, development, and well-being. To be effective change agents, we must embrace an ecological perspective of our clients' situations by understanding both the complex multidimensionality of multiple systems, and how issues on a systematic level can trickle down and impact individuals and their families. Social justice work is therefore about disrupting systems, the status quo, that have been built on and maintained unfair treatment and inequalities of resources and opportunities. While systems affect people, people can also affect systems (Cowan & Egan, 1979). We as psychologists and counselors are part of a system and therefore have the ability to change systems.

THE MEANING OF POWER IN SOCIAL CHANGE

Social change and power go hand in hand. Although power was noted as a principle of change, we would like to further examine the relationship between power and social justice. In social justice and human rights work, counselors and psychologists are constantly faced with issues of power. Who has the power? How does one handle one's power? What constitutes the constructive use of power to achieve social justice? How do we change the power base so that all people—regardless of socioeconomic status, gender, sexual orientation, religion, disabilities, ethnic, racial, or cultural background, and so on—receive equal resources, wealth, and opportunity?

When considering power in relationship to social change, there is an aim to help people move in a positive direction with a positive outcome (Homan, 2008). The use of power in social justice work is positive, intentional, and proactive. A primary aim in using one's power is to eliminate barriers that prohibit equality and fair treatment. An example of this occurred when

I (Fred) had a senior-level state position in the department of mental health as the regional director of a treatment program for adolescents and could use this position of power to advocate and change some of the policies that were inhibiting the rights of youth. Similarly, I (Rita) organized a meeting with students of color in a university graduate program and used this as a platform to recommend changes to university administration on the recruitment and retention of students of color.

The various definitions of power in social justice suggest that all individuals possess power (e.g., Robinson & Hanna, 1994; Rubin & Rubin, 1986; Wrong, 1995) and that power is purposeful and intentional. There are clear expectations in social justice counseling that when one uses one's power, it must be to provide benefits for clients and the larger social network and community. Often there is a collaborative use and sharing of power by various stakeholders (clients, families, and communities) working toward a mutual solution in developing new or improved conditions. For example, mental health professionals may encourage different ethnic groups in the United States (such as African Americans, Asian Americans, Native Americans, Latina/o Americans, Arab Americans, etc.) and gay rights organizations to join together to lobby against hate crimes and for the passing of tougher laws on hate crime and hate crime prevention.

The use of power in social justice work does not involve manipulation or coercion. It is more the case that power is shared cooperatively. For example, you and a group of colleagues are concerned that an administrator has been inadequately addressing issues of racial tension in the work environment. When the issue has been raised in the past, it has been ignored and brushed aside. As a collective group of concerned employees, you approach the administrator and suggest strategies to attend to these issues. This is a constructive and positive step, using a collective sense of power to address a brewing issue within your worksite. No one was forced to join the group of concerned colleagues, and the aim was for a positive result. Someone made the suggestion that moved a group of people to a desired outcome.

Although everyone has power, some people, by virtue of their positions or personality, have more power than others. The degree of power is dependent on the situation and the interplay among those involved. For example, as a group therapist you have power over the members of the group, establishing when to meet, for how long, who enters the group, parameters for psychological and physical safety within the group, and so forth. Or as a senior faculty member or higher-ranking supervisor in your workplace, you may have more authority by virtue of seniority.

Thus, power involves relationships among people, which can be either positive or negative. One's impact on others through the use of power relates to the degree of control one has over resources, money, information, food, and so forth, and the dependency other individuals have on those resources. For example, if your income from a job supports your family—pays the bills, buys the food, pays for transportation, clothing, and so on—the influence that your job supervisor has over you may be greater than if you did not need that income to pay your expenses.

Social change requires a degree of power to move individuals or groups in new directions. Sometimes our power is used to motivate or mobilize action steps conducive to change. Power in this situation is viewed as positive, since it can influence and impact change from an undesirable to a desired situation. When we are encouraging and activating people to promote social change, it is important that we respectfully use power. This requires respecting others while keeping a clear picture of the goals and avoiding using power for personal gain or interests.

Finally, working toward social change does not require us as helping professionals to do it alone. Working collaboratively with our clients and other stakeholders has the potential to strengthen our power and increase the chances of meeting our goals.

RESISTANCE TO CHANGE

People don't resist change. They resist being changed!

(Peter Senge)

Faced with the choice between changing one's mind and proving that there is no need to do so, almost everyone gets busy on the proof.

(John Kenneth Galbraith)

As we discussed, inherent in change are uncertainties and unpredictability. Not surprisingly, given the lack of clarity that may accompany change and shifts in power, some people are resistant to change. Change disrupts what we know, how we do things, and our ability to predict the future. Interestingly, even if individuals are aware that their situation is unhealthy, negative, or undesirable, they may still resist change, preferring to have order and certainty rather than the unexpected. For example, we often hear people talk about their dissatisfaction about their job or work, yet they do little or nothing to look for another job. Two old proverbs illustrate the ambivalence regarding change: One is "The devil you know is better than the devil you don't know," and the other, "jumping from the frying pan to the fire" depicts the caution involved in change.

Resistance is a natural part of change. Knowing the world we are in may be far easier than re-creating a new world that we don't know. Homan (2008) pointed out the difficulties in letting go of the time and energy one has invested so that all the skills to handle a particular situation are no longer pertinent. As mentioned previously, resistance may also manifest as individuals in positions of privilege, power, and leadership who are reluctant to share or give up their arrangement. Linked to giving up one's position are possible disagreements about reasons to change. Common factors related to resistance are unpredictability and fear of disruption.

In addition, there is uncertainty about outcomes. Social change is not guaranteed, and there may be many "twists and turns" along the way. The lack of clarity may create self doubt about the direction of change, one's ability, and one's future position. In fact, there may be grieving for the loss of one's status and the way things used to be. This may appear strange—that individuals would grieve over a dissatisfactory situation in their lives. But consider that people who were oppressed but had their basic needs such as food, shelter, and clothing taken care of during that experience may miss the safety and security of that aspect of the experience. The grief in this case would relate to the loss of the security and predictability of having those basic needs met; it would not take into account the other elements of the experience, where they now have the freedom to make their own choices and live their lives.

Dealing with Resistance

In counseling and psychotherapy, resistance refers to client behavior that has the potential to obstruct the therapeutic process and sabotage growth and positive change. Mental health professionals and counselors promoting social change will encounter similar types of resistance that inhibit the facilitation of human rights and equity. This happens both externally, from outside sources, and internally. Homan (2008) suggested that the most profound source of resistance to change is simply what we tell ourselves. Given this supposition, one way to minimize resistance would be to inform people about the reasons and goals for change. For example, "We are carefully examining the policies about suspension in this school, because 78% of the students suspended are students of color, even though they compose only 41% of the student body." This would be a clear and transparent sharing with parents and students about why there is an examination of the policy and why a change of policy and practice is being considered. Open communication has great potential for helping people understand what an issue is and why it is being considered, and to align themselves with the social justice goals.

A good example of resistance can be seen in the principles of resistance that Ridley and Thompson (1999) identified related to multicultural training. He noted that resistance is reflected in one's actual behavior and can thwart change, explaining that one must accept the costs and losses that accompany the change process. Ridley added that resistance can also manifest in avoidance, which I (Rita) saw when one graduate student refused to take a multicultural counseling class that I was teaching, saying the content was too threatening. Another aspect of resistance that Ridley identified is calling into question those who are attempting to resist change, sometimes directly and other times more passively, such as resisting doing tasks or assignments. Finally, he outlined subtle forms of resistance, where people change topics or deflect questions. We would add that in our opinion, resistance is heightened for individuals who have high needs for psychological safety and security driven by personal vulnerability; frequently such needs are manifested through controlling as much of their lives as possible.

Capitalizing on Resistance as a Positive Force

Dealing with resistance can be considered part of the work of social change. Rather than trying to avoid resistant clients or groups, the question for us as counselors and psychologists is how to align and find areas of agreement with those who are opposing change. Given our training in mental health and counseling, we are in a very advantageous position to understand unwillingness. In fact, we are highly trained to explore and interpret the actual source of resistance, fears of change, and associated anxieties. Are those who are resistant feeling vulnerable; are they misinformed; are they hostile? Using our insights regarding the roots of resistance, we can develop strategies that are person- or system-specific and address the motivation behind the actual resistance. This type of understanding and intervention strategy is critical in facilitating social justice.

SUMMARY

To successfully work with clients, families, or communities, social justice counselors and psychologists must have knowledge about how their clients perceive and relate to the world. Clients' worldviews may differ from that of the helping professional. Regardless of the differences in worldview, change agents must respect clients' worldviews and acknowledge that this is the pivotal point in fostering social change. Change agents can be effective only when they understand, recognize, acknowledge, and accept their clients' worldviews and life experiences. Any change must be approached from within the clients' worldview. Again, fully understanding, applying, and implementing the multicultural counseling competencies is a critical starting point for understanding clients and their families' worldviews. As mentioned in the multicultural counseling chapter, a few multicultural or cultural sensitivity training workshops will not be enough. To be multiculturally aware and competent requires deep self-reflection, examination, and exploration as well as an honest and genuine commitment to multiculturalism.

DISCUSSION QUESTIONS

1. After reading the chapter, please interpret in your own words the following passage from page 142:

   "Social justice and human rights work is closely intertwined with social change. This is in contrast to general change models (i.e., individuals changing personal behaviors . . .) . . . . We would define social change to include the changing or altering of systems . . . and structures . . . that hinder, obstruct, block, impede, and interfere with positive and optimal growth, development, opportunities and physical and psychological well-being for all individuals, families, groups, and communities."

2. How do you think global communications have impacted the idea of change in different parts of the world? What are some of the strengths? What are some of the obstacles?

3. Consider Prochaska and DiClemente's (1982) transtheoretical model of change (TTM):

   - Identify one of your personal challenges to change (you can use the one you used in the warm up exercise). Identify each of the stages you progressed through in making this change and your struggles, decisions, and outcomes.
   - Examine a community issue that you believe needs to change. Identify each of the stages in changing it, as well as your struggles and decisions and their outcomes.

4. This chapter discusses different meanings of power and the importance of using power in a proactive way.

   - What is your idea of power?
   - What type of power do you have as a student or in your work?
   - How would you be able to use your power proactively?
   - Can you identify others in your university or work site who have significant power? Are they using their power proactively in positive ways or not? What would you do to change the situation?

5. The chapter mentions one of the social change principles as, "Effective change agents combine learning and teaching" and discussed the problems of personal ego getting in the way of change.

   - Identify your challenges in these ideas.
   - How can you help others understand the importance of these two concepts?

REFERENCES

Bemak, F. (1996). Street researchers: A new paradigm redefining future research with street children. *Childhood, 3*, 147–156.

Bemak, F., & Conyne, R. (2004). Ecological group work. In R. K. Conyne & E. P. Cook (Eds.), *Ecological counseling: An innovative approach to conceptualizing person-environment interaction* (pp. 195–218). Alexandria, VA: American Counseling Association.

Brogan, M. M., Prochaska, J. O., & Prochaska, J. M. (1999). Predicting termination and continuation status in psychotherapy using the transtheoretical model. *Psychotherapy: Theory, Research, Practice, Training, 36*(2), 105–113.

Cowan, G., & Egan, M. (1979). *People in systems: A model for development in the human-service professions and education.* Pacific Grove, CA: Brooks/Cole.

DiClemente, C. C., & Hughes, S. L. (1990). Stages of change profiles in alcoholism treatment. *Journal of Substance Abuse, 2,* 217–235.

DiClemente, C. C., & Prochaska, J. O. (1985). Processes and stages of change: Coping and competence in smoking behavior change, In S. Shiffman & T. A. Wills (Eds.), *Coping and substance abuse* (pp. 319–343). San Diego, CA: Academic Press.

DiClemente, C. C., Prochaska, J. O., & Gillbertini, M. (1985). Self-efficacy and the stages of self-change of smoking. *Cognitive Therapy and Research, 9,* 181–200.

Homan, M. S. (2008). *Promoting community change: Making it happen in the real world* (4th ed.) Pacific Grove, CA: Brooks/Cole.

Hubble, M. A., Duncan, B. L., & Miller, S. D. (1999). *The heart & soul of change: What works in therapy.* Washington, DC: American Psychological Association.

Lam, C. S., McMahon, B. T., Priddy, D. A., & Gehred-Schultz, A. (1988). Deficit awareness and treatment performance among traumatic head injury adults. *Brain Injury, 2,* 235–242.

Lambert, M. J., Shapiro, D. A., & Bergin, A. E. (1986). The effectiveness of psychotherapy. In S. L. Garfield & A. E. Bergin (Eds.), *Handbook of psychotherapy and behavior change* (3rd ed., pp. 157–212). New York: Wiley.

McConnaughy, E. A., DiClemente, C. C., Prochaska, J. O., & Velicer, W. F. (1989). Stages of change in psychotherapy: A follow-up report. *Psychotherapy, 26,* 494–503.

Norcross, J. C., & Prochaska, J. O. (1986a). Psychotherapist heal thyself: The psychological distress and self-change of psychologists, counselors, and laypersons. *Psychotherapy: Theory, Research, Practice, Training, 23,* 102–114.

Norcross, J. C., & Prochaska, J. O. (1986b). Psychotherapist heal thyself: II. The self-initiated and therapy-facilitated change of psychological distress. *Psychotherapy: Theory, Research, Practice, Training, 23*(3), 345–356.

Prochaska, J. O. (1999). How do people change, and how do we change to help people? In M. A. Hubble, B. L. Duncan, & S. D. Miller (Eds.), *The heart & soul of change: What works in therapy* (pp. 227–258). Washington, DC: American Psychological Association.

Prochaska, J. O., & DiClemente, C. C. (1982). Transtheoretical therapy: Toward a more integrative model of change. *Psychotherapy: Theory, Research and Practice, 20,* 161–173.

Prochaska, J. O., & DiClemente, C. C. (1992). Stages of change in the modification of problem behaviors. In M. Hersen, R. M. Eisler, & P. M. Miller (Eds.), *Progress in behavior modification* (pp. 184–214). Sycamore, IL: Sycamore Press.

Prochaska, J. O., DiClemente, C. C., & Norcross, J. C. (1992). In search of how people change: Applications to the addictive behaviors. *American Psychologist, 47,* 1102–1114.

Prochaska, J. O., Norcross, J. C., & DiClemente, C. C. (1994). *Changing for good.* New York: William Morrow.

Ridley, C. R., & Thompson, C. E. (1999). Managing resistance to diversity training: A social systems perspective. In M. Kiselica (Ed.). *Confronting prejudice and racism during multicultural training* (pp. 3–24). Alexandria, VA: American Counseling Association.

Robinson, B., & Hanna, M. G. (1994). Lessons for academics from grassroots community organizing: A case study—the industrial areas foundation. *Journal of Community Practice, 1*(4), 63–94.

Rubin, H., & Rubin, I. (1986). *Community organizing and development.* Columbus, OH: Merrill.

Separation anxiety. (2009). *The Washington Post.* Retrieved from http://www.washingtonpost.com/wp-dyn/content/article/2009/03/15/AR2009031501669.html

Smith, M. L., Glass, G. V., & Miller, T. I. (1980). *The benefits of psychotherapy.* Baltimore, MD: Johns Hopkins University.

Wrong, D. (1995). *Power: Its forms, bases and uses.* New Brunswick, NJ: Transaction.

10

LEADERSHIP AND SOCIAL JUSTICE

*The ultimate measure of a man is not where he stands in moments of comfort
and convenience, but where he stands at times of challenge and controversy.*

(Martin Luther King Jr.)

A leader is a dealer in hope.

(Napoleon Bonaparte)

I must follow the people. Am I not their leader?

(Benjamin Disraeli)

*Don't tell people how to do things, tell them what to
do and let them surprise you with their results.*

(George S. Patton)

*A leader is best when people barely know he exists, not so good when people
obey and acclaim him, worse when they despise him. But of a good leader who
talks little, when his work is done, his aim fulfilled, they will say: We did it ourselves.*

(Lao-Tzu)

Leadership and learning are indispensable to each other

(John F. Kennedy)

WARM UP EXERCISE

1. *Where did you learn about leadership?*

2. *Recall when you have had an experience as a leader. What was it like?*

3. *When you have assumed leadership positions or watched others as leaders, what qualities did they exhibit that worked? What did they do that didn't work?*

4. *Who are leaders that you admire? Why do you admire them?*

5. *What are the things that are holding you back from being a leader on social justice issues?*

6. *If you could assume more leadership roles in your life, where in your life would you add this?*

There are many people who experience social justice and human rights violations. These people come from many different walks of life—they are of Muslim, Jewish, Christian, or Buddhist faith; they are gay or lesbian; they are Asian, African American, Latina/o, Arab, Native American, or biracial; they are immigrants and refugees; they are women and children, they are poor; they are uneducated; they are old and young and physically challenged. Regardless of where they come from, the experience of discrimination, racism, prejudice, oppression, and physical and psychological violation is the same—it is painful, it hurts, and it harms the very soul and spirit of human beings.

To eliminate, prevent, and intervene in social injustice and human rights violations, we as psychologists and counselors must be equipped with multiple skills, abilities, and capabilities. The previous chapter discussed being a change agent as a core component of social justice and human rights work. Leadership, advocacy, and empowerment are each components of social justice work. Leadership will be discussed in this chapter, and the other components—advocacy and empowerment—will be discussed in the next chapters (Chapters 11 and 12).

Each component is a critical tool in dismantling the various types of unfair, unjust, and unequal treatment and provides us with direction for what we must do as counselors and psychologists. The components of social justice are also vital tools in changing, establishing, re-creating, and developing equal and fair treatment and access to resources and opportunities for all people. It is essential that we, as helping professionals, assume leadership roles in implementing social change through advocacy and empowerment for those that we serve.

The chapter will begin with a discussion about the importance of leadership as it relates to social justice and human rights. To provide a foundation for understanding the significance of leadership in social justice work, the chapter will provide a brief overview of leadership types and styles followed by a discussion on leadership in psychotherapy and counseling. Finally a discussion on the leadership characteristics of a social justice and human rights mental health professional will be presented.

LEADERSHIP IN SOCIAL JUSTICE

With the rapid changes in society, there is an increasing need for helping professionals to develop leadership skills. In recognizing this need, the major psychology and counseling professional organizations (e.g., American Psychological Association, American Counseling Association) have held national conferences with leadership as a theme and have offered numerous workshops, presentations, and seminars on leadership. However, leadership skills and qualities have not been the focus in traditional training or licensure for psychologists and counselors. Although elements of leadership may be found in some of the courses at the doctoral level, there are rarely specific courses or sections of courses that focus on leadership or the infusion of leadership skills at the master's level. Most often, psychologists and counselors who assume leadership positions acquire leadership skills on the job after their graduate training.

For helping professionals working with social justice and human rights issues, it is important to have leadership skills. To advocate for and empower clients, psychologists and counselors must know how to motivate clients and communities and to take action and must know how to work collaboratively with clients, communities, agencies, service providers, institutions, and/or organizations. This requires a distinct kind of leadership that is unique to helping professionals who are working toward social justice and human rights. To fully understand the uniqueness of leadership in social justice and human rights, we will begin with a brief overview of traditional leadership models, followed by a discussion of the characteristics of social justice leaders.

LEADERSHIP MODELS

Webster's New College Dictionary (4th ed., 2008) defines a leader as "someone who is a guiding or directing head. Leadership is defined as an act or instance of leading or guidance" (p. 814). Much of the literature on leadership and leadership styles in the field of psychology and counseling relates to organizations or agencies.

Historical Overview

Great man studies. The earliest studies on leadership were called the "great man studies" (Short & Greer, 2002). All these studies focused on men in leadership positions. The methodology used in this approach was to identify universal personality traits of great military, political, and industrial male leaders. The assumption of using this approach was that the qualities and skills of great men were genetic traits and were identifiable, but could not be acquired through training or experience.

Trait approach. It was hoped that by using the trait approach (Mann, 1959; Stogdill, 1948) there could be a more precise measure of leadership characteristics. This approach assumed that leadership was a one-way process, so that only leaders could possess special leadership qualities. Leadership traits were identified through interviews, observations, tests, checklists, and rating scales. The identified leadership traits were grouped into five categories: (1) capacity (e.g., intelligence, alertness, verbal facility, originality, and judgment), (2) achievement (e.g., scholarship, knowledge, and athletic achievement), (3) responsibility (e.g., dependability, initiative, persistence, aggressiveness, self-confidence, and desire to excel), (4) participation (e.g., activity, sociability, cooperation, adaptability, and humor), and (5) status (socioeconomic, position, and popularity) (Mann, 1959; Stogdill, 1948).

There were two major criticisms to the trait approach. The first questioned the universality of traits and their transferability to different circumstances. Could a leader in one situation who possessed one or a combination of the above traits actually emerge as a leader in different circumstances? The second criticism was of the reliability and validity of the methodologies used in this approach. This was based on the lack of consistency among the measures employed to identify the leadership traits. Despite the concerns, the approach did, in fact, identify certain personality traits thought to be critical for leadership, including intelligence, responsibility, and participation (Short & Greer, 2002). A third criticism that we would add is that the leadership traits were identified exclusively among males, discounting the long history of women who have exhibited significant leadership capabilities.

Situational leadership. Given that the trait approach was unable to predict efficacy as a leader across different settings, the situational leadership approach emerged (Hersey & Blanchard, 1969).

This approach viewed leadership as a response to group characteristics, such as size, homogeneity, stability, satisfaction, and cohesion. Group characteristics were measured through interviews with leaders and group members, observations using sociometric instruments, ratings of group members' performance on stimulation exercises, and analyses of group procedures. Interestingly, situational leadership faced criticisms similar to those of the trait approach.

Behavioral approach. The behavioral approach focused on leadership behaviors as they were observed by group members (Short & Greer, 2002). A variety of settings were investigated, ranging from airliners to schools. The Leadership Behavior Description Questionnaire (LBDQ) was developed to observe leaders and consisted of two factors: consideration and initiating structure (Schriesheim & Stogdill, 1975). The consideration factor is the human relations dimension, referring to the leader's relationships and ability to relate to the group members. Thus, if Tania was in a leadership position, the consideration factor would examine how she related to others; was there a difference in how she related to women versus men, to older colleagues versus younger colleagues, to those with disabilities and those from different racial or ethnic backgrounds? In comparison, the initiating structure factor refers to the task dimension or the leader's ability to organize the work of the organization. Here we would look at how effective Tania is when she is working at the job itself and getting the work done.

Contingency theory. Contingency theory evolved from a combination of behavioral approaches, situational leadership, and personality traits. This new theory builds on the belief that leadership characteristics depend on a multitude of factors such as specific tasks, the presenting situation, leader and member relationships, leader personality, and group characteristics (Fiedler, 1969; Hersey, Blanchard, & Natemeyer, 1979; House & Mitchell, 1974; Tannenbaum & Schmidt, 1973). Therefore, when considering "What constitutes a leader?" contingency theorists would respond, "It depends" (Short & Greer, 2002).

Even so, there are different opinions held by contingency theorists with regard to whether it is possible for leaders to change their administrative and personal style in different situations. Some argued that it is not possible for leaders to change their style, and therefore it is better to place leaders in situations that match their personal leadership style and the demands of the situations (Fiedler, 1969). Others (e.g., Hersey & Blanchard, 1969) held a different position, postulating that leadership qualities and styles are adaptable and can change to fit the task and needs of the group in different situations.

LEADERSHIP STYLES

As we discussed in earlier chapters, leadership is typically not associated with mental health and counseling but is talked about more in the areas of organizational development and business. An organizational leader must be able to employ vision that moves an organization forward while also dealing effectively with individuals in the system. Therefore leadership skills include systems, interpersonal, instructional, and imagination skills. Six different leadership styles that are related to social justice work are listed in Table 10.1 and discussed in the following paragraphs.

Autocratic leadership. An autocratic leader is often viewed by followers as one who is distant and unapproachable, makes independent decisions,

Table 10.1 Six Different Leadership Styles Related to Social Justice Work
Autocratic leadership
Benevolent leadership
Bureaucratic leadership
Empowering leadership
Servant leadership
Transformative leadership

and has full control (Burke, Sims, Lazzara, & Salas, 2007). These leaders typically have difficulties delegating tasks and activities, since by doing so they diminish their control. I (Fred) encountered an example of such a leader when I was in Colombia consulting for a large social service agency. The director of the agency was highly authoritarian, staff were afraid to approach him or discuss problems they were having with him, and he remained very distant. These traits were in direct contrast to those of the deputy director, who laughed and engaged personally with her staff. Followers for this style of leadership tend to be docile, obedient, and passive; they follow orders, as did the staff in the Colombian social service agency.

Benevolent leadership. A benevolent leader is frequently viewed as having a parental style (Burke et al., 2007). The leader will listen to subordinates before making a decision. However, there is an expectation that laws and rules will be followed so as to maintain an orderly environment. I (Rita) have consulted for some social service agencies where the leaders were actually called "Mom" or "Dad." Similar to an ideal relationship between parents and their children, the relationship between the leader and the followers incorporates munificent qualities. The benevolent leader is seen as caring and approachable, but is still recognized to have the final say. This style is effective if the leader is highly skilled and the followers are dependent on those skills for direction and guidance.

Bureaucratic leadership. In contrast, a bureaucratic leader emphasizes managerial efficiency, focusing on order, clear policies, and rules (Uhl-Bien, Marion, & McKelvey, 2007). This leader will delegate only to those who are skilled and loyal and harbors expectations that followers are loyal to the organization. Bureaucratic leaders generally have good interpersonal and social skills so that they are approachable and are good listeners. Tasks and expectations are clearly defined, and individuals know which tasks and activities will be delegated.

Empowering leadership. The empowering leader is usually more democratic and has a participatory and collaborative approach (Burke et al., 2006). This leader is an active listener and clarifier. One potential dilemma for this type of leadership style is finding a balance between institutional demands, personal values, and human needs. The empowering leader is stylistically democratic, committed to making the organization more human, and willing to modify rules according to personal conscience. Followers expect to be able to participate in some of the decision making. This type of leadership is more consistent with social justice work, where one is balancing multiple factors while trying to empower others.

Servant leadership. Servant leadership is concerned with the quality of interaction within the organization as well as the impact of the organization on society (Avolio, Walumbwa, & Weber, 2009). Servant leaders will seek maximum development for employees, foster interdependent governance by peer teams, and encourage group decision making along with mutual responsibility and collegiality. Followers typically assume greater responsibility and work at high levels of trust and collegiality. Similar to empowering leadership, servant leadership is more aligned with social justice, cultivating autonomy, cooperation, and self-determined directions and decisions.

Transformative leadership. Finally, the sixth leadership style represents the highest level of consciousness and is rarely found. At this phase, leadership and followership are merged. All activity is interdependent in nature and global in concern. Leaders emphasize improving the balance between the world of material goods and the needs of each human being. The work is focused on issues related to ecology, human rights, reconciliation of conflicting groups, and the creative and humane use of technology. On a continuum of leadership for social justice and human rights mental health workers, the sixth leadership style is the ideal goal, surpassing even empowerment and servant leadership, and is characterized by its values, which are placed on equity, fairness, and human rights with regard to clients and organizations.

GENDER AND LEADERSHIP

Extensive research comparing leadership styles of women and men found both similarities and differences, finding that there are gender-influenced or gender-related but not gender-specific leadership styles (Tarule, Applegate, Earley, & Blackwell, 2009). A meta-analysis found a tendency for women to lead in a more democratic and participative way, while men tended to be more autocratic and directive (Eagly & Johnson, 1990). These differences may be attributed to a constellation of situations and behaviors and may not be solely due to gender stereotypes. Instead the findings suggest that women tend to lean toward interpersonal factors, focusing on the morale and welfare of the organization, while men tend to be more task oriented, emphasizing the performance and accomplishment of activities (Eagly & Johnson, 1990; Tarule et al., 2009).

Gender differences among men and women in leadership roles do not appear to be a function of biological differences, but may instead be based on numerous other factors. Some considerations include the underrepresentation of women in managerial positions, the inequalities of treatment of men and women inside organizations, salary differences, differences in status within organizations, and stereotypes that depict women leaders as caring and nurturing, all of which can influence how one leads (Bordas, 2007; Tarule et al., 2009). The ongoing underrepresentation of women in leadership and managerial positions may be related to women being viewed as a minority group and subsequently having a token status (Kanter, 1977), which may result in women being more critically analyzed about why and how they assume the role of a leader.

Women of color in leadership positions face additional challenges. Leadership theories and models have been constructed predominately from a White male perspective, creating both gender

bias and cultural bias (Bordas, 2007). Hence, women of color who are leaders experience more scrutiny and greater pressure to live up to expectations that are based on a White male perspective (Patal, 1992). This may become more pronounced when a woman leader is highly visible, and it can negatively impact how she is assessed, treated, and compared to her male counterparts. The concept of visibility and invisibility in leadership has been widely discussed (e.g., Applegate, Earley, & Tarule, 2009), and the importance of creating a safe environment has been noted, especially for leaders from marginalized groups.

COUNSELING LEADERSHIP

The six leadership styles listed above (see Table 10.1) relate to leadership toward social justice for counselors and psychologists in public and private agencies, institutions, and schools. Lewis, Lewis, Daniels, and D'Andrea (2003) stated that an effective leader in community agencies and organizations has the ability to assist people to realize their potential and contribute to the goals and purpose of an organization. This means that effective leadership can be partially viewed by how leaders facilitate the personal and professional development of people whom they supervise. This must be combined with vision, which is a core characteristic for leadership. Adding vision to this mix brings in elements of potential and growth, strategic planning skills, implementation strategies, and the ability to envision the future of the organization as a whole (Senge, 1990).

Although we agree that some of the perspectives on leadership qualities, such as intelligence, vision, organization, and good interpersonal skills, fit in with mental health social justice work, we would suggest that the traditional definitions of leadership are based on Western individualistic notions of leadership that do not adequately account for cultural and gender differences. These differences are especially important when working on issues of social justice and human rights, which may require additional leadership qualities and skills, and are particularly relevant when working within the framework of cultures that do not adhere to Western notions of individualism, independence, self-responsibility, self-reliance, self-importance, self-development, and so forth. It is important to note that as we discuss social justice leadership, we are intentionally avoiding imperialist leadership qualities, such as dominance, manipulation, a take-control attitude, "leading the way," "showing people how to," "having all the ideas," and so on. Instead we are working from a more egalitarian collaborative perspective to promote social change, power balances, and equity. These qualities are similar to some of the qualities of the empowering and servant leadership styles. In the next section, we will discuss some of our notions about leadership and leadership qualities and skills as they relate to social justice and human rights.

CHARACTERISTICS OF SOCIAL JUSTICE AND HUMAN RIGHTS LEADERS

The concept of authentic leadership has emerged, challenging traditional principles of leadership that focus on notions of power, dominance, and manipulation (Duignan & Bhindi, 1997). Authentic leadership examines empowerment through culture and community building, decision making, and the ability to build trusting environments (Block, 1993). Social justice leaders are unique in that they build these qualities, which form the basis of authentic leadership.

Authentic social justice leaders differ from general leaders since social justice supports a process built on respect, care, recognition, and empathy (Theoharis, 2007). Furthermore, social justice leaders intentionally emphasize and challenge historical, sociopolitical, and current social injustices (Theoharis, 2007). The intent of social justice leaders is to alter, change, and at times dismantle institutions and organizations that uphold social injustices by proactively addressing, reclaiming, sustaining, and advancing human rights, equity, equality, and fairness in social, economic,

political, educational, legal, and medical institutions, organizations, and systems (Goldfarb & Grinberg, 2002). Fine (1994) nicely describes social justice leaders as intentionally unearthing, disrupting, and transforming existing institutions and systems that are socially unjust. The role of social justice leaders is therefore to break the silence of social injustices and give voice to those who have been silenced (i.e., the oppressed, the disenfranchised, and the marginalized) while providing them with hope and vision of the future, of "what could be" instead of accepting "what is." As Fine (1994) states, social justice leaders denaturalize what appears to be natural (i.e., socially unjust systems and organizations).

Given our training as psychologists and counselors, we have learned about human relations, group dynamics, and communication and interpersonal skills, all of which are essential skills for authentic social justice leaders. For example, listening skills enable us to more effectively listen to clients', families', colleagues', and supervisees' ideas, needs, challenges, and concerns. We know how to create a safe environment in which others can share their dissatisfaction, discontent, frustrations, dreams, hopes, recommendations, and suggestions. A clear and insightful understanding of personal and organizational concerns and short- and long-range goals places psychologists and counselors in a key position to help individuals and groups resolve issues and move forward to achieve personal and organizational goals. Similarly, the combination of verbal and nonverbal communication skills enables social justice leaders to understand communication at multiple levels and help forge alliances and partnerships. We are in a distinctive position to facilitate the articulation of a clear vision that includes a commitment by all stakeholders.

Counselors and psychologists are also knowledgeable about group dynamics and group process. We are trained to be cognizant of interpersonal dynamics and to facilitate groups; these skills are essential in facilitating and promoting social change and human rights. Thus, sitting with a group of people considering a change in programming for homeless children, psychologists

Table 10.2 14 Characteristics of a Social Justice Leader

Genuineness

Authentic collaborator

Courageous risk taker

Challenges systems

Creative

Motivator

Humble, lacking ego

Responsible

A guide, not an expert

Generates empowerment

Understands self

Understands and appreciates differences in others

Able to use and understand research and data

Model for others

and counselors are at an advantage, because they not only understand the issues at hand, they also are skilled in group process and human relations. This type of training is essential for helping professionals and provides a tremendous foundation for social justice and human rights work.

Yet it is not only counseling and psychotherapy skills that one needs to be an effective social justice leader. Other skills and qualities are also necessary. Table 10.2 is a list of 14 qualities and characteristics that we see as essential.

14 CHARACTERISTICS OF A SOCIAL JUSTICE LEADER

1. **Genuineness.** We would suggest that authenticity is critical for social justice leaders and has the potential to generate deep-rooted trust and support. This is especially important as we forge relationships with clients, families, and communities with an aim for social change and human rights.

2. **Authentic collaborator.** We, as mental health professional leaders and counselors, must let go of the need to maintain control and power over our clientele. True partnerships mean sharing the vision, the ideas, the power, and the decision-making authority with all stakeholders (that is, clients, their families, and their communities). True collaboration, therefore, means social justice leaders are able to give, as well as receive, directions and instructions from stakeholders, thereby creating a shared collaborative leadership. An example of this was when we developed parent groups to support their children who were failing academically. In those groups, it was essential that everyone (including us) had an equal say over the agenda for group discussions, the content of the discussions, and the decisions of the group.

3. **Courageous risk taker.** Social change and improvements in human rights have never taken place without individuals taking risks. There is always a degree of risk taking when trying to create change. Therefore leaders who are counselors and psychologists must learn how to be courageous in challenging inequalities and unfair practices, treatment, and decisions. If we don't take the risk to speak out and take action, we are maintaining the status quo and more insidiously adding, perpetuating, reinforcing, and supporting the injustices. Therefore staying in one's comfort zone means maintaining and reinforcing the status quo.

4. **Challenges systems.** To achieve social justice and human rights requires leaders to challenge existing rules and regulations. Although a way of doing things may be what everyone expects and knows, it is essential for leaders to challenge the status quo and unfair and unequal ways of doing things and ways of treating individuals or groups of people.

5. **Creative.** To be a leader in social justice work means thinking beyond what is presented to us. We must explore ideas that extend past typical ways of addressing issues, think outside the box, and remain flexible as we engage in the process of change.

6. **Motivator.** A leader must have the ability to motivate and energize people. Benazir Bhutto, Nelson Mandela, Bantu Stephen Biko,

Golda Meir, Mahatma Gandhi, Indira Gandhi, Jesse Jackson, Aung San Suu Kyi, the Dalai Lama, Caesar Chavez, Abraham Lincoln, John F. Kennedy, Robert Kennedy, Martin Luther King Jr., and many others have been able to motivate national and international audiences. Most of us will be working on a much smaller scale as we focus on individuals and our local, regional, and state communities. So we do not have to move a nation or world, yet we still need to know how to motivate people toward social justice and human rights. This quality is similar to that described in the late Jerome Frank's work on persuasion and healing (Frank & Frank, 1991). Frank discussed how mental health professionals must be convincing and persuade clients that psychotherapy, as the selected means of treatment, is helpful. We would extend this to say that mental health professionals must be capable of persuasion and motivation that includes a human rights agenda. Part of being a motivator is instilling hope and belief in a promising and hopeful vision, so a social justice leader helps stakeholders move from accepting "what is" to believing in "what could be."

7. **Humble, lacking ego.** In our work, to help others become empowered we must learn to step aside and not interfere with client growth and development. A desired outcome in social justice mental health work is for the client or stakeholders to become self-reliant and no longer need us. This requires that we, as helping professionals, not let our own issues of being needed get in the way, and that we allow clients to move on. Part of this process of stepping out of the way involves having the humility to step aside, recognizing that we are not always the ones who know it all and understand our clients' problems better than the clients themselves. Rather, we are partners in the process of change. Therefore, we must accept and recognize our own limitations while truly acknowledging others' strengths and growth, while *letting go of our egos.*

8. **Responsible.** We live in a world where it is easier to blame others than to take responsibility for our behavior and actions. We hear endless stories from the media of instances of blaming

others, such as an individual suing McDonald's because the coffee was too hot and the individual got burnt. True leadership is the ability to own up to mistakes, errors, and ideas and plans that did not work, instead of blaming someone else or the system. We must also model taking ownership for our behavior and action for our clients and stakeholders.

9. **A guide, not an expert.** A social justice leader must assume a role as a guide rather than an expert. An authentic partnership and redistribution of power requires a guide to facilitate a process of justice and change, not an expert who is always in charge and makes decisions. An aspect of assuming a guiding role stems from Carl Rogers's (1957) work that emphasized trust as a core element in the therapeutic relationship. Therefore social justice leaders must acknowledge that their clients and stakeholders have something to contribute, and hence utilize community skills, expertise, and resources.

10. **Generates empowerment.** Leaders in social justice are empowerment enhancers. It is essential in striving for social justice and human rights that leaders work toward empowerment for each person and all people, not just for some.

11. **Understands self.** To be effective social justice leaders, we must first understand our own sociopolitical values, beliefs, attitudes, worldviews, and privileges. This understanding is similar to that required for us to acquire the multicultural counseling competencies. An understanding of how and what we believe helps us to be clear about how we are best able to help others and prevents our own biases and prejudices from obstructing this process. For example, if a psychologist has negative feelings about immigrants because she is embarrassed about her own immigrant parents, she may have difficulty working with a client who has migrated from El Salvador or Sudan and needs help adjusting to the U.S. culture. Therefore, as a helping professional, you must *know thyself* to be an effective social justice worker.

12. **Understands and appreciates differences in others.** As leaders in the field of social

transformation, we must not only understand ourselves but also have a deep and authentic appreciation of and respect for our clients, their families, and the communities that we work with. Thus, it is important to know, understand, acknowledge, and accept others' history and the influence of history on their lives today, the sociopolitical and sociocultural issues that impact their daily lives, and the psychological and ecological factors that impact them as people and groups of people.

13. **Able to use and understand research and data.** It is essential that social justice leaders use data and research to drive their work. Leadership regarding social change should not be based only on personal opinion but be supported by data. For example, if a mental health professional knows about the destructiveness of lead paint on intellectual functioning and is aware of the research, she can both educate her clients and assist clients in a low-income housing project to better advocate for themselves using the research findings.

14. **Model for others.** It is essential that leaders for social change become models for others to emulate. In many respects leaders working toward social justice are paving the way and have many eyes watching them. Being a role model for others is an important step to cultivate the next generation.

These 14 leadership qualities for social justice leaders provide a challenge for any of us in the mental health field who are trying to facilitate social transformation. Each quality by itself is a challenge, yet given our training as counselors and psychologists, we are in an ideal position to already be well versed in these skills.

DISCUSSION QUESTIONS

1. What qualities must a leader have?

2. What are some of the qualities that social justice counselors and psychologists must have?

3. What characteristics do you already have that enable you to be an active counselor/ psychologist social justice leader?

4. How do you think your role as a leader will affect (positively or negatively) your clients?

5. How do you think your graduate program has been helping you sharpen your role as a leader? Be specific.

   a. Take a look at the mission statement.
   b. What classes have you taken?
   c. Is leadership infused in classes and your graduate program?
   d. Have you been able to put into practice some of these concepts in the community and schools?

6. Think of a social justice and multicultural leader in the mental health profession.

   a. What makes this leader distinctive from other mental health professionals?
   b. What skills does this person have?
   c. How has this person impacted the community and the profession?

7. What are some of your fears or concerns about becoming a leader and advocate?

REFERENCES

Applegate, J. H., Earley, P. M., & Tarule, J. M. (2009). Support for women leaders: the visible and invisible. In C. A. Mullen (Ed.), *Leadership and building professional learning communities* (pp. 151–160). New York, NY: Palgrave Macmillan.

Avolio, B., Walumbwa, F., & Weber, T. (2009). Leadership: Current theories, research, and future directions. *The Annual Review of Psychology, 60,* 421–449.

Block, P. (1993). *Stewardship: Choosing service over self-interest.* San Francisco, CA: Berrett-Koehler.

Bordas, J. (2007, Fall). How Salsa, soul, and spirit strengthen leadership. *Leader to Leader, 46,* 35–41.

Burke, S., Sims, D., Lazzara, E., & Salas, E. (2007). *Trust in leadership: a multi-level review and integration. Leadership Quarterly, 18,* 606–632.

Burke, S., Stagl, K., Klein, C., Goodwin, G., Salas, E., & Halpin, S. (2006). What type of leadership behaviors are functional in teams? A Meta-analysis. *The Leadership Quarterly, 17,* 288–307.

Duignan, P. A., & Bhindi, N. (1997). Authenticity in leadership. An emerging perspective. *Journal of Educational Administration, 35,* 195–209.

Eagly, A. H., & Johnson, B. (1990). Gender and leadership style: a Meta-analysis. *Psychological Bulletin, 108*(2), 233–256.

Fiedler, F. E. (1969). Style or circumstance: The leadership enigma. *Psychology Today, 3*(4), 34–43.

Fine, M. (1994). Dis-stance and other stances: Negotiations of power inside feminist research. In A. Gitlin (Ed.), *Power and method: Political activism and educational research* (pp. 13–35). London: Routledge.

Frank, J. D., & Frank, J. B. (1991). *Persuasion and healing: A comparative study of psychotherapy* (3rd ed.). Baltimore, MD: Johns Hopkins University Press.

Goldfarb, K. P., & Grinberg, J. (2002). Leadership for social justice: Authentic participation in the case of a community center in Caracas, Venezuela. *Journal of School Leadership, 12,* 157–173.

Hersey, P., & Blanchard, K. H. (1969). Life-cycle theory of leadership. *Training and Development Journal, 23,* 26–34.

Hersey, P., Blanchard, K. H., & Natemeyer, W. E. (1979). Situational leadership, perception, and the impact of power. *Group and Organization Studies, 4,* 418–428.

House, R. J., & Mitchell, T. R. (1974). Path-goal theory of leadership. *Journal of Contemporary Business, 10*(3), 81–97.

Kanter, R. M. (1977). Some effects of proportions in group life: Skewed sex rations and responses to token women. *American Journal of Sociology, 82,* 965–990.

Lewis, J. A., Lewis, M. D., Daniels, J. A., & D'Andrea, M. J. (2003). *Community counseling: Empowerment strategies for a diverse society.* Pacific Grove, CA: Brooks/Cole.

Mann, R. D. (1959). A review of the relationships between personality and performance in small groups. *Psychological Bulletin, 56,* 241–268.

Patal, D. (1992, January). Minority status and the stigma of "surplus visibility." *Education Digest, 57*(5), 35–37.

Rogers, C. R. (1957). The necessary and sufficient conditions of therapeutic personality change. *Journal of Consulting Psychology, 21*(2), 95–103.

Schriesheim, C., & Stogdill R. (1975). Differences in factor structure across three versions of the Ohio State leadership scales. *Personnel Psychology, 28*(2), 189–206.

Senge, P. M. (1990). *The fifth discipline: The art and practice of the learning organization.* New York, NY: Doubleday.

Short, P. M., & Greer J. T. (2002). *Leadership in empowered schools: Themes from innovative efforts* (2nd ed.). Upper Saddle River, NJ: Merrill Prentice-Hall.

Stogdill, R. M. (1948). Personal factors associated with leadership: A survey of the literature. *The Journal of Psychology, 25,* 35–71.

Tannenbaum, R., & Schmidt, W. H. (1973). How to choose a leadership pattern. *Harvard Business Review, 51*(3), 162–180.

Tarule, J. M., Applegate, J. H., Earley, P. M., & Blackwell, P. J. (2009). Narrating gendered leadership. In D. R. Dean, S. Bracken, & J. Allen (Eds.), *Women in Academic Leadership: Professional Strategies, Personal Choices, 2,* 31–49. Sterling, VA: Stylus.

The Webster's New College Dictionary. (2008). 4th ed. Cleveland, OH: Wiley.

Theoharis, G. (2007). Social justice educational leadership and resistance: Toward a theory of social justice leadership. *Educational Administration Quarterly, 43*(2), 221–258.

Uhl-Bien, M., Marion, R., & McKelvey, B. (2007). Complexity leadership theory: Shifting leadership from the industrial age to the knowledge era. *Leadership Quarterly, 18*(4), 298–318.

11

ADVOCACY AND SOCIAL JUSTICE

Never be afraid to raise your voice for honesty
and truth and compassion against injustice and lying and greed.
If people all over the world . . . would do this, it would change the earth.

(William Faulkner)

Vision without action is a daydream. Action with without vision is a nightmare.

(Japanese proverb)

It only takes a single idea, a single action to move the world.

(Unknown)

Human progress is neither automatic nor inevitable . . . . Every step
toward the goal of justice requires sacrifice, suffering, and struggle;
the tireless exertions and passionate concern of dedicated individuals.

(Martin Luther King Jr.)

WARM UP EXERCISE

1. *Draw a horizontal line on a piece of paper. On the line, mark the dates and events where you advocated for an issue. This is your **Advocacy Line.***

2. *Draw a horizontal line under your **Advocacy Line.** Make a mark on the line with every event that you wished you had advocated for but didn't. This is your **Advocacy Wish Line.***

3. *Below the **Advocacy Wish Line** list the issues that you would hope to advocate for in the future. This is your **Advocacy Vision List.***

This chapter will discuss advocacy as it relates to multiculturalism and social justice. We will begin with an overview of the history of advocacy in psychology and counseling; this will be followed by a discussion of advocacy strategies and the application of advocacy skills to social justice work.

HISTORICAL OVERVIEW OF ADVOCACY

In the past decade, *advocacy* has become a buzz-word in the helping professions. As Gladding and Newsome (2004) stated, advocacy is a growing trend in counseling and hence the resurgence of literature on the topic (e.g., Bemak, 2000; Bemak & Chung, 2005, 2007, 2008; House & Martin, 1998; Kiselica & Robinson, 2001; Lewis, Arnold, House, & Toporek, 2002; Lewis & Bradley, 2000; Myers, Sweeney, & White, 2002; Stone & Hanson, 2002; Toporek & Liu, 2001). In the past decades the American Psychological Association (APA) and the American Counseling Association (ACA) have established committees, published special journal issues, and developed website resources on advocacy tools and competencies.

Despite the more recent attention to advocacy in psychology and counseling, it is not a new concept in the field. Advocacy began in the 1700s, when there was a public movement to improve treatment for people who were mentally ill (Brooks & Weikel, 1996). In 1908, Clifford Beers advocated for the mentally ill (Kiselica & Robinson, 2001), while at the same time Frank Parsons (1909) introduced vocational counseling as a means to address unemployment for youth who dropped out of school. A half-century later, social activism took root (e.g., civil rights movement, feminist movement) in the United States, causing debate in the helping professions about the role of advocacy for therapists and counselors.

Wright (1992) documented the history of advocacy in the APA for psychology as a profession as well as for client rights. As a result of oppression, racism, and discrimination, both multicultural

counseling (e.g., Arredondo et al., 1996; Atkinson, Thompson, & Grant, 1993; Leung, 1995) and feminist therapy (e.g., Comas-Díaz, 1987; Ennis, 1993) have strongly emphasized the role of advocacy in the helping professions. Community psychology and counseling (e.g., Lewis, Arnold, House, & Toporek, 2002; Lewis & Lewis, 1983; Lewis, Lewis, Daniels, & D'Andrea, 1998; Prilleltensky, 1997) have also emphasized the importance of incorporating advocacy as a critical role of helping professionals.

During the 1970s, community mental health advocacy gained recognition as a component of counseling. This changed in the late 1980s and 1990s, when advocacy and social change diminished in importance, and the counseling field strove to establish credibility and public acceptance by increasing the focus on accreditation and credentialing (McClure & Russo, 1996). Critics claimed that incorporating an advocacy role into the counseling profession was unrealistic and inappropriate (Weinrach & Thomas, 1998) and created issues of professional boundaries, dual roles (Toporek, 2000), and authoritarianism (Sollod, 1998).

Based on these criticisms many work settings neither supported advocacy nor viewed it as part of client services, viewing it instead as a potential threat, since empowered clients may challenge the politics, procedures, and structure of organizations, agencies, and institutions (Bemak & Chung, 2005). Other concerns were raised about incorporating advocacy into work with clients that could generate client dependency (Pinderhughes, 1983), foster client powerlessness (McWhirter, 1994), and potentially be viewed as condescending and disempowering to clients (Toporek, 2000).

Even so, in 2002, the ACA endorsed the advocacy competencies (Lewis, Arnold, House, & Toporek, 2002) as a step toward acknowledging the importance of advocacy work in counseling. The endorsement of the advocacy competencies has contributed to the ongoing current debate about the importance of advocacy as a significant aspect of helping professionals' work and the need for counselors and psychologists to address social injustices in their work (Bemak & Chung, 2005; Myers, Sweeney, & White, 2002).

TYPES OF ADVOCACY ACTIVITIES

The advocacy competencies (Lewis et al., 2002) provide a range of advocacy and empowerment strategies for working with clients and students in community, systems, and social and political advocacy. Advocacy in the helping professions includes a broad range of activities, from policy advocacy for the profession to advocating for clients and assisting clients to advocate for themselves. Professional organizational advocacy can be seen in matters that relate specifically to the profession, such as legislation, licensure, managed care, and prescription (Toporek, 2000) and in advocacy within professional organizations, such as the endorsement of multicultural counseling competencies in accreditation and standards of ethics (Arredondo et al., 1996; D'Andrea & Daniels, 1995; Sue, Arredondo, & McDavis, 1992).

Myers et al. (2002) provide a comprehensive review of and recommendations for advocacy in the helping profession. Illustrations of client advocacy can be seen when counselors and psychologists help in fighting against racism and discrimination against different ethnic, racial, cultural, and other diverse and disadvantaged groups in the United States (e.g., Astramovich & Harris, 2007; Chen-Hayes, 2000; D'Andrea & Daniels, 2000; Goodman & Waters, 2000; Herring, 2000; Sanders, 2000) as well as globally. Myers et al. (2002) stated that counseling and advocacy (regardless of the type) should not be viewed as mutually exclusive, but rather be seen as complementary and intertwined with work one does with clients and for the profession.

Even so, during the past 15 years, with the exception of multicultural counseling and feminist counseling, the term *advocacy* has generally been used to refer to activities that affect legislation and policy and enhance the credibility of the profession, rather than activities that promote change that addresses social inequities and

institutional changes that impact the lives and psychological well-being of clients. Even with the call for advocacy in the recent literature (e.g., Bemak, 1998, 2000; Bemak & Chung, 2005, 2007, 2008; House & Martin, 1998; Kiselica & Robinson, 2001; Lewis et al., 1998; McWhirter, 1994; Myers et al., 2002; Ratts, DeKruyf, & Chen-Hayes, 2007), there is still a significant gap between the theoretical discussion about the need for advocacy and actual training and practice. The next section will discuss the importance of advocacy in social justice work and the challenges and realities of actually being an advocate in the mental health field, and examine the need for advocacy in training and supervision.

SOCIAL JUSTICE AND HUMAN RIGHTS ADVOCACY

Why Is Advocacy Critical in Social Justice Work?

Since the 1960s and 1970s, there has been hesitation by helping professionals to incorporate advocacy into the role of mental health workers, psychologists, and counselors. While some mental health professionals continue to support the role of advocacy in the profession, many others are adamantly against it. The opposition's argument is rooted in traditional beliefs about the helping professions, and argues that the focus of counseling is on helping individuals with their personal and intrapsychic problems. Should there be injustice or patterns of unfairness or inequities in the client's world, the traditional position of counselors and psychologists has been to explore the internal processes of the client, change behavior to more effectively adapt or adjust, and assist with a shift in cognition so that the client's reactions change.

An example of this can be seen with Ade, a client who emigrated from Somalia and works as a baker. At work, he has three coworkers who are continuously making hostile comments such as, "Go back to Africa," or "Bet you never had food like this in Somalia land," or "You're making problems for us here, all you people coming over here and taking our jobs. I have a friend that could have used this job instead of you." Ade is very upset about his coworkers and is losing sleep worrying. On the advice of members of his church, he sought out a psychologist for help. A psychologist whose perspective is that her role is to help the client adjust might help Ade gain new perspectives on his colleagues (e.g., they are jealous, they are ignorant, they are threatened, they are scared, they are uneducated, etc.) so that the comments have less impact on Ade. The psychologist might also strategize with Ade about how to react differently, possibly doing or saying something differently that would help Ade feel better about the situation.

In contrast, a mental health professional with a social justice orientation would explore with Ade not only how to change his reactions to coworkers but also how to change the actual situation, so the comments and attitudes themselves are confronted. This would require exploring with Ade his comfort with and interest in changing the hostile circumstances in which he works, rather than just working with him to feel better with his own response. If Ade decides to try to change both himself and the situation, the next Somali or immigrant that comes to work at the bakery may not have to face the same situation or circumstances.

This example illustrates how emphasizing changing the client without considering the situation has the danger of leaving the psychosocial environment unchanged and intact. Introducing advocacy as an element in the psychotherapeutic process implies changing the status quo and makes the counselor or psychologist a social change agent. We would suggest that the inclusion of social transformation as part of the therapeutic process adds a dimension that is beyond the mainstream definition of working with clients one-on-one. Helping clients accept, adapt, and cope with institutional and societal barriers that have inhibited their quality of life and psychological well-being is more in line with our training as psychologists and counselors and our current skills and abilities.

It has been found (e.g., Prilleltensky, 1997; Sue, 1981) that due to the rapid changes in our society, methods of clinical interventions that used to work are no longer effective, given the presence of external factors that play a vital part in clients' growth and development. Politics and policies that impact people's lives—such as funding priorities for social service programs, legal decisions, going to war, unequal access to job promotion, continued racism and discrimination, career ladders, inequitable salaries, activities that are inaccessible access for physically challenged, and failing to provide health care benefits for gay and lesbian partners—all play major roles in clients' psychological well-being.

We as psychologists and counselors have been denying the impact and interrelationship of environmental factors on and with our clients. There are huge issues such as poverty, abuse, violence, drugs, academic failure, racism, sexism, homophobia, and so forth that greatly affect our clients' lives and their world (see Table 11.1). If we ignore these larger issues, and don't discuss with clients the toll that these social, political, and cultural factors take on them, we ignore a large and powerful aspect of our clients' lives. In fact, advocating for social justice issues means that, as helping professionals, we help clients figure out how to self-promote and participate in changing these social, political, and cultural issues. In addition, we actively promote change within the domain of our own personal lives through our professional associations and through political activism. In the example of Ade, the exploration of how to challenge the pattern of hostile and racist comments has an aim to change the situation itself rather than just Ade.

Advocacy is thus an important part of our work. We would suggest that adhering to our traditional roles as therapists and counselors contributes to maintaining and reinforcing the status quo, so that we end up politically supporting the social injustices, inequalities, and unfair treatment of certain groups of clients (Katz, 1985; Pack-Brown, Thomas, & Seymour, 2008). In fact, we would contend that advocacy is an ethical and moral obligation for psychologists and

Table 11.1 Boy Hangs Himself after Experiencing Anti-Gay Bullying

An 11-year-old boy hanged himself in April of 2009 after being bullied by his classmates for allegedly being gay. The boy's name was Carl Joseph Walker-Hoover, and he was a student at New Leadership Charter School in Springfield, Massachusetts. Carl's mother had been trying for weeks to get the bullying to stop, but the school did nothing to recognize the problem. Carl never stated that he was gay, but students learn at an early age to use anti-LGBTQ language to hurt their peers.

Not only is anti-LGBTQ harassment common among youth, but bullying in general is quite prevalent as well. Carl would have turned 12 on April 17, which was the day of the 13th annual National Day of Silence. On this day each year, thousands of students take a vow of silence to take action against anti-LGBTQ bullying at their school. If the schools start addressing these problems, they can save other children's lives and keep parents from having to deal with the type of grief that Carl's mother is experiencing.

Source: Presgraves (2009).

counselors and is part and parcel of being an effective mental health professional.

One of the arguments against incorporating advocacy in the helping profession is that the profession is a science, and as scientific disciplines, psychology and counseling should not take positions. We would argue that working with people to ensure that they receive equal and fair treatment, equivalent opportunities, and equal access to resources is not just a science but involves humanitarian values and beliefs and a moral obligation. People do not live in isolation but rather within an increasingly complex environment, and their psychological make-up is clearly intertwined with social, political, and cultural issues that are rooted in modern society. An example of this can be seen in the research that has shown racism having a significant bearing on psychological health (e.g., Constantine, 2006; Steele, Spencer, & Aronson, 2002; Sue, 2003).

One example I (Fred) recently experienced that illustrates the connection between person and environment was during a consultation for the Ministry of Health in Northern Ireland. Sadly, Northern Ireland has a very high rate of youth suicide. The government has been valiantly attempting to develop and introduce new intervention programs, yet the high rates of suicide remain constant. A colleague and I were invited to visit Northern Ireland to do an assessment and make recommendations for a plan of intervention. We visited numerous programs in the Catholic and Protestant sectors of Belfast and Derry (or Londonderry, depending on one's political affiliations), visited community centers under the protection of local community members, met with top health and mental health officials in Northern Ireland, and made several recommendations to the government. It was clear to us that the government's basis for designing suicide prevention programs and interventions had been on individual psychotherapy, without regard to the impact on people of the *troubles,* which is the term used to denote the sectarian conflict. My colleague and I were clear in our recommendations to the Ministry of Health officials that the *troubles* permeated every meeting we held and were in the forefront of any discussions about suicide, whether it was with local citizens—Catholic or Protestant—or mental health workers.

Based on our assessment, we recommended holding community and group meetings to discuss the loss, grieving, suicide, and feelings of despair that were so dominant in the Northern Ireland communities we visited. We suggested beginning with intrasectarian groups and gradually moving to intersectarian groups, all focusing on youth suicide and facilitated by neutral parties. This was flatly rejected by the health administrators and viewed as being potentially volatile and not within the purview of a health department. Interestingly, as time passed and other attempts at intervention failed, two years later our recommendations were being touted as the next step in mental health treatment, with substantive regional discussions about how to design and implement community interventions to address this very difficult and frightening problem facing youths across sectarian groups within the Northern Ireland community. We use this example only to illustrate the importance of taking a serious psychological problem and linking it back to the relevant factors within the larger community.

No different than Northern Ireland, individuals, regardless of where they live, cannot avoid the influence of society on their mental health and psychological well-being. As counselors and psychotherapists, we do not work in a vacuum that isolates individuals from their surrounding world. It is essential in our work that we acknowledge, recognize, and act on factors that have bearing on the psychological well-being and quality of life of our clients, their families, and their communities. Sometimes this involves assuming an advocacy role, which is consistent with Lerner's (1972) contentions: he talked about how the helping profession created a false dichotomy between social action and psychotherapy. According to Lerner, the aim and outcome of psychotherapy and social action is the same, with the difference being that psychotherapy is aligned with having intrapsychic obstacles, while social action is aligned with external obstacles. Lerner outlined the dichotomy between those who work on their clients and those who work for their clients.

Working for clients, counselors and psychologists are in a unique position to incorporate advocacy as part of their work. Given the fact that being a counselor or psychologist means having status and credibility that is rooted in institutional power and privilege, one can influence practices, procedures, and policies. Not only do mental health professionals understand the intrapsychic complexities of human suffering and pain, and not only are they knowledgeable about interpersonal dynamics and organizational

skills, but they also have access to resources, policymakers, and avenues for change that are not frequently accessible to clients. Understandably, not all counselors or psychologists will have the time or energy to effect major institutional or policy changes, yet all have the capability to facilitate some type of social change work, such as simply educating clients about their situation and their rights, or teaching them advocacy skills (Kiselica & Robinson, 2001). Adopting advocacy as part of psychotherapy has the potential to make a difference and create a better world that goes beyond an individual client.

Although we acknowledge the importance of advocating for policy change and funding for the profession that affects and benefits clients, we suggest that it is also important that advocacy be incorporated more directly with clients as well. Although eliminating barriers toward services, funding, and policy is essential, of equal importance is to use advocacy as a tool to eliminate institutional and societal barriers that obstruct clients' psychological growth, development, and well-being. This type of advocacy approach has a more direct effect on the clients, their families, and communities. In doing this more direct type of advocacy work, it is essential that counselors and psychologists be clear regarding the reasons and intentions for employing advocacy and aware of the impact of their advocacy work on clients.

Providing an example of this is a White colleague we know who is a professor at a major university and is highly supportive of African American graduate students. Although the African American students' work and level of responsibility are similar to those of other ethnic and racial groups in the graduate program, it is well known by students and faculty alike that our White colleague is overly supportive of African American students. When African American students hand in their papers late, she relaxes their deadlines; when African American students miss a class, she relaxes her grading standards for attendance. What in fact she does not do is hold African American students equally accountable for their behaviors and actions, and to the same standards, as other students. When we probed this issue with her and her colleagues, it became clear that she had grown up in a home where her father was a blatant racist and hated African Americans. "I will never do what my father did, never!" Her awareness of why and how she is advocating for African American students, and the ramifications of having different standards for African Americans than for other students, present an interesting challenge for the professor.

We would suggest that in this situation, the impact of lesser standards for one group than another is a disservice rather than a help and may have long range implications. This professor who unwittingly set up different standards for African American students has created a situation where there are serious implications for the African American students as well as all other students in the program. Thus, if psychologists and counselors are doing advocacy work because of personal unresolved issues or guilt about family members or their own privilege, then the use of advocacy may be inappropriate and at times, even detrimental to clients and families. Thus, we must be aware of our own issues and countertransference that may be disguised as advocacy when we work toward social justice.

DEFINITION OF ADVOCACY IN SOCIAL JUSTICE WORK

According to Merriam-Webster's Online Dictionary (http://www.m-w.com/dictionary/Advocate), *advocacy* is defined as "the act or process of advocating or supporting a cause or proposal, one that pleads the cause of another, and one that supports or promotes the interests of another." *Social justice advocacy* can be defined as "the belief that individual and collective actions are necessary to fight injustices that lead toward improving conditions for the benefit of both individuals and groups" (House & Martin, 1998). To advocate for clients can be viewed as an act of speaking up or taking action that leads toward environmental changes on behalf of clients (Kiselica & Robinson, 2001). This concept,

along with leadership and empowerment, helps to frame social justice and human rights for psychologists and counselors. To effectively combat and dismantle social injustices and human right violations, advocacy is an essential component of the work.

QUALITIES NECESSARY FOR EFFECTIVE ADVOCACY IN SOCIAL JUSTICE WORK

Possessing solid clinical and counseling skills is not the only prerequisite for helping professionals who want to become effective advocates. As one of my (Rita) students in a multicultural counseling class told me, "I used to think that the most important information that I would gain from the graduate counseling program was solid counseling skills, but I learned that the skills are not relevant if I also do not have solid multicultural awareness, knowledge, and competencies." An extension of this would be to add social justice skills, which many of our students now talk about as being as important as multicultural competencies.

Thus, being an advocate requires the core counseling skills and multicultural competencies, along with energy, commitment, motivation, passion, persistence, tenacity, flexibility, patience, assertiveness, organization, resourcefulness, creativity, a multisystems and multidisciplinary perspective, and the ability to deal with conflict and negotiate and access systems. It also requires an understanding of social change models and organizational dynamics, such as individual and institutional barriers to change, organizational collaboration, interdisciplinary collaboration, and client partnerships. On a personal level, it demands humility coupled with a profound dignity and respect for others.

Advocacy requires a balance of talents at several levels. One must be able to do hands-on work directly with clients, families, and communities while also being able to contribute to changing social policy in meetings, through scholarship, and through research. Both of the authors of this book have worked on different levels to create social change. For example, when I (Fred) directed the Massachusetts Department of Mental Health Region I adolescent treatment program for "untreatable" adolescents, I had morning meetings with the state commissioners of mental health, youth services, social services, and education to discuss funding, policies, and changes across the state. Then in the evening I went to the program's residential facility to eat dinner with the residents and staff and to speak to residents about their lives, their families, and how they were doing in school. Sitting with a 16-year-old emotionally disturbed adolescent requires a different set of skills than negotiating budgets with a state commissioner.

I (Rita) did similar work, meeting with community groups of refugees in the morning to talk about their needs, rights, concerns, and challenges as new members of U.S. society, and then meeting with policy makers, ESL teachers, and directors of social services and community agencies in the afternoon to share the refugee community's concerns. These later meetings set the stage for the refugee community to have a direct dialogue with service providers and policy makers to work collaboratively on how state agencies could be culturally responsive to new migrants. Talking to the refugees themselves required one set of skills, whereas discussions with policy makers and administrators required an entirely different set of skills and political savvy.

Kiselica and Robinson (2001) indicated that, supplementing the qualities for effective advocacy mentioned above, there is a need for commitment, appreciation, and a desire to alleviate human suffering. They stipulate that helping professionals must have compassion, sensitivity, and empathy for their clients and a commitment to improve the clients' life circumstances. We would add that it is very important for senior level psychologists and counselors in the field who have incorporated advocacy into their work to mentor and guide younger counselors and psychologists, junior faculty, and students. This can be achieved through supervision at various sites where counselors and psychologists work, through training sessions, through data analysis to identify injustices and inequities, and through publications that can reach a larger mass audience.

TYPES OF ADVOCACY AND ADVOCACY TASKS AND ACTIVITIES

Ezell (2001) identified 13 different types of advocacy and provided a comprehensive review of each kind. The types were wide-ranging, from case advocacy that focuses on advocacy for individuals, to class advocacy that focuses on groups of individuals who share the same problem, to policy advocacy that involves attempts to influence legal, social, economic, and governmental programs and policies. Lewis and Lewis (1983) looked at advocacy from a different vantage point, citing three levels of advocacy. They identified the first level as *here and now advocacy,* which is an instant response to an immediate situation; the second level as *preventive advocacy,* which is an action taken to prevent injustices against a group of individuals; and the third level as *citizen advocacy,* which is the movement to encourage others to take on social issues.

Toporek and Liu's (2001) model of advocacy incorporates both empowerment and social action as dimensions of advocacy. The model presents a continuum with empowerment on one end and social action at the other end. Both empowerment and social action take into account the sociopolitical context. Empowerment involves not only individuals, but may also include their families and/or communities. With the assumption that clients do not have the skills or knowledge to generate social change, the role of the counselor and psychologist is to initially assist clients in achieving their goals. However, they conclude that the purpose of empowerment is to enable clients to become independent from the counselor or psychologist, thus becoming truly empowered.

On the other end of the continuum is social action. The mental health professional's role in social action is external to counseling activities and involves active removal of barriers encountered by clients, their families, and their communities. Social action differs from empowerment in that social action is conducted at a macro social level, targeting issues that affect clients, such as legislation or policies. Empowerment in social justice will be discussed in more detail in the next chapter.

In addition to knowing the types and models of advocacy, it is important to look at how to proceed as an advocate. Promoting advocacy requires an ability to have an organizational perspective and see the larger systemic picture, thereby maintaining and holding on to the goal of one's advocacy work. Since advocacy and social change are difficult, it is also important to consider who might be one's potential allies who can assist in gaining momentum and partnerships to create social change. For example, when I (Fred) was trying to make significant changes in a large complex organization, I found that the state deputy commissioner, rather than the commissioner, was an ally who would help promote the change.

To effectively implement advocacy strategies, it is also critical to acquire skills to create systemic change. Doing advocacy therefore necessitates that psychologists and counselors act and be proactive on behalf of their clients, partnering with clients to challenge sometimes longstanding and undisputed traditions, policies, procedures, and notions that create and reinforce unfair treatment and inequalities. Becoming an advocate is not automatic; it requires organizational and communication skills. Thus, in our graduate training program, we actually provide a class on social justice where we help students develop systemic and organizational advocacy skills. (See Chapter 15 for an in-depth discussion of this program.)

As advocates, we must take it upon ourselves to dispute and challenge the status quo and the traditional models of changing the individual to fit the system, and instead assert and act to change the larger environment and surrounding socioecological systems. Within the advocacy framework, both the helping professional and the client are instrumental in promoting this change. Lewis et al. (1998) purport that advocacy serves two primary purposes: (a) increasing clients' sense of personal power, and (b) fostering environmental change that reflects greater responsiveness to their personal needs (p. 172).

To provide helping professionals with ideas on the type of advocacy work that can be done, Kiselica and Robinson (2001) presented a list of advocacy initiatives compiled from various sources (e.g., Baker, 1981, 2000; Kiselica, 1995, 2000; Kiselica & Ramsey, 2000) that ranged from ambitious to modest types of advocacy

Table 11.2   Types of Social Justice Advocacy

1. Arguing for better services
2. Pushing for increased clients' rights in the agency
3. Negotiating with agencies
4. Giving testimony to decision makers
5. Lobbying individual policymakers
6. Litigating or seeking legal remedies
7. Representing a client in an administrative hearing
8. Influencing administrative rule making in other agencies
9. Teaching advocacy skills to clients to solve a problem

(Continued)

Table 11.2 (Continued)

10. Educating clients on their rights
11. Educating the public on an issue
12. Monitoring other agencies' performance
13. Conducting issue research
14. Organizing coalitions
15. Influencing media coverage of an issue
16. Mobilizing constituent support
17. Political campaigning
18. Facilitating client access to information provided by institutions
19. Mediating between clients and institutions
20. Negotiating with outside agencies and institutions to provide better services for clients
21. Influencing policy makers through educational lobbying efforts
22. Directing complaints regarding inadequate services or oppressive policies to funding agencies
23. Using the Internet to

  - Market counseling services
  - Access online audio- and video-based help
  - Deliver multimedia-based assessment and information resources that match the ethnicity, age, and sex of the user
  - Reach clients who have transportation difficulties or live in geographically remote areas
  - Improve client access to self-help groups
  - Supplement traditional face-to-face counselor supervision with long-distance, electronic supervision
  - Expand opportunities for communication among counselors

Sources: Ezell (2001), Kiselica & Robinson (2001).

initiatives. Yet, each different type of advocacy has its own impact. Their examples ranged from talking to newspaper reporters and making television appearances to challenging cultural biases in standardized testing by publishing articles and books on the issue. Their suggested activities are important to note, in that advocacy does not necessarily mean holding demonstrations, lobbying, political campaigning, or mobilizing constituent support, but can happen by many other means. For example, I (Rita) contacted a journalist at a major newspaper and talked to him about the psychosocial adjustment challenges of refugees. The goal and the outcome of talking to the journalist were for him to write an article about the plight of refugees and therefore educate the public, as well as to bring awareness and attention of the issue to policymakers. This led to better social services for this population. Table 11.2 provides a list of different types of advocacy activities.

CHALLENGES AND REALITIES OF SOCIAL JUSTICE ADVOCACY

Being an advocate is not easy. One can experience burnout, become emotionally drained, or be seen as a troublemaker and be alienated. Some have identified that advocacy actually put their jobs at risk, and some have become the targets of backlash or harassment from colleagues (e.g., Bemak & Chung, 2005, 2007, 2008; Dinsmore, Chapman, & McCollum, 2000; Kiselica & Robinson, 2001). Even so, there is a great degree of personal satisfaction (Kiselica, 1998, 1999) in being an advocate, and there is a critical need to act in this capacity (Bemak & Chung, 2005, 2007, 2008).

It is inevitable that advocacy will create problems. Challenging the status quo and pushing for change has the potential to produce personal and professional difficulties. Taking on a system by becoming an advocate for social equity requires assuming a very different position than that of the traditionally defined counselor or psychologist. In our experience, there is typically resistance and resentment toward advocates for rocking the boat.

The story of a new counselor in a community agency recently came to our attention. As a new employee in a substance abuse treatment facility, she inherited a senior group cotherapist and several groups. In the groups, members were accustomed to being lectured at by the therapists and told exactly what they would talk about in each group therapy session. It was clear to the new counselor that the group members had little say about what happened in the group and no authority or power to change the dynamics. The clients felt powerless.

In an attempt to empower the members, the counselor set out to try to change these dynamics, asking group members what they felt was important to discuss in the group therapy sessions related to their substance abuse. Her advocacy for their empowerment led to dissension with her cotherapist; meetings with the agency director who talked about "how things are done here"; and resentment from her peers, who had serious concerns about the upstart new employee. The aim of the counselor was certainly not to create friction and animosity from colleagues but rather to fit in as a team player. Rather than be obstinate or refuse to recognize historical practices as "given practices," she questioned current practices in an attempt to improve services and advocate for fairness and equity that could empower and more fully benefit the clients (Bemak & Chung, 2005).

As in the case described above, it is risky to advocate, challenge, and confront supervisors and organizations to move toward social equity. Challenging the politics, procedures, and very practices in the place where we work may lead to negative repercussions (Bemak & Chung, 2005). Yet, our question would be, "How can we not do this work?" Consequently, an important aspect of being a successful advocate is figuring out how to sustain good professional relationships while challenging supervisors and organizations to adopt goals that benefit all clients, including those who are most marginalized or disenfranchised.

Nice Counselor Syndrome (NCS)

The NCS (Bemak & Chung, 2008) is typically manifested by many good-hearted, well-intentional psychologists and counselors who are commonly viewed as being the "nice" person at the agency, school, or organization. These professionals live up to their reputation of being nice people by the manner in which they consistently strive to promote harmony with others while avoiding and deflecting interpersonal conflicts in the school or organization in which they work. For example, the NCS in the school setting is evident in counselors who are noted to be comfortable assuming the roles of mediator and problem solver when working with students, parents, and other school personnel. The value these counselors place on being viewed as nice people by others prevents them from being willing to implement multicultural/social justice advocacy and organizational change services that predictably result in interpersonal disagreements and conflicts with other school personnel, especially those interested in maintaining the existing educational status quo (Bemak & Chung, 2008, p. 374).

Many counselors and psychologists experiencing NCS may truly believe in the importance of promoting educational equity for all students, and particularly students from marginalized groups. However, their overarching concern to be perceived as being nice people, who promote acceptance, peace, and interpersonal harmony at any cost, leads them to shy away from addressing, initiating, and confronting issues of equity and from advocating for fair treatment and access to opportunities and resources. NCS may therefore be said to be characterized by those counselors and psychologists who demonstrate a willingness to help perpetuate the status quo by conforming to the expectations and needs of others in order to be perceived as the "nice guy" (Bemak & Chung, 2008).

MOVING BEYOND NCS TO BECOME SOCIAL JUSTICE ADVOCATES

As we consider the challenges and realities of being advocates, it is essential to anticipate the personal and professional ramifications. For example, fear may be a personal obstacle, that is, fear of being disliked, or of being subjected to personal or negative peer pressure, or of being targeted for professional ostracism. This frequently happens when we do not conform to the traditional role of helping in a nice, noncontroversial, supportive, and friendly manner, which may lead to our being labeled as troublemakers (Bemak & Chung, 2008). There is also concern about professional character assassination. Colleagues or administrators may discredit counselors

or psychologists who practice advocacy, and this may lead to their jobs being jeopardized (Bemak & Chung, 2008).

Another personal obstacle is apathy. Personal apathy helps counselors and psychologists to avoid controversy and conflict with their coworkers and therefore leads them to be complacent about what exists and supportive of the status quo. Professional obstacles may include professional paralysis (Bemak & Chung, 2008): When psychologists or counselors think about the magnitude of social injustices, they may feel overwhelmed and confused with the complexity of these problems. This may lead to the professional thinking, "What can I do to make a difference? After all I'm just one person."

To simply adopt advocacy as part of one's role without any preparation or advanced consideration is similar to walking into a lion's den. Psychologists and counselors who are advocates must walk a fine line, trying to support causes of equity, justice, and fairness while keeping their jobs. It is essential that mental health professionals and counselors acquire skills to balance the institutional realities of working within systems where they may have minimal power with responding to and acting on issues for which they have ethical and moral responsibility to advocate for social justice for their clients. Critically important is to figure out strategies to deal with the institutional and individual barriers. Bemak and Chung (2005, 2008) discuss the types of skills needed for counselors to be effective advocates within educational settings. These

Table 11.3 13 Recommendations for Counselors as Advocates

1. *Define your role:*
   Include responsibilities and tasks of counselor that contribute to success.

2. *Emphasize equity and equal opportunity:*
   Distribute support, time, and resources evenly.

3. *Restructure intervention strategies:*
   Reach out to the larger community with intervention strategies.

4. *Teach clients their rights:*

   Provide tools that promote constructive change for clients that lead toward social justice, equal opportunities, and parity.

5. *Formulate partnerships with clients:*

   Formulate partnerships with clients who may lack the skills and knowledge to self-advocate.

6. *Align with clients to gain access to existing resources within their environments:*

   Know about organizational systems that are helpful in promoting positive change toward equity.

7. *Form alliances with others in your clients' environment:*

   Work with individuals who will work toward social change and decreasing inequities.

8. *Utilize data to change your role and incorporate advocacy:*

   Gather data and factual information that support a changing role, and advocate for that change.

9. *Encourage training in leadership and advocacy skills:*

   Know about organizational structure and change, and encourage trainings in organizations and graduate programs.

10. *Collaborate with other mental health professionals:*

    Collaborate with others in the mental health field to compile data that you can use to advocate for change.

11. *Participate in reform efforts:*

    Become a participant who contributes to these important efforts.

12. *Promote social action within a sociopolitical context:*

    Understand of how to promote social action within the sociopolitical domain.

13. *Collaborate with community agencies that provide other services:*

    Generate team support by utilizing additional resources.

Source: Bemak & Chung (2005).

skills can also be adapted to and used in community settings. Table 11.3 shows Bemak and Chung's (2005) 13 recommendations for counselors as advocates.

EXAMPLE OF ADVOCACY

A counselor, Gerard, took a new job and began providing counseling in a mental health clinic. After six months he noticed an increasing number of clients coming to the mental health clinic concerned about various issues, but all of them complained about headaches and stomachaches.

At first, Gerard helped clients specifically with their mental health problems, which included trouble concentrating, marital conflict, a growing anxiety about driving after witnessing a pedestrian being hit by a car, and behavioral problems in school. He did this without consideration of their headaches and stomachaches. Yet Gerard noticed that all the persons who came to see him also mentioned their physical ailments.

As more clients came for counseling with an assortment of mental health problems, Gerard continued to hear about the headaches and stomachaches. He grew concerned about the consistent pattern and decided to investigate to see if there might be some reason for the physical problems. He soon learned that all his clients lived near a chemical waste plant that had been taken over by a new owner one year before. Gerard began to gather information about the plant, the new owner, and the environmental effects of the kind of toxic waste that was being processed at the plant. He soon learned, from readings and public health officials, that there was a potential for serious mental and physical reactions to the waste and that the new owner had a track record of fines and citations for not following safety guidelines.

At this point Gerard took on a role as an advocate on two levels. First, on a systemic level, he began to question the practices of the chemical plant through letters to the editor of the local newspaper, calls to elected officials, meetings at the state level, and contacts with the public health department. Second, rather than discount the information he had gathered from his investigations, he decided to share it whenever a client complained about headaches or stomachaches. He told clients about the potential dangers of the chemicals being processed locally and provided information about the track record of the plant owners. If, in counseling, clients indicated that they wanted to do something about the situation, Gerard would help them explore avenues for action and advocacy. In this way, he himself became an advocate for his clients, and he simultaneously helped them self-advocate if they wanted to take action.

must move forward and beyond the traditional approach of focusing solely on the intrapsychic, accept and recognize the impact of sociopolitical factors on our clients and their families, and determine how our advocacy can effectively address those issues. As we take on this work, it is important that we attempt to clearly understand our own issues and processes and that we are clear about how we are taking on the advocacy role and why we are becoming advocates. As advocates, we must learn how to work cooperatively with other professionals and clients. As we do the work, it is essential that we exercise patience for the process of social change, since advocacy, similar to psychotherapy and counseling, is a process.

Acknowledging that advocacy is one of many roles we play as mental health professionals is important. Since not every activity and action with clients falls under the umbrella of advocacy, we must have a clear working definition of advocacy that guides our actions and interventions. A framework for advocacy is to keep in mind that it is a goal-seeking endeavor, and that the advocacy process involves obtaining, modifying, and promoting change to accomplish the targeted goal(s). The process of advocacy perpetuates social change and change in the status quo (Ezell, 2001). Being an advocate requires intentionality, a plan, and targeted efforts to generate change—social, economic, legal, cultural, and policy change.

CONCLUSION

In summary, as counselors and psychologists, surely part of our job is to advocate with an aim to create a just society in which all people have equal opportunities and resources to pursue their potential; to ensure that programs, services, procedures, and policies are accessible and efficient for all people; to establish and protect balanced and equal rights and entitlements; and to eliminate the negative and unethical impacts of social, economic, and political influences. We

DISCUSSION QUESTIONS

1. Take a look at the advocacy competencies endorsed by ACA in 2003.

   - What are some of things you are already doing as an advocate, either at your place of work or personally?
   - What are your strengths as an advocate?
   - What are some competencies endorsed by ACA that you lack?
   - What are some competencies that you are willing to work on to improve?

2. Analyze the following statement from this chapter: "We would contend that advocacy is an ethical and moral obligation for psychologists and counselors and part and parcel of being an effective mental health professional."

   - How would you argue this position in front of other mental health professionals who take the position that counseling and psychotherapy do not involve advocacy work and who argue that advocacy is not part of the role of mental health professionals?
   - Give an example of a situation in which you would be effective incorporating advocacy in your work as a mental health professional.

3. The chapter describes some characteristics of social justice workers. Three of the characteristics are humility, profound dignity, and respect for others.

   - How would you identify each of these characteristics in your own work and personality if you were faced with a situation where two teenage gang members were sent to your office, because both girls were found drawing graffiti on a wall in their middle school?
   - How would you show respect?
   - How would you display humility?
   - What would be one of your personal challenges?

4. According to Lewis and Lewis (1983), the three levels of advocacy actions are here and now, preventive advocacy, and citizen advocacy. Identify what your preferred level is, and identify some actions you could take at the other two levels.

5. Advocacy is described as challenging the status quo, and therefore it has the potential to produce personal and professional difficulties. Reflect on your own fears and concerns about being an advocate and risk taker and about creating interpersonal and organizational tension.

6. Describe a situation in which you have seen empowerment used on a personal, social, systemic, or political level.

REFERENCES

Arredondo, P., Toporek, R., Brown, S. P., Jones, J., Locke, D. C., Sanchez, J., & Stadler, H. (1996). Operationalization of the multicultural counseling competencies. *Journal of Multicultural Counseling & Development, 24*, 42–78.

Astramovich, R., & Harris, K. (2007). Promoting self-advocacy among minority students in school counseling. *Journal of Counseling and Development, 85*(3), 269–277.

Atkinson, D. R., Thompson, C. E., & Grant, S. K. (1993). A three-dimensional model for counseling racial/ethnic minorities. *The Counseling Psychologist, 21*, 257–277.

Baker, S. B. (1981). *The school counselor's handbook.* Boston, MA: Allyn & Bacon.

Baker, S. B. (2000). *School counseling for the twenty-first century* (3rd ed.). Columbus, OH: Merrill.

Bemak, F. (1998). Interdisciplinary collaboration for social change: Redefining the counseling profession. In C. C. Lee & G. R. Walz (Eds.), *Social action: A mandate for counselors* (pp. 279–292). Alexandria, VA: American Counseling Association.

Bemak, F. (2000). Transforming the role of the counselor to provide leadership in educational reform through collaboration. *Professional School Counseling, 3*, 323–331.

Bemak, F., & Chung, R. C-Y. (2005). Advocacy as a critical role for urban school counselors: Working toward equity and social justice. *Professional School Counseling, 8,* 196–202.

Bemak, F., & Chung, R. C-Y. (2007). Training counselors as social justice counselors. In C. C. Lee (Ed.), *Counseling for social justice* (2nd ed., pp. 239–258). Alexandria, VA: American Counseling Association.

Bemak, F., & Chung, R. C-Y. (2008). New professional roles and advocacy strategies for school counselors: A multicultural/social justice perspective to move beyond the nice counselor syndrome. *Journal of Counseling and Development, 86*, 372–381.

Brooks, D. K., & Weikel, W. J. (1996). Mental health counseling: The first twenty years. In W. J. Weikel & A. J. Palmo (Eds.), *Foundations of mental health counseling* (pp. 5–29). Springfield, IL: Charles C Thomas.

Chen-Hayes, S. F. (2000). Social justice advocacy with lesbian, bisexual, gay, and transgendered persons. In J. Lewis & L. Bradley (Eds.), *Advocacy in counseling: Counselors, clients and community* (pp. 89–98). Greensboro, NC: ERIC Counseling and Student Services Clearinghouse.

Comas-Díaz, L. (1987). Feminist therapy with Hispanic/Latina women: Myth or reality? *Women & Therapy, 6*(4), *The politics of race and gender in therapy* [Special issue], 39–61.

Constantine, M. (2006). Racism in mental health and education settings: A brief overview. In M. G. Constantine & D. W. Sue (Eds.), *Addressing racism* (pp. 3–14). Hoboken, NJ: Wiley.

D'Andrea, M., & Daniels, J. (1995). Promoting multiculturalism and organizational change in the counseling profession: A case study. In J. G. Ponterotto, J. M. Casas, L. A. Suzuki, & C. M. Alexander (Eds.), *Handbook of multicultural counseling* (pp. 17–33). Thousand Oaks, CA: Sage.

D'Andrea, M., & Daniels, J. (2000). Youth advocacy. In J. Lewis & L. Bradley (Eds.), *Advocacy in counseling: Counselors, clients and community* (pp. 71–78). Greensboro, NC: ERIC Counseling and Student Services Clearinghouse.

Dinsmore, J. A., Chapman, A., & McCollum, V. J. C. (2000, March). *Client advocacy and social justice: Strategies for developing trainee competence.* Paper presented at the Annual Conference of the American Counseling Association, Washington, DC.

Ennis, C. Z. (1993). Twenty years of feminist counseling and therapy: From naming biases to implanting multifaceted practice. *The Counseling Psychologist, 21*(1), 3–7.

Ezell, M. (2001). *Advocacy in the human services.* Belmont, CA: Brooks/Cole.

Gladding, S. T., & Newsome, D. W. (2004). *Community and agency counseling* (2nd ed.). Upper Saddle River, NJ: Prentice-Hall.

Goodman, J., & Waters, E. (2000). Advocating on behalf of older adults. In J. Lewis & L. Bradley (Eds.), *Advocacy in counseling: Counselors, clients and community* (pp. 79–88). Greensboro, NC: ERIC Counseling and Student Services Clearinghouse.

Herring, R. (2000). Advocacy for Native American Indian and Alaska Native clients and counselees. In J. Lewis & L. Bradley (Eds.), *Advocacy in counseling: Counselors, clients and community*

(pp. 37–44). Greensboro, NC: ERIC Counseling and Student Services Clearinghouse.

House, R., & Martin, P. (1998). Advocating for better futures for all students: A new vision for school counselors. *Education, 119,* 284–291.

Katz, J. H. (1985). The sociopolitical nature of counseling. *The Counseling Psychologist, 13*(4), 615–624.

Kiselica, M. S. (1995). *Multicultural counseling with teenage fathers: A practical guide.* Thousand Oaks, CA: Sage.

Kiselica, M. S. (1998). Preparing Anglos for the challenges and joys of multiculturalism. *The Counseling Psychologist, 26,* 5–21.

Kiselica, M. S. (1999). Confronting my own ethnocentrism and racism: A process of pain and growth. *Journal of Counseling and Development, 77,* 14–17. Belmont, CA: Brooks/Cole.

Kiselica, M. S. (2000, April). *Keynote address: The mental health professional as advocate: Matters of the heart, matters of the mind.* Great Lakes Regional Conference of Division 17 of the American Psychological Association, Muncie, IN.

Kiselica, M. S., & Ramsey, M. L. (2000). Multicultural counselor education: Historical perspectives and future direction. In D. C. Locke, J. E. Myers, & E. L. Herr (Eds.), *The handbook of counseling* (pp. 433–452). Thousand Oaks, CA: Sage.

Kiselica, M. S., & Robinson, M. (2001). Bringing advocacy counseling to life: The history, issues, and human dramas of social justice work in counseling. *Journal of Counseling and Development, 79*(14), 387–398.

Lerner, B. (1972). *Therapy in the ghetto: Political impotence and personal disintegration.* Baltimore, MD: Johns Hopkins University Press.

Leung, S. A. (1995). Career development and counseling: A multicultural perspective. In J. G. Ponterotto, J. M. Casas, L. A. Suzuki, & C. M. Alexander (Eds.), *Handbook of multicultural counseling* (pp. 549–566). Thousand Oaks, CA: Sage.

Lewis, J., Arnold, M., House, R., & Toporek, R. (2002). *ACA advocacy competencies.* Retrieved from http://www.counseling.org/Publications/

Lewis, J., & Bradley, L. (2000). *Advocacy in counseling: Counselors, clients and community.* Greensboro, NC: ERIC Counseling and Student Services Clearinghouse.

Lewis, J. A., & Lewis, M. D. (1983). *Community counseling: A human services approach.* New York: Wiley.

Lewis, J. A., Lewis, M. D., Daniels, J. A., & D'Andrea, M. J. (1998). *Community counseling:*

Empowerment strategies for a diverse society (2nd ed.). Pacific Grove, CA: Brooks/Cole.

McClure, B. A., & Russo, T. R. (1996). The politics of counseling: Looking back and forward. *Counseling and Values, 40,* 162–174.

McWhirter, E. H. (1994). *Counseling for empowerment.* Alexandria, VA: American Counseling Association.

Myers, J. E., Sweeney, T. J., & White, V. E. (2002). Advocacy for counseling and counselors: A professional imperative. *Journal of Counseling and Development, 80,* 394–402.

Pack-Brown, S. P., Thomas, T. L., & Seymour, J. M. (2008). Infusing professional ethics into counselor education programs: A multicultural/social justice perspective. *Journal of Counseling & Development, 86,* 296–302.

Parsons, F. (1909). *Choosing a vocation.* Boston, MA: Houghton Mifflin.

Pinderhughes, E. B. (1983). Empowerment for our clients and for ourselves. *Social Casework, 64*(4), 331–338.

Presgraves, D. (2009, April). *11-year-old hangs himself after enduring daily anti-gay bullying.* Retrieved from http://www.glsen.org/cgi-bin/iowa/all/news/record/2400.html

Prilleltensky, I. (1997). Values, assumptions, and practices: Assessing the moral implications of psychological discourse and action. *American Psychologist, 52,* 517–535.

Ratts, M., DeKruyf, L., & Chen-Hayes, S. (2007). The ACA advocacy competencies: A social justice advocacy framework for professional school counselors. *Professional School Counseling, 11*(2), 90–98.

Sanders, J. L. (2000). Advocacy on behalf of African-American clients. In J. Lewis & L. Bradley (Eds.), *Advocacy in counseling: Counselors, clients and community* (pp. 15–24). Greensboro, NC: ERIC Counseling and Student Services Clearinghouse.

Sollod, R. N. (1998). Unexamined religious assumptions. *American Psychologist, 53*(3), 324–325.

Steele, C. M., Spencer, S. J., & Aronson, J. (2002). Contending with group image: The psychology of stereotype and social identity threat. In M. Zanna (Ed.), *Advances in experimental social psychology* (pp. 379–440). New York, NY: Academic Press.

Stone, C. R., & Hanson, C. (2002). Selection of school counselor candidates: Future directions at two universities. *Counselor Education and Supervision, 41*(3), 175–193.

Sue, D. W. (1981). *Counseling the culturally different: Theory and practice.* New York, NY: Wiley.

Sue, D. W. (2003). *Overcoming our racism: The journey to liberation.* San Francisco, CA: Jossey-Bass.

Sue, D. W., Arredondo, P., & McDavis, R. J. (1992). Multicultural counseling competencies and standards: A call to the profession. *Journal of Counseling and Development, 70,* 616–624.

Toporek, R. L. (2000). Developing a common language and framework for understanding advocacy in counseling. In J. Lewis & L. Bradley (Eds.), *Advocacy in counseling: Counselors, clients and community* (pp. 5–14). Greensboro, NC: ERIC Counseling and Student Services Clearinghouse.

Toporek, R. L., & Liu, W. M. (2001). Advocacy in counseling. In D. B. Pope-Davis & H. L. K. Coleman (Eds.), *The intersection of race, class, and gender in multicultural counseling* (pp. 385–413). Thousand Oaks, CA: Sage.

Weinrach, S. G., & Thomas, K. R. (1998). Diversity-sensitive counseling today: A postmodern clash of values. *Journal of Counseling and Development, 76*(2), 115–22.

Wright, R. H. (1992). The American Psychological Association and the rise of advocacy. *American Psychologist, 23*(6), 443–447.

12

THE MYTHS AND REALITIES OF EMPOWERMENT

You may never know what results come of your actions, but if you do nothing there will be no result.

(Mahatma Gandhi)

We become successful by helping others become successful.

(Unknown)

WARM UP EXERCISE

1. Have you ever advocated for something? What happened?

2. What were the barriers to your advocacy?

3. Do you have any heroes or heroines who advocated for something they believed in? Can you identify the qualities that made them effective advocates?

Social justice, social change, and empowerment cannot be separated. An outcome of social justice and human rights within the context of mental health is a shift of power, with clients and stakeholders gaining more say and influence over their lives and the lives of others. To be effective in empowering people, one must recognize the way power influences individual, family, and community social justice and human rights. One must also recognize and understand that powerlessness creates obstacles to personal, social, and community growth and development as well as other ongoing disadvantages, such as lack of access to opportunities and equal rights.

Rappaport (1987) stated that empowerment is personal mastery and control over one's life, caring about others, and the ability to exert political and social influence.

At the root of empowerment is the concept of power, as we discussed in Chapter 9 on social change. May (1972) based power on the character of the relationship, describing five types of power that incorporate both destructive and constructive elements. May explained how the destructive aspects of power include exploitation and manipulation. The other forms of power he described as being either constructive or destructive, depending on how they were used. Competitiveness could be used in either a positive or negative manner, while nutritive power, or having power for others, and integrative power, or power with others, could also be used in helpful or unhelpful ways.

In psychology and counseling, one aims to support and foster an outcome for clients in which they acquire power and subsequently become empowered on *personal, social, systemic,* and *political* levels. When we offer counseling from a social justice framework, the outcome and goals expand to include not only *personal* empowerment, but also *social, systemic,* and *political* empowerment. Thus, when we counsel and advocate with and for clients' rights, we are aiming to support clients in gaining a say over their own lives as well as affecting the world around them. A way to consider this is to think about, for example, a Latina in-home program supervisor who came for counseling because she experienced unfair treatment and discrimination by staff from other agencies. The counselor could have simply focused on her feelings of helplessness and frustration and successfully aided her in coping with the situation. To address the social aspects of her situation meant exploring and supporting her interest to challenge the individual(s) who were discriminating against her and trying to work things out. This would be empowerment on a social level.

The counselor may also want to emphasize systemic empowerment by exploring what she wants to do with the knowledge that many of the

other Latina women in her agency had also experienced unfair treatment and were frustrated and angry. If she wanted to advocate and challenge the discrimination beyond her own experience to improve the interagency relationships and address the broader issue within the larger human services programs, this would constitute systemic empowerment. Systemic empowerment is complemented by the supervisor's interest in advocating politically. The counselor could assist and support the supervisor's interest in advocating for Latina women to be represented on various interagency committees that could attend to this issue and introduce new actions and policies; this would be political empowerment.

As we discussed in previous chapters, traditional psychotherapy and counseling originate with a focus on the client without much regard for the impact of sociopolitical forces and ecological factors that contribute to the problems faced by clients and their families. Therefore, historically, helping professionals have not been involved in their clients' worlds outside of the personal processes that are explored in psychotherapy and counseling sessions. Working toward social justice and human rights involves a significantly broader awareness and emphasis on the intersecting factors that impact a client's life and attention to the rights of others, requiring client empowerment that goes beyond intrapsychic processes.

Thus, empowerment involves the helping professional working within the clients' everyday life experiences and associated injustices. The socioeconomic, sociocultural, sociohistorical, sociopolitical, and ecological contexts of a client's life are essential elements to incorporate into counseling (Bemak & Conyne, 2004; Toporek & Liu, 2001). McWhirter (1994) underscored this, emphasizing that empowerment must take into account the sociopolitical context within which clients live. It follows that in moving toward social equity and equal rights, clients must have influence in these dimensions that affect their lives.

Consequently, empowerment acknowledges the central role of power dynamics at societal, community, cultural, familial, and individual levels (Pinderhughes, 1983). To ignore the importance of power in a broader context is to ignore a crucial influence in empowerment. Simply recognizing oppression, discrimination, poverty, racism, and so forth and how a client manages these issues in his or her life is not enough. Rather counselors and psychologists must act on social injustices, such as oppression or discrimination, by expanding their traditional roles and developing awareness of and action on social, political, and economic barriers encountered by marginalized and disenfranchised clients (McWhirter, 1994).

AUTHENTIC EMPOWERMENT

Empowerment is a term that is commonly used nowadays. Counselors and psychologists regularly talk about empowering individuals, families, and communities, and are in agreement that empowerment is a good thing. The concept and term are used regularly in discussions about clients and psychological interventions. No one is against empowerment, and everyone supports empowering others as a goal. Yet the casual and everyday inclusion of empowerment as part of counseling and psychotherapy, in our opinion, has diminished its potency. We have been struck by how some proponents of empowerment have difficulty letting go of control, giving up elements of their own power in therapeutic encounters, or actually supporting clients to "run with" their newfound power. At times, well-intentioned therapeutic encounters have fallen short of the goal of empowerment. Thus, when we consider empowerment, we have used the term *authentic empowerment*.

As clients grow and begin to experience authentic empowerment, there may be an accompanying assertiveness or challenging of the counselor or psychologist, which may present difficulties for the mental health professional. Although a decreased dependence on and eventual end of the need for us as counselors or psychologists is clearly a goal of therapy, the reality

that we are not needed, and that our clients have attained true autonomy and self-mastery, may raise strong countertransference reactions, resulting in conscious or unconscious resistance to the client's empowerment.

AUTHENTIC EMPOWERMENT AND ADVOCACY

Authentic empowerment is seen as a dimension of advocacy in which the helping professionals assist clients in achieving goals and eliminating barriers that prevent clients and families from attaining fair treatment and equal quality of life. Initially counselors and psychologists may educate clients about their circumstances, teach them advocacy skills, and collaborate with them in an effort to achieve social justice, with the outcome being that clients master the skills to advocate for themselves. Authentic empowerment occurs when counselors and psychologists are genuinely cultivating and supporting the client in developing personal authority and a command of themselves and their ability to positively influence the world around them. Clients begin to have a more profound sense of self, with a deeper understanding about what this means for improving themselves and the world around them, resulting in advocacy activities. The advocacy that comes along with social justice and human rights begins with the resolution of personal issues that allows clients to gain a sense of self that provides a base from which to help and care for others.

FACTORS IN EMPOWERMENT

Becoming an advocate for empowerment to promote social justice is not an automatic process. It takes time, commitment, and certain attributes. Below we will describe 10 factors that we consider key in fostering empowerment (see Table 12.1).

1. **Personal commitment.** To facilitate empowerment, one must have a personal investment in the issue at hand. Being personally involved and

dedicated to the social justice issue leads to empowerment of the self and empowerment of others. The commitment to change has a direct relationship with empowerment. Therefore, if people are committed to equal marriage rights for gay and lesbian couples, it is more likely that they will become empowered in pursuit of this goal.

2. **Hope.** When we have hope, or the belief that there will be a positive outcome as a result of our actions, then there will be a greater potential for empowerment. In contrast, the absence of viable success or progress toward creating change and justice has the potential to deflate and disempower. Thus, even small successes at reaching social justice goals generate faith that actions will result in positive outcomes. For example, if a woman is being sexually harassed at her workplace, she may go to see a psychologist to work on her feelings of anger and fear. If, in counseling, she realizes that many women are experiencing the same issues, she may decide that she wants to take action with the supervisors to address the broader issue of harassment within the workplace. If she takes action within the workplace and the sexual harassment decreases, the likelihood is that she will feel empowered by seeing that things in fact can change.

3. **Social support.** When one knows that there are others who will join in and support the movement and take action to promote human rights and social justice, it facilitates empowerment. This is also true if individuals have a social support network to join them. This means that if I recognize that my peers and colleagues encounter similar problems, and I know that they will join in the effort to create change, I feel empowered.

4. **Common goals.** Shared goals are a factor that contributes to empowerment. When one shares the same vision for social justice with others, there is a sense of mutuality and empowerment. Knowing that there are others who feel upset over toxic emissions by a chemical plant in a particular community helps those involved to know there is support and to feel empowered to take action.

5. **Available action.** When there is a prospect of taking action, it helps solidify feelings of empowerment and a sense that there can be change. For example, when several high school students were caught with alcohol, the principal gave harsher penalties to the African American students involved than to the White students. A number of African American parents were upset and approached the school board. Knowing that there was this available action to take helped the parents feel empowered.

6. **Not being afraid of conflict or tension.** Tackling social justice and human rights issues creates dissonance and challenges existing structures. Being able to handle tension and conflict is critical in facilitating empowerment. If one avoids interpersonal tension, it will be disempowering.

7. **Comfort with discomfort.** Challenging existing structures to promote equity, access, and fairness has the potential to generate confusion and chaos. Having the capacity to adapt and accept a disorderly world while change is happening is an important factor in feeling empowered.

8. **Understanding process.** Empowerment requires us to understand how change happens and to have a good sense of process. Progression and change take time, so one must be patient and accepting in order to feel empowered.

9. **Historical successes.** We base our experiences of empowerment on the past. If we have had small successes in creating change in the past, or observed others having successes, then we are much more likely to feel empowered.

10. **Having a role model who was empowered.** Having someone who stood for social justice and human rights who is a role model is important. An exemplary figure who has tackled the issues of change to improve society helps to foster empowerment. Role models could be someone living locally in one's neighborhood or national or international figures such as Martin Luther King Jr., Harriet Tubman, John F. Kennedy, Nelson Mandela, the Dalai Lama,

Table 12.1 10 Key Factors for Fostering Empowerment

Personal commitment

Hope

Social support

Common goals

Available action

Not being afraid of conflict or tension

Comfort with discomfort

Understanding process

Historical successes

Having a role model who was empowered

Aung San Suu Kyi, Mahatma Gandhi, Mohammed Ali, Cesar Chavez, Frederick Douglass, Sitting Bull, Shirin Ebadi, Rosa Parks, Jackie Robinson, or Harvey Milk.

CASE STUDY EXAMPLE OF SOCIAL JUSTICE AND AUTHENTIC EMPOWERMENT

To illustrate social justice, advocacy, and empowerment, we would like to present a real life case study example of how psychotherapists and counselors utilized advocacy to assist their clients toward empowerment and social justice work. For this study, the two authors of this book received funding from the Martha Holden Jennings Foundation to conduct a project that aimed to improve academic performance with high-risk students through family involvement. The project was based in a school located in a low-income urban area that was identified as having high numbers of students who lived in poverty, qualified for free and reduced-price meal programs, and had very low school performance. The aim of our project was to improve academic achievement and student performance for students at the highest level of risk for academic failure in the school.

Research has shown that family involvement helps raise students' academic performance (Jeynes, 2007). This project specifically targeted disengaged and marginalized families, generating a counseling intervention support group for caretakers, including parents and grandparents. The longer-term goal for the group was to have the families assume ownership and responsibility for the project and become engaged and active in the students' education.

"Disengaged families" were defined as those families not actively engaged in their children's school lives and having little or no contact with school personnel. All the families, in fact, had long-standing records of not responding to repeated attempts by school administrators, counselors, and teachers to reach them and discuss their children's school performance and behavior (Bemak & Cornely, 2002).

Initially the school principal was extremely hesitant about the project, worried that parents would mobilize and challenge her leadership and authority. After several meetings where we advocated for the potential positive outcomes of the project, the principal relented and gave permission to implement it. Students involved in the study were selected based on the following criteria: poor academic performance, behavioral problems, and little or no family contact with school personnel. Working with the school counselors, ten students were identified who were failing seventh grade and whose families had no involvement with the school.

Our next step was to contact the parents and guardians of these ten children. Contacting the parents was a major challenge, since one of the criteria for selection was that parents or guardians had a history of ignoring any attempts by the school to reach them. After numerous telephone calls and follow-up visits to homes, we were able to persuade eight parents/guardians to attend a meeting to discuss their children's school performance.

At the first meeting we discussed the goals for the project. Participants were initially suspicious, hesitant to speak, and distrustful of attending another meeting where they were talked "at." Rather than tell the parents and guardians what we were going to do at the meetings, we encouraged them to help us define what would be most helpful in order to support their children in school. In effect, they defined our project rather than the project defining them, and they were intrigued with the idea that they would set the agenda and the goals for our meetings.

The experience of being valued participants was quite unique for these parents and guardians, and as the first meeting progressed, the participants became animated and excited as they defined the agenda and goals for the meeting. After a highly productive discussion and unanimous agreement that "this meeting was very different from any other meeting they had ever been to," the question was posed to the group about how often to meet. The group itself decided that they *wanted* to meet on a regular basis every two weeks.

In the parents/guardians group there was no regular set agenda; instead there was an open forum in which the members set the agenda for each meeting within the framework of improved academic performance of the children. Meetings were facilitated by us (Fred and Rita). At first, parents and guardians kept asking us to "tell them what to do" since they were accustomed to participating in that manner. Aiming toward *authentic empowerment* and equity, we continually asked them as a group to set the agenda, group rules, and norms. Members agreed that they were all concerned about their children and began discussions about how to improve their school performance.

As the participants talked about their children, discussions evolved into sessions of sharing about their personal lives and challenges, fears, difficulties, and challenges they faced as parents and grandparents. Relationships within the families were discussed, as were personal issues that had been unresolved, such as prior incarceration, homelessness, prostitution, and drug abuse. These sessions led toward self-healing and a greater awareness and skill in providing support for their children's education.

One day, one of the mothers expressed frustration about not having time, energy, or knowledge of how to help her child in school. "I work many jobs and long hours, so when I get home I am exhausted. My kids, they all come running up to me yelling and carrying on, so I just run to my bedroom, lock the door, and turn on loud music. They just bang away at my door, but I ignore it." Through the meetings and group support, this mother learned how to come home and balance time with her three children while finding a moment for her to catch her breath that her family agreed to.

The meetings were held regularly on a bimonthly basis for the entire school year. Each meeting involved working out transportation for those members without transport or gas money, university student volunteers to provide childcare for younger children, and volunteer tutors. During the entire academic year, not one of the parents or guardians, students, or volunteers dropped out of the program. In fact, as the year progressed, a second parent for some of the participating children started to regularly attend the meetings, and other parents of other children joined the group. After a few months, there was a waiting list to join, generated by interested students and parents/guardians. The group of parents and grandparents decided that everyone had to make a commitment to attend the meetings, and that anyone who missed two meetings in a row without a good reason would not be permitted to remain in the group.

Meetings were held in the school gym. Several activities were conducted simultaneously. In one corner of the gym, we (Fred and Rita) met with parents and guardians to discuss parenting as well as associated personal, family, and work-related problems. These sessions were most often deeply personal, with tears, hugs, and a tremendously supportive environment. In another section of the gym, the children—divided according to age level and/or school subject—worked on their homework and studies with volunteer tutors. Yet another area of the gym was designated for younger siblings who required childcare and were looked after by other university student volunteers. The set-up in the gym resembled a living room, where all family members were present and visible to each other, and there were multiple ongoing activities. At times, everyone joined together for a large community meeting that allowed parents and guardians, children, and volunteers to speak together about issues, common goals, and the program.

As the project progressed, the students began to improve their performance in school, and the parents, guardians, and grandparents began to feel empowered. The stories of life challenges in the groups and community meetings affected family relationships and changed interactions with children, and the group became a safe and supportive haven in a trying world. Mothers, fathers, and grandparents collectively brainstormed about how to overcome each other's problems, gave helpful advice to each other, and encouraged one another to make significant changes.

Members talked about the group as a life-changing experience. One mother shared how joining the group was a turning point in her life. The phrase took root, and the members named the group and the project "Turning Point." Upon hearing the name for the group, the children also wanted an identity, so we had a community meeting to decide about the name for their portion of the program. They decided collectively to use the term "TP" since it was a "cooler" term than "Turning Point," demonstrating that not only the parents but also the children took ownership and gained a say in their lives. As the word got around, students would wait outside the school building to request to be part of the TP. The Turning Point parents/guardians decided that any students could be involved in the project, the only criterion being that a family member or guardian must also attend.

At the end of the school year, an event occurred that mobilized the Turning Point group, even though their children were not among those involved. On the last day of school, administrators sent letters to parents of students who needed to repeat a grade, informing them that their children would be held back for another year. These parents were in total shock, since they had had no idea that their children were doing poorly academically. Because the letters were sent on the last day of school, it was impossible for parents to discuss the matter with teachers or the school principal, since the school was closed.

The Turning Point group was outraged when this occurred. They were irate over how school administrators had handled the situation, and they brainstormed how to tackle the problem. As a group, they decided to contact other parents in their neighborhood and circulate a petition about the principal's decision and a demand for a meeting with parents and the principal about this issue. They also decided that rather than stage a demonstration, a small group of parents should contact the state department of education to talk to the superintendent.

Before the beginning of the new academic year, the parents were informed that a new principal had been assigned to the school. It is unclear whether this was a direct outcome of the work of the Turning Point group. Regardless, it reinforced the parents' conviction that they could take control of the situation, be empowered, advocate, and create change toward equity.

Measured results of the project were significant at a very high level. Parents became more positive and provided discipline and attention to their children, children communicated more openly and positively with parents and grandparents, disruptive behaviors both in school and at home significantly decreased, and grades and attendance dramatically improved. Furthermore, the parents and guardians of the Turning Point group became empowered, and they empowered others to stand up for their rights.

This case example illustrates advocacy, leadership, and *authentic empowerment,* where individuals truly defined strategies, goals, and directions for their own positive healthy growth. The group was a disenfranchised and impoverished population that historically had had no say about their children, their children's education, or their own lives. Given the opportunity to take leadership roles, to advocate for each other and eventually with the school system, and to become empowered, they excelled.

DISCUSSION QUESTIONS

1. Can you identify one or two myths of empowerment?

2. Discuss the definition of *empowerment* presented in the chapter.

3. What are some of the components of empowerment that will be important in your work as a mental health professional?

4. Analyze the following statement: "Simply recognizing oppression, discrimination, poverty, racism, etc., and how clients manage these issues in their lives is not enough."

   a. Identify a current issue that is affecting your local area.
   b. Design some strategies that you could employ as a mental health professional to address those injustices.
   c. What elements of empowerment would you use?

5. Choose one of the 10 key factors in fostering empowerment, and reflect on how this is important in the process of empowering yourself and others.

6. Using the example of Turning Point in the chapter, identify the factors that were important to fostering empowerment in the group members.

7. The chapter describes the importance of resolving personal issues in order to help others. List two or three personal social justice resolutions that you could include in your daily practice to make sure you are working toward authentic empowerment with your clients.

REFERENCES

Bemak, F., & Conyne, R. (2004). Ecological group work. In R. K. Conyne & E. P. Cook (Eds.), *Ecological counseling: An innovative approach to conceptualizing person-environment interaction.* Alexandria, VA: American Counseling Association.

Bemak, F., & Cornely, L. (2002). The SAFI model as a critical link between marginalized families and schools: A literature review and strategies for school counselors. *Journal of Counseling and Development, 80,* 322–331.

Jeynes, W. H. (2007). The relationship between parental involvement and urban secondary school student academic achievement: A meta-analysis. *Urban Education, 42,* 82–110.

May, R. (1972). *Power and innocence.* New York, NY: Norton.

McWhirter, E. H. (1994). *Counseling for empowerment.* Alexandria, VA: American Counseling Association.

Pinderhughes, E. B. (1983). Empowerment for our clients and for ourselves. *Social Casework, 64*(4), 331–338.

Rappaport, J. (1987). Terms of empowerment/exemplars of prevention: Toward a theory for community psychology. *American Journal of Community Psychology, 15*(2), 121–145.

Toporek, R. L., & Liu, W. M. (2001). Advocacy in counseling. In D. B. Pope-Davis & H. L. K. Coleman (Eds.), *The intersection of race, class, and gender in multicultural counseling* (pp. 385–413). Thousand Oaks, CA: Sage.

13

INTERDISCIPLINARY COLLABORATION AS A MEANS OF ACHIEVING SOCIAL JUSTICE

I offer you peace. I offer you love. I offer you friendship. I see
your beauty. I hear your needs. I feel your feelings. My wisdom flows from the
Highest Source. I salute that Source in you. Let us work together for unity and love.

(Mahatma Gandhi)

WARM UP EXERCISE

1. *What professional disciplines do you think are linked to counseling and psychology?*

2. *Describe how each of the professional disciplines you listed in #1 links with counseling and psychology.*

3. *What would counselors and psychologists learn from collaborating with professionals from the disciplines you listed in #1?*

4. *How would you reach out and collaborate with someone from another discipline? Discuss strategies you might use to do this.*

5. *Describe a project that you might propose with colleagues from another discipline.*

A major key in working toward social justice is for counselors and psychologists to work across disciplines. In moving toward a social justice model, it is critical that mental health professionals and counselors look beyond the exclusionary view toward other professional disciplines. Historically the mental health field has been isolated, related to the European American focus on individual psychotherapy, as previously discussed in this book. The emphasis on individual work promotes a narrow and linear perspective that traditionally excludes other professional disciplines. This is especially true because the profession's constricted emphasis on individual interventions, rooted in traditions of psychopathology and a disease model, gives it little cause to find benefit from other professional areas.

When one moves beyond this restricted definition of mental health and counseling to include a broader view inclusive of the socioecological, community, sociohistorical, sociopolitical, psychosocial, and family contexts of counseling and psychotherapy, there is a natural linkage with other professional disciplines and greater compatibility with a social justice model framework. Social work, sociology, psychology, public health, education, medicine, psychiatry, anthropology, geography, ethnic studies, women's studies, nursing, law, geography, economics, and political science intersect with mental health issues and counseling in ways that can contribute to alleviating problems from a holistic perspective that combines human rights and social justice.

Working with individuals, families, groups, or communities on human rights violations and social injustices is a complex, multidimensional, and multifaceted issue. Although our professional discipline provides us with a solid understanding and foundation for working on these diverse issues, it gives us only one viewpoint. The other disciplines mentioned above offer other perspectives on the problems faced by individuals, groups, families, and communities in our society. Particularly when broadening our work to include efforts leading toward human rights and social justice challenges, it is helpful to move beyond the psychological realm and incorporate other perspectives. For example, we (Fred and Rita) have done extensive collaboration with sociologists, cultural anthropologists, public health officials, and international lawyers, to better understand the problems faced by urban children, refugees, and other marginalized groups. Their training and work in sociology, anthropology, public health, and law gives new and different ways to examine research with this population and develop prevention programs, offering us a far wider understanding of the issues at hand than our psychological training allows.

Thus, work toward eliminating human rights violations and social injustices from a multidisciplinary perspective helps us gain a more holistic understanding of the situation and a broader approach to deal with these challenges. The same could be said for a counselor or psychologist counseling a homeless family; the mental health professional might collaborate with the housing office, employment programs, the local school, juvenile services, and a public health official. Or a counselor might be working with a client in foster care, and therefore might need to collaborate with social worker, case manager, psychiatrist, teachers, and so forth.

The interdisciplinary collaboration with people from other disciplines requires a change in the function and role of the counselor or psychologist, who becomes a partner in addressing social issues and inequities in contemporary society. This necessitates a reexamination of the fundamental philosophical principles underlying counseling and psychology and a reconceptualization of strategies to engage individuals, groups, communities, institutions, and societies in the process of change and growth. Simultaneously, it requires a critical examination of training for mental health professionals and counselors that incorporates ways to effectively implement techniques that work toward social justice and human rights across professional disciplines. We would suggest that contemporary counseling and psychology, as a profession, has been markedly deficient in linking to the larger society and world in embodying the principles of social change and advocacy that addresses the social, political, cultural, and economic problems faced by hundreds of millions of people globally, making it critical to redefine the role of counselors and psychotherapists as partners in achieving social justice.

THE IMPORTANCE OF COLLABORATING ACROSS DISCIPLINES

As this chapter points out, we believe that it is essential to collaborate with professionals from other areas of specialization. This relates to an important fundamental belief that there is a relationship among social, cultural, psychological, educational, political, health, historical, and economic problems, especially as we attend to human rights and social justice, that directly impacts the need for a changed role for counselors and psychologists. Bronfenbrenner (1986) clearly wrote about the association between social, psychological, and educational needs, on the one hand, and mental health on the other; his conclusions were derived from his work in schools. In addition, Heath and McLaughlin (1987) argued that the scope of problems in distressed schools and families is so complex that to solve them we must collaborate with community resources, while Bemak (1998) contended that interdisciplinary collaboration is a means of working for human rights and social change.

It has been pointed out that the development of new models to address multifarious problems requires multidimensional, multifaceted, and interdisciplinary partners to achieve positive results and change (Boyer, 1990). In fact, major foundations such as the Ford Foundation, Annie E. Casey Foundation, and W. K. Kellogg Foundation have been funding projects aimed at interagency and interdisciplinary cooperation leading toward new collaborative directions for mental health professionals and necessitating a careful examination of reforms that incorporate interdisciplinary interventions and research. We strongly emphasize the need to incorporate interdisciplinary collaboration into mainstream counseling

and psychotherapy as a means of working toward social change and social justice.

Since there is a history of advocacy in counseling and psychology (Bemak & Chung, 2005; Lewis & Bradley, 2000), interdisciplinary collaboration would be an extension of contemporary counseling and psychology and would be compatible with the values, professional mission, and contemporary issues of the profession. A recent example of infusing interdisciplinary collaboration into the work of counselors is seen in the work of the Education Trust, an educational advocacy group based in Washington, D.C. In the mid-1990s, a group of about 15 counseling experts from around the United States met periodically for 18 months to redefine the role of school counselors. Based on their work and funding from the DeWitt Wallace–Readers Digest Fund, six universities were eventually funded to implement the National Initiative to Transform School Counseling. With an underlying focus on social equity and social justice, one of the major areas of emphasis of these grants was to collaborate across disciplines to improve graduate-level training, in-service training, and a redefinition of the school counselor's role by public school systems and state educational systems.

THE NEED FOR INTERDISCIPLINARY COLLABORATION THAT MOVES TOWARD SOCIAL JUSTICE

Incorporating social justice and human rights is a major shift that challenges contemporary practice and beliefs in counseling and psychology. As previously stated, the profession currently values theories based on European American belief systems with explicit and implicit emphases on individuals. This way of defining the profession has little bearing on its sociopolitical context, and to change requires that current paradigms be deconstructed.

One example of shifting paradigms is the standardization of graduate training programs. There are set criteria for certification and licensure in the counseling and psychology fields. These criteria do not include room for innovative interdisciplinary programs that would support interventions that go beyond traditional counseling and psychotherapy. Furthermore, curricula for training counselors and psychologists in areas such as teamwork, leadership, social action, poverty, public health, sociology, anthropology, policy, and advocacy are not generally included in the framework of graduate training. Critics of licensure and certification label the standards as rigid and insular, with the result being that university faculties are unable to plan new and innovative coursework and programs of study (Aubrey, 1983; Thomas, 1991; Weinrach, 1991). Consequently the introduction of new coursework is inhibited, and programs continue to perpetuate the status quo regarding skill development, creating fundamental structural barriers that prohibit the introduction of new concepts and fail to keep pace with the changing needs, roles, and functions of the profession. In contrast, one program that has incorporated some fundamental changes is the Counseling and Development program at George Mason University, which is discussed in Chapter 15.

Maintaining the status quo is consistent with what we believe is a flawed assumption that counseling/psychology, as a profession, can effectively stand alone. As previously mentioned, there is little to no attention paid to interdisciplinary collaboration in counseling and psychology training programs, practice, supervision, or consultation. Theories and strategies remain encapsulated in a limited professional framework. Practitioners narrowly explore solutions to psychological problems without acknowledging the value of other professional disciplines' perspectives. Simultaneously, the depth and complexity of modern society's problems and interpersonal violence are growing for many of our clients, students, families, schools, institutions, agencies, and communities and cannot be viewed through the lens of only one discipline. Viewing societal problems through only one discipline creates an erroneous egocentric viewpoint that can ultimately result in counselors and psychologists

providing substandard services and treatment to their clients, and hence may lead to harmful and unethical practice. Even so, counselors and psychologists have little or no exposure to new paradigms of training and practice that value a multidimensional system that would encourage and support interdisciplinary efforts of cooperative teams. To change the status quo and establish interdisciplinary efforts that enhance social justice and human rights, we would suggest four areas of considerations as follows:

1. **Realignment of Power**

We believe that the psychologists and counselors in partnership with other professional disciplines could assume an active role in working across disciplines with a focus on planned social change. A stance like this would more effectively adapt to the rapidly changing dynamics in society. It would require systematic interventions that influence basic social structures and impact individual and social values, attitudes, behaviors, and policy. The idea of an active and redefined role is a particularly sensitive issue, since social change involves a realignment of power and position within society, so that if one profession gains power in stimulating social change, the entire dynamic system experiences changes in interrelationships and societal impact. An example of such a realignment of power might occur through collaboration among the mental health disciplines (psychology, counseling, psychiatry, and social work) with an aim to change mental health public policy, requiring shared power among the respective professions. Another example might be with counselors and psychologists who may forge alliances with public policy officials, public health officials, sociologists, and housing officials to discuss building healthy communities in low-income housing areas. This would require a shift in traditional power bases that allows equitable input from the respective disciplines toward a greater shared goal.

These examples show how the realignment of power necessitates that other professions will also need to redefine their roles and positions, particularly as they interact with each other, possibly experiencing a loss or gain of power and influence. This, in effect, changes the accepted status quo as new paradigms are established through the change in political and social structures. When shifting models to incorporate interdisciplinary collaboration, it means that some participants who have been accustomed to being in positions of power must share their decision-making and authority. In these shifts of power, it is of utmost importance to acknowledge that in some situations other professional disciplines may have necessary expertise, and hence, counselors and psychologists must let go of power and control in order to meet the greater goals. Again, the focus is on interdisciplinary collaboration and not individual egos.

For an illustration of this letting go, consider the traditional relationship between counseling/psychology and the field of psychiatry. Both of us (Fred and Rita) have sat on mental health interdisciplinary teams with psychiatrists who, by virtue of their professional degrees, were assigned to head the teams. Both of us have also headed teams that included psychiatrists. In the first example, psychiatrists were chiefs of the teams because of their training as psychiatrists, rather than because of any expertise or skills they had. This is consistent with historical practice, in which psychiatrists have been the dominant force in mental health and have had the ultimate say about what happens on interdisciplinary teams of nurses, psychologists, social workers, and counselors. In a more equal interdisciplinary partnership, a psychiatrist would not be the overriding individual with the final say, but rather one member of an interdisciplinary team, who could contribute his or her expertise and knowledge from training in the field of psychiatry toward the solution of a problem. This would be a dramatic shift from current existing structures that are steeped in hierarchical models of authority and expertise, and would, in our opinion, more effectively utilize the respective areas of expertise on a team.

Another illustration is evident in the functioning of interdisciplinary teams in school systems. I (Fred) have been involved in numerous school-based projects that incorporated outside community human services agencies, businesses, and parents. These partnerships forged alliances with schools to address school problems. One example was the Anne Arundel County School system (Annapolis, Maryland), where I received a grant funded by the state department of education to work with the schools, community agencies, and parents to reduce violence in the schools and community. Teams were formed and met for almost two years with an aim to reduce violence. Interestingly, power shifts occurred as interdisciplinary teams collaborated on addressing school and community issues. The principals' roles changed so that they each became one of many players rather than the person at the helm fully in command and responsible for designing strategies to address school and community violence. Parents became highly involved, and their opinions were valued as much as those of the school counselor, principal, and human services agency personnel. The change to a shared authority and shared decision making shifted the dynamics of a hierarchical school system to one with more equal participation, in which participants cooperated to solve problems that were based in the school community.

2. Hope: A Key Ingredient

Another important aspect of creating change through interdisciplinary collaboration is to foster hope and a vision of change. Hope has been identified as a precondition for enduring action. In fact, hope has been found to contribute to 15% of treatment outcome (Lambert & Bergin, 1994). It may be stated that without aspirations, hope, and vision, the momentum for change is lost. To design a program such as the Anne Arundel County project, focused on reducing violence in an inner city low-income community, requires fortitude, patience, and skills as well as a belief in the possibility of change. Without the hope that violence could in fact be reduced in Annapolis, the parents, school staff, and human services agency personnel would have been disillusioned, and in our opinion, the project wouldn't have worked. Penn and Kiesel (1994) described the role of the African American psychologist as one who defines hope and can discern a future that supports a commitment to unity and solidarity. We would suggest that this definition is generally applicable to all counselors and psychotherapists in their role as social change agents.

3. The Ecological Context

As a result of the multitude of problems facing our society, counselors and psychologists are presented with individuals, families, groups, and communities who face obstacles to generating fulfilling lives in the pressures and effects of the world and contributing life circumstances around them. Social, economic, political, and cultural forces have great influence on how and what a counselor does (Bemak & Conyne, 2004; Bronfenbrenner, 1986; Kasambira & Edwards, 2000; Shiraev & Levy, 2010). As mental health professionals and counselors, we are challenged to address these issues with clients on a broader basis than can be provided with individual counseling alone. We would suggest that this requires cross-disciplinary work. For example, when we (Rita and Fred) have worked in the area of refugee mental health, we have systematically found it important to collaborate with attorneys, immigration lawyers, health care officials, probation officers, social service providers, school personnel, and political scientists on policies, interventions, program development, and community planning, all of which take into account different aspects of the refugees' lives that impact their mental health.

The reconceptualizing of the problem within an ecological context will accompany a redefinition of the traditional counselor role that will demand challenging existing systems. These systems continue to perpetuate and inadvertently contribute to personal and social problems while maintaining social inequities in various forms. To effectively address these issues, it is essential that counselors and psychotherapists work across disciplines with attention and care to the larger ecological context.

Working within a sociopolitical and cultural domain and attempting to change the existing structures may prove to be difficult. This is particularly true since the core of counseling and psychology has been facilitating change for clients on an individual, group, or family basis. To address the environmental milieu, which we contend has great significance in creating and contributing to the problems presented by individuals, families, and groups, presents a new set of problems and difficulties. Even so, ironically, although the mental health profession has promoted individual transformation, as a profession with the potential for significant impact, it has been fairly stagnant and inept at addressing larger social issues. This may be seen within the context of Boyer's (1990) work, in which he coined the term *scholarship of application.* He carefully described the need for researchers to investigate the application of knowledge through problem definition and solutions that are beneficial to both individuals and institutions, and he discussed his idea about how important it was not only to contribute to society, but to reshape it. This is particularly striking given the context of the shifting psychological and social problems that accompany national and global trends and the opportunity for the counseling and psychology professions to contribute to a changing world.

4. One Step Behind

In one sense, mental health may be regarded as one of the professional areas that has the most potential to promote psychosocial change. Yet we would suggest that as a profession, we are one step behind by not keeping pace with the relevant shifts in social, economic, cultural, political, and technological developments that critically impact society. We would propose that the reason the mental health profession is not considered a major force in social transformation relates in part to its lack of formalized or consistent attention to interdisciplinary collaboration as a means to address complex modern problems.

In part, this relates to stereotypes in other disciplines that characterize psychology and counseling within the Western framework of individual counseling, intrapsychic issues, and psychopathology, without acknowledging the impact of the community and external factors. For example, we both (Rita and Fred) have been working on issues of child trafficking. It is not surprising that we are the only psychologists/counselors on the interdisciplinary team. Similarly, it is not surprising that there is a danger of school counselors being relegated to "clerk work" and becoming obsolete (Bemak, 2000), and of psychologists and counselors not being regularly consulted about larger concerns, such as discrimination, racism, or the effects of terrorism within troubled communities.

Consequently, to keep pace with rapidly changing times, the profession must reexamine the basic tenets of counseling and psychotherapy. This self-scrutiny would assist in more adequately addressing the problems of contemporary society and, in our view, lead to a greater emphasis on interdisciplinary collaboration as a means to social and political change.

RECOMMENDED ACTIONS AND STRATEGIES

To change one's outlook and incorporate interdisciplinary perspectives requires a new way of thinking. It means letting go of the singular perspective that is predominant in the field of psychology and counseling, which generally excludes other disciplines. This would most certainly need to be accompanied by a major shift in theory and practice. It also requires rethinking about territoriality, which has implications for authority, funding, and responsibility. Breaking down these well-established boundaries is a monumental task, yet one that is necessary and essential for the advancement of social justice.

To move in this direction, psychologists and counselors must let go of the narrowly prescribed viewpoint that their way of thinking, which originates in the roots of the profession, is the only perspective that will provide answers for understanding human behavior and larger societal issues. Acknowledgment that a mental health point of view is one of many perspectives, rather than all encompassing, requires a significant shift in one's belief system as well as humility, acceptance, acknowledgement, and respect

for other ways of perceiving the world and its problems. We strongly believe that psychologists and counselors must take off their blinders and assume a leadership role in proactively forming positive partnerships with other disciplines. It would be incumbent on the mental health community to take this leadership role, given their training and skills in human relations and group leadership. The potential results would include a more effective outcome for their clients, families, communities, and society at large.

GUIDING PRINCIPLES FOR INTERDISCIPLINARY COLLABORATION

To promote interdisciplinary collaboration as an essential component for social change, we are suggesting 17 guiding principles that are noted below (also see Table 13.1). Although there is overlap in some of the guiding principles, we believe that each area is significant enough to warrant an independent categorization.

1. **Develop professional identification.** Although psychology is well established in its professional identity, one of the criticisms of the counseling field relates to its search for a professional identity (Hanna & Bemak, 1997). Both psychology and counseling remain rooted in individual Western psychotherapy. Before psychologists and counselors expand beyond their own professional discipline and begin cooperative partnerships with other professional disciplines, there must be a clear identification and collective agreement on the role and definition of counselors and psychologists that integrates long-standing identities with contemporary roles.

Conflict within and between the counseling and psychology professions has been evident during the last decade. Divisions within the counseling field have been evident in disagreements within the American Counseling Association (ACA) and subsequent separation of the Association of School Counselors Association and the American Mental Health Counselors Association from ACA, while conflicts continue to exist within the psychology field, such as some of the tensions between counseling and clinical psychology. A redefinition and clarification may help delineate similarities and differences from a broader perspective for the counseling and psychology fields as well as delineate counseling as a professional discipline, differentiating it from other professions such as psychology, social work, marriage and family therapy, and psychiatry, and more clearly defining the similarities and differences between counseling and clinical psychology, thus more clearly articulating the state of the profession.

2. **Reduce interprofessional conflict, hostility, and mistrust.** Various disciplines remain skeptical and distrustful about the potential for contributions by other professional disciplines. Territory has been well defined by different disciplines, including psychology and counseling, as have approaches to social, economic, cultural, and political problems. The differences in approach coupled with the lack of appreciation or acknowledgement for other perspectives provide a basis for conflict and disagreement between various professional groups and agencies.

A good example of this conflict is evident in the case of a troubled family that is involved with multiple human services agencies. The 16-year-old son is missing school and has been referred to the department of youth services for stealing a car, his 14-year-old sister receives individual counseling from a local mental health clinic, another sister sees the school counselor weekly, and the parents are enrolled in a job training program and counseling in order to become financially independent and get off welfare. The fact that the department of youth services, the department of social services, the local school, and a mental health clinic are all working with different members of this family would provide a tremendous opportunity for a more comprehensive intervention that would address the broader scope of the family problems. As the system now stands, the likelihood is that each of these distinct agencies will develop its own strategies and provide interventions that do not account for other interventions that are ongoing in the larger family system. We would suggest that the problems are interrelated and need an interdisciplinary approach,

requiring that causal factors rather than symptoms should be attended to, and that cross-disciplinary mutual trust and respect must be fostered and maintained.

3. **Provide broader solutions beyond those of narrowly defined mental health work.** When counselors and psychologists use multidisciplinary perspectives to address problems, there are significant changes that must take place in understanding the role of counseling and psychotherapy. An acknowledgement that other disciplines have their own value systems, perceptions, and theoretical base is the foundation to address problems. Appreciating the additional contribution to understanding the problem in a broader manner that goes beyond the mental health issues is also an essential component. Thus, this new viewpoint requires not only acceptance of or tolerance for other professional disciplines, but an actual mutual respect and openness to what another profession may have to contribute to the understanding and resolution of presenting issues. For example, when I (Fred) collaborated with a good friend who is a Swiss sociologist in working with urban youth at risk, he talked about space within urban areas as being a key in defining and fostering at-risk behaviors, a viewpoint that greatly expanded my conceptualization of the problem.

Others have supported this way of thinking. Adler (1986) argued that the melding of different professional cultures to problem-solve increases effectiveness, while Bergan (1995) and Caplan, Caplan, and Erchul (1995) asserted that this held true for school problems. Given this change in thinking, it is crucial to acknowledge that the most effective solution may not rest solely within the traditional mental health domain.

4. **Plan cooperative, mutually defined projects and goals.** A critical element in promoting social justice through cooperating across disciplines is to engage all parties from the different professional areas in planning an agreement about outcomes and objectives. This facilitates a shared responsibility and equal participation that is crucial to the outcome. Furthermore, cooperation engenders not only shared goals but also a coownership

of them that is mutually agreed upon, especially since a body of cooperating parties plans the project. Thus, in developing a school-community-family partnership program in an urban school area, we brought in school officials, parents, and community members who all contributed to developing the plan and process to implement the plan. As we proceeded with the project, it was clear that the entire group owned the project, rather than us (Fred and Rita) owning it.

This is significant in that all the respective disciplines become equal partners in sharing their expertise early on in the planning process. As multidisciplinary groups move beyond traditional boundaries, they begin to examine problems that were formerly seen only through the mental health lens through a more holistic perspective. For any one of the disciplines to impose its authority during the planning phase, based on the belief that the particular discipline is more valued or carries more influence than any other discipline, would undermine the mutual cooperation and negatively affect the interdisciplinary partnerships.

5. **Develop and implement projects and goals that support and facilitate cooperative partnerships.** Planning projects as described in #4 above is only the first step. Of equal importance is the development and implementation of the project. Each of these two steps, the planning and then the development and implementation, are critical in the fostering and continuance of truly cooperative interdisciplinary teams aiming to meet the goals of broader, more comprehensive interventions. The process by which an interdisciplinary team works together to overcome traditional professional boundaries, problem-solves, and endeavors toward the same objectives is vital to cultivating a hardy and vigorous collaborative work environment.

6. **Reconstruct professional roles.** Within the mental health field, as in all professional disciplines, there is a set of values, beliefs, and explicit and implicit norms about the profession. The culture of counseling and psychology has been passed on for generations and carries a philosophy that is very well established in the field.

One of the interesting aspects of working across disciplines is the notion that in order to reconstruct professional partnerships that are mutually inclusive, counselors and psychologists must deconstruct historical and modern assumptions about their function and role, and recreate a new role definition that will work within the framework of interdisciplinary teams. To redefine professional roles, mental health professionals must dismantle traditional boundaries and forge ahead into unfamiliar territory. A natural byproduct of this will be increased discomfort and anxiety, as professional counselors and psychologists develop new definitions for new times that embrace working with other professions. It further taxes mental health professionals to work with uncertainty in a more complex cross-disciplinary fashion, but this will be fundamental in planning and developing interdisciplinary interventions.

7. **Share power and decision making.** One of the most important elements of interdisciplinary collaboration is the process for planning and developing programs. With developing collaboration, all parties must have equal opportunities for contribution and participation. In contrast, when a hierarchical interdisciplinary group is formed, there is disparity in influence, input, and a true acceptance of various professional perspectives. Consequently, shared power and decision making are crucial to viable interdisciplinary partnerships.

We would agree with Friend and Cook (1996), who identified parity and shared decision making as the distinguishing features of collaborative teams. Noteworthy in this discussion is the mental health field, which is notorious for its hierarchy, with psychiatry typically assuming the role as the dominant authority. This is particularly interesting, since psychiatrists have the least amount of training in direct psychotherapy and counseling as compared to the other mental health professionals (e.g., counselors, psychologists, social workers, marriage and family therapists). In fact, psychiatry emphasizes the physiological and biomedical elements of mental illness (as opposed to mental health) and utilizes disease as the framework for understanding all psychological or psychiatric problems. Consequently, the medical model that considers problems within a diagnostic framework is the predominant voice in interdisciplinary mental health coalitions, carrying mental illness forward as the stronger viewpoint. A more equal power distribution would consider the medical model as one voice in the discussion, rather than as the authoritative notion of what constitutes a problem and how to treat it.

It should be mentioned that power differentials are also evident within other professional disciplines and have the potential to negatively impact the efficiency of the multidisciplinary team. It has been the experience of both authors that designating a facilitator, rather than a "leader" who is chosen by virtue of her or his profession, has proven to be the most formidable way to circumvent the potential for power-driven problems when working across disciplines in teams. Designated facilitators have the ability to encourage cooperation that best utilizes the knowledge and expertise of all team members. This works better than drawing on team members' "profession power" to make final decisions.

8. **Create exchanges that foster interprofessional collaboration.** One way to enhance interprofessional partnerships is to organizationally create specific programs for interprofessional exchanges. These programs become embedded within the institutional structure and become part of public and private agencies, organizations, departments, institutions, and school infrastructures.

The programs can be designed across disciplines to maximize exposure to other professional disciplines and outlooks. For example, I (Fred) was consulting in Nicaragua and designed, with the minister of education and minister of social services, a year-long pilot staff-exchange program between the two ministries that aimed to more efficiently address the problems of troubled youth who were orphaned as a result of the war. I replicated a similar type of exchange between two Maryland social service agencies and an urban school district. The exchange aimed to collaboratively work with aggressive troubled youth by assigning staff to office space and projects that were team driven rather than agency based. A condensed version of this may be to introduce an "interprofessional exchange day," whereby agencies and schools designate days as informal open houses for other professionals, or agencies could even have formalized, one-day professional exchanges.

Similarly, I (Rita) have been involved with a seven-country project on human trafficking. The team consists of anthropologists, child researchers, geographers, economists, educators, public policy personnel, and international lawyers. The interdisciplinary international team discussed policies regarding research protocols on children, challenges in implementation of child protection laws and child rights, and national and international policies on the rights of vulnerable children.

9. **Reconstitute rewards and incentives.** Typically, scholarly, professional, or merit rewards are based on accomplishments that are limited to excellent work within one's own discipline. A guiding principal for better interdisciplinary collaboration would be to revamp this system to develop a system of rewards and incentives that support interdisciplinary partnerships aimed at social change.

For example, there could be awards given by professional associations at the county, regional, state, or national level honoring the best social change project that utilized an interdisciplinary approach, or there could be an award for best innovative interdisciplinary project, paper, or presentation to create societal change. Another idea would be to initiate university awards and grants, agency awards, or school-based awards that promote social change through multidisciplinary work. One way to further standardize cross-disciplinary rewards and incentives would be to have the grants and rewards cofunded by more than one organization.

10. **Relocate offices to foster teamwork.** Physical space is another important dimension in promoting interdisciplinary teams working toward social justice. It would not be difficult to reassign offices in a way that places staff in cooperating

agencies together. This would better reflect a team approach to problems, as opposed to approaches centered on individual agencies, schools, or organizations that provide offices only for their own personnel.

We would suggest that a fundamental value shift to support interdisciplinary teams working together to mutually address problems could be enhanced by agencies and organizations reallocating office space so that staff, some of the time, would be housed in another organization's office. This basic shift in physical space as a base of operations would champion the team approach. This has been achieved in a number of places. The two authors have instituted this concept by creating a family space within a school that was meaningful and contributed to the goals of the school, locating mental health clinics within health and social services offices, and housing mental health personnel in schools.

11. **Rethink and reallocate funding schemata.** Funding is almost always awarded directly and solely to one agency, school, or organization, which has the ultimate responsibility for and authority to use the money in ways that their organization best sees fit. It is far less usual to develop alternative funding methods that enhance the development of interdisciplinary work.

Two possibilities come to mind to illustrate this point. First, funding could be used within agencies, organizations, or schools to fund individual staff to designate a portion of their time to participate in a collaborative interdisciplinary project. Thus, the work site becomes the motivator and supporter of the interdisciplinary work.

The second possibility is illustrated in an example from an urban school district, which committed a substantial start-up budget to a school-community-family project. This project was placed under my (Fred's) jurisdiction while I was based at a university and was an outsider to regional politics. I assumed responsibility for administering the grant and allocating funding to multiple agencies and the school district to work with at-risk youth. This was significant in that the funding was not for one agency or the school district, but rather funds

were administered by me, a neutral outside party, whose investment was in children and families, not territory and turf.

Funding that supported collaboration by multiple agencies that had joint responsibility to implement the project underscored a commitment to the interagency team concept and generated an allocation of resources, staff, and funding to the team. This was truly a team-based grant that brought together regional human services agencies and the regional educational school district. The outcome of this funding experiment was a new collaborative effort that required cooperative programming, shifted job responsibilities, and called for resource commitment by respective organizations to support a collaborative structure. This project and others like it have the potential to develop completely new paradigms that are accompanied by major shifts in the allocation of resources, resulting in far more effective service delivery to meet the complex problems accompanying mental health and social justice issues.

12. **Provide training that involves the entire team.** Similar to reconceptualized funding schemata oriented toward collaborative projects, training geared toward interdisciplinary teams is also essential. Activities for interdisciplinary partnerships should be consistent with the desired outcome (e.g., a team approach to addressing larger problems).

Traditionally, training has involved compartmentalized groups from one agency or school, and rarely does one see someone from another agency or institution participating in training that is offered at a specific agency, organization, or school. To have team members from different disciplines join together and participate in training aimed at specific problem areas, rather than training aimed at specific professional discipline areas, creates the potential for tremendous cross-disciplinary fertilization and exchange of ideas.

For example, I (Fred) implemented a three-day start-up training for a new interdisciplinary team working with low-income at-risk inner city families. The team began the training by redefining the roles and relationships of the team members.

Following this in-depth discussion, and breaking down institutional and personal barriers, mutual project goals were established. Keeping the objectives in mind, the team examined their current tasks and responsibilities and explored how to redefine those tasks and responsibilities in order to be more effective in achieving their goals. The training utilized activities described by Johnson and Johnson (1997) for building effective teams, including activities to develop collaborative skills, group processing, positive interdependence, personal accountability, and direct communication.

Interestingly, discussion about the barriers that inhibited collaboration resulted in those obstacles being dissolved. As the traditional institutional barriers came down, roles and relationships were redefined and reshaped, leading to both a new vision and new common language that crossed organizational boundaries. This became the cornerstone for the identification of the team as a newly constituted body with a cohesive direction and objectives. The team goals were developed during the training based on Villa and Thousand's (1988) premise that commonly agreed upon goals result in positive collaboration.

13. **Develop interdisciplinary university training at the graduate level.** To have mental health practice incorporate interdisciplinary work, it is essential that there be exposure to cooperative partnerships at the university level for graduate students in training. We would suggest that interdisciplinary collaboration must begin at the university level and that cross-disciplinary training models be established as prototypes that can be developed and imbedded as part of the training. This is important in addressing the complex issues related to social justice and human rights within the context of mental health.

Currently, graduate-level training is encapsulated in discipline-specific work that is perpetuated throughout the profession and basically unchallenged. To begin at an early stage of professional development (i.e., during graduate-level university training) would assist future professionals in developing skills for and acceptance of interdisciplinary activities. Interestingly, 15 years ago, graduate training, coursework, and applied practica that were multidisciplinary in nature were identified as having long-range implications for facilitating cooperation (Golightly, 1987; Humes & Hohenshil, 1987).

An excellent example of cross-departmental training was developed at the graduate school at the University of Utah. This program included prospective teachers, special educators, counselors, administrators, and school psychologists (Welch et al., 1992). Another unique example is the doctoral program in the College of Education and Human Development at George Mason University, where all the PhD students are admitted to the graduate school and have a specialization in their area of concentration (e.g., counseling, special education, educational leadership, etc.). Before beginning their specialization courses, all students take six courses as a cohort group, studying topics such as leadership, ways of knowing, organizational development, research, and so forth.

14. **Develop an understanding of change theory and its application to counseling and psychotherapy.** For mental health professionals to work effectively in new ways with colleagues from other disciplines and to promote social change, there must be an understanding of organizational and systemic change, similar to the understanding that students develop in the program at George Mason University described above. Frequently, psychologists and counselors talk about changing communities, contributing to the larger society, or promoting equity and human rights, but their efforts often fall short due to their lack of training and skills in social change.

We would suggest that to try to do social justice work within the mental health field without the tools that come with training, supervision, and experience will only produce failure and frustration. Therefore counselors and psychologists must have an understanding of how change works and exposure to theories about social change and mental health. Readings to better understand how to facilitate change could include Alinsky (1971), Bemak and Chung (2005), Hanna and Robinson (1994), Prilleltensky and Prilleltensky (2003), and so forth.

An example of how to institutionalize training in this area is in the graduate program in counseling and development at George Mason University, where we have instituted a master's-level class called Counseling and Social Justice in an attempt to provide a theoretical base and training ground for future mental health professionals who will contribute to larger-scale social change. Yet, simply having a theoretical understanding of change is not sufficient preparation for actually implementing it, so we would further contend that one must also learn how to put social change theory into practice. Therefore any training must include application, and this is provided by the program's master's level courses that have social justice projects as part of the curriculum (e.g., career counseling with the homeless) and the doctoral-level internship course in social justice. Fundamental to these examples is the need for training that provides a comprehensive understanding of theory and practical application. A detailed description of the Counseling and Development Program at George Mason University is found in Chapter 15, which discusses graduate training programs.

15. **Create publications that foster interdisciplinary collaboration.** Professional publications that encourage and promote interdisciplinary work are sparse. Furthermore, most collaborative publications are written by colleagues from the same discipline and subsequently published in their respective professional journals. There is a perpetuation of professional isolation, since the readers of journals constitute only the colleagues in that particular professional discipline. In the authors' experience, even when one is involved in cross-disciplinary projects, there is little cross-fertilization of scholarly publications. Therefore another guiding principal we would recommend is for individuals to publish across professional disciplines.

For example, it would be helpful for community-based psychologists and community agency counselors to collaborate with school counselors, school psychologists, and school administrators to write in educational administration journals about research and recommendations

regarding the linkage between the support of a family intervention program and academic performance in schools. This would be a deviation from having such work published only in family therapy journals or school counseling journals, which typically would not be read by school administrators and therefore would be unlikely to ever impact the school professionals—and administrators—who are in the unique position to develop, promote, and fund family intervention programs in their schools.

16. **Collaborate on cross-disciplinary presentations.** Another area that is important in fostering interdisciplinary collaboration is the development of professional presentations with colleagues outside one's own profession. Both authors have had numerous experiences where they have worked with colleagues from areas outside of counseling and psychology, including anthropologists, sociologists, public health officials, educators, psychiatrists, physicians, nurses, economists, geographers, international lawyers, businessmen and businesswomen, and political scientists. In some of these instances we have presented our work and findings with our colleagues at both their professional meetings and our professional meetings. In some cases, such as our work with human trafficking, we find ourselves as the only professionals from a psychological background, and hence we add a valuable perspective to the conversation.

A more specific example is when I (Fred) received a grant to decrease school violence and aggression in a major urban school system. The major thrust of the grant was to develop a comprehensive school-community-family partnership that involved school counselors, mental health agency-based counselors and social workers, school principals, central and regional office school administrators, teachers, various community agencies representatives, social workers, psychologists, nurses, parents, and business people. Rather than presenting the success of this project myself independently at the American Counseling Association and American Psychological Association annual meeting, I invited a sampling of professionals and individuals involved with the project to participate and copresent. In turn, the school administrator invited the other participants to present at her professional meeting. The result—that we not only worked together daily but also collaborated to present this work at a major national forum, was highly beneficial and consistent with the design of the project. In fact, presenting together contributed to even greater collegial relationships and greatly enhanced the project.

Another example is when I (Fred) was invited in two different years as a featured speaker to address the national conference of the National School Board Association's Council of Urban Boards of Education.

17. **Research, evaluate, and document.** Many projects require a final report. Interestingly, the final report does not regularly translate into a more formal evaluation to determine the project's viability for replication or suggestions for modification or continuation. We would strongly suggest that when considering interdisciplinary projects, it is of great importance that there is cross-disciplinary research, evaluation, and documentation that have application to the practice. This is especially true since cross-disciplinary work has not been documented or proven to be effective, and evaluating the efficacy of this type of work will lead to a better understanding of best practices and the viability of this type of intervention. Completing a more thorough and in-depth evaluation would require cooperation among universities, agencies, and institutions to bridge the gap between practice and research. Furthermore, the evaluation and measurement of interdisciplinary partnerships has both short- and long-term benefits and is crucial in understanding the short- and long-term benefits of and obstacles to interdisciplinary work.

Table 13.1   17 Guiding Principles for Interdisciplinary Collaboration

1. Develop a professional identification.
2. Reduce interprofessional conflict, hostility, and mistrust.
3. Provide broader solutions beyond those of narrowly defined mental health work.
4. Plan cooperative, mutually defined projects and goals.
5. Develop and implement projects and goals that support and facilitate cooperative partnerships.
6. Reconstruct professional roles.
7. Share power and decision making.
8. Create exchanges that foster interprofessional collaboration.
9. Reconstitute rewards and incentives.
10. Relocate offices to foster teamwork.
11. Rethink and reallocate funding schemata.
12. Provide training that involves the entire team.
13. Develop interdisciplinary university training at the graduate level.
14. Develop an understanding of change theory and its application to counseling and psychotherapy.
15. Create publications that foster interdisciplinary collaboration.
16. Collaborate on cross-disciplinary presentations.
17. Research, evaluate, and document.

CONCLUSION

We are in the beginning of a new century. The 21st century presents an opportunity for next steps and another major transition in our attempts to improve our surrounding world and attend to social injustices. The passage further into this century offers the mental health field a unique opportunity to reexamine itself and review the parameters and scope of how various professional disciplines can more effectively contribute to a better world.

Historically, there was a call in the mental health field for social action as a core professional responsibility; this can be seen in early projects in impoverished inner cities, advocating for the rights of mental health clients, or working with youth facing family and school problems. Modern times have significantly changed the ecological context from these earlier days. Even so, some things have remained consistent in that the cultural, sociopolitical, and economic domains continue to influence peoples' lives, and psychologists and counselors have an opportunity to impact these situations in a broader context than one individual at a time.

It is only logical with changing modern issues that the role, structure, and function of the counseling profession transform and adapt to better address the complexities of the 21st century and keep up with the times. Joining with other professions and collaborating with other departments, agencies, and institutions that go beyond the all-important but limited scope of counseling and psychotherapy will be crucial to the mental health profession's ability to make a significant contribution to social change and a better world.

DISCUSSION QUESTIONS

1. Take a look at the role of an indigenous healer in a different culture from yours.

   a. Describe the healer's role. Analyze the healer's power, influence, and credibility and the hierarchy within which the healer works.

   b. What are some roles of this healer that are different from roles of healers viewed from a Western perspective?

   c. How does the healer interrelate with other "professionals" in the community?

2. A student is referred to you. Mohammed is fairly new to this country. He came from Pakistan two years ago. Although he is fluent in English, he seems to struggle in most of his classes, with teachers reporting a decline in his grades. He does not pay attention in class, and he ignores teachers' instructions, especially those of female teachers. You try to schedule a parent conference meeting, and you find out Mohammed's mother does not visit the school, since she feels her English is not good. Mohammed's father recently moved back to Pakistan, so his parents are separated right now. After talking to Mohammed's mother on the phone, you find out they are not covered by health insurance, and since the boy's father left the country, they are at risk of losing their house. Your supervisor encourages you to plan a special meeting to review Mohammed's case.

   a. What are some of the main issues that come to your mind in this case?

   b. Who would you invite to the meeting? Consider Mohammed's relatives, school staff, community services, social services, and so forth.

   c. What topics would you want to address during the meeting?

3. Critically analyze your graduate program curriculum. What are some of the components missing to incorporate knowledge and experience in interdisciplinary work?

4. Your supervisor just chose you to be in charge of creating an at-risk youth prevention program for culturally and linguistically diverse adolescents. Be creative and describe what your program would consist of, using the following guidelines.

a. You have the chance to choose five professionals from different professional disciplines to start with you on this initiative. Which professionals would you like to have in your team? List at least ten in order of preference. Discuss.

b. What are some of the preconceptions you may have about each profession? Explain.

c. How would you present your case to your supervisor that those are the professionals your program needs?

d. What are some of the challenges you may encounter?

5. What do the authors mean when they talk about "taking off the blinders" and assuming a leadership role in proactively forming positive partnerships with other disciplines?

a. What are some of your own blinders? List four to five blinders.

b. List at least three actions you will be implementing in your daily work to be proactive in collaborating with other disciplines.

REFERENCES

Adler, N. J. (1986). *International dimensions of organizational behavior.* Boston, MA: Kent.

Alinsky, S. D. (1971). *Rules for radicals.* New York, NY: Random House.

Aubrey, R. (1983). The odyssey of counseling and images of the future. *The Personnel and Guidance Journal, 62,* 78–82.

Bemak, F. (1998). Interdisciplinary collaboration for social change: Redefining the counseling profession. In C. C. Lee (Ed.), *Counselors and social action: New directions* (pp. 279–293). Alexandria, VA: American Counseling Association.

Bemak, F. (2000). Transforming the role of the counselor to provide leadership in educational reform through collaboration. *Professional School Counseling, 3*(5), 323–331.

Bemak F., & Chung, R. C-Y. (2005). Advocacy as a critical role for urban school counselors: Working toward equity and social justice. *Professional school counseling, 8,* 196–202.

Bemak, F., & Conyne, R. (2004). Ecological group counseling: Context and Application. In R. K. Conyne & E. P. Cook (Eds.), *Ecological counseling: An innovative approach to conceptualizing person-environment interaction* (pp. 219–242). Alexandria, VA: American Counseling Association.

Bergan, J. R. (1995). Evolution of a problem-solving model of consultation. *Journal of Educational and Psychological Consultation, 6,* 111–123.

Boyer, E. (1990). *Scholarship reconsidered: Priorities of the professorate.* Princeton, NJ: Carnegie Foundation for the Advancement of Teaching.

Bronfenbrenner, U. (1992). Ecological Systems Theory. In R. Vasta (Ed.), *Six theories of child development* (pp. 187–250). Philadelphia: Jessica Kingsley Publishers.

Caplan, G., Caplan, R. B., & Erchul, W. P. (1995). A contemporary view of mental health consultation: Comments on "Types of Mental Health Consultation" by Gerald Caplan (1963). *Journal of Educational and Psychological Consultation, 6,* 23–30.

Friend, M., & Cook, L. (1996). *Interactions: Collaboration skills for school counselors* (2nd ed.). White Plains, NY: Longman.

Golightly, C. J. (1987). Transdisciplinary training: A step forward in special education teacher preparation. *Teacher Education and Special Education, 10,* 126–130.

Hanna, F. J., & Bemak, F. (1997). The quest for identity in the counseling profession. *Counselor Education and Supervision, 36*(3), 194–206.

Hanna, M. G., & Robinson, B. (1994). *Strategies for community empowerment: Direct action and transformative approaches to social change practice.* Lewiston, NY: Mellen.

Heath, S. B., & McLaughlin, M. W. (1987). A child resource policy: Moving beyond dependence on school and family. *Phi Delta Kappan, 68*(8), 576–580.

Humes, C. W., & Hohenshil, T. H. (1987). Elementary counselors, school psychologists, school social workers: Who does what? *Elementary School Guidance and Counseling, 1,* 37–45.

Johnson, D. W., & Johnson, F. P. (1997). *Joining together: Group theory and skills* (6th ed.). Englewood Cliffs, NJ: Prentice-Hall.

Kasambira, K. P., & Edwards, L. (2000, June). *Counseling and human ecology: A conceptual framework for counselor educators.* Paper presented at the

8th International Counseling Conference, San Jose, Costa Rica.

Lambert, M. J., & Bergin, A. E. (1994). The effectiveness of psychotherapy. In A. E. Bergin & S. L. Garfield (Eds.), *Handbook of psychotherapy and behavior change* (4th ed., pp. 143–189). New York, NY: Wiley.

Lewis, J. A., & Bradley. L. (Eds.). (2000). *Advocacy in counseling: Counselors, clients, & community.* Greensboro, NC: Educational Resources Information Center Counseling and Student Services Clearinghouse.

Penn, M. L., & Kiesel, L. (1994). Toward a global world community: The role of black psychologists. *Journal of Black Psychology, 20*(4), 398–417.

Prilleltensky, I., & Prilleltensky, O. (2003). Synergies for wellness and liberation in counseling psychology. *The Counseling Psychologist, 31,* 273–281.

Shiraev, E. B., & Levy, D. A. (2010). *Cross-Cultural Psychology: Critical Thinking and Contemporary* Applications (fourth edition). Boston, MA: Allyn & Bacon.

Thomas, K. R. (1991). Oedipal issues in counseling psychology. *Journal of Counseling and Development, 69,* 203–205.

Villa, R., & Thousand, J. (1988). Enhancing success in heterogeneous classrooms and schools: The power of partnerships. *Teacher Education and Special Education,* 144–154.

Weinrach, S. (1991). CACREP: The need for a mid-course correction. *Journal of Counseling and Development, 69,* 491–495.

Welch, M., Sheridan, S. M., Fuhriman, A., Hart, A. W., Connell, M. L., & Stoddart, T. (1992). Preparing professionals for educational partnerships: An interdisciplinary approach. *Journal of Educational and Psychological Consultation, 3*(1), 1–23.

PART V

SOCIAL JUSTICE APPLICATIONS

14

Social Action Research: A Critical Tool for Social Justice Work

Some people dream of success, while others wake up and work hard at it.

(Unknown)

Some men see things as they are and say
why—I dream things that never were and say why not.

(George Bernard Shaw)

Whatever affects one directly, affects all indirectly. I can never be what I ought to be
until you are what you ought to be. This is the interrelated structure of reality.

(Martin Luther King Jr.)

WARM UP EXERCISE

1. *When have you ever used research? What purpose did the research serve?*

2. *How do you imagine that research could help with social justice issues? Give some examples.*

3. *How might you present data and research findings to help change a particular situation? Are there aspects of presenting the findings that would be important in promoting change?*

4. *How does research fit into counseling clients? Is there ever a time you would use research in your clinical work?*

(Continued)

(Continued)

5. *What would be some easy ways to collect data related to your work as a counselor or psychologist?*

6. *What kind of activities or assignments would help you learn best about social justice in a graduate training program?*

Data are important to demonstrate the efficacy of the work we do as counselors and psychologists. In order to collect data, it is important that mental health professionals have a fundamental understanding of social action research. This chapter will address the importance of understanding and doing basic research as a means of promoting social justice. We will begin with a discussion about the link between research and social change; this will be followed by a discussion of relevant research methodologies. The remainder of the chapter will focus on the implementation of social action research by psychologists and counselors doing social justice work.

WHY RESEARCH?

Utilization of research is a critical tool in working toward eliminating social injustices and human rights violations. Often, helping professionals do not see the advantages of research and consequently disregard the use of research data. Some are even put off by or afraid of research and hold the view that research has little relevance to their work. Others are actually negatively predisposed toward research (Robinson, 1994). The counseling field's long-standing ambivalence about research (Sprinthall, 1981) continues today and contributes to a belief of some that there is no connection between research and practice. Our belief is that there must be a link between research and application that is crucial in social justice counseling. We would argue that to change systems and to improve the quality of life and psychological

well-being of clients, families, schools, and communities, data, statistics, and research findings are important tools.

Prilleltensky (1997) proposed that knowledge from research must be a springboard for social action. This may be especially true in Western societies, where the worldview is based on scientific findings and such evidence is regarded as the absolute truth. Therefore, it is important that social justice counselors and psychologists embrace and acknowledge research as an effective and valuable tool that is as much a part of their work as anything else they do. An example of how research data can be gathered in a simple and reliable manner, and used for social change, is presented below.

USING RESEARCH DATA IN SOCIAL CHANGE

For counselors and psychologists to be effective change agents, they must speak the language of the systems they want to change. Speaking the language involves understanding the organizational culture and knowing what to study within that environment to acquire data for social change. For example, high schools in the United States are primarily interested in the academic performance and achievement of the students, since schools are largely evaluated on test scores. In the time of high-stakes testing, one important method for promoting and improving academic performance is through counseling strategies and interventions that enhance the psychological well-being of clients/students. A problem in fully utilizing the school counselor or school psychologist has been the lack of administrative support for mental health interventions, given administrators' focus on academic performance instead.

Rather than continue to struggle with defining their role from a narrow mental health perspective, it would make a great deal of sense for counselors and psychologists working in schools to systematically document their counseling sessions' effect on academic performance. Thus, even though the counseling sessions may target issues such as peer relationship problems, family tensions, bullying, the impact of community violence, or drug abuse and prevention, the data collected on individual, group, and family interventions could be linked to improvements in academic grades, school attendance, school drop-out rates, and disciplinary referrals. The data speak to the language of the school environment and assist administrators to see the scientific evidence of how counseling is linked with improved academic performance and achievement.

An example of this can be seen in the study done by Bemak, Chung, and Sirosky-Sabado (2005), who found that significant academic improvement resulted from group counseling with eight high school girls who were at high risk of failure and dropping out of school. The data examined were based on academic records and attendance, which for all eight girls improved. It is important to note that this did not involve sophisticated statistical analysis or complicated methodology, but rather simple data gathering. Furthermore, the data collected were important to the school itself, and collecting them had unqualified support from school administration.

Data gathering that involves contrasting conditions prior to counseling interventions with conditions after counseling interventions is straightforward and easily done. The above example examined students' tardiness, school attendance, disciplinary referrals, disruptive behavior in classroom, grades, levels of family involvement, and so forth, which are all easy to measure. The data gathered provided evidence about the impact of counseling interventions on meeting the overall academic goals of the school, resulting in administrative support for the counseling.

Research, therefore, does not have to be based on strict empirical quantitative methodology but can use easily implemented research methodologies.

CREATIVITY IN RESEARCH: THE USE OF MULTIPLE RESEARCH METHODOLOGIES

Historically, social science research has been dominated by a scientific and objectified view (Bemak, 1996; Tyler, 1991). This perspective has cultivated a mistaken impression that there is little or no connection between research and practice. Although we believe that traditional empirical quantitative and qualitative research has a place in social justice research, we would argue that traditional empirical research methodologies are not the only research tool that is effective in social justice work.

At times, social justice work requires gathering information in innovative and creative ways. To gather data about social issues, social justice counselors and psychologists must move beyond traditional research design and methodology, using methodologies such as the case study method and social action research, as well as ethnographic methodologies. Each of these methodologies provides important information, and these methods can be easily used by professionals who are not researchers. In addition, it is possible to combine research designs, such as employing both quantitative and qualitative methodologies concurrently, and to use other types of mixed methodologies. All of these methodologies fall under the umbrella of research and can be just as rigorous, reliable, and valid as empirical research designs (Kumar, 2007).

We believe that conducting and utilizing research is an important role for counselors and psychologists whose aim is to work toward intervening in, eliminating, and preventing social injustices and human rights violations. The type of research design employed is dependent not only on what one is investigating but also on one's ability to access support and guidance from supervisors and colleagues for conducting research. Collecting data and analyzing results are crucial steps in the work of a social justice mental health professional. The ultimate aim in doing research within a social justice framework is to focus on studies that are helpful in investigating social justice issues and can be applied to create change for clients and larger systems. It is important that conducting research is seen as helpful and useful, rather than an added task and hindrance.

Counselors and psychologists do not have to undertake research by themselves, especially if they have little or no experience in research. There are tremendous resources for collaboration with university faculty and doctoral students in counseling and psychology, as well as with agencies and schools that may be looking for outcome data, and with colleagues from other disciplines. Collaboration with others has the potential to bring in other material and human resources, which are invaluable in conducting research. An example of this can be seen with a psychologist who wants to conduct research on the efficacy of a gang prevention strategy but does not have the research skills to set up a study. There are several avenues the psychologist might pursue. One is to track down a faculty member in a nearby university who has an interest in this area and develop a partnership. A second option is to contact state and local agencies and departments that have been working in this area to explore codesigning a research project. A third option would be to contact a school where there may be gang activity and see if the school's counselor, psychologist, or social worker would be interested in developing a partnership and research program. Any of these strategies would have the potential of generating a collaborative team approach and incorporate others who have skills in research.

An important consideration for counselors and psychologists who want to use social action research as a tool for understanding social issues and promoting social change is research design. The philosophy, mission, and purpose of social action research are in line with the values and beliefs inherent in social justice, yet empirical designs may not be compatible with conducting research for social change. Social action research differs from the traditional research methodologies that focus on developing, generating, or providing evidence for a specific theory, model, technique, or intervention. Rather, social action research focuses on creating social change and taking action (Reason & Bradbury, 2001) and can be used in conjunction with traditional methodologies. The next section will present a brief overview of the history and aims of social action research and discuss the relationship of social action research to social justice work.

WHAT IS SOCIAL ACTION RESEARCH (SAR)?

History of Social Action Research

To understand the importance of social action research (SAR) in psychology and counseling and its potential to contribute to social justice and human rights, it is important to know the history of SAR. SAR is not a new concept, since participatory forms of inquiry aimed at solving practical problems have existed throughout time (Hall, 2001) and can be traced dating as far back as Aristotle (Eikeland, 2001). For example, Marxist philosophy conveyed the message that the important thing is not necessarily to understand the world, but to change it. Many action researchers trace the origins of SAR to the work of Kurt Lewin in the 1930s and 1940s. Lewin has been credited with coining the term *action research* (Adelman, 1993), which has been adopted worldwide. The concept has been used for everything from political liberation and emancipation to education reform to assessment of development institutions, such as governments, nongovernmental organizations (NGOs), and multinational bodies such as the World Bank (Gaventa & Cornwall, 2001).

An excellent example of action research was Freire's (1970) work. He employed participatory research practice in the liberation of the oppressed in Brazil. John Dewey used action research in the progressive education movement in the United States (Noffke, 1994), while in the United Kingdom SAR was used to instigate curriculum reform (Elliott, 1997). Similarly, in Australia a movement toward collaborative curriculum planning

(Kemmis & Grundy, 1997) was fostered based on action research. The range of issues and countries where action research has been conducted demonstrates the global adoption and widespread use of social action research (Reason & Bradbury, 2001).

It has also been suggested that the foundation of SAR is based on the liberating perspectives of gender (e.g., feminist movement) and race (e.g., civil rights movement) (Bell, 2001; Maguire, 2001). Both movements were aimed toward consciousness-raising and challenged the structures and practices of the power base. Both movements had goals similar to those of action research. The feminist and civil rights movements both underscored empowerment as a primary goal that would radically change the existing power structure. In addition, both movements aimed to dramatically redefine the power relations within the existing systems with an aim toward greater social justice, equity, and democracy for everyone, regardless of gender and race.

Others claim that action research is rooted in experiential learning and psychotherapy (Schein & Bennis, 1965). It has been argued that psychotherapy and counseling are forms of mutual inquiry due to the dimension of process, which is so prevalent in many forms of psychotherapy and counseling (Rowan, 2001). This would be especially applicable to group work and to existential and humanistic psychotherapeutic approaches, where the therapeutic dynamics are essential to the healing process. An example of this can be seen in England, where *clinical inquiry,* a term coined by Schein (2001), resulted in the development of communities of learning (Senge & Scharmer, 2001). The learning communities were based on humanistic approaches and developed through experimentation, resulting in the advancement of cooperative inquiry (Heron, 1971).

In the 1960s and 1970s, social scientists throughout the world developed greater awareness about social injustices and human rights violations. Many felt an imperative to act as they witnessed the suffering of others (Gustavsen, 2001). As worldwide exposure increased, many social scientists challenged their traditional training and the universities and institutions where

they worked as they searched for ways to respond to global human rights violations. Concurrently some social scientists grew increasing dissatisfied with their traditional training and lack of institutional support to address the social injustices. The awareness of the injustices and institutional obstacles to address these issues has caused some to leave academia. For example, the Rosca Foundation for Research and Social Action was one of the first NGOs in Colombia; it was founded by a group of social scientists who had left their university positions to work in cooperation with peasants and Indians toward social justice (Fals Borda, 2001).

The movement to address social injustices forced social scientists trained in traditional research methodology to reexamine standard research practices and ask whether traditional methods were applicable to issues of social injustice. Embedded in the challenging of conventional research protocols was the search for a better understanding of human rights. New methods were developed for information gathering, such as collecting stories, testimonies, narratives, and oral histories. Conceptions of groups of respondents and research participants broadened from the traditional idea of a sample composed of accessible individuals or students to include a wider range of people, such as freedom fighters, indigenous peoples, the mentally ill, and so forth. Data and information were obtained through direct involvement, intervention, or insertion into the process of social action rather than through a narrowly restricted process that would involve using questionnaires or even observation (Fals Borda, 2001). Those in the movement to change research therefore discovered a way to bring about a convergence between the popular thought of everyday people and academic science. The integration of the two led to more comprehensive and applicable knowledge, especially by and for the underprivileged classes that were in need of scientific support to create change.

The challenges to traditional research methodologies paralleled the growth of social scientists' moral conscience and personal ethical standards. Many felt that it was essential to incorporate the worldwide, national, regional, and local social injustices into their research agendas. To exclude these issues was considered by many not only to be a violation of ethical standards but also to conflict with their moral conscience. Therefore a situation was created where the "head and heart" had to work together in a marriage that involved a holistic epistemology (Gustavsen, 2001). This created an upheaval in research where many action researchers rejected what had once been important in their career advancement and promotion, and they redefined the parameters of research. Many of the social action researchers found themselves creating partnerships with people who were the subjects of the research, and they with the subjects to build toward social transformation and the betterment of the larger society.

SAR encompasses many theoretical orientations and inspirations. It has drawn on pragmatic philosophy (Greenwood & Levin, 1998; Levin & Greenwood, 2001), critical thinking (Carr & Kemmis, 1986; Kemmis, 2001), the practice of democracy (Gustavsen, 2001; Toulmin & Gustavsen, 1996), liberationist thought (Fals Borda, 2001; Selener, 1997), humanistic and transpersonal psychology (Heron & Reason, 2001; Rowan, 2001), constructionist theory (Lincoln, 2001; Ludema, Cooperrider, & Barrett, 2001), systems thinking (Flood, 2001; Pasmore, 2001), and complexity theory (Reason & Goodwin, 1999). With the diverse sources that inspired SAR and its inclusion of individuals, communities, organizations, and the larger society, there was an ability to examine issues at both micro and macro levels. Stylistically and methodologically, SAR is highly compatible with counseling and psychotherapy that is aimed toward social justice and has the flexibility and versatility to be employed to address social injustices and inequities.

The Goal of Social Action Research

The ideas about action research arose when social scientists started doing experiments in the field rather than in the laboratory. Traditional scientific research is based on research methodology that is rigorous, variables that can be controlled, methods that can be replicated, and results that

have general applicability. Scientific researchers have also been typically viewed as individuals who are based at universities and research institutions, research centers, and research divisions of companies. The researcher characteristically has training and a background in research, belongs to an organization or institution that has a clear research agenda, and typically develops and implements studies by asking questions through written or oral means, observing people or groups of people, or conducting experiments. One concern about this type of research has been the minimal connection between the researcher's thinking or hypotheses and the concerns and experiences of the groups being studied (Heron & Reason, 2001). Therefore it could be claimed that traditional research is, in many instances, theoretical rather than practical.

Contrary to conventional research design and methodology, SAR argues that theory alone has little power to create change and that there is a need for a far more complex interplay between theory and practice (Gustavsen, 2001). It has been argued that the outcome of empirical research does not help people find ways to act or change their lives. In contrast, SAR is conducted not only to develop theory but also to contribute directly back to application. For example, transformative participatory evaluation (TPE) aims to enhance political power and social justice in oppressed communities, taking a political stance and promoting change (Whitmore, 1998). Thus findings from SAR are conducive to action.

SAR has been defined as "a participatory, democratic process concerned with developing practical knowing in the pursuit of worth-while human purposes, grounded in a participatory worldview" (Reason & Bradbury, 2001, p. 1). It is research in which everyday people address concerns, issues, and challenges that occur in their daily lives, and in the process, they generate knowledge about their situation. The intent is that the new knowledge will lead to action that changes the situation. The focus is first on problem solving and then on the generation of knowledge, so that the ultimate goal will lead to improvement or changes in a community's or society's institutions, organizations, structures, and systems. Thus, SAR leads to the reduction or elimination of inequalities, unfair treatment, social injustices, and human rights violations. The outcome of SAR knowledge is subsequently embedded in cycles of action-reflection-action over time (Rahman, 1991), and it is through the process of doing SAR that the problem-solving phase evolves into a more basic social and cultural transformation (Hall, 1981).

Four Common Characteristics of Social Action Research

There are four common characteristics of SAR that have relevance to social justice counselors and psychologists (Stringer, 1999). They are described as (a) democratic, (b) equitable, (c) liberating, and (d) life-enhancing.

Democratic characteristics in SAR refer to the value and weight of respondents' contributions in the research and involve everyone engaged in the research. Thus, research about the prevention of substance abuse at a treatment facility would include the residents, the staff, and the administration as participants in developing and implementing the research methodology and protocol. Their participation in the research would carry equal importance.

A second common characteristic in social action research is that it is *equitable*. A basic assumption is that everyone has something of worth to contribute. In SAR, no discrimination is made on the quality of respondents, and there is a belief that everyone can contribute something of merit and value. For example, the authors were funded to work on a grant in an inner city middle school targeting improved academic achievement through family involvement for students at the highest levels of academic failure. Meeting with parents, grandmothers, guardians, and caretakers of the identified students was a slow process that steadily attracted more and more participants. Interestingly, not one of the adults had *ever* previously engaged with school personnel,

because they had previously felt discounted and devalued in school. This project grew into a tremendous success, in large part because everyone's opinions, concerns, and ideas were valued and appreciated. A grandmother to whom no "official" had ever listened, a former drug addict who was trying to mother her young adolescent daughter, a mother who would lock herself in her bedroom in frustration and anger over her failure to adequately "manage" her four children, and a former prostitute whose oldest daughter was in a juvenile detention facility were but a few of the parents and guardians who became core members of the research and intervention team. Each one of them felt that in the program they were all valued, heard, and respected, and that program meetings provided a place and opportunity to voice their concerns, tell their stories, and create changes.

A third common characteristic is that SAR is *liberating*. The idea that through the research one can change one's condition and become free from oppression and negative circumstances is a powerful belief. SAR has the potential to provide this liberation. An example of this was when I (Fred) was working in an Upward Bound program; this program was developed by President John F. Kennedy to address poverty. One of the aims of Upward Bound was to work with failing and marginalized high school youth and their families to improve academic performance and secure entrance into college. In working with the families, I continually encountered hopelessness and desperation. To circumvent this, I conducted SAR to gather data that would be helpful in promoting change for the families and students.

Working in one community, the parents and I had repeated discussions about what they would like to change for their children and in their community. As a result of these discussions, one parent decided to run for political office. The process of watching the parent body and the Upward Bound students plan, organize, and campaign for a previously depressed, unemployed father was remarkable. The belief and action taken as a result of the collective work and related research was thoroughly liberating for the research participants and provided hope to move beyond their limiting circumstances, which led to the motivation and courage to actively change the debilitating conditions that they faced at that time. Hence, this was research in action.

The fourth characteristic that can be generalized to all SAR and social justice is *life-enhancing*. To grow and expand one's life, one's world, and one's relationships is to enrich one's life. SAR offers a possibility to do just that—to embody new and healthier aspects in one's life. It allows one to pursue broader horizons with the possibility of reaching a fuller potential.

Counselors and psychologists working toward social justice must understand the design, implementation, and application of SAR. Instead of using the traditional research methods they were trained in, counselors and psychologists must utilize SAR and extend themselves to incorporate new methodologies, reconsider control groups, and assess how to apply their findings to create social change. The implementation of SAR for helping professionals requires a new set of skills, adaptation of traditional research methodologies, and often an unlearning of old techniques and learning of research techniques that are consistent with social justice and social change work.

RELATIONSHIP BETWEEN SOCIAL JUSTICE, SOCIAL ACTION RESEARCH, AND COUNSELING AND PSYCHOLOGY

Both SAR and social justice minded helping professionals have the same aim in working toward social justice. As previously discussed, the root of SAR is the collection of information and knowledge that helps challenge social inequalities and injustices. Similarly, psychologists and counselors are engaged in a process of change by the very nature of their work. The desired outcome for both SAR and social justice counseling work is to disrupt the status quo, so that *all* members of society have equal opportunities and access to resources to improve their quality of life. SAR and counseling and psychotherapy begin with an interest in the problems facing individuals, groups, families, communities, and institutions, and both have an objective of helping people gain better awareness, understanding, and skills to improve and change their conditions.

Therefore the use of SAR as a means for helping clients is a natural process to facilitate change and has similarities to the process of counseling and psychotherapy. The anticipated outcome in both SAR and counseling is not simply to generate knowledge or awareness, but to actually assist clients to improve their quality of life, their psychological growth and development, and their psychological and social well-being. This is done through change, empowerment, and an emphasis on a broader ecological context.

Similar to counseling and psychotherapy, SAR deals with social issues that affect the quality of life of individuals, families, groups, schools, communities, and societies. These issues are wide-ranging. Related to psychological well-being, SAR might explore issues such as education, failing grades, school dropout, unemployment, poverty, teen pregnancies, the relationship of community environment to crime, the impact of physical health on psychological well-being, or how to design community housing that is conducive to mental health. Other issues could include community development, disabilities, domestic and community violence, sexism, immigration, gun violence, postwar stress, religion and spirituality as it relates to healthy development, substance abuse, sexual and psychological abuse, HIV/AIDS, or other effects of oppression and discrimination on psychological well-being (see Table 14.1 for an example of the potential consequences of bullying). The purpose of SAR in investigating any of the above areas is to bring about change by improving the social and cultural circumstances of affected people, families, communities, and institutions. Undertaking the research not only helps counselors and psychologists know the results of their work but also helps clients know the outcomes. When engaging in SAR, there is a cooperative involvement so that in instances where there is a lack of social justice or human rights, clients or others are motivated to assist in improving a given situation and therefore are willing to help create change. This presents a different paradigm from that provided by traditional research. In SAR, the researcher, counselor, or psychologist is not independently deciding what to study and how to study an issue but rather includes the clients and clients' families and communities to be involved in the process of reflection and change.

Thus, the parallels between SAR and counseling and psychotherapy are evident. Both address the social injustices inflicted on clients with a philosophical foundation that is based on a moral and ethical obligation to work for social justice. When one looks at the broader social context, it appears superficial to adhere to the traditional psychotherapy and counseling assumptions that we are working solely with the intrapsychic dynamics of the client while ignoring other social, political, cultural, historical, ecological, and spiritual influences on the client. Thus, counseling and psychotherapy working toward social justice engage in a process of change through the therapeutic encounter itself. Analogous to this is SAR, where the actual process of the research is conducive to change. Therefore, SAR is an ideal tool to be utilized by social justice counselors and psychologists.

APPLICATION OF SOCIAL ACTION RESEARCH IN COUNSELING AND PSYCHOTHERAPY

Education and Democratization as a Basis of Social Action Research

Of utmost importance for counselors and psychotherapists conducting SAR is collaboration. A key component of the collaborative partnerships is education and training about the investigated issues and findings. Providing education about social injustices and human right violations is a proactive step in teaching community members about salient issues. Embedded in education and SAR is democratization, whereby all people have an equal say in concerns about the community. One way for psychologists and counselors to participate and to promote democratization is by providing information and knowledge based on research findings back to the community. The actual facts about one's own life and community, based on the results of the

Table 14.1　Family Suspects that Bullying Led to Young Girl Taking Her Own Life

12-year-old Maria Herrera took her own life after being bullied at school. According to her mother, Mercedes Herrera, Maria was harassed and beaten up by her classmates. Mercedes tried to talk to the school about the harassment, but the school did not address the issue. She later found Maria hanging by a belt in a closet at their house. Maria later died at the hospital. Maria had told her guidance counselor a year before that she wanted to commit suicide, but the counselor did nothing, according to Mercedes. Mercedes also said she made at least 20 complaints to the school about the bullying, but the school has no record of this. The Department of Education stated they had no record of Maria being the victim of persistent bullying or of Mercedes filing any complaints. The family said they are considering legal action against the school. According to research, girls who are consistently bullied are 32 times more likely to be depressed and 10 to 12 times more likely to contemplate or attempt suicide than girls who are not bullied.

Source: Family blames bullying for suicide. (2008).

research, engender the possibility for people to change their communities. The collaboration thus creates participatory democracy built from the bottom up.

An example of this would be a project that I (Fred) designed in collaboration with service providers, professionals, and community members in a large county in the Washington, D.C., area. I was funded to work on violence prevention in a high school that was identified as being at high risk, with significant failure on test scores, school dropout, and violence. I organized a meeting with representatives from the department of social services and the department of mental health, the high school counselor, and the principal. The meeting generated a multiagency perspective about the problem and an agreement to investigate the relevant issues. A joint research survey was developed and administered by the three organizations to better understand the concerns. The findings showed that the community had fears about lack of employment, had a pervading sense of a lack of police protection, and was concerned that there was a lack of care for public areas in the community.

Based on the findings, rather than have mental health professionals see clients individually for counseling, the group organized an intervention program in cooperation with community members. New job training was initiated, community police were assigned to become more visible, and a group of community residents began to take responsibility for the care and beautification of self-selected public areas in the community. The result of this SAR caused a collective and participatory response and action with community members and the researchers, facilitating important change within the community. As a result, reports of referrals for counseling derived from fear of violence at the high school significantly diminished. Unlike actions that would have resulted from traditional research methods, these results and actions are consistent with the unique approach of SAR in tackling problems, whereby mental health professionals and counselors, in partnership with clients, families, schools, and/or communities provide innovative ways to present and address problems (Fals Borda, 2001).

From Professional to Student: Fundamentals in Social Action Research

SAR research emphasizes partnerships between those interested in changing some aspect of their lives and the researcher/social justice counselor/psychologist. The helping professional becomes an authentic collaborator with the people/clients/students/stakeholders. Teamwork creates equal partnerships that have mutual goals for personal, social, and cultural transformation. In this unique research cooperation, the counselor or psychologist does not take on the role of the expert but rather assumes the role of student, and the clients educate the helping professional about their situation. This process was illustrated in an article I (Fred) wrote in which I described my experience conducting research regarding street children in Brazil. In the article, entitled "Street Researchers: A New Paradigm Redefining Future Research With Street Children" (Bemak, 1996), I described the changing role of the street researcher:

> If the street researcher is successful in entering this world it will be through the guidance of street children, who will not only be the research subjects, but at times assume the responsibility of teachers and even protectors from potentially dangerous situations. Thus, the role of the street researcher is multifaceted, causing a relinquishing of the predisposed subjective reality as "The Professional." Street researchers are not only social scientists but also novices in a new culture who must learn new ways to communicate, norms and rules that govern the culture, how the street child culture interacts with the surrounding environment, and how to remain safe within the context of a potentially threatening world. All this is done by accepting the teachings of "the subjects" who are much younger and poorer with far less formal education. (pp. 151–152)

Therefore, helping professionals must give up their roles as the leaders or experts, since there will be times when grassroots or community leaders or the clients themselves may assume the leadership role, as the street children did in the Brazilian example. This causes a change in one's role as a helping professional, moving to that of a collaborator or facilitator rather than an expert who knows everything about the issues at hand. A driving force for the shift in roles is the underlying premise that the client(s), who have a daily experience of the situation being researched, are the people closest to the situation and therefore are the most qualified and competent authorities on the issues.

The shift in role and authority when doing SAR may create confusion for the counselor or psychologist. With the adoption of social change as part of counseling or psychotherapy, professionals may be unclear about how to incorporate social action into their work. It is also an interesting shift to listen to the voices of clients, whose knowledge has not been typically represented in research design, decision making, or with regard to power inequities. Therefore, for SAR to be effective, it is critical that there be cooperation with members of the research team and clients in defining problems and solutions; it is a form of participatory coinquiry. An outcome of coinquiry is that clients and community members become jointly responsible for building knowledge as well as decisions about how to use the research findings. This becomes important in promoting equity and fairness as one changes social and cultural institutions, organizations, systems, and structures. In summary, the shift in the role of the researcher is a core value for SAR and has the potential to lead to true empowerment of clients. In essence, SAR "is not only a research methodology, but also a philosophy of life" (Fals Borda, 2001, p. 31).

Social Action Research Requires Thinking Outside the Box

One requirement for SAR is versatility. As previously discussed, conducting SAR research requires going beyond traditional methodology and includes reviewing family archives, oral traditions, testimonies, and collective memory as investigative strategies. This form of gathering information has been described as *thick analysis,* since it combines research methods that enable social scientists to inquire into language, culture, traditions, religion, social and cultural relations, and historical and political realties (Bell, 2001). Although rigorous research is considered to be important, it has been argued that it is equally important to use methods that allow for collaboration that equalize the relationship between researcher and participants (Bell, 2001).

One might say that SAR is about the right to speak and voice one's opinions. It allows oppressed groups to speak out. Because it gives them a voice, SAR provides participants (clients) with the power and space to decide for or against action and for or against breaking silence, and to identify what and how to study in a way that will improve life conditions. Bell (2001) captures the essence of this:

> By dealing in voices, we are affecting power relations. To listen to people is to empower them. . . . The telling of, listening to, affirmation of, reflecting on, and analysis of personal stories and experiences from the ground up are potentially empowering action research strategies. (p. 62)

When we undertake SAR, we are not looking to generate academic theories, nor are we aiming to develop theories about making change or taking action. We are not looking for new knowledge or empirical data. Rather, SAR is a search for liberation, a search for greater freedoms and parity, a search for dismantling unfair and discriminatory practices that all lead toward an improved and more equitable world. The hope is to acquire practical knowledge that can be applied to everyday life and can contribute to an improved social, cultural, economic, political, psychological, and spiritual quality of life for people and communities, leading to broader and more equitable relationships and existence. To this end, SAR is about creating new forms of understanding, since action without reflection and understanding is blind and becomes simply theory and does not change oppressive or unfair conditions. SAR demands participation and thus is only possible with, for, *and* by identified persons and in communities where the research itself may be beneficial. Counselors and psychologists can play a vital role in this process.

AN EXAMPLE OF SOCIAL ACTION RESEARCH IN THE UNITED STATES

An example of a cooperative SAR project can be seen in a national study funded by the National Institute of Mental Health (NIMH) to investigate the serious problems facing Amerasians (children of Vietnamese mothers and American fathers) who have relocated to the United States In the 1980s and early 1990s, this population of adolescents was presenting unique problems for resettlement agencies in the United States because of their historical background of being shunned and rejected in Vietnam. With great hopes to "finally go home," many Amerasians migrated to the United States in the 1980s only to find themselves without English language skills, rejected by Vietnamese refugees in the United States and unable to locate their biological fathers. Their dream of returning to their fathers' homeland and gaining peace of mind was more of a myth than a reality. We (Fred and Rita) were asked to undertake the first comprehensive national study of Amerasians (Bemak & Chung, 1998, 1999).

The study was developed in collaboration with 12 randomly selected agencies throughout the United States. These agencies were involved in assisting in the relocation of Vietnamese refugees. The directors of the agencies, other professionals who had worked extensively with this population, and Amerasians (who were not to be respondents in the study) participated in designing the research methodology. The agencies also participated in the process of sharing the research findings with the Amerasians and their communities. The jointly developed questionnaire was administered on-site at the 12 locations, where groups of 15 Amerasians completed the questionnaire at each site. Given the highly emotionally charged questions, following each administration of the questionnaire, the researcher spent two hours debriefing the respondents.

Interestingly, all of the sites reported that the acts of filling out the very personal questionnaire (which covered the Amerasians' past and present lives, adjustment to the United States, and future aspirations) and participating in the subsequent debriefing, in and of themselves, created a process whereby change occurred in the respondents and the respective staff at the various agency sites. This offers excellent examples of collaborating in the design and administration of the questionnaire and providing participants in the study with an opportunity to tell and listen to each others' stories and reflect on their lives. As a result of the study, both the agency staff and the Amerasian participants reflected on changes they wanted to make personally, socially, and—in the case of staff—programmatically.

The research with the Amerasians is a good example of how SAR can fully involve participation by the members of the targeted community, the organization or institution serving them, and the university researchers. The cooperation began with the development of the research project and continued through every stage of the research. This is contradictory to pure science research models where respondents are viewed as passive subjects. In SAR, participants, respondents, and subjects are seen as active change agents, and studies are conducted *with* the people rather than *on* the people (Heron & Reason, 2001).

Basic to SAR is the belief that everyday people are capable of developing their own ideas and can work together in collective research teams to understand the problem and find methods to change their situation. Three different kinds of activities may be involved in this process. First, there may be an inquiry into the nature of the problem in order to understand the causes and context of the problem. Second, people may organize themselves as community units. Third, people may mobilize themselves for action by raising their awareness of what should be done on moral and political grounds (Fals Borda, 2001).

SOCIAL ACTION RESEARCH IN A GLOBAL CONTEXT

As a result of research collaboration and democratization, counselors and psychologists incorporate the role of change agent into their work. Breaking the cycle of oppression; ending exploitation, racism, terror, violence, and the monopolization of power and resources; and providing clients with an opportunity to have a voice in their present and future all are cornerstones in the helping professional's role.

SAR is not limited to a specific country but can be implemented worldwide, as we mentioned in the historical overview of SAR. As Walters (1973) poignantly stated about SAR with regard to the racism and exploitation experienced by African Americans in the United States, "Research is a tool to dismantle the master's house and to achieve social justice" (p. 206). The same statement may be applied to racism in Australia, South Africa, Brazil, the United Kingdom, various other European countries, and so on. The next section provides an example of using social action research in a global context.

Example of Global SAR: An Asian Case Study

While living in Asia, I (Rita) was involved in working with community members who lived in the poor rural areas. The communities encountered various problems due to political oppression. People lived in unsanitary conditions with little food and resources. They were constantly faced with dilemmas such as trying to figure out how to spend their small weekly incomes. Given unhygienic conditions and little money to buy food, families were forced to decide whether to spend the weekly income on food or to buy soap so they would not get sick. Communities were regularly confronted with sociopolitical obstacles. It soon became obvious that the government's work in providing a better quality of life for the community was just lip service without any real attention. The real source of the problem was living in a dictatorship and being under constant fear of social injustices and potential human rights violations, such as being arrested and detained without any provocation, reason, or legal recourse. Although I was aware of the source of the problem, it was evident that community members had minimal awareness about their exploited situation. They just thought life was tough.

In an attempt to address this, I began to gather relevant information in collaboration with community and spiritual leaders. This was a step toward defining the actual problem within the larger ecological context, examining the elements that maintained and exacerbated the problem. We gathered information by listening to and recording community members' stories and testimonials. As we began to collate the information and understand the systematic themes that emerged from our research, we began to present the information to community members. Sometimes this would happen in the village square after dinner when people gathered or at other informal gatherings, and other times in more formal meetings when community members would gather to share their collective stories and discuss recurrent themes of oppression, discrimination, disempowerment, and feelings of hopelessness and helplessness.

I was simultaneously providing counseling and doing SAR, joining in the evening activities to discuss social justice issues, and helping to creatively facilitate these meetings, sometimes through discussion, sometimes through political theatre, sometimes through story telling. Community members, both adults and children, became engaged in this process and were excited to act out their oppressive experiences as testimonials or political theatre. This inevitably would stimulate a discussion, whereby the entire community would share, explore, analyze, explain, and eventually educate each other about what had happened and what it meant to the individual, the family, and the entire community.

This had multiple effects on the community. First, community members realized that others had experienced similar events and reacted in a similar manner. They also learned about the injustices in relationship to their own lives and community, and simultaneously realized that this situation was generalized. As they learned from the SAR, they also began to understand the need for change. As a result of the SAR project, the community made decisions to change and began brainstorming as a community on strategies to promote change.

Stringer (1999) describes the final stage of SAR as one in which communities review again, reanalyze, and once again modify their responses, based on the information gathered through the research. As we (the community and spiritual leaders and I) facilitated the meetings, the community reexamined their situation and reconsidered a response for change. Thus, the SAR not only gathered important information and provided counseling to community members, but of equal importance, it assisted community members to better understand and analyze the problem, supported their ideas and decisions, encouraged their responses, and enabled them to examine different strategies to address the problem.

Political theatre and social action research. Working with illiterate communities, I (Rita) found that the technique of weaving political theatre into the activities of the community as an aspect of SAR in counseling and psychotherapy has multiple effects. It helps gather information through psychologically charged stories and contributes to open testimonials, where people share emotional experiences through their stories. The cathartic nature of the enactment provides another therapeutic outlet for painful emotions and the release of repressed feelings, contributing to individual, family, and community healing.

For example, I assisted community members in writing the skits and performing the political theatre. Through these theatrical plays, the entire community became more aware of the unjust life realities (the problem) that affect entire communities, and they gained knowledge regarding the actual source of the problem. The plays evoked questions, such as how and why life was as it was, and this was followed by discussion, exploration, examination, and theorizing.

An outcome of this process of research and intervention is substantive reflection by community members about what to do. As I facilitated community reflections and discussions of the various political theatre skits, ideas and strategies and action steps to improve community problems were developed by community members as they reevaluated and reviewed their life circumstances.

Throughout the process I took a secondary role, gathering information, helping facilitate the political theatre when needed, facilitating debriefing and reflection on the political theatre, and occasionally contributing to discussions. It is important to note that my ideas and values were not imposed at any stage in this process. Instead, political theatre as an aspect of SAR raised awareness, and through awareness created social action and change. The decision to create change originated with the people in the community.

CONCLUSION

SAR is a new dimension for counselors and psychologists who are not researchers. It is at the crux of working toward social justice and requires a redefinition of the role and scope of the job done by counselor and psychologists. Using SAR, not only are they clinicians and counselors, but they are also educators who bring findings back to their clientele, researchers who form partnerships to work with clients and students, and leaders who use their skills in interpersonal relations to facilitate social change with multiple stakeholders. Being advocates is intrinsic to the added scope of their work and propels counselors and psychologists to become political and social activists in the larger social and political context. The inclusion of SAR in the therapeutic work that counselors and psychologists are trained to do is part of the Multi-Phase Model (MPM) of Psychotherapy, Counseling, Human Rights, and Social Justice. Bringing SAR into the world of the helping professional builds on their vision of and commitment to working toward social justice and human rights.

DISCUSSION QUESTIONS

1. How is action research different from the traditional models of research? Explain.

2. What are your main fears or worries when you think about doing research? Be specific.

3. Do you see yourself applying action research in your work site? Why would you do this? Can you name a specific topic you would like to investigate?

4. What does it mean to "speak the language" of the systems one wants to change? What actions would you need to take in your current job—or if you are not working right now, a possible future job—to more effectively "speak the language"?

5. What is your stereotype of a typical researcher? What is your idea of a social action researcher? Describe.

6. Four main characteristics of social action research (SAR) link to its use by social justice counselors and psychologists is that: it is democratic, equitable, liberating, and life-enhancing. Bearing these characteristics in mind, consider this scenario: The local high school has regular incidents of school violence. In fact during the past year there have been six gun incidents. How would you apply SAR and these four characteristics in collecting information and studying the problem? Answer the following questions:

   a. Where would you start?

   b. Who would you interview? Who would the participants be?

   c. How would you weigh the importance of the teachers' and administrators' responses relative to the students' and parents' responses and the maintenance staff's responses?

   d. What goals and outcomes would you hope for after your SAR findings are shared? How would the four characteristics be reflected in the goals and outcomes?

REFERENCES

Adelman, C. (1993). Kurt Lewin and the origins of action research. *Educational Action Researcher, 1*(1), 7–25.

Bell, E. E. (2001). Infusing race into the US discourse on action research. In P. Reason & H. Bradbury (Eds.), *Handbook of action research: Participative inquiry and practice* (pp. 48–58). Thousand Oaks, CA: Sage.

Bemak, F. (1996). Street researchers: A new paradigm redefining future research with street children. *Childhood, 3*, 147–156.

Bemak, F., & Chung, R. C-Y. (1998). Vietnamese Amerasians: Predictors of distress and self-destructive behavior. *Journal of Counseling and Development, 76*(4), 452–458.

Bemak, F., & Chung, R. C-Y. (1999). Vietnamese Amerasians: The relationship between American fathers and psychological distress and self-destructive behavior. *Journal of Community Psychology, 27*(4), 443–456.

Bemak, F., Chung, R. C-Y., & Sirosky-Sabado, L. A. (2005). Empowerment groups for academic success (EGAS): An innovative approach to prevent high school failure for at-risk urban African American girls. *Professional School Counseling, 8*, 377–389.

Carr, W., & Kemmis, S. (1986). *Becoming critical: Education, knowledge and action research* (3rd ed.). London: Falmer Press.

Eikeland, O. (2001). Action research as the hidden curriculum of the western tradition. In P. Reason & H. Bradbury (Eds.), *Handbook of action research: Participative inquiry and practice* (pp. 145–155). Thousand Oaks, CA: Sage.

Elliott, J. (1997). School-based curriculum development and action research in the UK. In S. Hollingsworth (Ed.), *International action research: A casebook for educational reform* (pp. 17–28). London, UK: Falmer Press.

Fals Borda, O. (2001). Participatory (action) research in social theory: Origins and challenges. In P. Reason & H. Bradbury (Eds.), *Handbook of action research: Participative inquiry and practice* (pp. 27–37). Thousand Oaks, CA: Sage.

Family blames bullying for suicide. (2008, April). WABC-TV Education News. Retrieved from http://abclocal.go.com/wabc/story?section=news/education&id=6080573

Flood, R. L. (2001). The relationship of "systems thinking" to action research. In P. Reason & H. Bradbury (Eds.), *Handbook of action research: Participative inquiry and practice* (pp. 133–144). Thousand Oaks, CA: Sage.

Freire, P. (1970). *Pedagogy of the oppressed.* New York, NY: Seabury Press.

Gaventa, J., & Cornwall, A. (2001). Power and knowledge. In P. Reason & H. Bradbury (Eds.), *Handbook of action research: Participative inquiry and practice* (pp. 70–80). Thousand Oaks, CA: Sage.

Greenwood, D., & Levin, M. (1998). *An introduction to action research: Social science research for social change.* Thousand Oaks, CA: Sage.

Gustavsen, B. (2001). Theory and practice: The mediating discourse. In P. Reason & H. Bradbury (Eds.), *Handbook of action research: Participative inquiry and practice* (pp. 17–26). Thousand Oaks, CA: Sage.

Hall, B. (1981). Participatory research, popular knowledge, and power: a personal reflection. *Convergence, 14*(3), 6–19.

Hall, B. L. (2001). I wish this were a poem of practices of participatory research. In P. Reason & H. Bradbury (Eds.), *Handbook of action research: Participative inquiry and practice* (pp. 171–178). Thousand Oaks, CA: Sage.

Heron, J. (1971). *Experience and method.* Guildford, UK: University of Surrey.

Heron, J., & Reason, P. (2001). The practice of co-operative inquiry: Research 'with' rather than 'on' people. In P. Reason & H. Bradbury (Eds.), *Handbook of action research: Participative inquiry and practice* (pp. 179–188). Thousand Oaks, CA: Sage.

Kemmis, S. (2001). Exploring the relevance of critical theory for action research: Emancipatory action research in the footsteps of Jurgen Habermas. In P. Reason & H. Bradbury (Eds.), *Handbook of action research: Participative inquiry and practice* (pp. 91–102). Thousand Oaks, CA: Sage.

Kemmis, S., & Grundy, S. (1997). Educational action research in Australia: Organizations and practice. In S. Hollingsworth (Ed.), *International action research: A casebook for educational reform* (pp. 40–48). London, UK: Falmer Press.

Kumar, M. (2007). Mixed methodology research design in educational technology. *Alberta Journal of Educational Research, 53*(1), 34–44.

Levin, M., & Greenwood, D. (2001). Pragmatic action research and the struggle to transform universities into learning communities. In P. Reason & H. Bradbury (Eds.), *Handbook of action research: Participative inquiry and practice* (pp. 103–114). Thousand Oaks, CA: Sage.

Lincoln, Y. S. (2001). Engaging sympathies: Relationships between action research and social constructivism. In P. Reason & H. Bradbury (Eds.), *Handbook of action research: Participative inquiry and practice* (pp. 124–133). Thousand Oaks, CA: Sage.

Ludema, J. D., Cooperrider, D. L., & Barrett, F. J. (2001). Appreciative inquiry: The power of unconditional positive question. In P. Reason & H. Bradbury (Eds.), *Handbook of action research: Participative inquiry and practice* (pp. 179–187). Thousand Oaks, CA: Sage.

Maguire, P. (2001). Uneven ground: Feminism and action research. In P. Reason & H. Bradbury (Eds.), *Handbook of action research: Participative inquiry and practice* (pp. 59–69). Thousand Oaks, CA: Sage.

Noffke, S. (1994). Action research: Towards the next generation. *Educational Action Research, 2*(1), 9–18.

Pasmore, W. (2001). Action research in the workplace: The socio-technical perspective. In P. Reason & H. Bradbury (Eds.), *Handbook of action research: Participative inquiry and practice* (pp. 38–47). Thousand Oaks, CA: Sage.

Prilleltensky, I. (1997). Values, assumptions, and practices: Assessing the moral implications of psychological discourse and action. *American Psychologist, 1,* 95–110.

Rahman, M. A. (1991) The theoretical standpoint of PAR. In O. Fals Borda and M. A. Rahman (Eds.), *Action and knowledge: Breaking the monopoly with participatory action-research* (pp. 13–23). New York, NY: Apex Press, and London, UK: Intermediate Technology.

Reason, P., & Bradbury, H. (2001). *Handbook of action research: Participative inquiry and practice.* Thousand Oaks, CA: Sage.

Reason, P., & Goodwin, B. (1999). Toward a science of qualities in organizations: Lessons from complexity theory and postmodern biology. *Concepts and Transformation, 4*(3), 281–317.

Robinson, E. H. III. (1994). Critical issues in counselor education: Mentors, models, and money. *Counselor Education and Supervision, 33,* 339–345.

Rowan, J. (2001). The humanistic approach to action research. In P. Reason & H. Bradbury (Eds.),

Handbook of action research: Participative inquiry and practice (pp. 114–123). Thousand Oaks, CA: Sage.

Schein, E. H. (2001). Clinical inquiry/research. In P. Reason & H. Bradbury (Eds.), *Handbook of action research: Participative inquiry and practice* (pp. 228–237). Thousand Oaks, CA: Sage.

Schein, E. H., & Bennis, W. (1965). *Personal and organizational change through group methods: The experiential approach.* New York, NY: Wiley.

Selener, D. (1997). *Participatory action research and social change.* Ithaca, NY: Cornell Participatory Action Research Network, Cornell University.

Senge, P., & Scharmer, O. (2001). Community action research: Learning as a community of practitioners, consultants and researchers. In P. Reason & H. Bradbury (Eds.), *Handbook of action research: Participative inquiry and practice* (pp. 238–249). Thousand Oaks, CA: Sage.

Sprinthall, N. A. (1981). A new model for research in service of guidance and counseling. *Personnel and Guidance Journal, 62,* 491–495.

Stringer, E. T. (1999). Action research (2nd ed.). Thousand Oaks, CA: Sage.

Toulmin, M., & Gustavsen, B. (Eds.). (1996). *Beyond theory: Changing organizations through participation.* Amsterdam, Netherlands: John Benjamins.

Tyler, F. B. (1991). Psychosocial competence in developing countries. *Psychology and Developing Societies, 3*(2), 171–192.

Walters, R. (1973). Toward a definition of black social science. In J. A. Ladner (Ed.), *The death of white sociology* (pp. 190–212). New York, NY: Random House.

Whitmore, E. (1998). *Understanding and practicing participatory evaluation.* San Francisco, CA: Jossey-Bass.

15

A MODEL HIGHER EDUCATION TRAINING PROGRAM: COUNSELING, MULTICULTURALISM, AND SOCIAL JUSTICE/HUMAN RIGHTS

The time is always now.

(Unknown)

It only takes a single idea, a single action to move the world.

(Unknown)

WARM UP EXERCISE

1. *How was social justice built into the mission statement for the graduate program that you either teach in or attended as a graduate student?*

2. *What courses covered topics in social justice? What were those topics?*

3. *What classes could add or have added more content in social justice? How and where would you do this?*

4. *How could you build social justice into practicum, internship, and externship experiences?*

(Continued)

(Continued)

5. What field experiences could you build into courses in a graduate training program that would help students learn about social justice?

6. What kind of activities or assignments would help you learn best about social justice in a graduate training program?

Although the psychology and counseling field acknowledges the need to incorporate social justice issues in its graduate training programs, very few programs have actually done this (Vera & Speight, 2003). Currently there are few psychology and counseling graduate training programs that focus on social justice and human rights. In fact, there are only a handful of graduate training programs that address these issues, including those at Boston College and at George Mason, Penn State, Marquette, Ball State, and Loyola universities (Talleyrand, Chung, & Bemak, 2007). These programs have incorporated a social justice philosophy into their mission statement and recruitment efforts. Their recruitment initiatives address an underrepresentation of students of color in their counseling and counseling psychology training programs.

Boston College's counseling psychology program has endorsed a developmental contextual framework (Lerner, 1995) as a theoretical foundation for their training program. Their aim is to train their graduate students to conceptualize problems from individual, contextual, and developmental perspectives. Students learn to create treatment and prevention programs that address problems at individual and systemic levels. Typically, this approach has not been recognized within the counseling and psychology professions, so there has not been an endorsement of this emphasis in graduate training programs (Talleyrand et al., 2007).

The universities incorporating social justice and human rights in graduate training are unique in the field. All of these programs have moved from "discourse to action" (Hartung & Blustein, 2002) in an effort to create a level playing field

for all people. However, a majority of graduate training programs do not have training in social justice and human rights. Instead, professionals who are committed to these issues must learn on the job. Rarely in counseling and psychology graduate training programs does one discuss social justice and human rights in relationship to practice. When they are mentioned, it is generally in the context of a philosophical discussion and typically is embedded in the multicultural counseling or cross-cultural psychology class. It would be rare to hear about social justice in a course on human development, counseling children, principles and practices of school counseling, abnormal psychology, diagnosis and treatment, mental health consultation, or group counseling or group psychotherapy.

There is also an absence of social justice considerations in practicums and internships; the Western model is the dominant paradigm for this important experience, which provides the culmination of one's training to become a degreed professional. Typically, during this definitive moment in training, there is an overemphasis on individual counseling that is conducted through the evaluation of tapes and transcripts of individual sessions without regard to human rights issues.

We would argue that to not reflect on the issues of social justice and human rights beyond the discussions that may occur in the multicultural counseling or cross-cultural psychology courses is a glaring deficit in training. The ignoring of social justice as an integral issue in mental health training contributes to a perpetuation of the injustices that continue to occur in our societies and to our clients. Consequently, we believe that it is critical to address social justice and human rights issues during all aspects of training, thus eliminating the myth or shortsighted assumption that social justice and human rights practice can be picked up on the job. Furthermore, we would strongly suggest that if training programs are serious about incorporating social justice and human rights issues, then it is crucial that these themes be infused throughout all phases of training programs, from the beginning foundation and introductory courses to the culminating practicums and internships. Failure to integrate these issues throughout all aspects of the program is paying lip service to these potent issues and inadvertently adding to and maintaining social injustices and potential human rights violations.

This chapter will describe the George Mason University Counseling and Development Program, which not only has social justice in the mission statement but also infuses social justice and human rights issues throughout the curriculum of both the master's and doctoral programs. The aim of this chapter is two-fold: (1) to discuss the process and procedure of including social justice in a graduate training program, and (2) to illustrate that social justice can be effectively infused and implemented at *all* levels of graduate training. The chapter will end with recommendations for infusing social justice in other graduate training programs for mental health professionals.

THE COUNSELING AND DEVELOPMENT PROGRAM AT GEORGE MASON UNIVERSITY

The Counseling and Development (C&D) Program at George Mason University (GMU) is presented as an example of how a graduate program that trains mental health professionals might appear when it emphasizes training in social justice and human rights. This program is the work place of both authors of this book, who were instrumental in developing and creating the current program. We hope that describing the process involved in changing the C&D program to incorporate social justice will assist other counseling faculty to

examine their own processes and practices. To fully appreciate the challenges to the program and the changes made to it, we begin with the program history, then discuss the program's development and changes, and finally discuss the current status of this program and recommendations. Challenges in the development and implementation of the C&D social justice and human rights program will be discussed throughout this chapter.

PROGRAM HISTORY

The C&D is housed in George Mason University's College of Education and Human Development (CEHD). Prior to 2000, the program had a traditional counseling graduate training program that included master's and doctoral programs. The doctoral program was somewhat unusual in that it was housed in a generalized doctoral program that was generic for the entire graduate school. All doctoral students took a cluster of 8 credits in general culture (courses entitled Ways of Knowing, Leadership Seminar, and Doctoral Seminar) with doctoral students from all the educational disciplines. They also took 12 credits in research methods, and in collaboration with a faculty member, each student designed an individualized course of studies (21 credits) in her or his selected professional specialization and minor area that included an additional 12 credits. Interestingly, prior to our joining the faculty in 2000, the C&D Program only had one doctoral level specialization course, meaning that students majoring in counseling had to design a program of studies including coursework from other areas, such as conflict resolution, psychology, sociology, social work, criminal justice, public administration, and so forth.

In 1999, the C&D Program was at a unique crossroads. The entire former faculty had left, forcing a decision from administrators about whether or not to continue the program. In the meantime, while the administration was deciding what to do with the program, they hired two interim visiting faculty to "hold up" the program.

Although the two faculty were committed to the program, since they received their doctoral degrees from CEHD, they were also overwhelmed. Eventually, a decision was made to hire new faculty and continue the program, resulting in the two authors joining the faculty. At the same time, the two interim faculty were hired on a permanent basis, creating a new program with a total of four faculty in 2000. The changes to the program began the first year with the four faculty. Two additional entry-level faculty were subsequently hired, one in 2001 and one in 2004. The two new faculty each had significant experience in the field of multiculturalism and social justice but limited university background. Of the six faculty members, three are persons of color.

Both authors had prior knowledge of the state of the C&D program and knew that this was an opportunity to design their ideal program. They presented the vision for a social justice focused program to the CEHD administration prior to accepting positions, and the CEHD's agreement to this focus became part of the package for accepting the positions. We made it clear that we had no interest in joining the faculty simply to continue with the existing curriculum and mission. We showed how the traditional C&D program was dated and hence not effective in addressing current social issues. Both of us had strong backgrounds in multiculturalism and social justice (Talleyrand et al., 2007), and we had both worked nationally and internationally to address issues of poverty, mental illness, and juvenile delinquency. Our clients had included refugees and immigrants, street children, youth and families identified as being at risk, the mentally ill, prison inmates, and survivors of war and torture. We had extensive cross-cultural experience that included work with Asian American, African American, and Latina/o community mental health centers and on Native American Indian reservations. In addition, both of us had had unique opportunities to live and work internationally, with Fred Bemak having worked in 30 countries in Africa, Asia, Europe, Latin America, and the South Pacific; and Rita Chi-Ying Chung having lived in 4 countries prior to coming to the United States and worked in 10 countries in Asia, the Pacific Rim, Europe, and Latin America.

As previously mentioned, the administration had concerns about the status of the C&D program and was very interested in our vision for it. We were both offered support to bring our new ideas to the program. The other two faculty who were hired at that time had experience at the state level but minimal experience nationally or internationally or as faculty members. Interestingly, after the administration had interviewed each of us, they interviewed the other two prospective full-time faculty. The interview included questions about the candidates' views on the change that we (Fred and Rita) had presented. Their assessment of the potential faculty's attitudes, thoughts, and beliefs about program change was based on the new ideas that we (Fred and Rita) had discussed during our interviews, with an assumption that the program would change dramatically.

Thus, a clearly articulated vision had been introduced to the administration and became embedded in the thinking about the future of the C&D Program. In the second year of the new program, a fifth faculty member was hired. In fact, individuals were attracted to the C&D program because of the social justice mission statement. Remarkably, all faculty hired during this two-year period were open to and supportive of our new ideas and led the way to discussions about the shape and direction for the future C&D Program.

The development of the C&D program will be described in seven levels:

- Level 1: Defining the Mission Statement
- Level 2: Course Revisions and Curriculum Changes (for both the master's and doctoral level courses)
- Level 3: Walking the Talk
  - ○ application of social justice through work done by Counselors Without Borders
  - ○ design and implementation of the Professional Dispositions
- Level 4: Program Admissions
- Level 5: Student and Program Assessment

- Level 6: Faculty Retreats
- Level 7: Student Involvement and Contributions

LEVEL 1: DEFINING THE MISSION STATEMENT

The year 2000 (the first year with the four new faculty) was the year of building, planning, and discussion. As an initial step in the planning process, the faculty scheduled a series of retreats to discuss the mission and direction for the program. During the first year, three retreats were held, two of them overnight. The outcome of the retreats was a newly defined mission for the program. The new mission was focused on five major components: social justice, multiculturalism, internationalism, advocacy, and leadership. The mission statement reads as follows:

The Counseling and Development Program is committed to preparing counselors who promote the social, psychological, physical, and spiritual health of individuals, families, communities, and organizations in order to contribute to the advancement of global well-being. The program strives for national and international excellence in implementing a counseling perspective that provides a foundation in basic counseling skills and focuses on social justice, multiculturalism, internationalism, advocacy, and leadership. It is our belief that a global perspective on development across the life span, and an understanding of and appreciation for multiculturalism, diversity, and social justice are integral to the preparation of professional counselors, requiring that they are prepared to assume leadership roles, be proactive change agents, and become advocates for social, cultural, economic, and political justice. The program is committed to accomplishing this mission by promoting the interconnectedness of teaching, research, service, and professional practice through interdisciplinary teams. Faculty members will facilitate a continued tradition of international, national, and regional leadership through collaborative partnerships, projects, research, publications, presentations, consultation, and training.

It is important to comment on the process by which the group of faculty came together to discuss a dramatically different vision for a program that had been steeped in traditional individual Western ethnocentric counseling. Previously, there had been a sporadic and inconsistent attention to issues of diversity, but social justice had not been considered as part of the training program, and leadership and advocacy were rarely mentioned within the context of multiculturalism and social justice. In addition, our two colleagues were traditionally trained and had each held traditional mainstream school counseling positions, into which they had built creative, but institutionally restricted, innovations. Thus, to propose social justice, multiculturalism, internationalism, advocacy, and leadership to our colleagues was a challenge to the practice and constructs they had held during their professional careers.

Interestingly, our colleagues resonated with the ideas about social justice and became excited about the possibilities of building on their previous work. Although they had not previously conceptualized or acted on concepts of social justice and multicultural counseling, they found that these were beliefs they held but had not known how to enact or formulate in their work. Although faculty were excited about this change, we wanted to ensure that everyone was talking about the same concept. Therefore, faculty were asked how they defined each of the five mission components, and how each component related to them personally and professionally. Not surprisingly, the definitions differed, although there were some common elements. For example, one faculty member expressed confusion over the differences between social justice and social change. Faculty also had different definitions of multiculturalism. For example, one faculty member believed that multiculturalism should include special education and disabilities as a major component. There was also lack of understanding about why we should extend our work globally. We realized that it was important to spend time discussing each of the five mission components to ensure that we had consensus about the ideas we were discussing and that we were all at the same starting point for building our program.

Discussing the five mission components helped our colleagues gain a fuller understanding of each of the components in relation to our graduate program in counseling and their professional work. As a result of a deeper exploration of these concepts, seriousness grew about how to incorporate these ideas into the program mission and the training. The outcome of the discussions was that our two colleagues supported and were excited about these ideas and found their voice through the concepts of social justice, multiculturalism, internationalism, advocacy, and leadership, which helped articulate some of their unexpressed convictions. Discussions were both intensive and extensive; belief systems and worldviews were reevaluated, and values were examined within the framework of the counselor's work and role. Thus, the final mission statement was tried and tested until there was overall consensus.

An essential aspect of considering the mission statement was the belief that it must have significance and drive the graduate program. Faculty agreed that the mission statement was the absolute foundation for the program, providing a basis for the philosophy, teaching, training, and scholarship of both the faculty and students. Thus, the process of developing a mission statement was not meant to be an exercise in futility, where the final document was thoroughly discussed and debated, only to be shelved and forgotten. Rather, it generated a starting point in establishing a program identity that could be used as a basis from which to design coursework. We want to underscore the importance of spending the necessary time to fully discuss and explore the mission statement with all faculty; it is essential to come together and reach mutual consensus about a mission statement and coursework. Although this process took a year, it was a very worthwhile year of learning for everyone.

It was a year later that the fifth member of the C&D Program was hired. During a highly competitive search process, applicants were carefully screened to identify a candidate who appeared, through work and scholarship, to be aligned with the program mission. Subsequently, the search process was not based on finding someone who could teach a prescribed set of courses or had a research focus in any particular area, but instead on finding someone who believed in and was committed to the mission of the program. The interview process reflected the demand for philosophical consistency; a significant portion of the interview focused on reactions to the philosophy and ideas about how the candidate might instill these concepts into graduate level training and practice. In fact, the faculty member who was hired shared that a key attraction to the program for her was the mission statement and philosophy of the program, which was consistent with her personal and professional philosophy.

LEVEL 2: COURSE REVISIONS AND CURRICULUM CHANGES

With the hiring of a fifth faculty member in the second year of the program, the next step was to align the curriculum and courses with the mission. This was a monumental task, where faculty agreed to tailor the areas of program concentration and each individual course. The consensus was that the mission should be reflected and infused in each class, and students must be aware of and understand the relationship of the mission to their coursework. Thus began a yearlong process of program redesign and development of new courses on both the master's and doctoral level courses.

Approximately 90% of the curriculum underwent major changes. Rather than discuss all the details, it may be helpful to just list a few examples of the major revisions that better linked the program to the mission of social justice, multiculturalism, internationalism, advocacy, and leadership. This section is divided into two parts, with the first part being master's degree program revisions and the second part being doctoral degree program revisions.

Master's Level Program Revisions

1. **The Advanced Human Growth and Development course** had been taught from a traditional Western framework. Culture had been an afterthought in this course and was periodically mentioned without intent or focus. The new Human Growth and Development course was transformed into a cross-cultural human growth and development class, with an emphasis on culture, social justice, and human rights. This was in line with changing U.S. demographics, globalization, and current social justice issues, such as poverty, gun violence, immigration, interpersonal violence, and the impact of child labor and human trafficking. The new course involves discussions on how social justice and human rights issues influence and affect the psychological and physical well-being of individuals throughout their lives. Infusing these factors into the Human Growth and Development course provides a more responsive approach to the knowledge that counselors and psychologists must have about human development from a broader multicultural, cross-cultural, social justice perspective.

2. **The Introduction to Research course** had been housed as a generic course in CEHD. There had been long-standing complaints from counseling students that the examples used in the class and the focus of the course were not in line with the counseling field in general and more specifically with the C&D Program's mission. An outcome of this was that the C&D Program developed a new class in research for counseling students, with a focus on using and understanding data as a means of advocacy for clients and ultimately to create change. Assignments in the course also include research projects on social justice issues.

3. **A Foundations in Counseling class** was created to provide an overview of the field of counseling. This course not only provides an overview of the entire field but is the beginning fundamental class that introduces the mission and philosophy of the program. Upon completing this class, all the students clearly understand the program's mission and how their roles as counselors will fulfill that mission. In addition, this class includes faculty introductions in which all of the counseling faculty speak about their research and scholarship and how it is related to the mission.

4. **A Counseling and Social Justice class** was developed, since it was critical to provide the tools for students to be able to effectively promote social justice issues. An important distinction about the social justice class is that it is *separate* from the multicultural counseling class. Although the two classes have similar aims, the Counseling and Social Justice class builds on the Multicultural Counseling class and ties together the philosophy of the program with knowledge and skills that are not typically taught in multicultural classes or counseling programs.

A major component of the course is a social justice internship, for which students go out in the field to do hands-on work in social justice. This assignment requires students to work in different organizations and agencies on social justice issues. For example, students developed a "Tunnel of Oppression" universitywide exhibition open to all students on campus. The aim of the exhibition was to educate individuals on a specific social justice and human rights issue. The exhibition consisted of various creative illustrations of the issue, and it also provided resources and materials regarding the issue. Every student in the C&D program attended this exhibition as part of their other classes, while the students in the Counseling and Social Justice class were involved in debriefing small groups of students from across campus about the exhibition.

Another example was the development of a gang prevention program for the American School Counselor Association (ASCA); the program is now available on ASCA's website. Students from the class also decided to pass on bringing in food for the traditional end-of-semester party, and instead took food and clothing as a contribution to the local food bank and homeless shelters.

These examples are just three out of hundreds. All of the social justice internships aim to teach counselor trainees about taking steps toward social justice and being creative in the process. Helping students to move out of the traditional ways of thinking and to be imaginative and flexible as social justice advocates and change agents is a key component to instilling skills for change. Furthermore, these projects demonstrate to students that they can make a difference and instill in them the value of giving back to the community (see Chung & Bemak, in press a).

5. **The Career Counseling class** not only teaches career theories from a multicultural and social justice perspective but also has students do hands-on counseling with disenfranchised populations. For example, Fred was working with a regional homeless shelter and had the students in class provide career counseling to the homeless population. This has become a regular assignment in the class, and the offer of students providing career counseling has been extended to other community agencies, including domestic violence shelters and prisons. This type of hands-on project helps students frame social justice within the context of career counseling (see Bemak & Chung, in press a).

6. **The Principles and Practices of School Counseling class** was redesigned to incorporate the key issues of the Transformation of School Counseling initiative that focused on academic success for *all* students. This initiative was led by The Education Trust in the mid-1990s with a 14-month national assessment to reshape and transform school counseling. The assessment found that there was a lack of consistency between counselors' training and practice, that there were no interdisciplinary linkages in their training, and that there was an absence of training in leadership, advocacy, multicultural, and collaboration skills. As a result, four years of grant funding were provided to develop national prototypes for future training programs. I (Fred) was involved during all the phases of the Transformation School Counseling initiative, and I (Rita) was involved in the grant implementation phase. Each of us has carried the findings of the Transformation of School Counseling into our work with C&D, so that the

C&D Program's mission includes leadership, advocacy, data-driven social change, multiculturalism, and social justice.

7. **The Practicums and Internships** were redesigned to more effectively reflect the program's new mission. Typically, students develop counseling skills through these experiences. In the new program, other assignments were included that emphasized the program's mission. These assignments might involve developing prevention programs to promote social change, developing a program evaluation for a social justice intervention or prevention project through the use and collection of data, and leadership and advocacy activities. Furthermore, students have to demonstrate proficiency in multiculturalism, social justice, advocacy, and leadership.

One outcome of the course revisions was that the number of credits required for degrees in both the Community Agency Counseling (CAC) and School Counseling (SC) Programs increased. This was due to a commitment by the program to facilitate training that went beyond traditional certification standards, which typically require only a single course in multicultural counseling. Proficiency in other areas that are key foundations of the C&D Program's mission—social justice, advocacy, and leadership—is not required in the accreditation standards, and thus typically not required in coursework. Yet, since each of these fundamental concepts is core to the mission, courses were added, revised, and changed to incorporate these concepts into the required training program.

Doctoral Level Program Revisions

At the doctoral level, CEHD at George Mason University has a program of studies that is generalized. As mentioned previously there had been only one course that was specifically related to counseling for counseling doctoral students. The new doctoral curriculum included the existing counseling course entitled Emerging Issues in Counseling and additional courses in line with the mission. Two courses added were Advanced Multicultural Counseling and Advanced Group Counseling. In addition, three advanced internships were added, one in counseling leadership, one in multicultural counseling, and one in social justice. Examples of key revisions of the C&D concentration of courses at the doctoral level are as follows:

1. **An Advanced Multicultural Counseling course** was designed to facilitate a deeper understanding and operationalization of the multicultural counseling competencies through the respective areas of knowledge, awareness, and skills. This course goes beyond the master's level course content in the area of cultural diversity by developing advanced skills, techniques, and interventions in working across cultures; examining, on a deeper level, one's own cultural heritage and biases; exploring racial and ethnic identity development in the context of work as a clinical supervisor or professional counselor or psychologist; and developing skills in conducting race dialogues,. Students are required to conduct a series of race dialogues in schools and communities (e.g., churches, community centers, etc.) with people they do not know who come from a different racial and ethnic group than their own. The race dialogues promote an intense and honest discussion about racism, prejudices, and biases; they are aimed at giving students skills that will be useful for their future careers as multicultural social justice leaders, faculty, and professionals. The course advanced ideas about how to apply multicultural counseling work within a social justice/human rights framework.

2. **The Advanced Internship in Counseling Leadership** was developed to provide training to link leadership with counseling and social change. This course goes beyond the master's level Counseling and Social Justice class to explore in depth theories of leadership, leadership development, qualities of leadership, and the association between being a leader and social change. Furthermore, the class provides an internship experience where students assume a leadership role in public and private organizations and systems that are aimed at facilitating change. The course is different from the traditional mental health internships, where the emphasis is on counseling rather than cultivating leadership skills to facilitate social justice.

3. **The Advanced Internship in Multicultural Counseling** was created to fully expand the program focus on multicultural counseling to an intensive, advanced hands-on practice experience. This internship provides the student with an experience that exclusively emphasizes multicultural counseling and supervision, examining every therapeutic encounter through a multicultural lens and with a perspective on the relationship between multicultural counseling and social justice. This course differs from the master's level internship in that it focuses on the doctoral student providing supervision as well as counseling. This is particularly important since supervision is a key role for individuals with doctoral degrees, and they must be knowledgeable and skilled in doing social justice mental health work from the position of a supervisor.

4. **The Advanced Internship in Social Justice** was designed as an advanced internship experience that stressed the integration of coursework done in leadership, advocacy, and multiculturalism toward a model of social justice and human rights. National agencies and organizations that are providing human services for underserved populations are designated as sites for the interns, and students undertake a wide variety of internship projects, including developing and implementing mental health based social justice prevention and intervention programs, evaluating existing programs, and working on national, state, and regional policies. At this level, students are expected to take a major leadership role in the design, implementation, and evaluation of social justice programs.

LEVEL 3: WALKING THE TALK: APPLICATION OF SOCIAL JUSTICE WORK THROUGH COUNSELORS WITHOUT BORDERS

Counselors Without Borders (CWB) began in response to a need for social justice after Hurricane Katrina. Two months after Hurricane Katrina, at a national conference for professors and supervisors in the counseling field, the president of the national association (Association for Counselor Education and Supervision) asked an audience of around 700 supervisors and counselor educators how many people had gone to the Gulf Coast to help after the devastation of Hurricane Katrina. A few people in the room raised their hands, and it quickly became apparent that they had gone to the Gulf and helped there with critical tasks that did not include counseling. Simultaneously the news media were continually portraying the failures of the U.S. Federal Emergency Management Association (FEMA), Red Cross, and U.S. Substance Abuse and Mental Health Services Administration (SAMHSA) to provide basic services as well as mental health support.

Given the gravity of the situation, I (Fred), at that moment of seeing that only a handful of my peers had been to the Gulf, decided to bring a large team and provide the critically needed mental health counseling. An easily accessible resource pool that was available at that time was my students, all of whom would eventually do practicum and internship work and receive supervision. Since there was a paucity of mental health professionals on the Gulf, and since there were prohibitive restrictions for selecting counselors to work there (federal agencies and Red Cross required that counselors be licensed and be committed to work in the disaster area for two or more weeks), and since there was a severe need, I decided to invite a team of 16 advanced graduate students, who had excelled in social justice and multicultural work, to work with me to provide counseling on the Gulf. Rita was also invited to join the CWB team as another faculty supervisor.

All of the students agreed to participate in advanced intensive training about trauma and disaster mental health and to gain familiarity with the culturally diverse groups living on the Gulf, and all agreed to two to three hours of clinical group supervision *daily* while on site on the Gulf. Simultaneously I contacted the state professional mental health association and the Mississippi Department of Mental Health and offered to bring a team to provide counseling

services. The team went to Mississippi and saw over 600 clients from the African American, White, and Vietnamese American communities. We worked closely with the Mississippi Department of Mental Health and state psychological and counseling associations, and we served at six disaster sites across the Gulf Coast, actually teaming with the SAMHSA mental health team as well as medical doctors, nurses, educators, and social service providers.

Similarly, during the California wildfires there was a scarcity of mental health services being provided to the American Indian tribes and the Latina/o population. CWB, comprised of a team of university graduate students and two faculty supervisors, partnered with colleagues and students from a local university in San Diego who joined the CWB team. Once again the focus was on providing counseling to underserved groups, and the work was underscored by social justice multicultural issues. The combined CWB went into low-income communities and schools, including those on Indian reservations, providing culturally responsive counseling services to over 1,000 clients. The format was similar to that used on the Gulf Coast, with an intensive period of training before departure and daily supervision on site.

Basically, CWB was established to provide counseling in situations where it was critically needed. Services were not being offered in either of these areas, and walking the talk involved taking strong steps to rectify the social injustices that existed in these situations (see Bemak & Chung, 2011). Due to the important work of CWB, a DVD was made to encourage other counseling and psychology training programs to establish a similar type of experience for their students (Bemak & Chung, in press b).

Professional Dispositions. An initial aim of the new program was to make sure that students fully understood and embraced the mission. Also, a later goal of equal importance to faculty was that students would be able to operationalize the mission of the C&D program rather than just having the "book knowledge." To ensure that students were not just saying or doing what they thought was expected of them and giving correct answers, the first author (Rita), with the support of the other faculty, developed a set of ethical standards that were based on the ACA ethical standards. The ACA standards were expanded to incorporate professional dispositions that emanated from the C&D mission statement, and these became standards for all students in the C&D Program. These were named Professional Dispositions; they are core to the courses and are included in course syllabi as expectations for professional conduct. Thus, the Professional Dispositions (see Table 15.1) provide a guideline of ethical standards and behavior for all students in the program.

Typically, graduate programs in counseling and psychology evaluate students on their papers, examinations, writing skills, research abilities, clinical skills, and presentations. Many students are highly proficient at these tasks but may have attitudes or behaviors that are troublesome to faculty. This issue has been discussed thoroughly in the literature and remains a constant problem in mental health graduate level training (Bemak, Epp, & Keys, 1999; Forrest, Elman, Gizara, & Vacha-Haase, 1999; Wilkerson, 2006).

Concerns about certain students' professional, personal, and interpersonal qualities are no different in the C&D Program at George Mason University than in other counseling and psychology programs throughout the world. The Professional Dispositions that were developed for the C&D Program are somewhat different from comparable standards in other programs, in

Table 15.1 C&D Program's Professional Dispositions

The American Counseling Association code of ethics requires counselors and counselor trainees to maintain standards of professional competence and possess good moral character. Therefore, the Counseling and Development Program in the College of Education and Human Development at George Mason University requires its students to exhibit the following:

Communication Skills	*Professionalism*
Clear presentation and demonstration of multicultural competencies in counseling skills	Commitment to multiculturalism and diversity
	Commitment to social justice as it relates to counseling
Clear oral communication	Respect of multiculturalism and diverse cultures
Clear written communication	Demonstration of openness, willingness to learn, and positive attitude about multiculturalism and diverse cultures
Clear ability to demonstrate effective and supportive helping skills	Commitment to the psychological well-being, health, and wellness of all people
Clear ability to demonstrate effective listening skills	Sound judgment
Collaboration	Integrity and honesty
Respect for the opinion and dignity of others	• Ability to accept personal responsibility • Ability to receive and reflect upon constructive criticism • Positive attitude
Ability to collaborate with others	• Ability to meet deadlines • Ability to maintain confidentiality with clients, students, and colleagues
Ability to demonstrate effective interpersonal skills	• Appropriate assertiveness • Ability to manage stress
Ability to participate as a colleague and team member in all aspects of professional training	• Ability to meet requirements as stated in course syllabi • Adherence to ACA ethical guidelines

that they are reflective of the core mission and values that underscore social justice, multiculturalism, internationalism, advocacy, and leadership. The dispositions are tailored toward the promotion of a social justice human rights multicultural philosophy, and they promote openness, fairness, integrity, tolerance, and equity. Students who decide to apply to and enroll in the C&D Program clearly understand the mission, so they are making decisions about adopting the Professional Dispositions when they enroll.

One example of a dispositional problem can be seen with a student in a multicultural class who stated that she ran a group for Latina girls. The Latina girls told the graduate student that they were experiencing racism and discrimination from one of the teachers. The graduate student told the multicultural class that she did not believe the girls, because the teacher that they mentioned was her friend, and she knew that the teacher was in "no way" racist. Furthermore, the Latina girls were known to be "trouble-makers." The graduate student proudly shared with the multicultural counseling class that she "straightened the girls out" by letting them know that their perception of their teacher was "all in their minds." When the first author (Rita, who was the instructor for the class) asked the student whether anything was done to investigate the girls' allegations, the student became defensive. When Rita continued probing the situation and suggested to the student an objective point of view where she could have investigated the girls' allegations, the student became angry and belligerent. The remarkable response by the student to Rita was, "You mentioned that racism is a volatile issue, quite frankly I [as a school counselor] don't get paid enough to deal with these types of situations."

Despite this attitude and overall demeanor, this student wrote excellent papers, was well prepared, gave good class presentations, and regularly attended class and participated. Yet, she had this type of attitude and reaction to a serious problem raised by Latina girls in the school, that is, she initially discounted the girls based on a personal relationship with the teacher who was accused of discriminating against them. Clearly, the student was angry and defensive, was not open to hearing from the instructor or classmates that she may have responded to the situation in a biased manner, and was not willing or open to hear constructive feedback. Typically this would not constitute a disposition problem in traditional programs, but with the Professional Dispositions geared toward openness, self-awareness, and the promotion of social justice, this student faced dispositional problems within the C&D Program, despite academic excellence in other areas.

Another example of a dispositional problem can be seen with a girl from Africa who recently immigrated to the United States and told her school counselor (another student in the C&D Program) that in her culture it was believed that when people pass away, their physical body may be dead, but their spirit continues to live. The school counselor told the girl not to mention this to anyone because she would sound "crazy." Once again, ethical standards do not question counseling students' values that do not embrace cultural differences, but with the C&D Professional Dispositions, this raised some serious questions about the counseling student's response. These sad but interesting examples cause us to reflect on what students are learning in graduate training and what is acceptable in terms of the more intangible qualities, attitudes, and beliefs that students carry when they graduate.

Another way to consider this is that graduate students, who are generally intelligent and fair-minded people, can easily "talk the talk," but they cannot always "walk the walk." This prompted me (Rita) to take the lead in developing the Professional Dispositions as a method of ensuring that students are accountable, ethically sound, and in line with the ethical standards and values that are inherent to the George Mason University's C&D Program. The entire faculty supported the Professional Dispositions and agreed on adopting them as a foundation to the program. Hence, students may get a grade of A in a course due to their performance on assessments and assignments, but may require remediation in other areas if they violate any of the Professional Dispositions. The student in the first example could theoretically receive an Incomplete or F grade for the class, but would be provided with faculty support and guidance to learn constructive ways to address the Professional Dispositions. If the behavior continued, such a student might be placed under review and on probation.

Along with the C&D Professional Dispositions, there is a list of steps that faculty, administration, and staff must follow if students are accused of violating the Professional Dispositions. The dispositions are designed to proactively educate students about their ethical behavior, and there is a set of action steps to take if unethical behavior continues. The action steps range from being required to demonstrate an improvement in attitude or behavior, to being on probation, and even to being counseled out of the program. The dispositions are mentioned throughout the program, discussed during the admissions interview process, posted on the website, attached to syllabi, and carefully reviewed in detail during the Foundations in Counseling course. Hence, students are fully aware of the dispositions from the first moment they interview for the program to their final internship class.

It is important to note that the dispositions are in no away a method of silencing students who may have other viewpoints. Other viewpoints are welcomed, but the underlying message to all students and faculty is that although there may be differences in viewpoints and worldviews, there must be at least an openness to listen and hear others' points of view. If there is disagreement, it must be voiced with the utmost respect. For example, when the Professional Dispositions were presented in a multicultural counseling class, one of the students mentioned that she felt she needed to monitor what she said in class—that the dispositions hindered her in freely expressing her opinions. A class discussion occurred about this issue, and it was agreed upon by all that the dispositions would not be a hindrance or silence anyone from speaking, but

rather be used as a guideline toward openness and respect for diverse thoughts and opinions.

LEVEL 4: PROGRAM ADMISSIONS

Previously, C&D students were accepted into the graduate program based on traditional requirements that were in line with the George Mason University CEHD. With the new mission statement and intentional efforts to recruit and retain students with qualities of leadership, potential for advocacy, and a high level of interest in and commitment to social justice and cultural diversity, the C&D program changed the admissions criteria. The revised admissions requirements incorporated an assessment of how prospective students had responded to issues of cultural diversity, social justice, and human rights in their prior personal and work experience. An assessment of a candidate's awareness and openness about these issues is important in determining the student's coherence with the program philosophy and training. An assessment is also made of applicants' current ability and potential for leadership and advocacy: Can this candidate carry forward the mission statement of social justice, multiculturalism, internationalism, advocacy, and leadership? References, interview ratings, application essays, values, and attitudes carry significant weight for admissions, which are less reliant on grade point averages and Graduate Record Examination scores. Those applicants who make the first cut are invited to a group interview and are asked about their reactions to the C&D mission and their values in relationship to it. They are also evaluated with respect to the interpersonal skills they exhibit during the group interview. Another part of the admissions interview includes a writing sample reacting to an aspect of the C&D mission.

The admission criteria go far beyond test scores and grades, which may be culturally biased and may not be a good indication of a candidate's potential as a future professional. Based on these new admissions criteria, the program expanded the percentage of students of color admitted, progressing in three years from 3% students of color to 35% students of color. The new mission statement and revised admissions criteria and process were instrumental in attracting students of color and students committed to the multicultural social justice mission. Concurrently, the faculty has changed from 90% White to 50% faculty of color.

LEVEL 5: STUDENT AND PROGRAM ASSESSMENT

Although students' progress is reviewed throughout the program, there is a more formal assessment at a program midpoint and at the conclusion of the program. The review and assessment criteria consist of traditional assessments evaluating grades and skills as well as the student's adherence to the program mission. Near the end of the program, students submit a professional portfolio that includes evidence of their mastery of elements of the program, such as skills and multicultural competencies; evidence to demonstrate their linkage of course theory to practice; and substantiation of how the five components of the C&D mission were incorporated throughout their program of study.

In addition, the program is currently developing an assessment tool to evaluate the quality of training. The questionnaire will evaluate the effectiveness of the program and will explore areas such as students' ability to utilize their training in the internship and work environment and their ability to operationalize the social justice components of the training in their internship sites and work places. It will also include an assessment of how students in this program differ from those in traditional graduate training programs. Furthermore, a questionnaire is currently being developed to assess the long-term impact of the training; it will ask graduates how they incorporate multicultural and social justice work in their current workplace.

LEVEL 6: FACULTY RETREATS

Much of our discussion so far has been about program development and students. It is also important to acknowledge the hard work and process by which faculty developed a program that incorporated social justice, multiculturalism, internationalism, advocacy, and leadership. Frequently universities ignore the faculty in describing their graduate programs and maintain a focus on students and program content. One commitment by the C&D Program was to ensure that the all faculty was included and participated fully in the development of the program, especially since it valued positive and healthy faculty relationships as a basis for creating a positive and healthy program environment. As mentioned earlier, the faculty had several retreats, three of them overnight. The overnight retreats, combined with several full-day retreats, assisted the faculty in attaining full consensus about the mission of the program and how to operationalize the mission.

A fascinating aspect of this process was that once the program had been redesigned, courses rewritten, and full approval granted by the appropriate university committees, the faculty realized that it would be important to step back and reflect on their own process, their relationships, and reactions to key concepts such as multiculturalism and social justice. Thus, a faculty retreat was structured to discuss several questions:

- Where are we now?
- How has the process of revamping the program affected you?
- How have you incorporated the five C&D components into your teaching, research, and practice?
- What concerns did and do you have, what challenges have you come across, and what do we need from each other at this point in time?

In one of the faculty retreats, there was an exploration of personal beliefs and worldviews related to issues of White privilege, racial identity, multiculturalism, and social justice. This was a profound experience, with a frank and honest discussion about faculty positions, feelings, and worldviews about these key issues in the program and in relationship to their own lives.

Finally, the faculty made several presentations about the development of the C&D Program at national conferences, such as the Columbia University Winter Roundtable and the annual meetings of the Association for Counselor Education and Supervision and the American Counseling Association. In each of these, the presenter shared the process of developing a new program and mission as well as his or her personal reactions and responses to the process. Later presentations also included students, who shared their perspectives on being part of a program that focused on social justice and multiculturalism (Bemak, Chung, Talleyrand, Jones, & Daquin, 2011). In fact, a DVD (Chung & Bemak, in press b) has just been made about the C&D Program that includes both faculty members' and students' reactions to the uniqueness of the C&D Program's mission.

LEVEL 7: STUDENT INVOLVEMENT AND CONTRIBUTIONS

Students have also been involved in the infusion of the C&D mission into all the C&D courses. As part of the first social justice class, students were asked to develop ideas on how the five elements of the mission could be infused into all the courses. Students' ideas were presented to faculty during a faculty retreat. Faculty took the students' recommendations seriously, infusing some of their ideas into the design of the courses. Also, town hall meetings have been established to maintain a continual dialog with students. In addition, the graduate counseling student organization, Chi Sigma Iota (CSI), has organized multiple social justice activities. They organized a walk for the homeless and a suicide prevention walk, cosponsored bringing a production of *The Exonerated* to George Mason University, and raised money for the victims and families of the Virginia Tech shooting. These are just some examples of CSI social justice activities.

Challenges in the Transformation

Although the C&D Program was fortunate to have both administrative and faculty support in transforming a traditional program into a program that endorses social justice and multiculturalism, there have also been challenges. One of those challenges was the difference in students' responses to faculty of color and White faculty when intensively exploring social justice and cultural diversity issues. Some students were more resistant to hearing straightforward, sensitive information about subjects such as White privilege or cultural biases from faculty of color than from White faculty.

Another challenge related to students knowing what to do with new information about social justice, human rights, and multiculturalism. Although every student entered the program knowing and accepting the C&D mission, their level of understanding and personal skills varied, so that operationalizing the principles of multiculturalism, social justice, and human rights in their personal and professional lives was sometimes very difficult. A real in-depth examination of these issues created intense personal challenges for students and presented complex and difficult class discussions. (See Chapter 8 for more on students' multicultural social justice journeys.) Students would find themselves confronting friends, partners, spouses, and family members about things they learned in the program, which would manifest in feelings of confusion and chaos within the classroom. Related to the problems of changing relationships and having differing values from others were some difficulties with practicum and internship placements. Finding supervisors who shared the program mission and values was sometimes difficult. The program had to educate supervisors about its mission and its expectations for students in field placements who were working from a social justice and multicultural framework.

Another difficulty was finding part-time adjunct faculty who agreed with the program mission and were willing and able to infuse the major components of multiculturalism, social justice, internationalism, advocacy, and leadership as a core part of their teaching. To rectify this, faculty held meetings with full- and part-time faculty and created mentoring pairs between full-time and part-time faculty who taught similar courses to ensure that the mission statement was incorporated in all the classes.

We acknowledge that the C&D Program was fortunate to have administrative support for the program changes, and that there was no major resistance exhibited by any of the program faculty. We also realize that this may not be the case for other programs and departments who wish to infuse these values into their teaching, research, and training; they may come across resistance and barriers to adopting a social justice training program. To address these concerns, the next section provides recommendations for counseling and psychology faculty who are interested in making similar changes and developing a social justice multicultural focus.

RECOMMENDATIONS

There are a number of recommendations that we have for successfully designing and implementing a social justice mission into counseling and psychology training programs. Although the recommendations are based on a counseling program, we believe that they are applicable to other psychology training programs such as counseling, community, or clinical psychology, given a departmental commitment to multiculturalism and social justice.

Consensual agreement regarding the meaning of social justice. There are so many definitions for social justice that it is important to spend time coming to mutual faculty understanding and agreement about what social justice means. This takes time and patience, and we emphasize that faculty must agree not just on a dictionary definition, but rather on the need to examine underlying values, biases, and beliefs about what constitutes social justice and how this would translate into graduate training.

Soliciting administrative support. Garnering support from deans and central administration is essential in changing a department to include social justice. A go-ahead from a dean authorizes

a department to move ahead and explore how to build in social justice constructs. This is important to explore and acquire at the beginning of the process so there is a fundamental understanding by faculty members that the inclusion of social justice is acceptable.

Gaining support from collaborating agencies, centers, and organizations. Every department works closely with outside agencies, centers, and organizations. Whether it be from funding agencies, field placement sites, collaborating centers or institutes, or something else, the outside support for instilling social justice into the training can be very helpful in approaching university administrators.

Spending time on faculty retreats. Meetings of one or two hours cannot possibly capture the complexity of amalgamating social justice into an existing graduate training program. Training programs have established histories, ways of doing things, and principles and values that focus the training. It is essential that faculty take the time to deeply consider changes to the curriculum and their own personal commitment to social justice training. Even though many counselors and psychologists would agree that social justice is an important issue, there are different views about how to describe social justice and how to build social justice into graduate training. Faculty retreats allow time to exchange ideas about how social justice can be built into classroom instruction and offer a place to support and mentor faculty as they start their social justice journey.

Working closely with adjunct faculty and field supervisors. Adjunct faculty and field supervisors are not involved in full-time department meetings. Frequently they are less engaged and committed to the program and may feel somewhat distant from the department. To remedy this at GMU, all adjunct faculty and field site supervisors are told, upon hire, about the mission of the program and the need for them to incorporate the mission into their teaching. It is also explained that there is a full-time point person to assist them with the social justice component of the program should they want support. Of course, they have academic freedom to include social justice and cultural diversity into the course material or supervision as they see fit, but including it is a requirement of the position. To supplement this, there are periodic adjunct faculty meetings where teaching and supervision are discussed.

Empowering students. In a training program that emphasizes social justice, it is essential that there is coherence for faculty and students. It is important to model and practice what one is doing in training by making sure that students have input into the program. Built into the C&D Program are events such as town hall meetings, where all attendants have a chance to voice their opinions; social justice events and projects sponsored by the student honor society; and social justice events sponsored by the faculty, such as working on the Gulf Coast following Hurricane Katrina or in California after the San Diego wildfires (as previously described in the section about Counselors Without Borders).

Building cooperative partnerships. Partnerships at the local, state, national, and international levels to address social justice issues are also important. Thus faculty are role models in establishing linkages with professional associations, committees of those associations, other universities, mental health agencies and organizations, schools, nonprofit organizations, nongovernmental organizations (NGOs), and so forth.

Assessment and evaluation. Self-evaluation of the successes and remaining gaps in the revised graduate training program are essential. Faculty must develop measures to evaluate the impact and quality of the revised program. Issues to assess could include students' academic training in relationship to their social justice development, changes in their personal values, their level of understanding of how to implement social justice in counseling, and so forth. The assessment could be done through the use of both quantitative (e.g., surveys, questionnaires) and qualitative (e.g., semistructured interviews) research methodologies. It may also be helpful to conduct exit interviews for students graduating from the program and follow-up assessments with former graduates to evaluate whether they are integrating social justice into their work.

SUMMARY

In summary, the development of the George Mason University Counseling and Development Program involved hard work and commitment by each and every faculty member. The program is an example of a unique mission of social justice that reflects the beliefs of the faculty and screens prospective student applicants to ensure they are dedicated to the mission. The emphasis on social justice, multiculturalism, internationalism, advocacy, and leadership required tremendous work, time, and energy from faculty and involves being engaged in a continuous process. We believe it provides a good example for you, the reader, to see one model of a program that has successfully incorporated social justice and human rights into the core of training, and we hope that elements in this chapter may have applicability to the graduate training or supervision work that you are doing.

REFERENCES

Bemak, F., & Chung, R. C.-Y. (2011). Post-disaster social justice group work and group supervision. *Journal for Specialists in Group Work, 36*(1), 3–21.

Bemak, F., & Chung, R. C.-Y. (in press a). Classrooms without walls. *Journal of Humanistic Counseling, Education, and Development.*

Bemak, F., & Chung, R. C.-Y. (in press b). *Counselors without borders* [DVD]. Microtraining and Multicultural Development, a division of Alexander Street Press. Available from http://emicrotraining .com

Bemak, F., Chung, R. C.-Y., Talleyrand, R. M., Jones, H., & Daquin J. (2011). Implementing multicultural social justice strategies in counselor education training programs. *Journal of Social Action in Psychology and Counseling, 3*(1), 29–43.

Bemak, F., Epp, L., & Keys, S. (1999). Impaired graduate students: A process of graduate program monitoring and intervention. *International Journal for the Advancement of Counselling, 21,* 19–30.

Chung, R. C.-Y., & Bemak, F. (in press a). Use of ethnographic fiction in social justice graduate counselor training. *Counselor Education and Supervision.*

Chung, R. C.-Y., & Bemak, F. (in press b). *Incorporating social justice into your program.* Microtraining and Multicultural Development, a division of Alexander Street Press. Available from http://emicrotraining.com/

Forrest, L., Elman, N., Gizara, S., & Vacha-Haase, T. (1999). Trainee impairment: A review of identification, remediation, dismissal, and legal issues. *The Counseling Psychologist, 27,* 627–686.

Hartung, P. J., & Blustein, D. L. (2002). Reason, intuition, and social justice: Elaborating on Parson's career decision-making model. *Journal of Counseling and Development, 80,* 41–47.

Lerner, R. M. (1995). *America's youth in crisis: Challenges and options for programs and policies.* Thousand Oaks, CA: Sage.

Talleyrand, R. M., Chung, R. C-Y., & Bemak, F. (2007). Incorporating social justice in counselor training programs. In R. L. Toporek, L. H. Gerstein, N. A. Fouad, G. Roysircar, & T. Israel (Eds.), *Handbook for social justice in counseling psychology: Leadership, vision, and action* (pp. 44–58). Thousand Oaks, CA: Sage.

Vera, E. M., & Speight, S. L. (2003). Multicultural competence, social justice, and counseling psychology: Expanding our roles. *The Counseling Psychologist, 31,* 253–272.

Wilkerson, K. (2006). Impaired students: Applying the therapeutic process model to graduate training programs. *Counselor Education and Supervision, 45*(3), 207–307.

PART VI

SOCIAL JUSTICE IN A GLOBAL WORLD

16

SOCIAL JUSTICE IN A MULTICULTURAL AND GLOBAL WORLD: ADVANCING THE SOCIAL JUSTICE AGENDA

*The world is too dangerous to live in—not because of the people who do evil,
but because of the people who sit and let it happen.*

(Albert Einstein)

A scholar who loves comfort is not fit to be called a scholar.

(Confucius)

WARM UP EXERCISE

1. *How have things going on in other parts of the world affected your life? Think of three examples.*

2. *What are social injustices that you are aware of that have happened or are happening in other parts of the world?*

3. *Think of people you know or have met who came from a country other than your own. Have you ever spoken to these people about their home country, their experiences in their homeland, and their sense of similarities and differences with life in your country? If so, what did you learn about their experience in relationship to social justice? If not, why do you imagine you did not speak about these differences and experiences of justice?*

We can see the effects of globalization wherever we look in today's world.

Similarly, the realities of social and economic injustices and inequities continue to have a strong presence in our contemporary world. When we as counselors and psychologists begin to link these two strongly influential contemporary themes together and commence examining social justice from a global perspective, many questions arise. Why should those of us based in the United States be concerned with social injustices outside of our own country? Why should those of us based in the United States spend our resources in other countries, when we could be spending them our own country? Why should I, as a counselor or psychologist, be concerned with issues other than those of my individual client? How does globalization relate to mental health work and to me?

There is much to be done in the United States and elsewhere related to social justice. The previous chapters have discussed and outlined why social justice is critical in the mental health field and have presented data to illustrate the degree of inequality in modern society. In this final chapter, we would like to discuss the importance of expanding social justice issues beyond one's own local, regional, and national environment and examine how to incorporate a global perspective into our social justice mental health work. This is especially important in the 21st century, as the world is shrinking. Globalization has impacted so many dimensions of our society, yet in the mental health field, we still have paid minimal attention to internationalizing our work. Although Marsella (1998) has made revolutionary first steps in expanding psychology to an international context, few have picked up on this, and the field has not continued exploring the implications of globalization for mental health. This chapter is meant to further explore these questions and pose some initial answers about why and how globalization and mental health link.

WHY ADDRESS SOCIAL JUSTICE ISSUES FROM A GLOBAL PERSPECTIVE?

When we examine the facts, the connection between globalization and mental health become clearer. Around the world there are 1.3 billion people living on less than one dollar a day. Three billion people, almost half the world, earn less than two dollars a day and have no access to sanitation. Another 1.6 billion people do not have access to electricity, causing over 1 million people in the developing world to die annually due to water-borne diseases and inadequate sanitation (Shah, 2010b). UN-Habitat (2008) states that poor hygiene and lack of sanitation account for 1.6 million deaths a year globally. Twenty percent of the population in developed nations consumes 77% of the world's goods, including 45% of all meat and fish. In contrast, the poorest one fifth of all nations consumes only 5% of all meat and fish. Similarly, the disparity in consumption in other areas is significant. Twenty percent of the population in developed nations consumes 58% of the world's total energy (the poorest fifth consume less than 4%), 84% of all paper (the poorest fifth, 1.1%), have 74% of all telephone lines (the poorest fifth have 1.5%), and own 87% of the world's vehicles (the poorest fifth own less than 1%) (Shah, 2010b). In addition, a mere 12% of the world's population who reside in developed industrial countries uses 85% of its water (Shah, 2010b).

Pointedly, the total wealth of the top 8.3 million people around the world rose 8.2% to $30.8 trillion in 2004, giving them control of nearly a quarter of the world's financial assets. When one looks more closely at this figure, it is found that approximately 0.13% of the world's population controls 25% of the world's assets (Shah, 2010b).

Facts such as these have an impact on the social and psychological well-being of individuals, families, communities, regions, states, and countries as well as on international relations. Concerns about social issues further contribute to social ills and problems. For example, there are approximately 2.2 billion children in the world. Of those children, almost one half, or 1 billion children, live in poverty. Of the 1.9 billion children in the developing world, there are 640 million without adequate shelter (that is 1 in 3), 400 million with no access to safe water (1 in 5), and 270 million with no access to health services (1 in 7) (Shah, 2010b). Globally, 120 million children do not have access to education, and in 2003, 10.6 million children (which is equivalent to the total population of children in France, Germany, Greece, and Italy) died before they reached the age of 5 (Shah, 2010b). Lack of access to safe drinking water and adequate sanitation cause the deaths of 1.4 million children each year, while 2.2 million children die every year because they are not immunized. Fifteen million children (an amount equal to the total child population of Germany or the UK) become orphans annually because their parents or guardians die of HIV/AIDS (Shah, 2010b). These figures are alarming and need to be a cause for concern about the social conditions within the child's family and community as well as internationally.

Research has also shown a relationship between poverty and violence (Postmus & Hahn, 2007). The World Health Organization's report on violence (WHO, 2002) shows staggering statistics on the level and degree of violence worldwide. For example, it is estimated that in 2000, 1.6 million people, including approximately 57,000 children, died due to violence; violence was also one of the leading causes of death for people aged 15–44 years; in some countries, one in four women reported sexual violence by an intimate partner; and approximately 4% to 6% of elderly people experience some form of abuse in the home (WHO, 2002). In fact, the 20th century was one of the most violent periods in human history. More than half of the people who lost their lives to conflict throughout the world were civilians (WHO, 2002).

When you look at the compilation of these alarming statistics, you may be wondering, "How does this affect me?" Even if you feel moved by the statistics, there may still be another important question, which is, "Well, what can I do about it? How can I make a difference?" In this next section,

we will examine these statistics in more detail and discuss the relevance of global social justice issues to the United States.

THE INTERSECTION OF GLOBAL ISSUES AND U.S. ISSUES

We would suggest that there is a clear and marked intersection between global social issues and U.S. social issues. To begin, we will examine the economic impact on the U.S. economy to provide a foundation for understanding social issues and mental health. It is interesting to note that in our experience, there has only been minimal work done that links economics with social and mental health concerns (Marsella, 1998). This has left counselors and psychologists estranged from the larger impact of economics on mental health. In this section we would like to explore and connect the relevance and importance of the economy with counseling and psychotherapy and social justice.

Approximately 62% of the world economy interacts with the United States; that is, 62% of all the wealth in the world is affected by what happens in the United States (Chung, 2005). The United States has more millionaires and billionaires than any other country in the world. In fact, the top 400 income earners in the United States make as much in a year as the entire population of the 20 poorest countries in Africa (over 300 million people). Of the top 200 corporations in the world, the United States has the most with a total of 82. The combined sales of all 200 corporations are 18 times the size of the combined annual income of the 1.2 billion people (24% of the total world population) who are living in extreme poverty (Shah, 2010b).

Even though the United States has only 4.6% of the world's population, approximately 50% of the world's worth is in the United States, and 30% of the world's resources are consumed by the United States (Shah, 2010b). In the 1990s, the average U.S. citizen was consuming 30 times more resources and goods than a citizen of India.

Only 20% of the world's population lives in developed nations, yet they use two thirds of all the resources. Concurrently, the poorest 40% of the world's population accounts for 5% of global income (Shah, 2010b).

The disparities in these statistics are astounding, and the question still remains: How does this affect me, the individual, the layperson, a mere counselor or psychologist? I am not involved in any corporations, I own few stocks, and I am not in the top income bracket. I don't have exposure to people from other parts of the world who are poor, diseased, uneducated, or hungry, and I occasionally contribute to local charities. We would suggest that these responses are appropriate in many respects—counselors and psychologists are not in the mental health field because it is a high-income profession. Rather, many go into mental health work to be helpers and healers. We are in the profession because we care about people. That care and concern for others correlates with a need to be involved not only locally and regionally but also nationally and internationally. To illustrate our belief in this need for international work, let's break down these statistics into more meaningful day-to-day activities.

The Impact of U.S. Consumption on the World

Living in a developed industrial nation, we consume resources and products that have moved beyond what we need to meet our basic needs and that now include luxury items and technological innovations to improve efficiency. For example, Americans and Europeans together spend $17 billion a year on pet food, which is $4 billion more than the estimated yearly additional amount needed to provide everyone in the world with basic health and nutrition (U.N. Development Programme, 1998, p. 5). In fact, the United States spends more than $16.2 billion a year on pet food alone, and a total of $45.5 billion on the combination of pet food, veterinary services, and other pet care items (American Pet Products Association, 2009).

When looking at figures related to expenditures on meat, the average meat, poultry, and fish consumption by Americans is 200 pounds per year. Generally speaking, Americans eat eight ounces of meat per day, which is twice the global average (Bittman, 2008). Producing a quarter pound of hamburger requires 100 gallons of water, 1.2 pounds of feed grain, and energy equal to a cup of gasoline, causing the loss of 1.25 pounds of topsoil and producing a greenhouse gas emission equal to that of a six-mile drive in a typical U.S. automobile. Hence, the realistic estimate of the real cost of a hamburger was put at $35 (U.N. Development Programme, 1998). Related to meat consumption is the clearance of the Amazon rainforest for pasture to raise cattle. The land is not used to raise food for local consumption, but rather for beef that is exported to the United States. Furthermore, 70% to 80% of the grain produced in the United States is used to feed livestock, and more than one third of the world's grain harvest is used to feed livestock. Eight hundred million people suffer from hunger, and a good portion of corn and soy goes to cattle, pigs, and chickens (Bittman, 2008; Shah, 2010a).

Desserts and cosmetics are also important in developed countries. In 2002, Europeans spent $11 billion on ice cream, and Americans spent approximately $20 billion on ice cream, frozen desserts, and frozen novelties ("Cost of U.S. Appetite," 2002). Annual expenditures on cosmetics are $8 billion in the United States, which is $2 billion more than what is needed to provide basic education for everyone in the world (Shah, 2010b). Despite the volume of consumption, there has been little connection between increased consumption and increased happiness for Americans. The National Opinion Research Center of the University of Chicago found that the proportion of Americans who say they are "very happy" has remained at about one third since 1957, even though personal consumption has more than doubled (Durning, 1992). The Harris Poll also showed that only 33% of people described themselves as being "very happy" in 2010, down from 35% in 2008 and 2009 (Corso, 2010).

As we consume these resources, several questions arise. How are the products and resources we consume actually produced, and what are the macro and micro level impacts on the environment, society, community, and individuals? Who influences our choices of consumption, and who influences how and why things are produced or not produced? How do consumption habits change as societies change? What is the effect of the demands by wealthier nations and the rich on poorer nations? What is the impact of consumption and economics on our personal values? How does materialism influence our values and relationships with other people? How does mental health fit into these questions and issues?

Rich countries strip poorer countries of their natural resources, leaving a devastating imbalance of wealth throughout the world. According to the United Nations 2003 report, a third of the world's population will be slum dwellers within 30 years. UN Habitat (2008) defines a neighborhood as a slum if more than half of the households in the area suffer from one or more shelter deprivations. Shelter deprivation is defined as stark houselessness, deprivation with respect to certain basic amenities, deprivation in terms of quality of dwelling structure, and overcrowding within a dwelling structure as well as overcrowding of dwelling structures in a limited space. Currently, almost one sixth of the world's population lives in slum-like conditions, and 1 out of every 3 people living in cities of the developing world lives in a slum (Shah, 2010b; UN-Habitat, 2008). U.S. corporations extract huge profits from almost every corner of the world (Lewis, 2003). Relative to the percentage of the world's resources it consumes, the United States remains last among the industrialized countries in the amount it allocates for international development, giving exactly 0.11% of gross domestic product (Krieger, 2003).

It has been argued that the United States is spending more on its plans to research, develop, and deploy missile defenses than on international humanitarian and development assistance (Stiglitz & Blimes, 2008). For example, the United States has the largest military budget in the world at 46.5% of the world's total, and it is distantly followed by China (6.6%), France (4.2%), the UK (3.8%), and Russia (3.5%) (Shah, 2010c).

Furthermore, the cost of current wars exceeds the cost of the 12-year war in Vietnam; it is more than double the cost of the Korean War, and it is estimated to be almost 10 times the cost of the first Gulf War (Stiglitz & Blimes, 2008). Stiglitz and Blimes (2008) estimate that the operating cost of the war in Iraq is $12.5 million per month, and if you include Afghanistan, the cost is $16 billion. This is the same amount as the United Nations' annual budget. Between the fiscal years of 2007 and 2008, the total U.S. military budget increased by $50 billion (Shah, 2010c). The same amount could be used to close the poverty gap for U.S. children for a year and provide health coverage for 94,000 children for a year (Children's Defense Fund, 2004).

The United States' failure to seriously address poverty and social injustices globally is leading to resentment, anger, and aggression toward U.S. citizens. A small portion of what the U.S. government spends on its military could save lives and build friendships by providing humanitarian assistance in the form of food, health care, education, sanitation (Krieger, 2003), and psychological well-being. For example, the United States now spends over 50% of its discretionary budget on the military; in 2004, $453.7 billion was spent, or $37.8 billion a month. This figure equates to 8.7 billion a week, which is enough to provide child care for 1.4 million U.S. children of working families for a year. $1.2 billion a day is enough to provide health coverage for 845,000 U.S. children for a year; $51.6 million an hour is enough to provide Head Start for 7,400 U.S. children for a year; and $860,815 a minute is enough to fully immunize 1,300 U.S. children by age two (Children's Defense Fund, 2004).

On a global level, to date, the monies used to finance the war in Iraq could be used to fully fund global antihunger efforts for 7 years, a world-wide AIDS program for 18 years, or basic immunizations for every child in the world for 60 years (National Priorities Project, 2009). Figures such as these have a profound effect on social justice issues and have significant implications for mental health.

The United Nations Universal Declaration of Human Rights

In an effort to reduce or eliminate social injustices and to promote equality in global society, in 1948 the General Assembly of the United Nations (U.N.) adopted and proclaimed the Universal Declaration of Human Rights. (See the Appendix to Chapter 3 for a list of the 30 articles in the declaration.) According to the declaration, all member countries of the U.N., regardless of political status, were to publicize the declaration by disseminating, displaying, reading, and discussing them in schools and other educational institutions.

The Universal Declaration of Human Rights is a set of standards for all member countries. The U.N. emphasized that all member countries, in cooperation with the U.N., pledged to achieve the goals of the declaration and promote a universal respect for and observance of human rights and fundamental freedoms as outlined in the 30 articles. The essence of the declaration is that the foundation of freedom, justice, and peace is a result of a recognition of the dignity and equal rights of all individuals. Therefore, the declaration attempts to curtail barbarous acts and atrocities, respect fundamental human rights, and support freedom of speech and belief and freedom from fear and want. The declaration also stresses that human rights should be protected by the laws of each country, and suggests that it is essential to promote the development of friendly relations among countries.

It is important for psychologists and counselors to have a basic understanding of the Universal Declaration of Human Rights, especially as one works within the realm of human rights and social justice. Below is a summary of these rights with a discussion about their correlation with work as a psychologist or counselor.

The 30 human rights articles stipulate that all people—regardless of race, ethnicity, nationality, gender, language, religion, political or other opinion, national or social origin, property ownership, socioeconomic status, and birth or other status—are born free and equal in dignity and with a right to life, liberty, and security. Hence, no one shall be held in slavery or servitude in any form. The articles also specify that no one be subjected to torture or to cruel, inhumane, or degrading treatment or punishment, nor subjected to arbitrary arrest, detention, or exile. Underlying this premise is that all individuals are equal before the law and are entitled without any discrimination to fair and public hearing and to equal protection of the law. Essentially, all individuals are innocent until proven guilty.

Other aspects of the articles denote that people shall not be subject to arbitrary interference with their privacy, family, or home, nor face attacks on their honor or reputation. The articles also outline that all individuals have the right to freedom of movement and residence within the borders of their country, as well as the right to leave and return to their own country. Related to movement, the articles specify that people are permitted to abide in other countries to escape persecution, that everyone has the right to a nationality, and that individuals may not be denied the right to change their nationality.

Adult women and men, without any limitation due to race, nationality, or religion, have the right to marry. Marriage is held freely with the full consent of the people involved and protected by the society and the State. Along with the right to freedom of choice in marriage, the articles outline how everyone has the right to freedom of thought, conscience, and religion. In addition, all people have the right to freedom of opinion and expression, and if they so choose, they can impart information through any medium. Related to freedom of expression, everyone has the right to peaceful assembly and association and the right to take part in the government of their country, which should be based on the opinions and will of the people through free unhampered elections and open and accessible voting procedures.

The articles also address work, designating that all people have the right to work, to freely choose their employment, to have protection against being unemployed, and to work in just and acceptable working conditions. Equal pay for equal work, without discrimination, is everyone's right. Similarly, individuals have the right to form and join trade unions for the protection of their interests.

The 30 articles also cover basic needs, relaxation, and free time. Everyone has the right to leisure and rest. Additionally, having all the basic needs met is a fundamental right for individuals. A basic standard of living (e.g., food, housing, and clothing), medical care and appropriate social services, and security in special situations (e.g., unemployment, sickness, disability, widowhood, and old age) are all essential human rights that are necessary for an acceptable living standard. Both motherhood and childhood are entitled to special care and assistance, and children should be valued and have access to the same social protection whether born in or out of wedlock.

While parents have the right to choose the educational path for their children, education is a right for all and should be mandatory. Higher education is available on the basis of merit, and the purpose of education is to develop an individual's personality and to ensure or teach about the respect of others. The promotion of equality, acceptance, and friendship shall support the activities of the U.N. in the promulgation of peace.

Finally, all people shall have equal opportunities for creativity and community participation, and have protection for any inventions they create. Social and international functioning is a means to ensure that all put forth in the declaration is accomplished, knowing that statements in the declaration are not partial or beneficial toward any particular group or person, and that any attempt to destroy the proclamations of freedom and rights in the declaration is unacceptable.

Basically these rights set forth a foundation that is inherent in mental health and social justice work regarding freedom of choice, health care, work, marriage, creativity, psychological and physical safety, privacy, movement, expression, and political involvement. These issues are highly correlated with positive mental health and with social justice work by counselors and psychologists.

Before we examine social justice and mental health from a global perspective, it is important to examine this concept from our own backyard. What is happening in our own respective countries, and what is its applicability to the people's mental health? What role do we as counseling and psychology professionals have with respect to the U.N. Universal Declaration on Human Rights? What does this foundation of global human rights mean to us as mental health and social justice professionals?

WHY SHOULD MENTAL HEALTH PROFESSIONALS AND COUNSELORS BE INVOLVED?

The onset of globalization and rapid change has created an interconnectedness causing more understanding, contact, and accessibility between different cultures and countries, and creating a *global village*. The rapidity of globalization affects all aspects of modern day living, leaving no area of human life untouched. Rapid changes due to sophisticated communications, technology, and global travel have accelerated change in the global economy and created a financial interdependence that links different cultures, regions, states, and countries (Chung, 2005).

Unfortunately, as we move ahead with this rapid and yet exciting change, there is a simultaneous increase in global instances of social injustices and human rights violations (Chung, 2005). Women and children especially are identified as victims of these injustices (WHO, 2002). Globalization involves more than just economy and trade, as illustrated with some of the statistics we discussed earlier in this chapter, and there is a psychological component of it that affects psychological well-being (Sassen, 1998) and cultural practices (e.g., Appadurai, 2000; Giddens, 2000; Tomlinson, 1999). It is clear that the gap between rich and poor and between individuals, regions, states, and countries is widening, which in turn creates a dilemma, especially within the context of the Universal Declaration of Human Rights. Priorities in governmental funding that control access to health care services, and to expensive technology that saves or prolongs life, play an important role in globalization (Chung, 2005) and have significance for mental health and human rights.

Other human rights mental health concerns point to the development of conflict resolution strategies for peaceful coexistence among groups whose differing beliefs, values, and behaviors are influenced by their cultural and religious worldviews, gender, race, or ethnic backgrounds and socioeconomic situations (Mays, Rubin, Sabourin, & Walker, 1996). Tolerating those with a different religion or faith, accepting the role of women in long-standing male dominated cultures, or accommodating practices such as abortion or female genital mutilation are all examples of flash points and areas where there is a potential convergence of human rights and mental health. Given these significant differences and the resulting psychological concerns, there has been a call to the helping profession to be responsive to the demands of globalization and changes in newly multiethnic, multiracial, and multinational societies (e.g., Arnett, 2002; Leong & Ponterotto, 2003; Marsella, 1998; Mays et al., 1996; Paredes et al., 2008).

The United States is the largest technologically powerful economy in the world and leads the world in health technology, yet it has only 4.5% of the global population. Therefore, less than 5% of the world's population has approximately 50% of the world's wealth and consumes 30% of the world's resources (Shah, 2010b), making it evident that the United States is the superpower and hence has a major influence on a global level. Regardless of global attitudes toward the United States, it still exerts significant influence throughout the world. Given the status of the United States internationally, it may be argued that professional psychology and counseling associations based in the United States (e.g., American Psychological Association, American Counseling Association, American Mental Health Counselors Association, etc.) are in an advantageous position economically and politically compared with other counseling associations worldwide (Chung, 2005). With the status of being a U.S.-based organization comes the power to influence

mental health associations worldwide (Winslade, 2003) with the potential to not only to be effective, but also to play a major role in working to achieve global social justice and human rights.

Although the U.S. psychology and counseling fields have been criticized by others as being deeply rooted in the cultural values and behaviors of U.S. principles of individuality, abstract ideals, and rationality (Cheung, 2000; Kim, 1995; Leong & Ponterotto, 2003; Trimble, 2001), this should not prevent psychologists and counselors in the United States from acting globally. Pedersen (2003) stated that "American psychology is in danger of being left behind" because "U.S. psychologists know far less about psychology in other cultures than international psychologists know about us" (p. 400). Given our degree of consumption of global resources and our power to create change solely by the fact that we are living in the United States, we would suggest that it is our ethical and moral duty and responsibility to act beyond our local areas and expand to act in regional, national, and international spheres.

Throughout this book we have emphasized that individuals' lives are not linear and that our mental health profession needs to look at the broader picture to be aware of and understand the complexity and multidimensionality of human existence and the influence of social, environmental, and political factors on it. In this chapter we are extending this outlook one more step, to the global arena. How we conduct ourselves on a daily basis has an impact either directly or indirectly on others around the world. The immigrants for whom we provide counseling have ties to families adjusting in the United States and to family and friends in a home country. Their mental health has significance that ripples across international boundaries. For example, the client whom we help become more tolerant and accepting of Iraqis may discriminate less against people of Middle Eastern descent, and this has implications for Iraqis living here as well as their larger extended family networks living in Iraq.

The phone call we make to our senator or national association about torture by psychologists may contribute to influencing policy that has international implications for mental health professionals and human rights. Therefore, our actions may have bearing on mental health related policies, laws, and human rights issues on a global level. We would suggest that we cannot and should not ignore global issues of social injustices and human right violations, since they are so intricately linked to our own mental health and social justice work in our own local domain. If you are concerned and affected, even slightly, by the statistics that have been presented, then the question we would ask you is, "What are you going to do about it?" As Martin Luther King Jr., stated, "Our lives begin to end the day we become silent about the things that matter."

PRACTICAL STRATEGIES FOR PSYCHOLOGISTS AND COUNSELORS

A saying promoting social action that has been around for some time reads, "Think globally, act locally." The saying has relevance for psychologists and counselors who, in our opinion, must "think globally, act globally and locally." We resonate with the quote by Martin Luther King Jr., who called on people to become engaged in the fight for social justice, saying, "If not us, who? If not now, when?" If we as counselors and psychologists, with positions of power, excellent communication skills, and potential influence, do not step forward to question violations of social justice and human rights, then who will?

There are some strategies that we believe are relevant to the global work that psychologists and counselors can do related to mental health and social justice. Some ideas are noted below:

- Develop mental health training programs in partnership with international colleagues. These can be for training for work outside of your home country or training for international populations living in your home country.
- Develop cooperative university degree and certificate programs in psychology and counseling with colleagues from a university outside of your country.

- Write collaboratively with colleagues from other countries, and publish in overseas journals.
- Ask your professional organizations to include more globalization and social justice issues in the organization's agenda, conference presentations, and journal articles.
- Serve on committees that focus on international work.
- Lobby your legislative representative and officials to pass bills favoring international social justice and human rights.
- Volunteer your time and skills to work with international groups who need assistance and live locally.
- Educate your colleagues about international collaboration.
- Speak and write about your experiences, and the need for social justice for international groups with whom you have worked with overseas or locally.

In summary, globalization has created a smaller, more informed world. We are knowledgeable about the issues facing those who migrate to our geographic region and also very aware of what is going on in many parts of the world. The unique time we live in affords us tremendous opportunity to make a difference, especially in light of our training and skills. I (Rita) wrote once that we need to "speak up, speak out" against injustices (Chung, 2002). We would encourage you to do the same. We hope that what we have presented will inspire, motivate, and propel you to take action on social injustices at the local, national, and international levels. So instead of just talking the talk, let's walk the talk. This is a call for action (Chung, 2011).

DISCUSSION QUESTIONS

1. What do you believe is important in considering global issues for mental health practitioners?

2. Discuss how economics and politics relate to issues in the counseling field.

3. The United Nations has established the Universal Declaration of Human Rights. How do the precepts of this declaration relate to your work as a counselor, psychologist, or social worker?

4. Describe three strategies by which counselors, psychologists, and social workers can become involved in global concerns

REFERENCES

American Pet Products Association. (2009). *Industry statistics and trends.* Retrieved from http://www.americanpetproducts.org/press_industrytrends.asp

Appadurai, A. (Ed.). (2000). *Globalization.* Durham, NC: Duke University Press.

Arnett, J. J. (2002). The psychology of globalization. *American Psychologist, 57*(10), 774–783. doi: 10.1037/0003-066X.57.10.774

Bittman, M. (2008, January 27). Rethinking the meat-guzzler. *The New York Times.* Retrieved from http://www.nytimes.com/2008/01/27/weekin review/27bittman.html

Children's Defense Fund. (2004). *State of America's children.* Washington, DC: Author.

Cheung, F. M. (2000). Deconstructing counseling in a cultural context. *The Counseling Psychologist, 28*(1), 123–132. doi: 10.1177/0011000000281008

Chung, R. C.-Y. (2002). Combating racism: Speaking up and speaking out. In J. Kottler (Ed.), *Finding your way as a counselor* (2nd ed., pp. 105–108). Alexandria, VA: American Counseling Association.

Chung, R. C.-Y. (2005). Women, human rights and counseling: Crossing international boundaries. *Journal of Counseling and Development* [Special issue on women and counseling], *83*(3), 262–268.

Chung, R. C.-Y. (2011). *Social justice counselors in action: Walking the talk.* [DVD]. North Atlantic Region, Association for Counselor Educators and Supervisors (NARACES) Conference 2010 Keynote Presentation.

Corso, R. A. (2010, May). *Annual happiness index finds one-third of Americans are very happy.* Harris Interactive. Retrieved from http://www.harrisinteractive.com/NewsRoom/HarrisPolls/tabid/447/ctl/ReadCustom%20Default/mid/1508/ArticleId/394/Default.aspx

Cost of U.S. appetite for frozen desserts to exceed $20 billion in 2002. (2002). Retrieved from http://www.packagedfacts.com/about/release.asp?id=14

Durning, A. (1992). *How much is enough: The consumer society and the fate of the earth.* New York, NY: Norton.

Giddens, A. (2000). *Modernity and self-identity: Self and society in the late modern age.* Cambridge, UK: Polity Press.

Kim, U. (1995). Psychology, science and culture: Cross-cultural analysis of national psychologies. *International Journal of Psychology, 30*(6), 663–679. doi: 10.1080/00207599508246593

Krieger, D. (2003). *Economic justice for all.* Retrieved from http://www.globalpolicy.org/socecon/in equal/income/2003/0523forall.htm

Leong, F. T. L., & Ponterotto, J. G. (2003). A proposal for internationalizing counseling psychology in the United States: Rationale, recommendations, and challenges. *The Counseling Psychologist, 31*(4), 381–395. doi: 10.1177/0011000003031004001

Lewis, T. (2003). *The growing gap between rich and poor.* Retrieved from http://globalpolicy.org/socecon/inequal/2003/0801gap.htm

Marsella, A. J. (1998). Toward a "global-community psychology": Meeting the needs of a changing world. *American Psychologist, 53*(12), 1282–1291. doi: 10.1037/0003-066X.53.12.1282

Mays, V. M., Rubin, J., Sabourin, M., & Walker, L. (1996). Moving toward a global psychology: Changing theories and practice to meet the needs of a changing world. *American Psychologist, 51*(5), 485–487. doi: 10.1037/0003-066X.51.5.485

National Priorities Project. (2009). *Cost of war.* Retrieved from http://www.nationalpriorities.org/costofwar_home

Paredes, D. M., Choi, K. M., Dipal, M., Edwards-Joseph, A. R. A. C., Ermakov, N., Gouveia, A. T., & Benshoff, J. M. (2008). Globalization: A brief primer for counselors. *International Journal for the Advancement of Counselling, 30*(3), 155–166. doi: 10.1007/s10447-008-9053-1

Pedersen, P. B. (2003). Cultural biased assumptions in counseling psychology. *The Counseling Psychologist, 31*(4), 396–403. doi: 10.1177/001100000 3031004002

Postmus, J., & Hahn, S. (2007). The collaboration between welfare and advocacy organizations: Learning from the experiences of domestic violence survivors. *Families in Society, 88*(3), 475–484.

Sassen, S. (1998). *Globalization and its discontents: Essays on the new mobility of people and money.* New York, NY: New Press.

Shah, A. (2010a). *Global issues: Beef.* Retrieved from http://www.globalissues.org/article/240/beef

Shah, A. (2010b). *Global issues: Poverty facts and stats.* Retrieved from http://www.globalissues .org/article/26/poverty-facts-and-stats

Shah, A. (2010c). *Global issues: World military spending.* Retrieved from http://www.global issues.org/article/75/world-military-spending

Stiglitz, J., & Blimes, L. (2008). *The three trillion dollar war.* New York, NY: Norton.

Tomlinson, J. B. (1999). *The media and modernity.* Cambridge, UK: Polity Press.

Trimble, J. E. (2001). A quest for discovering ethnocultural themes in psychology. In J. G. Ponterotto, J. M. Casas, L. A. Suzuki, & C. M. Alexander (Eds.), *Handbook for multicultural counseling* (2nd ed., pp. 3–13). Thousand Oaks, CA: Sage.

UN-Habitat. (2008). *State of the world's cities 2008/2009: Harmonious cities.* London, UK: Earthscan.

United Nations (U.N). (2003). *Experts share strategies to stop child trafficking.* New York, NY: U.N. Special Session for Children.

United Nations Development Programme. (1998). *Human Development Report 1998.* New York, NY: Oxford University Press.

Winslade, J. (2003, March). *The impact of counselling in New Zealand.* Paper presented at the meeting of the American Counseling Association, Anaheim, CA.

World Health Organization. (2002). *World report on violence and health.* Geneva, Switzerland: Author.

17

CONCLUSION

If you are neutral in situations of injustice, you have chosen the side of the oppressor.
If an elephant has its foot on the tail of a mouse and you say that you are neutral,
the mouse will not appreciate your neutrality.

(Bishop Desmond Tutu)

You don't have to see the whole staircase—just take the first step.

(Martin Luther King Jr.)

A small group of thoughtful people could change the world. Indeed,
it's the only thing that ever has.

(Margaret Mead)

Adding social justice to our work as healers is challenging. It requires incorporating a new dimension into the already complex and difficult work of being a healer. Yet to remain neutral, to not respond to the issues of injustice that permeate many of our clients' lives, to remain passive and ignore those critical and influential components of someone's life, to not have a voice, is to allow—through one's inaction—the social injustices to continue. Being silent is to participate in the oppression, the violations, and the pain that have such power and impact in so many of our clients' lives. As Martin Luther King Jr. stated, "A time comes when silence is betrayal."

This book describes the next steps beyond multiculturalism in the mental health field. It speaks to the fifth force in mental health, social justice, and defines theory, application, research, and training of multicultural social justice counselors, psychologists, and social workers. The book is based on the premise that it is not acceptable or effective to simply look at mental health through the lens of Western psychology, which is rooted in individually oriented interventions and psychopathology. Rather the book presents a different paradigm that challenges us to think, act, and provide interventions through a systems-oriented ecological perspective that is underscored by social change as a driving force in change, growth, and healing. The foundation of multicultural social justice is based on clear precepts of justice, human dignity, equality, equity, freedom, cultural responsiveness, and fundamental human rights for all people. When we do multicultural social justice work, we mitigate the harms created by others' power and privilege.

Becoming a multicultural social justice mental health professional calls for the personal embodiment of social justice values. It is more than just work, since one cannot preach social justice values in the work setting without practicing them. Practicing as a social justice mental health professional pushes us to live the values in all aspects of our lives and necessitates that there be coherence in our personal and work value systems. This requires a careful examination of our own values; our own biases, prejudices, and privileges; and our own lives; and an assessment of how we personally remain silent in moments of injustice or step forward to promote dignity, equality, and freedom from oppression for all. It demands that we question ourselves about if, how, and when we are willing to take risks, which are fundamental to multicultural social justice counseling. Furthermore, social justice mental health work obliges us to examine our own power and privilege and how we access and utilize this in promoting social justice. Essentially, becoming social justice counselors, psychologists, and social workers challenges the very core of our being and frequently requires us to deeply reexamine our personhood.

The profound need for self-examination has roots in an article that we, the two authors, wrote a few years ago about how multicultural social justice counselors must move beyond what we call the "nice counselor syndrome" to become advocates for social justice (Bemak & Chung, 2008). In the article, we explained that our concern is not that mental health professionals are "nice" people, it is that the emphasis on being liked, appreciated, and approved of comes at the expense of social justice advocacy work. In reconsidering who we are and how we are as social justice mental health professionals, there is a need to adopt certain traits that are conducive to social justice work.

One cornerstone of doing multicultural social justice work is courage. Courage is the remedy for fear, and fear is ever present in today's world. Yet for social justice counselors, psychologists, and social workers, fear cannot become a predominant driving force. In order to be able to speak up, speak out, and question long-standing practices of injustice, one must be brave. In our experience, deeply believing in the fundamental principles of social justice will generate motivation and action. In turn, courage and motivation to promote fairness, equality, and dignity for every person can help transcend the culture of fear that we now live in and help promote social action and social change.

After a recent keynote presentation on social justice counseling, I (Rita) was asked, "How do you feed your soul?" The response for both authors is immediate—through passion; through commitment; through strong values and beliefs about equity, dignity, fairness, and equality; through hope in healing for a better more peaceful world; and of course, with the support of family, friends, and colleagues. We hope the book has motivated you to act and not just think about social injustices, stirred you emotionally, and given you the skills and knowledge to be a multicultural social justice counselor and psychologist. The book is intended as a call for action and a call for change. We believe the time is long overdue—it is the time to walk the talk! It is with these thoughts that we conclude our book and hope that the text has been helpful in your journey as a social justice mental health professional. We wish you a peaceful and passionate journey.

REFERENCES

Bemak, F., & Chung, R. C.-Y. (2008). New professional roles and advocacy strategies for school counselors: A multicultural/social justice perspective to move beyond the nice counselor syndrome. *Journal of Counseling and Development, 86,* 372–381.

INDEX

Note: Figures and tables are indicated by f and t after the page number, respectively.

ABOUT THE AUTHORS

Dr. Rita Chi-Ying Chung is a professor in the College of Education and Human Development at George Mason University. She received her undergraduate and graduate training in psychology at Victoria University in Wellington, New Zealand. Before coming to George Mason University, she was a faculty member at the Ohio State University.

Rita arrived in the United States from New Zealand in 1990 to do her overseas postdoctoral fellowship in the Department of Psychology at the University of California, Los Angeles (UCLA). After her two-year fellowship, she remained at UCLA as the project director for the first Chinese American epidemiological study funded by the National Institute of Mental Health. She has also been a consultant for the World Bank in Washington, D.C., and has held adjunct faculty positions at Johns Hopkins University and George Washington University.

Rita has over 80 publications in professional journals and book chapters in major psychology and counseling textbooks, and she has coauthored a book on refugee mental health. Her research focuses on multicultural, cross-cultural, and social justice issues in counseling; the psychological impact of racism; immigrant and refugee psychosocial adjustment and adaptation; the interrelationship of academic achievement and psychological stress on students of color; post-disaster counseling, and interethnic race relations. Her recent research has been on the psychosocial issues in child trafficking. Rita's work on trafficking of Asian girls into commercial sex work led to an invitation by the United Nations in New York to present on this topic.

Rita is also involved with the Counselors Without Borders; she co-led and cosupervised teams and groups of students working along the Mississippi Gulf Coast three months after Hurricane Katrina and on American Indian reservations and in Latina/o migrant communities after the San Diego wildfires. She also did post-disaster consultation and training in Thailand after the tsunami, in Burma after Cyclone Nargis, and in Haiti after the major earthquake in 2010. Rita has worked throughout the United States as well as in Asia, the Pacific Rim region, the United Kingdom, Europe, and South America. She has received numerous awards acknowledging her social justice and multicultural work from both state and national organizations.

Dr. Frederic P. Bemak is a professor in the College of Education and Human Development and the director and cofounder of the Diversity Research and Action Center at George Mason University. He received his master's and doctoral degrees in counseling from the University of Massachusetts, Amherst, and his bachelor's degree in psychology from Boston University. Fred has held administrative faculty appointments at Johns Hopkins University and the Ohio State

University as well as faculty appointments at the Federal University of Rio Grande do Sul (Brazil) and the University of Queensland (Australia).

Prior to his university work, Fred directed federal- and state-funded programs serving youth, including the University of Massachusetts Amherst Upward Bound Program and the Massachusetts Department of Mental Health Region I Adolescent Treatment Program. He was clinical director of a national training consortium based in the Department of Psychiatry at the University of Massachusetts Medical School that was funded through the National Institute of Mental Health. He was also a chief psychologist at Wing Memorial Hospital in Massachusetts.

Fred has done extensive consultation, training, and supervision with mental health professionals and organizations throughout the United States and internationally in 40 countries. His work has focused on cross-cultural counseling, refugee and immigrant mental health, social justice, counseling at-risk youth, and postdisaster counseling. Fred has been a Fulbright Scholar twice—once each in Brazil and Scotland; a World Rehabilitation Fund International Exchange of Experts Fellow in India; a Kellogg International Fellow, which involved work throughout Latin American and the Caribbean; and an American Psychological Association Visiting Psychologist. He has published over 80 book chapters and professional journal articles and coauthored four books, and he is the founder of Counselors Without Borders. Fred was recently the recipient of the American Counseling Association Gilbert and Kathleen Wrenn Award for a Humanitarian and Caring Person, and he has received multiple other awards for his multicultural social justice work.